English Dictionary

English Dictionary

Bloomsbury Books
London

List of Abbreviations

adj	adjective	*poss*	possessive
adv	adverb	*prep*	preposition
def art	definite article	*pron*	pronoun
demons	demonstrative	*sing*	singular
esp	especially	*vi*	intransitive verb
f	feminine	*vt*	transitive verb
inf	informal	*vt-vi*	transitive & intransitive verb
n	noun		
per	personal	*usu*	usually
pl	plural		

This edition published 1994 by Bloomsbury Books, an imprint of The Godfrey Cave Group, 42 Bloomsbury Street, London, WC1B 3QJ.

ISBN 1 85471 520 8

Printed and bound in France by Maury Eurolivres

A

a the indefinite article, used before a consonant. *see* **an**.
aback *adv* backwards; by surprise.
abacus *n* a square slab on the top of a column; a counting frame.
abandon *vt* to forsake entirely; to desert; to give oneself up to a desire or emotion.
abandoned *adj* deserted; depraved.
abase *vt* to bring low; degrade; disgrace.
abasement *n* degradation.
abash *vt* to put to confusion; to make ashamed.
abate *vt* to lessen. * *vi* to become less.
abatement *n* reduction; decrease
abbatoir *n* a public slaughterhouse.
abbess *n* a female superior of a nunnery.
abbey *n* (*pl* **abbeys**) a monastery or convent.
abbot *n* the male superior of an abbey or monastery.
abbreviate *vt* to shorten.
abdicate *vt* to resign voluntarily; to relinquish.
abdomen *n* the lower belly.
abduct *vt* to entice; to lead away by force.
abduction *n* the unlawful carrying off of a person.
aberration *n* a wandering from the right way; derangement of the mind.
abet *vt* to aid or to encourage (in evil).
abetter, abettor *n* one who abets.
abeyance *n*: **in ~** suspense.
abhor *vt* to shrink from with horror; to detest.
abhorrence *n* detestation.
abhorrent *adj* hateful.
abide *vi* to stay in a place; to dwell. * *vt* to wait for; to tolerate; to endure.
abiding *adj* permanent.
ability *n* the power to do a thing; skill; (*pl* **abilities**) the powers of the mind.
abject *adj* mean; vile.
abjure *vt* to renounce upon oath.
ablaze *adv* on fire; in a blaze.
able *adj* capable; skilful.
ablution *n* a washing away from; a cleansing.
ably *adv* with ability.
abnormal *adj* deviating from a fixed rule; irregular.
aboard *adv*, *prep* on board; in a ship.
abode *n* residence.
abolish *vt* to destroy; to do away with.
abominable *adj* hateful.
abominate *vt* to hate extremely; to abhor.
abomination *n* hatred; the object of hatred.
aborigine *n* the original inhabitant of a country.
abortion *n* a miscarriage, usually induced.
abortive *adj* fruitless.
abound *vi* to be, or have, in great plenty.
about *prep* around; near to; concerning. * *adv* around; nearly.
above *prep* to or in a higher place than; more than. * *adv* to or in a higher place.
above board *adv* without concealment or deception.
abreast *adv* side by side.
abridge *vt* to shorten; to condense.
abridgement *n* a summary of a text without loss of meaning; a shortening.
abroad *adv* at large; in a foreign country.
abrogate *vt* to repeal; to make void.
abrupt *adj* broken off; steep; sudden; curt in manner or speech.
abruptness *n* suddenness.
abscess *n* a gathering of pus in some part of the body.
abscond *vi* to fly from justice.
absence *n* the state of being absent; inattentive.
absent[1] *adj* not present; inattention.
absent[2] *vt* to keep oneself away from.
absentee *n* one who absents himself.
absolute *adj* unlimited; despotic.
absolutely *adv* unconditionally.
absolution *n* a freeing from guilt or its punishment.
absolve *vt* to free from, as from guilt or punishment; pardon.
absorb *vt* to drink in; to soak up; to engross.
absorbent *adj* imbibing; swallowing; able to soak up moisture.
absorption *n* act or process of imbibing or swallowing up; total interest in.

abstain *vi* to keep back from; to refrain.
abstemious *adj* sparing in food or drink; temperate.
abstinence *n* a refraining from anything, especially from strong drink.
abstract *vt* to draw from; to separate and consider by itself; to summarize.
abstract *adj* existing in the mind only; not concrete. * *n* a summary.
abstracted *adj* lost in thought.
absurd *adj* contrary to reason; ridiculous.
absurdity *n* the quality of being absurd; that which is absurd.
abundance *n* great plenty.
abundant *adj* abounding; plentiful.
abuse *vt* to ill-use; to insult.
abuse *n* misuse; insulting words.
abusive *adj* insulting.
abut *vi* to border; to meet.
abyss *n* a bottomless gulf; a chasm.
academic *adj* belonging to an academy or university; theoretical. * *n* a teacher or researcher in a university.
academy *n* a school of arts or sciences; a society of persons for the cultivation of arts and sciences.
accede *vi* to assent to; to comply with.
accelerate *vt* to hasten; to quicken the speed of.
acceleration *n* increase of velocity.
accent *n* a stress or modulation of the voice; a manner of speaking.
accent *vt* to express or note the accent of.
accentuate *vt* to emphasize.
accept *vt* to receive; to admit.
acceptance *n* reception; approval.
access *n* approach; admission.
accessible *adj* easy of approach; affable.
accession *n* the act of acceding; addition; succession to a throne.
accessory *adj* additional. * *n* an accomplice.
accident *n* a chance or unforeseen event; a mishap.
accidental *adj* happening by chance.
acclaim *n* praise; enthusiastic approval. * *vt* to applaud.
acclamation *n* a shout of joy or approval.
acclimatize *vt* to accustom to a new climate; to become used to.
accolade *n* a high honour; strong praise.
accommodate *vt* to make suitable; to adjust; to provide lodging for.
accommodating *adj* obliging.
accommodation *n* lodgings; loan.
accompaniment *n* the music played to accompany a singer or other performer.
accompany *vt* to go with; to perform music along with.
accomplice *n* an associate, especially in a crime.
accomplish *vt* to fulfil.
accomplished *adj* elegant; having a finished education; skilled.
accomplishment *npl* attainments.
accord *n* harmony; agreement. * *vt* to make to agree; to grant. * *vi* to agree.
accordance *n* agreement.
accordingly *adv* consequently.
accordion *n* a small keyed wind instrument.
accost *vt* to speak to first; to solicit.
account *n* a reckoning; a bill; narration. * *vt* to reckon; to value. * *vi* to give or render reasons; to explain (with for).
accountable *adj* liable to be called to account; responsible.
accountant *n* one skilled in accounts.
accoutrements *npl* military dress and arms; special equipment.
accredit *vt* to give credit or authority to.
accredited *adj* authorized.
accretion *n* enlargement by natural growth or by external additions.
accrue *vi* to come to; to result from.
accumulate *vt* to heap up. * *vi* to increase.
accumulation *n* a heap; a collection.
accuracy *n* correctness.
accurate *adj* done with care; exact.
accursed *adj* lying under a curse; doomed.
accusation *n* a charge brought against anyone.
accusative *adj*, *n* a case in grammar.
accuse *vt* to charge with a crime; to blame.
accused *n* a person charged with a crime.
accustom *vt* to make familiar with by use.
accustomed *adj* familiar by custom; usual.
ace *n* a unit; a single point on cards or dice; an expert.
acerbity *n* sourness; bitterness.
acetic *adj* sour; like vinegar.
ache *vi* to be in pain. * *n* a gnawing pain.

achieve *vt* to accomplish; to win.
achievement *n* an accomplishment through effort.
acid *adj* sharp or sour to the taste. * *n* a sour substance; one that with certain other substances forms salts.
acidity *n* sourness.
acknowledge *vt* to own the knowledge of; to own or confess.
acknowledgement *n* recognition.
acolyte *n* an attendant.
acorn *n* the fruit of the oak.
acoustics *n* the science of sound; the sound properties, good or bad, of a room or hall.
acquaint *vt* to make to know; to inform.
acquiesce *vi* to rest satisfied; to comply.
acquiescence *n* assent.
acquiescent *adj* resting satisfied; submitting.
acquire *vt* to obtain; to gain.
acquisition *n* acquirement; gain.
acquisitive *adj* fond of getting; eager to possess things.
acquit *vt* to set free; to absolve.
acquittal *n* a setting free from a charge.
acre *n* a quantity of land containing 4840 square yards.
acreage *n* the number of acres in a piece of land
acrid *adj* sharp to the taste or smell.
acrimonious *adj* full of bitterness.
acrimony *n* sharpness or harshness of temper or tone of speech.
acrobat *n* a rope dancer; a gymnast.
acronym *n* a word made up of initial letters or parts of words.
across *prep*, *adv* from side to side; over; crosswise.
act *vi* to be in action; to exert power; to conduct oneself. * *vt* to do; to perform; to play on the stage; to pretend. * *n* a deed; power; a part of a play; law, as an act of parliament; pretence.
acting *n* performance of a part in a play. * *adj* taking someone's place for a time.
action *n* a deed; operation; a gesture; a lawsuit; a battle.
actionable *adj* furnishing grounds for an action at law.
active *adj* busy; quick; lively.
activity *n* nimbleness; an occupation, work or leisure a person is engaged in.
actor *n* one who acts; a stage player.
actress *n* a female stage player.
actual *adj* real.
actuary *n* a specialist in insurance statistics.
actuate *vt* to put into action; to incite.
acumen *n* sharpness of perception; sagacity.
acute *adj* sharp; pointed; keen; sharp in sound or of hearing; intense; of supreme importance.
adage *n* a proverb; a maxim.
adagio *adj*, *adv* in music, slow; with grace. * *n* a slow movement.
adamant *n* any substance of impenetrable hardness; the diamond.
adapt *vt* to adjust or change to suit a purpose.
adaptability *n* the capability of being adapted.
adaptation *n* the result of adapting, e.g. a book for another medium.
add *vt* to join to; to find sum of.
addendum *n* (*pl* **addenda**) something added.
addict *vt* (usually passive with **to**) to be given to or dependent on. * n one addicted to something, e.g. drugs.
addition *n* act of adding; the thing added.
additional *adj* added on.
addled *adj* rotten; muddled.
address *vt* to direct; to speak to. * *n* verbal or written application; speech or discourse; tact; direction of a letter.
adept *n*, *adj* well skilled (person).
adequate *adj* sufficient; passable.
adhere *vi* to stick; to cling.
adherent *adj* sticking to. * *n* a follower.
adhesion *n* the act or state of sticking to; adherence.
adhesive *adj* sticking; sticky.
adieu *interj* farewell.
adipose *adj* fatty.
adjacent *adj* adjoining.
adjective *n* a word which qualifies a noun.
adjoining *adj* adjacent.
adjourn *vt* to postpone. * *vi* to leave off for a time.
adjournment *n* act of adjourning; postponement.

adjudge *vt* to decree.
adjudicate *vt* to adjudge; to determine judicially; to give a ruling on.
adjunct *n* something added or joined. * *adj* united with.
adjust *vt* to set right; to fit.
adjustable *adj* able to be adjusted.
adjustment *n* the act of adjusting; a settlement.
administer *vt* to manage; to dispense; to distribute.
administration *n* management; the executive part of a government.
admirable *adj* worthy of admiration; excellent.
admiral *n* the commander of a fleet or navy.
admiralty *n* a board for administering naval affairs.
admiration *n* wonder mingled with delight and respect; esteem.
admire *vt* to regard with delight or affection and respect.
admissible *adj* allowable.
admission *n* admittance; concession.
admit *vt* to allow to enter; to grant.
admittance *n* permission to enter; entrance; allowance; confession.
admonish *vt* to warn; to reprove.
admonition *n* gentle or solemn reproof.
adolescence *n* a growing up to adulthood; the age of youth.
adopt *vt* to take and raise as one's own (child); to embrace.
adorable *adj* worthy to be loved.
adoration *n* worship paid to God; profound reverence.
adore *vt* to worship; to love intensely.
adorn *vt* to deck with ornaments; to beautify.
adrenaline *n* a hormone secreted in glands in the kidney which is released by stress and increases the heart and pulse rate.
adrift *adv* at the mercy of circumstance; floating at random.
adroit *adj* skilful; clever.
adulation *n* servile flattery.
adult *adj* full-grown. * *n* a person grown to manhood.
adulterate *vt* to debase by mixture.
adulterer *n* a person guilty of adultery.
adultery *n* unfaithfulness to marriage vows.
advance *vt* to put forward; (in commerce) to pay beforehand. * *vi* to go forward. * *n* a going forward; progress.
advanced *adj* in the van of progress.
advancement *n* improvement; promotion in station, career, etc.
advantage *n* a favourable state; gain; a term in tennis.
advantageous *adj* profitable.
advent *n* arrival; the four weeks before Christmas.
adventure *n* a hazardous enterprise; an exciting experience. * *vt*, *vi* to risk or hazard.
adventurer *n* one who risks, hazards, or braves.
adventurous *adj* daring.
adverb *n* a word which modifies a verb, adjective or another adverb.
adversary *n* an enemy; an antagonist.
adverse *adj* hostile; contrary.
adversity *n* misfortune.
advertise *vt* to announce; to publish a notice of.
advertisement *n* information; a public notice promoting something.
advertiser *n* one who advertises.
advice *n* an opinion offered; counsel.
advisable *adj* fitting or proper to be done; expedient.
advise *vt* to counsel; to warn; to inform. * *vi* to deliberate or consider.
advised *adj* cautious; done with advice.
advisedly *adv* deliberately.
advocate *n* one who pleads for another; an intercessor. * *vt* to plead in favour of; to defend, esp in a law court.
adze *n* a kind of axe, with the edge at right angles to the handle.
aegis *n* protection; sponsorship.
aerate *vt* to put air or other gas into.
aerial *adj* belonging to the air; lofty. * *n* a device, antenna to receive and transmit radio waves.
aerie, eyrie *n* the nest of a bird of prey.
aeronaut *n* one who flies, sails or floats in the air.
aeronautics *n* the science of flight.
aeroplane, airplane *n* an aircraft with wings.

aesthetics the science or philosophy of art and the beautiful.
afar *adv* at, to or from a distance.
affability *n* geniality; friendliness.
affable *adj* courteous; accessible.
affair *n* a business matter; an event; a sexual relationship, usually temporary.
affect *vt* to act upon; to move the feelings of; to pretend.
affectation *n* an assumed air put on by a person; pretence.
affection *n* fondness; love.
affectionate *adj* tender; loving.
affidavit *n* a written declaration upon oath.
affiliate *vt* to adopt; to attach to a society or other body.
affinity *n* relation by marriage; liking; similarity; chemical attraction.
affirm *vt* to assert; to declare.
affirmation *n* a solemn declaration (instead of an oath).
affirmative *adj* positive; stating a thing to be true. * *n* that which expresses assent; the word 'yes'.
affix *vt* to fasten to. * *n* a syllable or letter added to a word.
afflict *vt* to grieve; to cause pain or sorrow.
affliction *n* distress; grief; pain.
affluence *n* abundance; wealth.
affluent *adj* wealthy; abundant.
afford *vt* to yield; to supply; to be able to spend, to grant.
affray *n* a fight; a disturbance; a tumult.
affront *vt* to insult; to offend. * *n* an insult.
afield *adv* to or in the field; far away.
afloat *adv*, *adj* floating; at sea.
afoot *adv* on foot; in motion; happening.
aforementioned *adj* mentioned before.
aforenamed *adj* named before.
aforesaid *adj* said before.
afraid *adj* struck with fear; feeling regret.
afresh *adv* anew.
aft *adj*, *adv* astern.
after *adj* later. * *prep* later in time than; behind. * *adv* later in time.
aftermath *n* the result or after effects usually of something unpleasant; a season's second crop of grass.
afternoon *n* the time from noon to evening.
afterthought *n* reflection after an act.
afterwards *adv* subsequently.
again *adv* once more.
against *prep* in opposition to; in expectation of.
agate *n* a hard quartz-like mineral.
age *n* a period of time; an epoch; the length of a person's life. * *vi*, *vt* to grow or make old; to show signs of advancing age.
agency *n* means; a specialized or specific business; the business of an agent.
agenda *npl* business to be transacted at a meeting.
agent *n* one who acts; a deputy.
agglomeration *n* a heap.
aggrandize *vt* to magnify; to increase in power, riches, etc.
aggravate *vt* to intensify; to exasperate.
aggravation *n* the act of aggravating; provocation.
aggregate *vt* to collect. * *adj* total * *n* the sum of parts.
aggression *n* the first act of hostility; attack.
aggressive *adj* inclined to attacking; prone to quarrelling.
aggressor *n* the person who starts hostilities.
aggrieve *vt* to pain; to vex.
aghast *adj*, *adv*. amazed; horrified.
agile *adj* nimble.
agility *n* nimbleness.
agitate *vt* to put in violent motion; to excite; to stir up.
agitated *adj* disturbed.
agitation *n* excitement; commotion.
agitator *n* one who excites discontent or revolt.
agnostic *n* one who disclaims any knowledge of God.
agog *adv* in eager excitement.
agonize *vi* to writhe with extreme pain.
agonizing *adj* giving extreme pain.
agony *n* extreme pain of body or mind; anguish.
agrarian *adj* relating to land and agriculture.
agree *vi* to be in concord; to suit.
agreeable *adj* suitable to; pleasing; grateful.
agreement *n* harmony; conformity; compact.

agriculture *n* the art or science of cultivating the ground.
aground *adv* stranded; on the shore.
ague *n* an intermittent fever with shivering.
ahead *adv* before; onward.
aid *vt* to help. * *n* help.
Aids *n* acronym for a complex medical condition, *a*cquired *i*mmune *d*eficiency *s*yndrome.
ail *vt* to pain. * *vi* to be in pain.
ailment *n* a pain; a disease.
aim *vi* to point with a weapon; to intend; to endeavour. * *vt* to level or direct as a firearm. * *n* intention; purpose.
aimless *adj* without aim.
air *n* the atmosphere; a light breeze; a tune; bearing (*npl*) affected manner. * *vt* to expose to the air; to dry.
air conditioning *n* a regulating system controlling temperature, freshness and humidity of air (in a building).
aircraft *n* any machine that flies in the air.
airily *adv* in an airy manner.
airing *n* an exposure to the air or to a fire; an excursion in the open air.
airline *n* a company or organization running aeroplanes for transportation.
airplane *see* **aeroplane**.
airport *n* a place where aircraft land and take off and undergo repairs.
air pump *n* a machine for pumping the air out of a vessel.
air raid *n* an attack on ground targets by military aircraft.
airtight *adj* so tight or compact as not to let air pass.
airy *adj* open to the air; fresh; casual; light-hearted.
aisle *n* a wing or side of a church; a passage in a church.
ajar *adv* partly open.
akin *adj* of the same kin; related to.
alabaster *n* a soft marble-like mineral.
alacrity *n* liveliness; eagerness.
alarm *n* a call to arms; sudden surprise; fright. * *vt* to give notice of danger.
alarming *adj* terrifying.
alarmist *n* one prone to excite alarm.
albino *n* a person with abnormally white skin and hair and pink eyes.
album *n* a book for autographs, sketches, etc; a long-playing record containing several items.
albumen *n* the white of an egg.
alchemy *n* an obsolete science, aiming at changing metals into gold, etc.
alcohol *n* pure spirit of a highly intoxicating nature produced by distilling or fermenting.
alcove *n* a recess.
alderman *n* formerly a magistrate of a town.
ale *n* a fermented malt liquor; beer.
alert *adj* vigilant; quick. * *vt* to warn.
alertness *n* briskness; activity.
algebra *n* the science of computing by symbols.
alias *adv* otherwise. * *n* (*pl* **aliases**) an assumed name.
alibi *n* the plea that one was elsewhere when a crime was committed.
alien *adj* foreign. * *n* a foreigner.
alienate *vt* to transfer to another; to estrange; to cause hostility towards.
alight *vi* to get down; to settle on.
alight *adv*, *adv*. on fire.
alike *adj* like; similar. * *adv* in the same manner.
aliment *n* nourishment; food.
alimony *n* an allowance to a woman legally separated from her husband.
alive *adj* living; lively.
alkali *n* a substance, as potash and soda, which neutralizes acids.
all *adj* every one. * *n* everything * *adv* wholly; entirely.
allay *vt* to ease; to assuage.
allegation *n* an assertion or statement made, often without having proof.
allege *vt* to assert, often without proof.
allegiance *n* loyalty.
allegorical *adj* figurative.
allegory *n* a story, etc which conveys a meaning different from the literal one.
allegro a word denoting a sprightly movement in music.
alleviate *vt* to make light; to assuage; to relieve pain.
alley *n* a narrow walk or passage.
alliance *n* state of being allied; league; the countries forming this.

allied *adj* united by treaty or marriage.
alliteration *n* the repetition of a letter at the beginning of two or more words in close succession.
allocate *vt* to distribute.
allot *vt* to give by lot; to apportion.
allow *vt* to let; to admit the truth or the possibility of; to grant.
allowance *n* a sum allotted; permission.
alloy *vt* to mix with baser metals. * *n* a mixture of metals.
allude *vi* to refer to.
allure *vt* to entice; to decoy.
allurement *n* temptation; enticement.
alluring *adj* attractive.
allusion *n* a hint; a reference.
alluvial *adj* deposited by water.
ally *vt* to unite by friendship, marriage, or treaty. * *n* an associate.
almanac *n* a calendar of days, weeks, and months, etc.
almighty *adj* omnipotent. * *n* God.
almond *n* the nut of the almond tree.
almoner *n* formerly a hospital social worker.
almost *adv* nearly.
aloft *adv* in the sky; on high.
alone *adj* solitary. * *adv* separately.
along *adv* lengthways. * *prep* by the side of.
aloof *adv* apart.
aloud *adv* loudly.
alpaca *n* a llama with long hair; cloth made from this hair.
alpha the first letter in the Greek alphabet.
alphabet *n* the letters of a language.
alpine *adj* pertaining to high mountains. * *n* a small plant growing on mountainsides.
already *adv* even now.
also *adv* likewise; too.
altar *n* an elevated stone on which sacrifices were offered; the communion table.
alter *vt* to change. * *vi* to vary.
alteration *n* partial change or variation.
altercation *n* a wrangle; an angry dispute.
alternate *adj* by turns. * *vt* to follow by turns.
alternative *n* a choice of two things.
although *conj* though.
altitude *n* height.
alto *adj* high. * *n* (in music) contralto.
altogether *adv* wholly.
altruism *n* devotion to others; unselfishness.
aluminium *n* a soft, white, light metal.
always *adv* at all times.
amalgam *n* a mixture of mercury with another metal, usually silver.
amalgamate *vt* to unite in an amalgam; to combine.
amass *vt* to form into a mass; to heap up.
amateur *n* a lover of any art or science or a participant in any sport or activity, but not a professional.
amaze *vt* to astonish.
amazement *n* wonder.
ambassador *n* a diplomatic representative of a country abroad.
amber *n* a mineralized yellow or yellow-brown fossil resin used for jewellery.
ambidextrous *adj* using both hands alike.
ambiguity *n* doubtfulness of meaning or interpretation.
ambiguous *adj* doubtful; obscure.
ambit *n* compass; scope.
ambition *n* desire for preferment or power.
ambitious *adj* aspiring.
amble *vi* to walk at a slow easy pace. * *n* an easy pace.
ambrosia *n* the imaginary food of the gods.
ambulance *n* a vehicle for transporting the sick or wounded.
ambulatory *adj* movable; walking.
ambush *n* the place or act of lying in wait in order to surprise.
ameliorate *vt* to make better.
amen *adv* so be it.
amenable *adj* easily led; co-operative; accountable.
amend *vt* to correct; to improve. * *vi* to grow better.
amendment *n* a change for the better; correction; reformation.
amends *npl* compensation; satisfaction; recompense.
amenity *n* pleasantness; agreeableness of situation.

amethyst *n* a precious stone of a bluish violet or purple colour.
amiability *n* sweetness of temper.
amiable *adj* loveable; pleasant; friendly.
amicable *adj* friendly; kind.
amid, amidst *prep* in the midst of.
amidships *adv* in or towards the middle of a ship.
amiss *adj* in error; improper. * *adv* improperly.
amity *n* friendship.
ammonia *n* volatile alkali.
ammonite *n* an extinct marine animal; its coiled shell found as a fossil.
ammunition *n* war stores and projectiles, e.g. bullets, rockets, fired from weapons; any helpful facts, etc, to be used in winning an argument.
amnesty *n* a general pardon.
amoeba *n* (*pl* **amoebae, amoebas**) a minute organism that constantly changes shape, found in fresh water.
among, amongst *prep* amidst.
amorous *adj* inclined to or showing love.
amorphous *adj* shapeless.
amount *vi* to mount up to; to result in. * *n* the sum total.
ampere *n* the unit of current in electricity.
amphibian *n* (*pl* **amphibia**) an animal able to live either on land or in water.
amphibious *adj* able to live in water or on land; (of a vehicle) built to operate on land and water.
amphitheatre *n* a building of an oval form, with rows of seats all round, rising one above the other.
ample *adj* spacious; abundant; sufficient.
amplification *n* enlargement.
amplifier *n* a device that amplifies or enlarges or makes the sound louder.
amplify *vt, vi* to enlarge; to make louder; to fill out.
amplitude *n* ampleness; extent; abundance.
amply *adv* fully; copiously.
amputate *vt* to cut off, as a limb.
amuck, amok *n, adv*: **to run ~** to attack all and sundry.
amulet *n* a charm against evils.
amuse *vt* to entertain; to beguile; to cause laughter.
amusement *n* diversion; entertainment.
amusing *adj* droll; diverting.
an *adj* the indefinite article, used before words beginning with a vowel sound.
anachronism *n* the error of assigning an event or circumstance out of its time.
anaemia *n* bloodlessness.
anaesthetic *adj* producing insensibility. * *n* a substance (drug or gas) which produces insensibility.
anagram *n* a word formed from the letters of another, e.g. rood from door.
analogous *adj* corresponding.
analogy *n* similarity.
analyse *vt* to resolve into its elements.
analysis *n* (*pl* **analyses**) a breaking up of a thing into its elements.
analyst *n* one who analyses.
anarchic *adj* without rule or government.
anarchist *n* one who opposes all forms of government.
anathema *n* an object of detestation.
anatomical *adj* relating to anatomy.
anatomy *n* the science dealing with physical structure of animals and plants; the art of dissection.
ancestor *n* a forefather.
ancestral *adj* relating or belonging to ancestors.
ancestry *n* lineage; descent.
anchor *n* an iron instrument that grips the sea or river bed and holds a ship at rest in water. * *vt* to hold fast by an anchor.
anchorage *n* a place where a ship can anchor.
ancient *adj* old; antique.
ancillary *adj* subservient or subordinate.
and *conj* a word joining words or phrases; also; in addition, consequently.
andante *adj* in music, with slow, graceful movement.
anecdote *n* a short often amusing story.
anemometer *n* an instrument for measuring the force of the wind.
aneroid *adj* a kind of barometer.
aneurysm *adj* dilatation of an artery.
anew *adv* once more.
anger *n* wrath. * *vt* to enrage.
angle *n* the inclination of two lines which meet in a point; a corner; a viewpoint.
angle *vi* to fish with hook and line.

angler *n* one who fishes with hook and line.
Anglican *adj* pertaining to the Church of England.
Anglicize *vt* to make English.
Anglophobia *n* an excessive hatred of English people, customs, etc.
angry *adj* full of anger; wrathful.
anguish *n* extreme pain, body or mind.
angular *adj* sharp-cornered; (of a person) thin and bony.
animal *n* a living being having sensation and voluntary motion.
animate *vt* to give life to; to enliven; to produce moving objects and figures by animation.
animated *adj* lively; living; (film, etc) made by animation.
animation *n* life; vigour; vivacity; the art of drawing objects and filming them to create moving images on film or tape.
animosity *n* violent hatred; active enmity.
ankle *n* the joint which connects the foot with the leg.
annals *npl* a yearly record of events.
annex *vt* to unite at the end; to subjoin; to take possession of.
annexation *n* the act of annexing.
annexe *n* an extension to a building, built on to it or erected nearby.
annihilate *vt* to reduce to nothing.
annihilation *n* the act of annihilating.
anniversary *n* a day on which some event is annually celebrated.
annotate *vt* to write notes upon.
announce *vt* to make known.
announcement *n* declaration.
annoy *vt* to hurt; to vex.
annoyance *n* act of annoying; state of being annoyed.
annual *adj* yearly; lasting a year. * *n* a book published yearly.
annuitant *n* one who receives an annuity.
annuity *n* a sum of money payable yearly.
annul *vt* to make of no effect; to repeal.
anoint *vt* to consecrate with oil; to rub with or apply oil to.
anomalous *adj* irregular; exceptional.
anomaly *n* irregularity.
anonymous *adj* nameless; unsigned.
another *adj* not the same.
answer *vt* to reply to; to suit. * *n* a reply; a solution.
answerable *adj* accountable.
antagonism *n* opposition; hostility.
antagonist *n* an opponent.
antagonistic *adj* hostile.
Antarctic *adj* of or near the South Pole.
antecedent *adj* going before. * *n* that which goes before; (*pl*) ancestors; a person's history.
antechamber *n* anteroom.
antedate *vt* to date before the true time.
antediluvian *adj* before the flood.
antelope *n* a kind of deer.
antemeridian *adj* before midday; a.m.
antenna *n* (*pl* **antennae**) one of the feelers of an insect; an aerial.
anterior *adj* prior.
anteroom *n* a room leading to another.
anthem *n* a piece of Scripture set to music.
anthology *n* a collection of poems or prose.
anthracite *n* a kind of coal which burns almost without flame.
antics *npl* buffoonery and posturing.
anticipate *vt* to forestall.
anticipation *n* act of anticipating; expectation.
anticlimax *n* a tame ending to a striking beginning.
anticyclone *n* an opposite state of atmospheric conditions to what exists in a cyclone, presaging good weather.
antidote *n* a remedy for poison or any evil.
antipathy *n* aversion; dislike.
antipodes *npl* the opposite side of the globe.
antiquarian *adj* pertaining to antiquaries.
antiquated *adj* old-fashioned; out of date.
antique *adj* old. * *n* an ancient relic, object of value or work of art.
antiquity *n* ancient times; great age; (*pl* **antiquities**) remains of ancient times.
antiseptic *adj* counteracting contamination.
antithesis *n* (*pl* **antitheses**) contrast.
antler *n* a branch of a stag's horn.
anvil *n* an iron block used by smiths.
anxiety *n* concern; worry.

anxious *adj* troubled; worried; eager.
any *adj* one indefinitely.
aorta *n* the artery leading from the heart.
apace *adv* fast.
apart *adj*, *adv* separate; aside; in pieces.
apartment *n* a room; a flat.
apathetic *adj* indifferent.
apathy *n* want of feeling; indifference.
ape *n* a monkey. * *vt* to mimic.
aperture *n* an opening.
apex *n* (*pl* **apexes, apices**) the summit.
apiary *n* a place where bees are kept.
apiece *adv* in a separate share.
aplomb *n* self-possession.
apocalypse *n* a disastrous happening.
apocryphal *adj* fictitious.
apologetic *adj* excusing.
apologize *vi* to make an excuse.
apology *n* that which is said in defence or as an expression of regret.
apoplexy *n* a shock involving paralysis.
apostasy *n* departure from one's faith or party.
apostate *n* one who renounces his religion or his party.
apostrophe *n* a mark (') indicating contraction of a word, or the possessive case.
apotheosis *n* a deification.
appal *vt* to dismay.
appalling *adj* causing dread or terror.
apparatus *n* (*pl* **apparatus**) tools or equipment for doing work or for a special purpose.
apparel *n* clothing. * *vt* to dress.
apparent *adv* evident; seeming.
apparition *n* a ghost or phantom.
appeal *vi*, *vt* to entreat; to carry to a higher court. * *n* entreaty.
appear *vi* to become visible; to seem.
appearance *n* act of coming into sight; semblance.
appease *vt* to pacify; to calm.
appellant *n* one who appeals.
appellation *n* a name; a title.
append *vt* to add; to attach.
appendage *n* something added; an external organ, e.g. a tail.
appendicitis *n* inflammation of the vermiform appendix of the bowels.
appendix *n* an adjunct; a supplement; a prolongation.
appertain *vi* to belong.
appetite *n* a desire or relish for food.
appetize *vt* to whet the appetite.
applaud *vt* to praise by clapping the hands.
applause *n* praise loudly expressed.
apple *n* a fruit.
appliance *n* the act of applying; the thing applied; a device or machine usually for domestic use.
applicability *n* relevance.
applicable *adj* suitable.
applicant *n* one who applies, e.g. for work.
application *n* the act of applying; perseverance; diligence.
apply *vt* to fasten or attach. * *vi* to suit; to make application.
appoint *vt* to fix; to nominate.
appointment *n* office; engagement.
apposite *adj* suitable.
appraise *vt* to fix or set a price or value on.
appreciable *adj* that may be appreciated.
appreciate *vt* to value; to be grateful to or thankful for. * *vi* to rise in value.
appreciation *n* the act of appreciating; a just valuation; approval; gratitude; a rise in value.
apprehend *vt* to take hold of; to arrest; to fear; to understand.
apprehension *n* seizure; dread.
apprehensive *adj* fearful.
apprentice *n* one who is learning a trade or occupation. * *vt* to bind as an apprentice.
apprise *vt* to inform.
approach *vt*, *vi* to come near. * *n* the act of drawing near; an avenue.
approbation *n* approval.
appropriate *vt* to take to oneself as one's own. * *adj* suitable.
appropriateness *n* peculiar fitness.
approval *n* praise; a favourable opinion.
approve *vt* to consider good; to sanction. * *vi* (with **of**) to express approbation.
approximate *adj* near; almost right or good. * *vt* to bring near. * *vi* to come near.
approximately *adv* nearly.
apricot *n* a stone fruit, allied to the plum.

April *n* the fourth month of the year.
apron *n* a garment worn in front to protect the clothes.
apt *adj* suitable; liable.
aptitude *n* natural facility.
aquarium *n* (*pl* **aquariums, aquaria**) a vessel or tank or building for aquatic plants and animals.
Aquarius *n* the water bearer, a sign in the zodiac.
aquatic *adj* living or growing in water; (*pl*) water sports.
aqueduct *n* a conduit made for conveying water.
aqueous *adj* watery.
aquiline *adj* hooked like the beak of an eagle.
Arab *n* a native of Arabia; an Arabian horse.
arabesque *n* a species of ornamentation consisting of fanciful figures in dance and music, and floral forms in art.
arable *adj* fit for ploughing and growing.
arbiter *n* an umpire.
arbitrarily *adv* by will or caprice only; despotically.
arbitrary *adj* despotic; capricious.
arbitrate *vi* to act as an arbiter; to decide.
arbitrator *n* a person chosen to decide a dispute; referee.
arboriculture *n* the art of cultivating trees and shrubs.
arc *n* a part of a circle or curve.
arcade *n* a covered passage containing shops.
arcane *adj* understood only with inside knowledge; secret; mysterious.
arch[1] *adj* chief; expert; roguish; sly.
arch[2] *n* a curved structure supporting a bridge or roof.
archaeology *n* the science of antiquities; knowledge of ancient art.
archaic *adj* antiquated; obsolete.
archbishop *n* a chief bishop.
archdeacon *n* a church dignitary, next in rank to a bishop.
archer *n* a person who shoots with a bow and arrow.
archery *n* the art of the archer.
archipelago *n* a sea abounding in islands.
architect *n* one who plans buildings.
architecture *n* the art or science of building.
archive *n* a record; (generally *pl*) public records.
archness *n* roguishness; slyness.
archway *n* a passage under an arch.
Arctic *adj* pertaining to the regions about the North Pole; frigid; cold.
ardent *adj* fervent; eager.
ardour *n* warmth; eagerness; passion.
arduous *adj* difficult.
arduously *adv* with effort.
area *n* any open surface; surface measurement; any enclosed or sunken space.
arena *n* an open space of ground for contests or games.
argue *vt, vi* to discuss; to dispute.
argument *n* a reason offered; a plea; a controversy.
argumentative *adj* prone to argument.
arid *adj* dry; parched.
Aries *n* the Ram, the first of the twelve signs in the zodiac.
arise *vi* to rise up; to come about.
aristocracy *n* government by the nobility; the nobility.
aristocrat *n* a noble.
arithmetic *n* the science of numbers; computation.
ark *n* a large floating vessel; a place of refuge.
arm *n* the limb from the shoulder to the hand; a weapon; (*pl*) war; armour; armorial bearings. * *vt* to furnish with arms. * *vi* to take up arms.
armada *n* a fleet of armed ships.
armament *n* a force armed for war; war equipment of an army, ship or vehicle.
armistice *n* a truce.
armorial *adj* relating to arms in heraldry.
armour *n* defensive arms.
armoury *n* a place for keeping arms.
armpit *n* the hollow place under the shoulder.
army *n* a body of men armed for war.
aroma *n* perfume.
aromatic *adj* fragrant.
around *prep* about; encircling. * *adv* on every side.
arouse *vt* to stir up.

arraign *vt* to indict; to censure.
arrange *vt* to put in order; to prepare for; to plan; to adjust a musical work for different instruments.
arrangement *n* orderly disposition; classification; agreement.
arrant *adj* downright; thorough.
array *n* order; apparel. * *vt* to draw up in order; to adorn.
arrear *n* (generally *pl*) that which remains unpaid.
arrest *vt* to stop; to apprehend. * *n* a seizure by warrant.
arrival *n* the act of coming to a place.
arrive *vi* to come; to reach; to succeed.
arrogance *n* haughtiness; insolent bearing.
arrogant *adj* haughty; overbearing; self-important.
arrow *n* a barbed shaft shot from a bow.
arsenal *n* a public establishment for making or storing weapons of war.
arsenic *n* a virulent mineral poison.
arson *n* the malicious setting on fire of a house, etc.
art *n* practical skill; cunning; profession of a painter, etc.
arterial *adj* pertaining to arteries; pertaining to a main road, railway, etc.
artery *n* a tube which conveys blood from the heart; a main road, etc, or means of communication.
artesian *adj* applied to wells made by boring.
artful *adj* skilful; crafty.
article *n* a separate item; composition (in newspaper); a part of speech, as *the*. * *vt* to bind by articles. * *vi* to stipulate.
articulate *adj* distinct; clear and intelligible. * *vi* to utter distinct sounds.
artifice *n* an artful device or deception.
artificial *adj* made by art; not natural.
artillery *n* cannon and heavy guns in general; the troops who manage them.
artist *n* one skilled in some art, especially the fine arts.
artistic *adj* characteristic of art; aesthetic.
artless *adj* unaffected.
as *adv*, *conj*, *prep* like; for example; because; in the same way; playing the part of.
asbestos *n* a mineral fibrous incombustible substance.
ascend *vi* to rise. * *vt* to climb.
ascendancy, ascendency *n* controlling power; sway.
ascendant *adj* superior. * *n* superiority.
ascension *n* act of ascending.
ascent *n* rise; upward slope.
ascertain *vt* to make certain; to find out.
ascetic *adj* unduly rigid in self-denial and self-discipline.
ascribe *vt* to attribute.
aseptic *adj* not liable to putrefy; rendered free of germs.
ashamed *adj* affected by shame or guilt.
ashen *adj* made of ash; pale.
ashes *npl* the remains of anything burned; (*fig*) a dead body.
ashore *adv*, *adj* on or to the shore.
aside *adv* on one side; apart. * *n* words spoken by an actor to an audience only.
asinine *adj* belonging to or resembling the ass; stupid.
ask *vt* to request. * *vi* to make inquiry.
askance, askant *adv* awry; obliquely.
askew *adv*, *adj* awry.
asleep *adj*, *adv*. sleeping.
aspect *n* appearance; outlook.
asperity *n* roughness; harshness.
aspersion *n* calumny, lie; (esp *pl*) slander; defamation.
asphalt *n* a kind of pitch used for paving.
aspirant *n* a candidate.
aspirate *vt* to pronounce with an audible breath; to add an *h* sound to.
aspiration *n* ardent desire; ambition.
aspire *vi* to aim at high things.
ass *n* a long-eared animal akin to the horse.
assagai, assegai *n* a light African throwing spear.
assail *vt* to attack.
assailant *n* one who assails; an attacker.
assassin *n* one who kills by surprise or secretly.
assassinate *vt* to murder by surprise or treacherously.
assault *n* an attack. * *vt* to assail.
assay *n* proof; analysis of ores. * *vt* to try.
assemblage *n* a collection of persons or things.
assemble *vt* to bring together. * *vi* to come together.

assembly *n* a gathering of people to consult together; a putting together of many parts to make a whole.
assent *n* consent. * *vi* to agree.
assert *vt* to affirm.
assertive *adj* affirming confidently.
assess *vt* to rate; to value or estimate amount, worth, etc.
assessable *adj* that may be assessed.
assessment *n* the act of assessing; the sum levied.
asset *n* a useful or valuable thing.
assiduity *n* close application; diligence.
assiduous *adj* constantly diligent.
assign *vt* to designate; to allot; to make over to another.
assignable *adj* that may be assigned.
assignation *n* an appointment to meet; a making over by transfer of title.
assignee *n* one to whom an assignment is made.
assignment *n* an allotment or legal transfer; a task assigned to someone.
assimilate *vt* to make like to; to digest.
assist *vt* to help. * *vi* to lend help.
assistance *n* help; aid.
assistant *n* one who assists.
assize *n* an assessment court; (*pl*) periodical courts for administering justice.
associate *vt* to join in company with. * *vi* to keep company with. * *n* a companion; a business colleague or partner.
association *n* act of associating; union.
assort *vt* to arrange. * *vi* to suit.
assortment *n* a varied collection.
assuage *vt* to allay; to calm.
assume *vt* to take for granted; to usurp. * *vi* to claim more than is due.
assumption *n* act of assuming; the thing assumed.
assurance *n* secure confidence; impudence; insurance.
assure *vt* to confirm; to insure.
assuredly *adv* certainly.
asterisk *n* a star-shaped mark used in printing (*) to indicate an omission, cross-reference, footnote, etc.
astern *adv* in or at the hinder part of a ship.
asteroid *n* a small planet.
asthma *n* a disease marked by shortness of breath.
astigmatism *n* a defect in the eyes preventing proper focusing.
astir *adv* awake or stirring; active.
astonish *vt* to amaze.
astonishment *n* amazement.
astound *vt* to astonish; to stun.
astrakhan *n* a rough cloth with a curled pile made from lambs bred in Astrakhan.
astral *adj* belonging to the stars.
astray *adv* straying.
astride *adv* with the legs apart or on either side of something.
astringent *n* a medicine that contracts the tissues. * *adj* binding; constricting; harsh; sharp; bracing.
astrologer *n* one versed in astrology.
astrology *n* the art of foretelling future events from the stars.
astronomer *n* one versed in astronomy.
astronomical *adj* pertaining to astronomy; very large.
astronomy *n* the science of the heavenly bodies.
astute *adj* shrewd; crafty.
astuteness *n* shrewdness.
asunder *adv* apart; into parts.
asylum *n* a place of refuge; an institution for the care of the insane.
at *prep* denoting nearness, presence or location.
atheism *n* the disbelief in the existence of God.
atheist *n* one who disbelieves the existence of God.
athenaeum *n* a literary or scientific club.
athlete *n* one skilled in exercises of agility or strength.
athletic *adj* pertaining to an athlete; strong; active.
athletics *npl* sporting events of track and field; physical exercises.
atlas *n* a collection of maps.
atmosphere *n* the air surrounding the earth; pervading influence.
atmospheric *adj* pertaining to the atmosphere.
atoll *n* a ring-shaped coral reef or islands.
atom *n* a minute particle, esp of a chemical element; anything extremely small.
atomic *adj* pertaining to or consisting of

atoms; pertaining to atomic energy, bomb, warfare. •
atone *vi* to make up for; to expiate.
atrocious *adj* abominable; very wicked.
atrocity *n* horrible wickedness.
atrophy *n* a wasting away.
attach *vt* to join; to affix. * *vi* to adhere.
attaché *n* one attached to the suite of an ambassador or a diplomatic mission.
attachment *n* fidelity; tender regard.
attack *vt* to assault. * *n* an assault; seizure by a disease.
attain *vi* to arrive at. * *vt* to reach; to gain.
attainable *adj* that may be attained.
attainment *n* accomplishment.
attempt *vt* to try to do. * *n* an essay; effort.
attend *vt* to wait on; to be present at. * *vi* to pay regard.
attendance *n* the act of attending; the persons attending.
attendant *adj* accompanying * *n* one who waits on or accompanies.
attention *n* heed; courtesy.
attentive *adj* heedful; courteous; diligent.
attenuate *vt* to make slender; to weaken.
attest *vt* to bear witness to.
attestation *n* testimony.
attic *n* a garret; a room or storing space under the roof of a house.
attire *vt* to dress. * *n* dress
attitude *n* posture; a position or viewpoint taken on some matter.
attorney *n* (*pl* **attorneys**) a law agent.
attract *vt* to draw to; to entice.
attraction *n* allurement; charm.
attractive *adj* having the power of attracting; enticing; pretty.
attributable *adj* that may be attributed.
attribute *vt* to ascribe, to impute. * *n* a quality; an adjectival word or clause.
attributive *adj* that attributes.
attrition *n* the act of wearing down by rubbing.
attune *vt* to put in tune; to adjust to or acclimatize.
auburn *adj* reddish brown.
auction *n* a public sale.
auctioneer *n* the person who sells at auction.
audacious *adj* daring; impudent.
audacity *n* daring; impudence.
audible *adj* that may be heard.
audience *n* an assembly of hearers; reception.
audit *n* an examination of accounts.
auditor *n* one who examines accounts.
auditory *adj* pertaining to the sense of hearing. * *n* an audience.
auger *n* a tool for boring holes.
aught *n* anything.
augment *vt* to make larger; to increase; * *n* increase; a prefix to a word.
augmentation *n* increase.
augur *n* one who foretold the future; a soothsayer. * *vt* to foretell.
august *adj* regal; imposing.
August *n* the eighth month of the year.
aunt *n* the sister of one's father or mother.
aureole *n* in art, a golden disk or halo round the head of saints.
auricle *n* the external ear; either of the two ear-like cavities of the heart.
aurora borealis *n* the northern lights or streamers.
auscultation *n* detecting heart conditions by listening to beats.
auspices *npl* omens; patronage.
auspicious *adj* fortunate; favourable.
austere *adj* stern; severe.
austerity *n* sternness; severity; living without luxuries.
authentic *adj* genuine.
authenticate *vt* to attest; to confirm.
authenticity *n* genuineness.
author *n* the writer of a book, etc.
authoress *n* a female author.
authoritative *adj* official; decisive.
authority *n* legal power or right; person exercising this power.
authorize *vt* to sanction.
autobiography *n* memoirs of a person written by himself or herself.
autocracy *n* absolute government by one person.
autocrat *n* an absolute ruler.
autograph *n* a signature.
automatic *adj* self-acting; carried out without conscious thought.
automaton *n* (*pl* **automata**) a self-moving machine, or a person acting like one.
autonomy *n* self-government.

autopsy *n* an examination of a dead body to discover the cause of death.
autumn *n* the third season of the year.
auxiliary *adj* helping. * *n* a person or thing that helps.
avail *vt, vi*. to profit. * *vi* to be of use. * *n* advantage; use.
available *adj* attainable.
avalanche *n* a vast snow slide.
avarice *n* greed of gain.
avaricious *adj* covetous; greedy.
avenge *vt* to take satisfaction for; to harm in retaliation.
avenue *n* an approach to; a broad street.
aver *vt* to assert.
average *n* medium. * *adj* medial; moderate; not outstanding in ability. * *vi* to form a mean.
averse *adj* disinclined.
aversion *n* dislike.
avert *vt* to turn aside or away from.
aviary *n* a place for keeping birds.
aviation *n* the art of flying.
aviator *n* one who flies aeroplanes.
avocation *n* a person's regular business or occupation.
avoid *vt* to shun.
avoirdupois *n, adj* a system of weight, in which a pound contains sixteen ounces.
avow *vt* to declare with confidence; to confess frankly.
avowal *n* an admission.
avowedly *adv* openly.
await *vt* to wait for; to expect.
awake *vt* to rouse from sleep. * *vi* to cease from sleep. * *adj* not sleeping.
awaken *vt, vi* to awake.
award *vt* to adjudge. * *vi* to make an award. * *n* a judgement; a reward or prize.
aware *adj* informed; cognizant.
away *adv* absent; at a distance.
awe *n* fear; fear mingled with reverence. * *vt* to strike with fear.
awful *adj* very bad; terrible.
awhile *adv* for some time.
awkward *adj* inexpert; inelegant; deliberately unhelpful; difficult.
awl *n* a tool for piercing small holes in leather.
awning *n* a canvas covering.
awry *adj, adv*. twisted; distorted; gone wrong.
axe *n* an instrument for hewing and chopping.
axiom *n* a self-evident truth.
axiomatic *adj* self-evident.
axis *n* (*pl* **axes**) the line on which a body revolves; a partnership.
axle *n* the pole on which a wheel turns.
azure *adj* sky-blue.

B

babble *vi* to talk idly; to prate. * *n* idle talk; murmur, as of a stream.
babel *n* confusion.
baboon *n* a large kind of monkey.
baby *n* a child just born; a young animal.
baby-sit *vt, vi* to look after a child during the parents' absence.
bachelor *n* an unmarried man; a graduate of a university or college.
bacillus *n* (*pl* **bacilli**) a microscopic organism; a microbe.
back *n* the hind or (in beasts) the upper part of the body. * *vt* to support; to cause to recede. * *adv* to the rear.
backbite *vt* to speak evil of secretly.
backbone *n* the spine; strength.
background *n* the ground behind; the setting of a picture or photograph; that which has taken place beforehand causing and leading up to an event, etc; social status.
backslide *vi* to degenerate; to relapse.
backward *adj* lagging behind; dull.
backwoods *npl* outlying forest districts.
bacon *n* pig's flesh cured and dried.
bacteriology *n* the study of bacteria.
bacteria *npl* microbes; germs.
bad *adj* wicked; immoral.
badge *n* a distinguishing mark or emblem.
badger *n* a burrowing quadruped. * *vt* to worry; to pester.
badminton *n* a game like lawn tennis played with shuttlecocks as balls.
baffle *vt* to frustrate; to defeat.
bag *n* a sack; a pouch; a purse.
bagatelle *n* a trifle.

baggage *n* luggage.
bagpipe *n* a musical wind instrument.
bail *vt* to liberate from custody on security for reappearance; to free (a boat) from water; to bale. * *n* security given for release; the small bar placed on the stumps in cricket.
bailliff *n* a subordinate civil officer; a landowner's or landlord's steward or agent.
bait *n* food to trap or lure animals or fish; an enticement. * *vt* to furnish with a lure; to harass, esp by verbal teasing.
bake *vt* to dry and harden by fire; to cook in an oven.
balance *n* a pair of scales; equilibrium; difference of two sums; the sum due on an account. * *vt* to bring to an equilibrium; to settle. * *vi* to hesitate.
balance sheet *n* a statement of assets and liabilities.
balcony *n* a railed or walled platform projecting from a window; an upper tier of seats in a theatre or cinema.
bald *adj* wanting hair; bare; paltry.
baldly *adv* nakedly; meanly.
baldness *n* state of being bald; meagreness.
bale *n* a bundle or package of goods. * *vt* to free a boat from water; (with **out**) to escape from aircraft by parachute; to bail.
baleful *adj* deadly.
balk, baulk *n* a ridge; a great beam; part of a billiard table. * *vt* to baffle.
ball *n* a round body; a bullet; a dance.
ballad *n* a narrative poem; a popular sentimental song.
ballast *n* heavy matter carried in a ship to keep it steady.
ballet *n* a theatrical dance.
balloon *n* a large bag filled with a gas which makes it float in the air.
ballot *n* a system of voting. * *vi* to vote by ballot.
balmy *adj* (of weather) pleasantly mild and calm.
balsam *n* soothing ointment.
baluster *n* a small column or pillar supporting a rail.
balustrade *n* a row of pillars joined by a rail.
bamboo *n* a tropical plant of the reed kind.
bamboozle *vt* to hoax; to confuse.
ban *n* a prohibition; an edict. * *vt* to curse; to forbid.
banal *adj* commonplace; vulgar.
banana *n* an edible plant with yellow fruit growing in hanging bunches.
band *n* that which binds; a company of people acting together, e.g. a group of musicians. * *vt* to unite in a troop.
bandage *n* a band; a cloth for a wound, etc. * *vt* to bind with a bandage.
bandit *n* a robber.
bandoleer *n* a shoulder strap for carrying cartridges.
bandy *vt* to exchange, esp words in anger; to pass to and fro.
bandy-legged *adj* having crooked legs.
baneful *adj* pernicious; poisonous.
bang *vt* to thump. * *n* a heavy blow.
bangle *n* a bracelet or anklet.
banish *vt* to drive away; to exile.
banishment *n* act of banishing; exile.
banister *n* a form of baluster that supports the uprights of a staircase.
banjo *n* a six-stringed musical instrument.
bank *n* ground rising from the side of a river, lake, etc; place where money is deposited. * *vt* to deposit in a bank.
banking *n* the business of a banker.
bankrupt *n* one who cannot pay his debts. * *adj* unable to pay debts; insolvent.
banner *n* a standard.
banns *npl* the proclamation of marriage.
banquet *n* a feast.
banter *vt* to chaff; to rally. * *n* raillery.
baptise *vt* to administer baptism to; to christen.
baptism *n* an immersing in or sprinkling with water as a religious ceremony.
baptismal *adj* pertaining to baptism.
bar *n* a bolt; obstacle; a long piece of wood or metal; a tribunal; a body of barristers; anything that prohibits or obstructs; a counter where liquors are served. * *vt* to prohibit.
barb *n* the notched tip of a fishing hook or arrow.
barbarian *adj* savage; uncivilized. * *n* a savage
barbarism *n* extreme cruelty, coarseness or ignorance; an impropriety of speech.

barbarity *n* the state or qualities of a barbarian; ferociousness.
barbarous *adj* cruel; inhuman.
barbed *adj* jagged with hooks or points.
barber *n* a hairdresser.
bare *adj* uncovered; empty; worn. * *vt* to make naked; to reveal.
barebacked *adj* unsaddled.
barefaced *adj* shameless.
barefoot *adj, adv* with the feet bare.
bargain *n* a gainful transaction; a cheap purchase. * *vi* to make a bargain.
barge *n* a flat-bottomed boat for freight used on canals and rivers; a canal pleasure boat. * *vi* to push in bodily.
bark *n* the outer rind of a tree; a barque; the noise made by a dog. * *vt* to strip bark off; to treat with bark; to make the cry of dogs.
barley *n* a species of grain used for making malt, beer, whisky, puddings, etc.
barmaid, barman *n* a woman, man who tends a bar.
barn *n* a building for storing grain, etc.
barometer *n* an instrument for measuring the weight of the atmosphere.
baron *n* a peer of the lowest rank.
baroness *n* a baron's wife.
baronet *n* the lowest order of hereditary titles.
barrack *n* (*usually pl*) buildings for housing soldiers. * *vt* to jeer loudly at.
barrage *n* a bar or dam constructed across a river; the firing of heavy artillery; a continuous onslaught as of words or blows.
barrel *n* a round wooden cask; the tube of a gun.
barren *adj* unfruitful; sterile.
barrenness *n* the state or quality of being barren.
barricade *n* a temporary fortification; a barrier. * *vt* to bar.
barrier *n* a fence; a bar.
barrister *n* a lawyer qualified to plead at the bar.
barrow *n* a small handcart; a burial mound.
barter *vi* to traffic by exchange. * *vt* to exchange in commerce. * *n* traffic by exchange.
baritone *n* a male voice between tenor and bass.
basalt *n* a dark volcanic rock, often found in columnar form.
base *adj* low; worthless. * *n* foundation; support; chief ingredient of a compound. * *vt* to place on a basis; to found.
baseball *n* an American game with four bases set in diamond shape, played with bat and ball.
baseless *adj* groundless.
basement *n* the ground floor.
baseness *n* meanness; vileness.
bashful *adj* modest; shy.
basic *adj* relating to a base; fundamental.
basil *n* an aromatic herb.
basilica *n* a hall or church with double colonnades.
basin *n* a broad shallow dish; a reservoir; a dock; the land drained by a river.
basis *n* (*pl* **bases**) a base; groundwork.
bask *vi* to lie in the sun.
basket *n* a wicker container.
bass *n* the lowest part in musical harmony; the lowest male voice.
bassoon *n* a musical wind instrument.
bastard *adj* illegitimate; not genuine. * *n* a person whose parents are unmarried.
baste *vt* to beat with a stick; to drip fat on meat while roasting; to sew with temporary stitches.
bastion *n* a fortification standing out from a rampart.
bat *n* a flying mammal like a mouse; a club used to strike the ball in cricket, etc. * *vi* to play with a bat.
batch *n* the quantity of bread baked at one time; a quantity.
bath *n* a place to bathe in; immersion in water.
bathe *vt* to immerse in water. * *vi* to take a bath.
baton *n* a staff; a truncheon; a thin stick used by a conductor of music.
battalion *n* a military body three or more companies strong.
batten *n* a board for flooring; strip of wood to fasten down the hatches; a plank. * *vt* to fasten with battens.
batter *vt* to beat with violence. * *n* a cooking mixture of flour, eggs and milk.
battery *n* a fully equipped artillery unit;

an apparatus for originating an electric current; a violent assault.

battle *n* encounter of two armies; a combat.

battlement *n* a parapet with openings to discharge missiles through.

battleship *n* a large warship furnished with heavy artillery.

bauble *n* a trifle.

bawl *vi* to shout; to weep loudly.

bay *adj* reddish-brown. * *n* an inlet on the shore of the sea or a lake; the laurel tree; the bark of a dog. * *vt* to bark at; (with **at**) with back to the wall.

bayonet *n* a dagger-like weapon fixed to a rifle.

bay window *n* a projecting window which forms a recess or bay within.

bazaar *n* a place of sale; a sale of articles for a charitable purpose.

be *vi* to exist; to remain.

beach *n* the shore of the sea. * *vt* to run (a vessel) on a beach.

beached *pa* stranded.

beacon *n* a flare; a signal of danger. * *vt* to light up.

bead *n* a little ball strung on a thread; a small drop of liquid; a small projection for sighting a gun.

beadle *n* a minor officer of a parish, church, or college.

beak *n* the bill of a bird.

beaker *n* a large drinking cup; a glass vessel.

beam *n* a main timber in a building; part of a balance which sustains the scales; a ray of light. * *vi* to shine; to smile broadly.

beaming *adj* emitting beams or rays; radiant.

bean *n* a name of several kinds of pulse or peas.

bear *vt* to carry; to suffer; to bring forth; to permit. * *vi* to suffer; to produce.

bear *n* a large shaggy quadruped.

beard *n* the hair on the chin, etc.

bearer *n* a carrier of anything.

bearing *n* manner, appearance and general behaviour.

beast *n* an animal; a brutal man.

beat *vt* to strike; to overcome. * *vi* to throb; to sail against the wind. * *n* a stroke; a rhythmic stroke of the heart; musical rhythm; the area patrolled by a police officer.

beatify *vt* to make happy; to pronounce a person worthy of canonization.

beating *n* act of striking; defeat.

beauteous *adj* beautiful.

beautiful *adj* full of beauty.

beautify *vt* to make beautiful; to adorn.

beauty *n* loveliness; elegance; a beautiful thing or person.

becalm *vt* to make calm.

because *conj* by cause of; on this account that; since.

beckon, beck *vi* to make a sign to approach by nodding, etc.

become *vi* to come to be. * *vt* to suit.

becoming *adj* fitting; graceful.

bed *n* something to sleep or rest on; the channel of a river; a layer; a stratum. * *vt* to lay in a bed; to sow. * *vi* to go to bed.

bedding *n* the materials of a bed.

bedeck *vt* to adorn.

bedraggle *vt* to soil by drawing through the mud.

bedroom *n* a sleeping room.

bedsit *n* one room with cooking and sleeping facilities.

bedstead *n* a frame for supporting a bed.

beef *n* the flesh of an ox or cow.

beefeater *n* a yeoman of the royal guard.

beeline *n* a direct line or way.

beer *n* a fermented liquor made from barley and hops.

beeswax *n* the wax secreted by bees for their combs.

beet *n* a vegetable with fleshy roots, yielding sugar.

beetle *n* a common insect; a wooden mallet. * *vi* to jut; to hang over.

beetle-browed *adj* having prominent brows.

befall *vt* to happen to.

befit *vt* to suit.

before *prep, adv* in front of; earlier than; rather than; onward.

beforehand *adv* in advance.

befriend *vt* to act as a friend to.

beg *vt* to ask in charity; to ask earnestly; to avoid answering a question; to take for granted.

beget *vt* to procreate; to produce.
beggar *n* one who begs. * *vt* to reduce to poverty; to be beyond, esp description.
begin *vi* to commence. * *vt* to enter on.
beginner *n* one who begins; a novice.
beginning *n* the first stage; commencement.
begrudge *vt* to envy the possession of.
beguile *vt* to dupe; to while away; to charm.
behalf *n* interest; support.
behave *vt* to conduct (oneself). * *vi* to act.
behaviour *n* conduct.
behead *vt* to cut off the head.
behest *n* a command.
behind *prep* in the rear of. * *adv* backwards.
behold *vt* to look upon; to regard with attention.
beholden *adj* obliged.
being *n* existence; a creature.
belabour *vt* to beat soundly.
belated *adj* arriving or made late.
belay *vt* (*naut*) to fasten a rope by winding round something.
belch *vt* to cast forth violently; to expel wind through the mouth.
beleaguer *vt* to besiege.
belfry *n* a bell tower.
belie *vt* to represent falsely; to fail to be equal to.
belief *n* faith; trust; opinion.
believe *vt* to accept as true; think.
belittle *vt* to make smaller; to disparage.
bell *n* a metallic vessel for making ringing sounds when struck; anything in the form of a bell. * *vt* to put a bell on.
bellicose *adj* pugnacious.
belligerent *adj* waging war; quarrelsome. * *n* a nation waging war.
bellow *vi* to roar like a bull. * *n* a roar.
bellows *npl* an instrument for blowing fires, supplying wind to organ pipes, etc.
belly *n* that part of the body which contains the bowels; the abdomen. * *vt, vi* to swell; to bulge.
belong *vi* to be the property of; to appertain to; to be a member.
belongings *npl* personal possessions.
beloved *adj* greatly loved.
below *prep* under; beneath. * *adv* in a lower place.
belt *n* a girdle; a band; a stripe; area, e.g. of trees.
bemoan *vt* to lament.
bemused *adj* muddled.
bench *n* a long seat; a long work table; seat of justice; body of judges.
bend *vt* to curve; to direct to a certain point; to adjust for one's own purpose. * *n* a curve.
beneath *prep, adv*. below; under.
benediction *n* a solemn blessing.
benefactor *n* a person who confers a benefit.
benefice *n* an ecclesiastical living.
beneficent *adj* kind; bountiful.
beneficial *adj* helpful; bringing about improvement.
beneficiary *n* a person who is benefited or assisted or gains.
benefit *n* an act of kindness; a favour; something that brings improvement; an allowance from government, an employer, etc. * *vt* to do a service to.
benevolence *n* kindness; active love of mankind.
benevolent *adj* kind; charitable.
benign *adj* gracious; kind.
bent *n* bias of mind; aptitude; a wiry grass.
benumb *vt* to deprive of sensation.
benzene *n* a liquid used to remove grease and as an insecticide.
bequeath *vt* to leave by will.
bequest *n* a legacy.
bereave *vt* to deprive of someone dear by death.
bereavement *n* loss by death.
berry *n* a pulpy fruit containing seeds.
berserk *adj* frenzied.
berth *n* a place in which a moored ship lies; a place for sleeping in a train, ship, etc. * *vt* to moor.
beseech *vt* to entreat.
beseechingly *adv* imploringly.
beset *vt* to surround; to attack from every direction.
besetting *adj* habitual.
beside, besides *prep* by the side of; near. * *adv* moreover.
besiege *vt* to lay siege to.

besotted *adj* infatuated.
bespatter *vt* to spatter over.
bespeak *vt* to speak for beforehand.
best *adj* the superlative degree of 'good'. * *adv* the superlative of 'well'. * *vt* to defeat; to beat.
bestial *adj* brutish.
bestiality *n* brutish conduct.
bestir *vt* to rouse oneself to action.
bestow *vt* to gift; to present with.
bestraddle *vt* to bestride.
bestride *vt* to stride over or across; to span.
bet *n* a wager. * *vt* to wager.
betide *vi* to befall; to happen.
betoken *vt* to imply; to foreshadow.
betray *vt* to prove false to; to entrap.
betrayal *n* act of betraying.
betroth *vt* to pledge in marriage.
betrothal *n* mutual promise to marry.
better *adj* comparative of 'good'. * *adv* comparative of 'well'. * *vt* to advance; to outdo.
between *prep* in the middle.
bevel *n* an instrument for setting angles.
beverage *n* a drink.
bevy *n* a flock of birds.
bewail *vt* to lament.
beware *vi* to take care.
bewilder *vt* to perplex.
bewilderment *n* perplexity.
bewitch *vt* to enchant.
bewitching *adj* fascinating.
bewitchment *n* fascination.
beyond *prep* on the farther side of; post; not within reach. * *adv* at a distance; further on.
bias *n* weight on one side; a bent; a prejudice. * *vt* to incline to one side.
biased, biassed *adj* prejudiced.
bib *n* a cloth or plastic cover tied round the neck (of a child) to protect clothing from food spillage.
Bible *n* the Holy Scriptures of the Christian faith.
biblical *adj* pertaining to the Bible.
bibliographical *adj* pertaining to bibliography.
bibliography *n* an account, description or reference list of books on a subject.
bibliomania *n* a passion for possessing books.
bibliophile *n* a lover of books.
bibulous *adj* given to tippling.
bicentenary *n* two hundred years.
biceps *npl* muscles of the forearm.
bicker *vi* to quarrel.
bicycle *n* a two-wheeled vehicle propelled by pedals.
bicyclist *n* one who rides a bicycle.
bid *vt* to ask; to order; to offer. * *n* an offer, as at an auction.
biddable *adj* obedient.
bidding *n* an invitation; a command.
biennial *adj* lasting for two years; taking place once in two years.
biennially *adv* once in two years.
bier *n* the frame on which a corpse rests or is borne.
bifurcate(d) *adj* forked or divided into two.
big *adj* great; large.
bigamist *n* one who commits bigamy.
bigamy *n* the crime of having two wives or husbands at once.
bigot *n* a person obstinately wedded to particular ideas.
bigoted *adj* prejudiced.
bigotry *n* intolerance.
bilateral *adj* two-sided.
bile *n* the bitter secretion of the liver; ill-nature.
bilge *n* the bulging part of a cask; the breadth of a ship's bottom.
bilge water *n* dirty water in the bilge of a ship.
bilingual *adj* in two languages.
bilious *adj* affected by bile.
bill *n* the beak of a bird; an instrument for pruning; an account of money due; draft of a new law; a poster or leaflet.
billet *n* a small note in writing; lodgings; a situation. * *vt* to quarter, as soldiers.
billet-doux *n* (*pl* **billets-doux**) a love letter.
billiards *npl* a game played on a table with balls and cues.
billion *n* a million of millions.
billow *n* a great wave of the sea.
bimonthly *adj* every two months.
bin *n* a receptacle.
binary *adj* twofold.
bind *vt* to tie; to oblige; to cover (a book); to make firm; to bandage. * *vi* to grow

hard, tight or stiff; to be obligatory.

binding *n* the cover and sewing of a book. * *adj* obligatory.

bingo *n* a gambling game with numbered cards for several people in which numbers called are covered by players until a card is full.

binocular *adj* adapted for both eyes. * *npl* field or opera glasses.

binomial *adj, n.* an algebraic expression with two terms.

biochemistry *n* the study of the chemistry of living organisms.

biogenesis *n* the doctrine that living matter springs only from living matter.

biographer *n* a writer of biography.

biography *n* written life of a person.

biologist *n* one skilled in biology.

biology *n* the study of the science of living organisms.

bipartite *adj* having two parts.

biped *n* an animal with two feet.

bird *n* a feathered, egg-laying vertebrate with wings.

birth *n* the act of bearing or coming into life.

birthright *n* any right to which a person is entitled by birth.

biscuit *n* a hard, flat, sweet or plain cake.

bisect *vt* to half.

bishop *n* the head of a diocese.

bishopric *n* the office of a bishop; a diocese.

bit *n* a morsel; the metal part of a bridle; a boring tool used with a brace.

bitch *n* a female dog or wolf.

bite *vt* to crush or sever with the teeth; to cause to smart; to wound by reproach, etc; to corrode. * *n* a wound made by biting; a mouthful.

biting *adj* sharp; piercingly cold; sarcastic.

bitter *adj* sharp to the taste; severe; painful.

bitterness *n* the quality of being bitter.

bitumen *n* a pitch-like substance.

bivalve *n* a two-valved animal.

bivouac *n* an encampment of soldiers for the night in the open air.

biweekly *adj* occurring every two weeks.

bizarre *adj* fantastic; odd; strange

black *adj* having no light; dark; gloomy; sullen; atrocious; wicked. * *n* the darkest colour. * *vt* to make black.

blackboard *n* a board for writing on with chalk.

blacken *vt* to make black. * *vi* to grow black or dark; to speak ill of.

blackguard *n* a scoundrel. * *vt* to revile.

blackleg *n* one who works during a strike.

blackmail *n* money extorted by threats. * *vt* to commit the crime of blackmail.

black market *n* illegal buying and selling when restrictions are in force.

blackout *n* total darkness when lighting has failed or been switched off; a loss of consciousness temporarily.

blacksmith *n* a smith who works in iron.

bladder *n* a membrane in animals containing the urine; a blister.

blade *n* a leaf; the cutting part of a sword, knife; the flat part of an oar.

blame *vt* to censure. * *n* censure; fault.

blameless *adj* free from blame.

blanch *vt* to make white. * *vi* to grow white.

blancmange *n* a white jelly.

bland *adj* mild; gentle.

blandish *vt* to soothe; to flatter.

blandishment *n* flattery.

blank *adj* white; empty. * *n* a void space.

blanket *n* a woollen covering.

blank verse *n* verse without rhyme.

blare *vi* to give forth a loud, harsh sound.

blarney *n* flattery; insincere talk.

blasé *adj* satiated; used up; bored.

blaspheme *vt* to speak irreverently of something held sacred.

blasphemous *adj* impious; irreverent.

blast *n* a gust of wind; the sound of a wind instrument; a violent explosion; harsh criticism. * *vt* to blight.

blatant *adj* noisy and loud; glaringly obvious.

blaze *n* a flame; a fire; brilliance. * *vi* to flame. * *vt* to noise abroad.

bleach *vt* to make white. * vi to grow white.

bleak *adj* dreary; dark and gloomy.

blear *adj* sore; dimmed.

blear-eyed, bleary-eyed *adj* sore or watery-eyed.

bleat *vi* to cry as a sheep. * *n* the cry of a sheep.
bleed *vi* to emit or lose blood. * *vt* to take blood from.
bleeding *n* a flow of blood; the operation of letting blood; the drawing of sap from a tree.
blemish *vt* to mar; to tarnish. * *n* a stain; dishonour.
blend *vt* to mix together. * *n* a mixture.
bless *vt* to make happy; to invoke a blessing.
blessed *adj* happy; holy.
blessing *n* a benediction; a prayer of thanks; good wishes.
blight *n* that which withers up or destroys wholesale; mildew. * *vt* to wither up; to blast; to cause failure.
blind *adj* destitute of sight; having no outlet. * *n* a screen; a pretext. * *vt* to make blind.
blindfold *adj* having the eyes covered.
blindly *adv* heedlessly.
blindness *n* want of sight; ignorance.
blink *vi* to wink; to twinkle. * *vt* to shut the eyes upon.
blinker *n* a flap to prevent a horse from seeing sideways.
bliss *n* perfect happiness.
blissful *adj* full of bliss.
blister *n* a watery bubble on the skin; a swelling as on paint. * *vt* to raise a blister; to castigate vigorously.
blithe *adj* joyful.
blizzard *n* a violent snowstorm.
bloated *adj* inflated.
blob *n* a small globe of liquid.
block *n* a heavy piece of wood; a lump of solid matter; a piece of wood in which a pulley is placed; buildings in a group; an obstacle. * *vt* to shut up; to obstruct.
blockade *n* a close siege by troops or ships. * *vt* to besiege closely.
blockhead *n* a stupid fellow.
blockhouse *n* a building used for defence.
blond, blonde *adj* having fair hair; of a fair complexion.
blood *n* the red fluid which circulates in animals; kindred. * *adj* pertaining to blood.
bloodless *adj* without blood; lifeless.
bloodshot *adj* inflamed.
bloodthirsty *adj* eager to shed blood.
blood vessel *n* an artery or a vein.
bloody *adj* stained with blood; cruel.
bloom *n* a blossom; a flower; state of healthy youthfulness. * *vi* to blossom.
blossom *n* the flower of a plant. * *vi* to bloom.
blot *vt* to spot; to stain; to dry. * *n* a spot or stain; a disgrace.
blotch *n* a spot or discoloured patch.
blotting paper *n* absorbent paper to dry up ink.
blouse *n* a loose upper garment.
blow *vi* to make a current of air; to pant; to bloom. * *vt* to impel by wind; to inflate. * *n* a blast; a blossoming; a heavy punch; a stroke; a misfortune.
blowpipe *n* a tube for heating flame by blowing air into it; a tube for blowing poison darts.
blubber *n* the fat of whales. * *vi* to weep noisily.
bludgeon *n* a short club.
blue *n* the colour of the sky; one of the seven primary colours; a university athletic distinction. * *adj* of a blue colour; sky-coloured; depressed. * *vt* to dye a blue colour.
blueprint *n* a print of plans, etc, photographed on a blue background; a plan used as a basis of future work.
bluestocking *n* a learned woman.
bluff *adj* hearty; blunt. * *n* a steep projecting bank. * *vt, vi* to persuade or deceive by a show of boldness or strength.
bluish *adj* slightly blue.
blunder *vi* to err stupidly. * *n* a mistake; an error.
blunt *adj* not sharp; unceremonious; rude; straightforward. * *vt* to make blunt or dull.
blur *n* a stain; a blot; a hazy impression. * *vt* to stain; to obscure.
blurt *vt* to utter suddenly or unadvisedly.
blush *vi* to redden in the face. * *n* a red colour in the face caused by shame, embarrassment, etc.
bluster *vi* to roar like wind; to swagger; to boast and bully. * *n* swaggering.
blustering *adj* noisy; windy.
boa *n* a large snake without fangs; a feath-

ery or fur scarf.

boar *n* the male of the pig or hog.

board *n* a strip of timber broad and thin; a table; food; persons seated round a table; a council; a group of people in charge of a company; the deck of a ship. * *vt* to cover with boards; to supply with food; to enter a train, bus, ship, etc.

boarder *n* one who receives food and lodging at a stated charge.

boarding house *n* a house where board and lodging are provided for payment.

boarding school *n* a school where the pupils are boarders.

boast *vi* to brag. * *vt* to magnify. * *n* a bragging utterance.

boastful *adj* given to boasting.

boat *n* a small open vessel, usually impelled by oars; a small ship.

boatswain *n* a petty officer or warrant officer on board ship.

bob *n* something that hangs or plays loosely; a short jerking motion; a woman's short haircut. * *vt* to move with a short jerking motion. * *vi* to play to and fro or up and down; to curtsey.

bobbin *n* a winding pin; a reel.

bode *vt* to portend.

bodice *n* the upper part of a dress; an inner vest; a corset.

bodily *adv* wholly; entirely.

body *n* the trunk or main part of an animal or human being; matter; a person; a dead person; a group of people; any solid figure.

bodyguard *n* one appointed to guard the safety of another.

bog *n* a marsh.

bogus *adj* sham.

boil *vi* to bubble from the action of heat; to seethe. * *vt* to heat to a boiling state. * *n* a sore swelling or tumour.

boisterous *adj* stormy; noisy; loud and high-spirited.

bold *adj* daring.

boldness *n* courage.

bole *n* the body or stem of a tree.

bolster *n* a long pillow. * *vt* to hold up; to give support to a person.

bolt *n* an arrow; a thunderbolt; a bar of a door. * *vi* to leave suddenly. * *vt* to fasten; to swallow hastily.

bomb *n* an explosive shell.

bombard *vt* to attack with continual fire and bombs; to attack with words and questions.

bombast *n* high-sounding words.

bombastic *adj* inflated; turgid; pompous.

bona fide *adv, adj* in good faith; genuine.

bond *n* that which binds; obligation; a legal deed; (*pl*) chains; a place where dutiable goods are stored. * *vt* to grant a bond in security for money; to store till duty is paid.

bondage *n* slavery.

bonded *adj* liable to pay duty.

bone *n* the hard part of the skeleton. * *vt* to take out bones from.

bonfire *n* an open-air fire.

bon mot *n* (*pl* **bons mots**) a witticism.

bonnet *n* a headdress.

bonny *adj* beautiful.

bonus *n* a premium; extra gift to shareholders; an addition to a salary.

book *n* a collection of printed sheets bound together. * *vt* to enter in a book; to reserve beforehand; to note a person's particulars for a minor offence.

booking office *n* an office where people buy tickets in advance.

bookish *adj* fond of study.

book-keeper *n* one who keeps accounts.

booklet *n* a little book.

bookmaker *n* a person who takes bets on events and pays out winnings.

bookseller *n* one who sells books.

bookworm *n* one who pores over books.

boom *n* a long pole to extend the bottom of a sail; a chain barrier across a river or harbour; a hollow roar; prosperity in commerce; in film studies, a long pole with a microphone at the end. * *vi* to roar; to make a loud, deep noise; to boost; to prosper.

boomerang *n* an Australian missile which when thrown returns to the thrower.

boon *n* a favour; something helpful; a plessing.

boor *n* a rustic; a rude, unhelpful person.

boorish *adj* clownish; rude.

boot *n* a covering for the foot.

booth *n* a temporary shed; a stall; a cubi-

cle for voting or for a telephone.
booty *n* spoil; plunder.
border *n* the outer edge of anything; the boundary line between two countries. * *vi* to approach near. * *vt* to surround with a border.
bore *vt* to make a hole in; to pester; to weary by being dull, uninteresting or repetitious. * *n* the hole made by boring; the diameter of a tube; a tiresome person; a great tidal wave.
boreal *adj* northern.
born *pp of* **bear** to bring forth.
borne *pp of* **bear** to carry.
borrow *vt* to ask or receive as a loan.
bosom *n* the breast; the seat of the affections. * *adj* beloved.
boss *n* a knob; a master; a manager. * *vt* to be domineering; to be or act as a boss.
botanic, botanical *adj* pertaining to botany.
botanist *n* one skilled in botany.
botany *n* the science which treats of plants.
botch *vt* to perform clumsily.
both *adj, pron* the two. * *conj* as well.
bother *vt* to annoy. * *vi* to trouble oneself. * *n* a trouble.
bothersome *adj* causing trouble.
bottle *n* a narrow-mouthed vessel of glass or plastic; the contents of a bottle.
bottom *n* the lowest part; the ground under water; foundation. * *vt* to found or build upon.
boudoir *n* a woman's private room.
bough *n* a branch of a tree.
boulder *n* a large roundish stone or rock.
boulevard *n* a wide street planted with trees.
bounce *vi* to spring or rush out suddenly; to rebound; to boast. * *n* springiness; a boast.
bouncing *adj* big; strong; boastful.
bound *n* a boundary; a leap. * *vt* to limit. * *vi* to leap. * *adj* obliged; sure; ready; destined.
boundary *n* a bounding line; a border.
bounden *adj* obligatory.
boundless *adj* unlimited.
bounteous *adj* liberal.
bountiful *adj* generous.
bounty *n* liberality; a premium to encourage trade; a reward.
bouquet *n* a bunch of flowers; a perfume from wine.
bourgeois *n* a middle-class citizen.
bout *n* a contest; a spell.
bovine *adj* dull, stupid.
bow[1] *vt* to bend. * *vi* to make a reverence. * *n* a bending of the head or body; the curved forepart of a ship.
bow[2] *n* a weapon to shoot arrows; the rainbow; a stick for playing on violin strings; a slipknot.
bowdlerize *vt* to expurgate.
bowed *adj* bent like a bow.
bowels *npl* the lower intestines.
bower *n* an arbour.
bowl[1] *n* a ball of wood; (*pl*) the game played with such bowls. * *vi* to play with bowls; to deliver a ball at cricket.
bowl[2] *n* a large roundish dish.
bow-legged *adj* bandy-legged.
bowler[1] *n* one who plays bowls; to deliver a ball at cricket.
bowler[2] *n* a stiff felt hat.
bowling green *n* a smooth lawn for the game of bowls.
bowman *n* an archer.
bowsprit *n* a spar projecting over the bow of a ship.
bow window *n* a bay window.
box *n* a case of wood, metal, etc; a seat in a theatre; a blow; a tree or shrub. * *vt* to put in a box; to strike. * *vi* to fight with the fists.
boxer *n* a pugilist.
boy *n* a male child.
boycott *vt* to refuse dealings with.
boyhood *n* the state of being a boy.
brace *n* a support; a bandage; a couple; a boring tool; (*pl*) suspenders. * *vt* to tighten; to straighten up; to strengthen.
bracelet *n* an ornament for the wrist.
bracing *adj* invigorating.
bracken *n* a species of fern.
bracket *n* a support for something fixed to a wall; a mark—() or []—in writing or printing to enclose words. * *vt* to place within or connect by brackets; to group.
bracketing *n* grouping together.
brackish *adj* salt; saltish.

brag *vi* to talk big. * *n* a boast.

braggart *adj* boastful. * *n* a boaster.

braid *vt* to weave together strands of hair, thread, etc. * *n* a plaited band.

braided *adj* edged with braid.

brain *n* the centre of thought and sensation; the soft matter within the skull.

braise, braize *vt* to cook in a covered pan.

brake *n* a device on a wheel to reduce speed or to stop motion; a type of wagon.

bran *n* the husks of ground corn.

branch *n* the offshoot of a tree; the offshoot of anything, as of a river, family. * *vi* to spread in branches; (with **out**) to broaden or increase one's activities.

brand *n* a burning piece of wood; a mark made with a hot iron; a trademark; a particular make (of goods). * *vt* to mark with a hot iron; to denounce.

brandish *vt* to shake; wave.

brandy *n* a spirit distilled from wine or fruit such as apricot, plum, etc.

brass *n* a yellow alloy of copper and zinc; brass section of an orchestra or band; impudence.

brassière *n* a woman's undergarment protecting and supporting the breasts; a bra.

brat *n* an ill-behaved child.

bravado *n* bluster.

brave *adj* daring; valiant. * *vt* to defy.

bravery *n* courage.

brawl *vi* to quarrel noisily. * *n* uproar.

brawn *n* the flesh of a boar; muscle; strength.

brawny *adj* muscular.

bray *vi* to make a loud harsh sound, as an ass. * *n* the cry of an ass.

brazen *adj* made of brass; impudent.

brazier *n* a worker in brass; a portable fire.

breach *n* the act of breaking; quarrel. * *vt* to make a gap in.

bread *n* food made of flour or meal baked.

breadth *n* width.

break *vt* to sever by fracture; to rend; to tame; to interrupt; to dissolve any union; to tell with discretion. * *vi* to come to pieces; to burst forth. * *n* an opening; a breach; a pause; the dawn.

breakage *n* a breaking.

breakdown *n* a failure or stoppage due to mechanical malfunction; a nervous or mental collapse; an analysing and classifying of a project, etc, into its separate parts.

breaker *n* a large, crested wave.

breakfast *n* the first meal in the day.

breakneck *adj* dangerously fast.

breakwater *n* a mole or bar to break the force of the waves.

breast *n* the fore part of the body; the conscience; the affections. * *vt* to face.

breastbone *n* the bone of the breast.

breath *n* the air drawn into and expelled from the lungs; life; pause; a gentle breeze.

breathe *vt, vi* to take breath; to live; to utter.

breathing *n* respiration.

breathless *adj* out of breath.

bred *pp* of **breed**.

breech *n* the hinder part (of a gun, etc); (*pl* **breeches**) garment for men.

breed *vt, vi* to bring forth; to educate; to rear. * *n* offspring; kind.

breeding *n* the raising of a breed; good manners.

breeze *n* a light wind.

brethren *npl* of **brother**.

breve *n* a note in music.

brevity *n* shortness.

brew *vt* to prepare from malt; to concoct; to scheme. * *vi* to make beer; to infuse tea. * *n* the mixture formed by brewing.

brewery *n* the place where beer brewing is carried on.

bribe *n* a gift to corrupt the conduct or judgment. * *vt* to gain over by bribes.

bribery *n* the giving or taking of bribes.

bric-à-brac *n* old curios.

brick *n* a rectangular block of baked clay or other material used in building.

bricklayer *n* one who builds with bricks.

bridal *n* a wedding. * *adj* belonging to a bride or a wedding.

bride *n* a woman about to be or newly married.

bridegroom *n* a man about to be or newly married.

bridesmaid *n* a woman who attends on a bride during a wedding.

bridge *n* a roadway across a river; a structure to carry people, vehicles, railways across; something that serves to fill a gap or helps communication; a platform on a ship from which the captain issues commands; a card game like whist. * *vt* to build a bridge over.

bridle *n* the headgear of a horse; a curb; a check. * *vt* to put a bridle on; to restrain.

brief *adj* short. * *n* a summary of a client's case; (*pl*) underpants without legs.

brigade *n* a group of two or more regiments.

brigadier *n* the officer who commands a brigade.

bright *adj* clear; shining; lively; clever.

brighten *vti* to make bright.

brilliance *n* the state of being brilliant; splendour.

brilliant *adj* sparkling. * *n* a diamond.

brim *n* the rim of anything.

brimful *adj* full to the brim.

brindled *adj* marked with brown streaks.

brine *n* salt water.

bring *vt* to lead; to fetch; to produce; to cause to happen.

brink *n* the edge; the margin; the moment before a happening, often a disaster.

brisk *adj* lively.

brisket *n* the breast of an animal.

briskly *adv* actively.

bristle *n* a stiff hair. * *vt, vi* to stand on end; to show anger.

brittle *adj* apt to break.

broach *n* a roasting spit. * *vt* to pierce, as with a spit; to tap; to open up.

broad *adj* wide.

broaden *vi* to grow broad. * *vt* to make broad.

broadside *n* a discharge of all the guns on one side of a ship.

brocade *n* a silk stuff with raised pattern.

brochure *n* a pamphlet.

brogue *n* a strong shoe formerly of raw hide; the Irish accent.

broil *n* a brawl. * *vt* to cook over a fire.

broken *adj* crushed; ruined.

broker *n* an agent who buys and sells for others.

brokerage *n* the business of a broker.

bromide *n* a drug; a platitude.

bronchi *npl* the tubes branching from the windpipe to the lungs.

bronchial *adj* belonging to the air tubes.

bronchitis *n* inflammation of the bronchial tubes.

bronze *n* an alloy of copper and tin; a colour.

brooch *n* an ornament to pin on a dress.

brood *vi* to sit on eggs; to ponder anxiously. * *n* offspring.

brook *n* a small stream. * *vt* to bear.

broom *n* a shrub with yellow flowers; a brush.

broth *n* a meat soup with vegetables.

brother *n* a son of the same parents; an associate; a fellow creature; a working or lay member of a male religious order.

brotherhood *n* the relationship of a brother; an association.

brow *n* the ridge over the eye; the forehead; the edge of a cliff.

browbeat *vt* to bully.

brown *adj* dusky; tanned. * *n* a colour resulting from the mixture of red, black, and yellow.

brownie *n* a junior Guide; a small nutty, chocolate cake.

browse *vt* to feed upon; to read through casually.

bruise *vt* to crush; to injure and cause discolouration of the skin without drawing blood. * *n* a skin discolouration from a blow.

brunette *n* a woman with a dark complexion and dark hair.

brunt *n* the main area to bear the shock of an attack, etc.

brush *n* an implement with bristles for cleaning by rubbing or sweeping or for painting; a skirmish; a thicket; the tail of a fox. * *vt, vi* to sweep; to touch lightly.

brushwood *n* small trees and shrubs growing together.

brusque *adj* abrupt; rude.

brutal *adj* cruel.

brutality *n* savageness; cruelty.

brute *adj* purely physical; sheer, as in brute force. * *n* a beast; a brutal person.

brutish *adj* brutal; sensual.

bubble *n* a fluid film enclosing air; a swindle. * *vi* to rise in bubbles.

buccaneer *n* a pirate.

buck *n* the male of deer, goats; a lively, stylish young fellow. * *vi* to jump violently.

bucket *n* a pail.

buckle *n* a strap or belt fastener. * *vt* to fasten; to bend.

buckshot *n* lead shot for hunting big game.

bucolic *adj* pastoral; rustic.

bud *n* a young shoot or flower. * *vi* to put forth buds.

budding *n* a method of grafting buds. * *adj* promising.

budge *vt* to move; to stir.

budget *n* a financial statement; an estimate for expenditure. * *vt, vi* to put on a budget; to plan; to make a budget.

buff *n* a yellow colour; the bare skin. * *adj* light yellow. * *vt* to clean or shine by rubbing.

buffer *n* anything for deadening the shock of collision, etc.

buffet[1] *n* a sideboard; a refreshment bar; a meal where people serve themselves.

buffet[2] *n* a blow; a slap. * *vt* to box; to contend against.

buffoon *n* a clown; one who plays the fool to amuse; a fool.

buffoonery *n* the antics of a buffoon.

bugle *n* a hunting horn; a kind of trumpet.

bugler *n* one who plays the bugle.

build *vt* to construct; to establish. * *vi* to form a structure. * *n* make; form.

building *n* an edifice; the art or trade of building.

building society *n* a financial company where deposits of money are paid interest and loans are made esp for house buying and mortgages.

bulb *n* a round root.

bulbous *adj* swelling out.

bulge *n* a swelling; a rounded projection. * *vt* to swell out.

bulk *n* size; the main mass; cargo.

bulky *adj* large and awkwardly shaped.

bull *n* the male of cattle, elephant and whale; an edict of the pope.

bulldog *n* a species of dog; a never-say-die person.

bullet *n* a metal missile shot from a firearm.

bulletin *n* an official report.

bullion *n* uncoined gold or silver.

bull's-eye *n* the centre of a target; a shot hitting this; any aim that is achieved.

bully *n* an overbearing quarrelsome fellow. * *vt* to insult and threaten.

bulwark *n* a rampart; a person or thing acting as a strong buffer.

bump *n* a heavy blow, or the noise of it; a lump produced by a blow. * *vt* to crash or knock against.

bumper *n* a full glass; a protective metal bar fixed at the front and rear of a vehicle to absorb shock.

bumptious *adj* self-assertive.

bun *n* a small cake; a round coil of hair worn at the nape of the neck.

bunch *n* a cluster.

bundle *n* a package. * *vt, vi* to tie in a bundle; to hurry off.

bungalow *n* a one-storeyed house.

bungle *vi* to botch. * *n* a clumsy performance.

bunion *n* a lump on the ball of the big toe.

bunk *n* a sleeping berth; a narrow bed.

bunker *n* a large bin; a sandpit hazard on a golf course; an underground shelter.

bunting *n* stuff of which flags are made; flags.

buoy *n* a floating navigation mark. * *vt* to keep afloat; (with **up**) to give support or encouragement to.

buoyancy *n* capacity for floating; cheerfulness; resilience.

buoyant *adj* floating; light; cheerful.

bur, burr *n* a prickly fruit, seed case or flowerhead.

burden *n* a load; something hard or wearisome to bear; a chorus. * *vt* to load; to oppress.

bureau *n* (*pl* **bureaux**) a writing table; a chest of drawers; a government office.

bureaucracy *n* government through state departments; unnecessary officialdom.

burgeon *vt, vi* to flourish; to grow rapidly and profusely.

burglar *n* a housebreaker.

burglary *n* the act of housebreaking.
burgundy *n* a red or white wine produced in Burgundy.
burial *n* the act of burying; interment.
burlesque *adj* comic. * *n* a caricature; a satirical play caricaturing some subject. * *vt* to turn into ridicule.
burly *adj* stout; portly; of a strong build.
burn *vti* to consume with fire; to be on fire; to rage fiercely. * *n* a hurt caused by fire; a rivulet.
burning *adj* fiery; vehement.
burnish *vt* to polish. * *n* polish.
burrow *n* a hole in the earth made by rabbits, etc. * *vi* to excavate.
bursar *n* a treasurer; a student who holds a scholarship.
bursary *n* a scholarship.
burst *vi* to fly or break open; to rush forth. * *vt* to break by force.
bury *vt* to put into a grave; to cover; to conceal.
bus *n* (*pl* **buses**) an omnibus.
bush *n* a shrub; a thicket.
business *n* occupation; concern.
busk *vi* to entertain for money.
bust *n* the bosom; the figure from head to chest in sculpture.
bustle *vi* to hustle. * *n* hurry.
busy *adj* occupied. * *vt* to employ.
busybody *n* a meddler.
but *conj, prep, adv* yet, except, only.
butcher *n* one who kills or sells animals for food. * *vt* to slaughter.
butler *n* a male servant in charge of a wine cellar.
butt *n* the end of a thing; a mark to be shot at; an object of ridicule; a cask of wine. * *vt* to strike with the head.
butter *n* the substance obtained from cream by churning. * *vt* to spread with butter; to flatter grossly.
buttercup *n* a wild yellow cup-shaped flower.
butterfly *n* a winged insect often brightly coloured; a showy person; a swimming stroke.
buttermilk *n* the milk that remains after the butter is separated.
button *n* a knob or disc for fastening; a badge. * *vt* to fasten with buttons.
buttress *n* a construction to support and strengthen a wall; a prop. * *vt* to support by a prop.
buxom *adj* jolly; large.
buy *vt* to purchase.
buzz *vi* to hum. * *n* a humming noise.
by *prep, adv.* used to denote the instrument, agent, or manner; at the rate of; not later than.
bye *n* in certain games, reaching the second round without playing an opponent in the first; a ball scoring a run in cricket without being hit by a batsman.
bygone *adj* past.
bylaw *n* a local law.
bypass *n* a road that skirts a town; a rechannelling, esp of blood flow into the heart. * *vt* to go round so as to avoid.
byre *n* a cow house.
bystander *n* a spectator.
byway *n* a side way.
byword *n* a common saying; a proverb.

C

cabal *n* an intrigue; a party clique. * *vi* to combine in plotting.
cabbage *n* a vegetable.
cabin *n* a hut; a room in a ship. * *vt* to confine.
cabinet *n* a closet; a showcase; the ministers of state.
cabinet-maker *n* a maker of furniture.
cable *n* anchor rope; a submarine telegraph wire. * *vt* to send by cable.
cackle *vi* to utter a cry (as of a hen); to chatter. * *n* clucking; idle talk or laughter.
cadaverous *adj* ghastly, deathlike.
cadence *n* a fall of the voice at the end of a sentence.
cadet *n* a younger brother; a military pupil.
cadge *vt vi.* to go about begging.
cadmium *n* a whitish metal.
Caesarean Section *n* the removal by surgery of a baby from the womb.
café *n* a small informal restaurant; a cof-

fee bar.

cage *n* a wire frame to confine birds or beasts.

cairn *n* a heap of stones as landmark or memorial.

cairngorm *n* a yellow-brown rock crystal as a gem.

caisson *n* a structure to raise sunken vessels; a structure used in laying foundations in deep water.

cajole *vt* to wheedle; to persude by smooth words.

cake *n* baked dough in various forms; fancy bread; a flat compact mass.

calamitous *adj* disastrous.

calamity *n* misfortune; disaster.

calcareous *adj* containing lime.

calculate *vt* to count; to think out; to estimate.

calculating *adj* scheming.

calculus *n* (*math*) a method of calculation.

calendar *n* a means of calculating years, months, days; an almanac; a list of coming events.

calf *n* the young of the cow; the fleshy lower part of the leg.

calibre *n* the diameter of the bore of a gun; quality.

calico *n* a cotton cloth, usually unbleached.

call *vt* to name; to summon. * *vi* to utter a loud sound; to make a short visit. * *n* a summons; a short visit; a bird's note; a need; a demand.

calligraphy *n* the art of writing.

calling *n* a vocation.

callipers *n, npl* compasses for measuring calibre; a metal support strapped to the leg for support.

callisthenics *n* exercises for strength or grace of movement.

callous *adj* hardened; unfeeling.

callow *adj* young and immature.

calm *adj* still; quiet; windless. * *n* tranquillity. * *vt* to soothe; to pacify.

calmness *n* composure, stillness.

calorie *n* a unit of heat; a unit measuring the energy of food.

calorific *adj* causing heat.

calumnious *adj* slanderous.

calumny *n* slander; defamination.

calve *vi* to give birth to a calf.

calypso *n* a West Indian story in song to a syncopated rhythm.

camber *n* the slight curve upward towards the centre of a road surface.

cambered *adj* curved.

cambric *n* a fine white linen.

cameo *n* a precious stone carved in relief.

camera *n* an apparatus for taking photographs or cinema and television pictures; a judge's private chamber.

camisole *n* an under bodice.

camp *n* the ground on which tents are pitched; the collection of tents; those who support a cause or party.

campaign *n* the operations of an army in war.

campaigner *n* an old soldier.

campus *n* the grounds (and buildings) of a university.

can[1] *n* a metal vessel; a tin.

can[2] *vi* (*past* could) to be able.

canal *n* an artificial watercourse for boats; a duct or channel in the body.

canard *n* a false rumour.

canary *n* a light wine; a song bird.

cancel *vt* to strike out; to delete; to annul; to undo or call off.

cancer *n* one of the signs of the zodiac; a malignant growth.

candelabrum n (*pl* **candelabra**) a branched ornamental candlestick.

candid *adj* frank; outspoken; fair and unprejudiced.

candidate *n* an applicant for a post or office; someone worthy to be chosen; someone taking an examination.

candidly *adv* sincerely.

candle *n* a stick of wax with a wick for lighting.

candlestick *n* a candleholder.

candour *n* frankness.

candy *vt* to conserve with sugar. * *n* a sweetmeat.

cane *n* a walking stick; the stem of some plants as bamboo; a thin stick for supporting plants. * *vt* to beat with a cane.

canine *adj* pertaining to dogs.

canister *n* a small box; an explosive shell.

canker *n* an ulcer; a blight.

cannabis *n* a drug from the hemp plant.

cannibal *n* a person who eats human flesh. * *adj* relating to cannibalism.
cannon *n* a large gun mounted on a carriage; a shot in billiards when the cue ball strikes two other balls; an impact and rebound. * *vt* to collide with.
cannonade *n* a bombardment.
cannot the negative of **can**.
canny *adj* cautious; wary.
canoe *n* a skiff driven by paddles.
canon *n* a decree; a law; a rule or criterion; a list of an author's works accepted as genuine; a cathedral cleric.
cañon, canyon *n* a narrow mountain gorge.
canonize *vt* to declare a person to be a saint.
canopy *n* a covering over a throne, bed, etc.
cant *n* insincere talk; jargon.
cantankerous *adj* cross.
cantata *n* a short oratorio.
canteen *n* a restaurant within or attached to a place of work, school etc; (the box holding) a full set of cutlery; a place in camp or barracks for the sale of food and drink; a flask for water.
canter *n* a moderate gallop. * *vi* to move at a moderate gallop.
cantilever *n* a large supporting bracket; a principle applied in bridge making.
canto *n* a division of a poem.
canvas *n* a coarse cloth; sails of ships; a painting.
canvass *vt* to solicit the votes of.
canyon *n* a long, narrow mountain gorge.
cap *n* a covering for the head; a top piece. * *vt* to put a cap on; to excel; to outdo.
capability *n* capacity; competence.
capable *adj* efficient; able.
capacious *adj* wide; roomy.
capacity *n* volume; ability.
cape *n* a headland; a sleeveless coat.
caper *vi* to skip. * *n* a leap; a prank.
capillary *adj* minute; hairlike. * *n* (*pl* **capillaries**) a small blood vessel.
capital *adj* chief; punishable with death. * *n* the top of a column; the chief city; wealth.
capitalist *n* a man of wealth.
capitalize *vt* to convert into capital.
capitation *adj, n.* per head especially of a tax.
Capitol *n* the US senate house.
capitulate *vi* to surrender on conditions.
caprice *n* a whim.
capricious *adj* fickle; unreliable.
Capricorn *n* one of the signs of the zodiac.
capsize *vt* to upset.
capstan *n* an apparatus for winding in anchors, etc.
capsule *n* a gelatin case containing a drug to be swallowed; a covering; the part of a spacecraft, often manned, that gathers information and is recovered later.
captain *n* a commander, a leader.
caption *n* a headline of a newspaper or book; the explanatory text under an illustration; a subtitle.
captivate *vt* to fascinate.
captive *n* a prisoner.
captivity *n* the state or condition of being a captive.
capture *n* arrest. * *vt* to seize.
car *n* a motor vehicle; the compartment for passengers on a train, aircraft, cable railway etc.
carafe *n* a glass water bottle.
caramel *n* burnt sugar as colouring matter; a caramel flavoured sweet.
carat *n* unit of purity for gold.
caravan *n* a company travelling together; a house on wheels.
carbide *n* a compound of carbon with a metal.
carbine *n* a cavalry rifle.
carbohydrate *n* a compund of carbon, hydrogen and oxygen found in sugar, starch etc.
carbolic *adj* an antiseptic acid obtained from coal tar.
carbon *n* pure charcoal.
carbonaceous *adj* containing carbon.
carboniferous *adj* carbon-bearing.
carbonize *vt* to convert into carbon.
carbuncle *n* a large boil.
carburettor *n* the device in an internal combustion engine making and controlling the mixture of air and fuel.
carcass *adj* the body of a dead animal.
card *n* a piece of pasteboard for various

purposes. * *vt* to comb wool, etc.
cardboard *n* a thick card.
cardiac *adj* pertaining to the heart.
cardigan *n* a knitted garment with front fastenings.
cardinal *adj* chief. * *n* a Roman Catholic dignitary.
care *n* solicitude; attention. * *vi* to be anxious; to have regard; to look after; to provide for.
career *n* a race; a profession. * *vi* to proceed rapidly and without control.
careful *adj* anxious; cautious.
careless *adj* heedless; thoughtless; carefree.
caress *vt* to fondle. * *n* an embrace.
caret *n* an omission mark, thus (^).
cargo *n* freight.
caricature *n* a ludicrous portrait. * *vt* to burlesque; to parody.
caries *n* bone decay; tooth decay.
carmine *n* a bright crimson colour.
carnage *n* slaughter.
carnal *adj* sensual; sexual; worldly.
carnally *adv* lustfully.
carnation *n* flesh-colour; a rose-pink flower.
carnival *n* a gala day; public merry-making; a travelling funfair.
carnivorous *adj* feeding on flesh.
carol *n* a song of joy, especially one sung at Christmas.
carotoid *n* one of two great arteries in the neck.
carousal *n* a noisy revel.
carouse *vi* to drink freely.
carp *vi* to find fault. * n a voracious fish.
carpenter *n* a worker in timber.
carpentry *n* the trade of a carpenter.
carpet *n* a woven cover for floors.
carpeting *n* cloth for carpets.
carriage *n* a vehicle; the price of carrying; behaviour; bearing.
carrion *n* putrid flesh.
carrot *n* a reddish vegetable of a tapering shape; something offered as a reward.
carry *vt* to bear; to convey; to gain; to behave.
cart *n* a vehicle with two wheels for carrying goods.
carte blanche *n* (*pl* **cartes blanches**) a blank paper; unconditional terms.
cartel *n* a challenge; a written agreement for the exchange of prisoners; a union formed to promote and achieve common aims.
cartilage *n* gristle.
cartography *n* science of making maps.
carton *n* a cardboard box.
cartoon *n* a humorous or satirical topical sketch; a comic strip often animated.
cartridge *n* a case containing the charge for a gun.
carve *vt* to cut; to engrave.
carver *n* one who carves; a large knife for carving.
cascade *n* a waterfall.
case *n* a box; a covering; an event; a suit in court; an ailment or disease being medically treated; the patient undergoing treatment; a form in the inflection of nouns. * *vt* to put in a case.
case-hardened *adj* callous.
casement *n* a hinged window.
cash *n* money. * *vt* to turn into money.
cashier *n* one who has charge of money. * *vt* to dismiss.
cashmere *n* a soft wool or woollen fabric woven from the hair of Kashmir goats.
casino *n* a gaming hall.
cask *n* a barrel.
casket *n* a jewel case.
casque *n* a helmet.
casserole *n* a covered dish for cooking; the food stewed in a casserole.
cassock *n* a garment worn by clerics and choristers.
cast *vt* to throw; to throw off; to let fall; to condemn; to model. * n a throw; a squint; a mould; a company of actors.
castaway *n* a shipwrecked person.
caste *n* social class and distinctions.
castigate *vt* to reprimand severely; to chastise.
casting *n* that which is cast in a mould; the allotting of actors to their roles.
cast iron *n* iron formed in moulds.
castle *n* a fortress; an imposing mansion.
castor *n* a small cruet; a small wheel.
castor oil *n* a medicinal oil used as a purgative.
castrate *vt* to geld.

casual *adj* accidental; occasional; informal; careless.
casually *adv* by chance.
casualty *n* an accident; the person injured or killed in an accident or a war.
cat *n* a domestic feline animal; a related animal such as a lion or tiger.
cataclysm *n* a deluge; an upheaval.
catacomb *n* an underground vault.
catalogue *n* a list; a register.
catapult *n* a sling.
cataract *n* a waterfall; a disease of the eye.
catarrh *n* a cold in the head, due to inflammation of a mucus membrane in the nose.
catastrophe *n* disaster; finale.
catch *vt* to lay hold on; to grasp; to entangle; to receive by contagion; to get. * *n* a grasping; a song; play on words; a type of fastening; a hidden obstacle.
catching *adj* infectious.
catechise *vt* to instruct by question and answer; to question.
catechism *n* a manual of instruction by questions and answers especially of religious tenets.
categorical *adj* positive.
categorically *adv* absolutely.
category *n* a class or order or division.
cater *vi* to provide provisions, etc.
catgut *n* a cord made from intestines of animals and used as strings for violins, harps, guitars, etc.
cathedral *n* the principal church in a diocese.
cathode *n* the negative pole of an electric current.
catholic *adj* universal; general. * *n* a member of the universal Christian Church.
catholicism *n* adherence to the Catholic Church.
cattle *npl* oxen; livestock.
caucus *n* a party organization or clique.
caulk *vt* to stop up seams of a ship.
causal *adj* implying cause.
causation *n* the relation of cause and effect.
cause *n* that which produces an effect; reason; origin; suit; an enterprise. * *vt* to bring about.
causeway, causey *n* a paved way.
caustic *adj* burning; biting; sarcastic.
caustically *adv* scathingly.
cauterize *vt* to sear or burn, especially in treating a wound.
caution *n* care; pledge. * *vt* to warn.
cautious *adj* wary; careful.
cavalcade *n* a procession of persons on horseback; a company of horsemen.
cavalier *adj* careless; haughty.
cavalry *n* mounted troops.
cave *n* an underground hollow. * *vt, vi* (with **in**) to collapse; to give in on yield.
caveat *n* a warning.
cavern *n* a large cave.
cavernous *adj* hollow.
cavity *n* a hollow place especially a hole in a tooth.
cease *vi* to leave off; to stop. * *vt* to put a stop to.
ceaseless *adj* incessant.
cede *vt* to give up.
cedilla *n* the mark (ç) of the soft c.
ceiling *n* the upper inside surface of a room.
celebrant *n* the officiating priest; one taking part in a religious ceremony.
celebrate *vt* to commemorate; to accord high praise to.
celebrated *adj* famous.
celebrity *n* fame; a famous person.
celerity *n* speed; quickness.
celestial *adj* heavenly.
celibacy *n* the unmarried state.
celibate *n* one vowed to celibacy. * *adj* unmarried.
cell *n* a small room; a cave; a unit mass in living matter.
cellar *n* an apartment underground.
cellophane *n* a thin transparent paper used as protective wrapping.
cellular *adj* consisting of cells.
cement *n* mortar; a bond of union. * *vt* to unite closely.
cemetery *n* a burial place.
cenotaph *n* a monument to one who is buried elsewhere.
censor *n* a critic; a supervisor (of books, films, etc) who advocates removal of anything obscene, treasonable etc.
censorious *adj* fault-finding.
censure *n* blame; reproof. * *vt* to judge;

to blame.
census *n* an official count of people.
cent *n* a coin worth a hundredth of a dollar.
centaur *n* a fabulous being, half man and half horse.
centenarian *n* one a hundred years old.
centenary *n* the hundredth anniversary or its commemoration.
centigrade *adj* divided into a hundred degrees.
centimetre *n* the hundredth part of a metre.
central *adj* at the centre; most important; principal.
centralize *vt* to move to the centre; to cause to be under a central jurisdiction, authority, government.
centre *n* the middle point; a nucleus. * *vt* to collect to a point. * vi to have as a centre.
centreboard *n* a movable keel.
centrifugal *adj* tending to fly from a centre.
century *n* a hundred years.
ceramic *adj* pertaining to pottery. * *npl* the art of pottery.
cereal *adj* pertaining to corn. * n a grain plant; a breakfast food from the grains of such a plant.
cerebral *adj* of the brain; requiring use of the brain.
ceremonial *adj* pertaining to ceremony. * *n* rites and their observance; form of duty.
ceremonious *adj* formal.
ceremony *n* outward rite; pomp; observance.
certain *adj* sure; particular.
certainly *adv* without doubt.
certainty *n* truth; fact.
certificate *n* a written testimony.
certify *vt* to declare; to attest.
cessation *n* stoppage.
cesspool *n* a receptacle for sewage.
chafe *vt* to warm by rubbing; to irritate (skin) by rubbing: to enrage.
chaff *n* the husk of corn; banter. * *vt* to banter; to make fun of laughingly.
chagrin *n* vexation.
chain *n* a series of links; a measure of length; (*pl*) bondage. * *vt* to confine with chains.
chair *n* a movable seat; an official seat; professorship.
chalet *n* a Swiss cottage; a ski lodge or holiday house modelled on this.
chalice *n* a cup; a communion cup.
chalk *n* a soft limestone. * *vt* to mark with chalk.
challenge *n* a defiance; a calling in question; a demand especially to fight; a task or request requiring special effort. * *vt* to defy; to call in question.
challenger *n* one who challenges.
chamber *n* an apartment; a public body.
chamberlain *n* an officer of state; a city treasurer.
chamois *n* a species of antelope; a soft leather.
champ *vt* to chew; to bite.
champagne *n* a brisk sparkling wine.
champion *n* a defender of a cause; a vindicator. * *vt* to uphold.
championship *n* state of being a champion; a contest held to find a champion.
chance *n* accident; opportunity; luck. * *vi* to happen. * *adj* casual.
chancel *n* the altar end of a church.
chancellor *n* the head of a university, court.
chancery *n* a division of the High Court.
chandelier *n* a branching lamp with many lights that hangs from a ceiling.
change *vt* to alter; to exchange. * n variety; small coins.
changeable *adj* variable; capricious.
channel *n* a watercourse; a narrow sea; a band of radio frequencies allotted for a purpose, such as broadcasting by a television station. * *vt* to groove; to convey; to guide.
chant *vti.* to sing; to intone. * *n* a song.
chaos *n* disorder; total confusion.
chapel *n* a place of worship.
chaperon *n* a lady guardian or escort.
chaplain *n* an army or navy clergyman.
chapter *n* a division of a book.
char *vt* to burn. * *n* a fish.
character *n* a letter or figure; the distinguishing attributes of a person or thing; nature; quality; a part in a play.

characteristic *adj* distinctive.
characterize *vt* to describe; to mark or be characteristic of.
charade *n* a word puzzle acted out in syllables followed by all of the word; a travesty.
charcoal *n* charred wood.
char *vt* to blacken by fire.
charge *vt* to load; to fill; to price; to entrust; to accuse; to command; to attack. * *n* care; cost; attack; order; accusation.
chargeable *adj* imputable.
chargé d'affaires *n* an ambassador's deputy.
charger *n* a large dish; a warhorse.
chariot *n* a state carriage.
charioteer *n* a chariot driver.
charitable *adj* benevolent; generous in giving; lenient.
charity *n* love; benevolence; generosity to the needy; a money-raising fund or institution.
charlatan *n* a quack.
charm *n* a spell. * *vt* to delight.
charming *adj* enchanting.
charnel house *n* a burial vault.
chart *n* a map; a table of information.
charter *n* a warrant; a hire. * *vt* to hire.
chary *adj* careful; cautious.
chase *vt* to pursue; to emboss. * *n* pursuit; hunt; a printer's frame.
chasm *n* a deep cleft.
chassis *n* the frame of a motor vehicle.
chaste *adj* pure.
chasten *vt* to discipline by punishment; to tame; to make repentant.
chastise *vt* to punish.
chastity *n* purity; virginity.
chat *vi* to gossip. * *n* talk.
château *n* a castle.
chattel *n* (*usu in pl*) belongings.
chatter *vi* to talk idly; to jabber. * *n* talk.
chauffeur *n* one employed to drive a car.
chauvinism *n* jingoism.
cheap *adj* of a low price; common; inferior.
cheapen *vt* reduce in price; to belittle.
cheat *vt* to deceive; to swindle. * *n* a trick; a swindler.
check *vti.* to stop; to curb; to chide; to control. * *n* position in chess; a control.
checkmate *n* the winning move in chess. * *vt* to frustrate.
cheddar *n* a brand of cheese.
cheek *n* the side of the face; impudence.
cheer *n* gaiety; happiness; good spirits; a shout of joy. * *vt* to brighten; to gladden; to applaud.
cheerful *adj* happy, blithe.
cheering *adj* encouraging.
cheerless *adj* gloomy; dejected.
cheese *n* the curd of milk dried and pressed.
cheeseparing *adj* mean.
chef *n* a head cook.
chemical *n* any substance obtained by a chemical process.
chemise *n* an undergarment worn by females.
chemist *n* one skilled in chemistry; a pharmacy.
chemistry *n* the science of the properties and nature of substances.
cheque *n* an order for money.
chequer *n* a square pattern; (*pl*) draughts.
chequered, checkered *adj* varied; fluctuating.
cherish *vt* to treasure.
cheroot *n* a kind of cigar.
cherry *n* a tree and its small red fruit; a bright red colour.
chess *n* a game played on a squared board.
chessman *n* a piece used in chess.
chest *n* a large box; the breast.
chestnut *n* a tree; its edible nut; its wood; a stale joke. * *adj* reddish-brown.
chew *vt* to masticate.
chic *n* style. * *adj* stylish.
chicane, chicanery *n* trickery.
chick, chicken n the young of birds.
chicken-hearted *adj* timid.
chickenpox *n* an eruptive fever.
chicory *n* a plant with a root that when ground is used for or with coffee.
chide *vti.* to reprove; to scold.
chief *adj* first; leading. * n a leader.
chieftain *n* the head of a clan.
chilblain *n* a painful swelling on the hands or toes produced by cold.
child *n* an infant; offspring.
childhood *n* the stage between birth and adolescence.

childish *adj* like a child; trifling.
childlike *adj* innocent.
chill *n* a cold fit. * *adj* cold. * *vt* to discourage.
chime *n* a harmony of bells; (*pl*) a set of bells. * *vi* to accord.
chimerical *adj* fanciful.
chimney *n* a smoke escape.
chimpanzee *n* a large ape.
chin *n* the lower part of the face.
china *n* porcelain.
chink *n* an opening; a crack. * *vt, vi* to jingle as of coins.
chintz *n* calico, patterned and coloured.
chip *n* a fragment. * *vt* to cut into chips.
chiropody *n* the treatment of the feet.
chirp *vi* to cheep.
chisel *n* a cutting tool. * *vt* to cut or engrave.
chiselled *adj* clear-cut.
chivalrous *adj* gallant; knightly.
chivalry *n* knighthood; gallantry.
chloride *n* a chlorine compound.
chlorine *n* a gaseous element used in bleaching and disinfectants.
chloroform *n* a volatile liquid anaesthetic.
chlorophyll *n* the green colouring matter of plants.
chocolate *n* a beverage and sweet from cacao; its colour.
choice *n* option; selection; preference. * *adj* select; precious.
choir *n* a band of singers; the place especially in church where they sit.
choke *vt* to suffocate. * *vi* to be blocked up.
cholera *n* a highly infectious and deadly disease.
choleric *adj* bad-tempered; peevish.
choose v*t* to prefer; to select.
chop *vt* to cut to pieces. * *vi* to turn suddenly. * *n* a piece of meat.
chopsticks *n* two wooden sticks used to eat especially by Chinese.
choral *adj* belonging to, sung by or written for a choir.
chord *n* three or more musical notes played together.
chorister *n* a singer in a choir.
chorus *n* a company of singers; musical refrain.
chosen *adj* select.
Christ *n* Jesus of Nazareth, the Christian Messiah.
christen *vt* to baptize; to name.
Christendom *n* the whole body of Christians.
Christian *n* a professed follower of Christ.
Christianity *n* the religion of Christians.
Christmas *n* the festival of Christ's nativity, December 25.
chrome, chromium *n* a hard metal used in steel alloys and electro-plating.
chronic *adj* permanent.
chronicle *n* a diary of events; history. * *vt* to record.
chronological *adj* arranged in order of happening.
chronology *n* the science of time; the sequence of events and their arrangement in order.
chronometer *n* a timepiece.
chrysalis *n* the grub stage of certain insects.
chubby *adj* plump.
chuck *vt* to tap under the chin; to toss; to pitch; to give up; to throw away.
chuckle *vi* to laugh in the throat; to exult. * *n* a half-suppressed laugh.
chum *n* a close friend.
chunk *n* a short thick piece.
church *n* a building consecrated to the worship of God; the body of clergy.
churchyard *n* a cemetery.
churlish *adj* surly; sullen.
churn *n* a vessel that is vigorously turned and shaken to make butter; a milk container.
chute *n* a sloping channel or slide for water, rubbish, logs etc.
cicatrix, cicatrice *n* a scar.
cider *n* fermented apple juice.
cigar *n* a roll of tobacco leaf for smoking.
cigarette *n* a paper cylinder of shredded tobacco.
cinchona *n* a tree whose bark yields quinine.
cinder *n* a burned coal.
cinema *n* a building where films are shown; the art or industry of film-making.
cinnamon *n* a tree and the aromatic spice

from it; a yellow-brown colour.
cipher, cypher *n* the figure 0; any numeral; a person or thing of no importance; a secret writing.
circle *n* a round figure; a group; its bounding line; a ring; a class. * *vt, vi* to move round; to enclose.
circuit *n* area; extent; journey of judges to hold courts; a detour; the path of an electric current.
circuitous *adj* roundabout.
circular *adj* round. * *n* a notice.
circulate *vi* to move in a circle; to pass from person to person or place to place. * *vt* to spread.
circulation *n* circulating; the area centred and the number sold, of a newspaper etc; the flow of blood through the arteries and the veins; currency.
circulatory *adj* circulating.
circumcise *vt* to cut off the foreskin.
circumference *n* the bounding line of a circle.
circumflex *n* an accent (^) on vowels marking contraction, etc.
circumlocution *n* a roundabout mode of speaking.
circumlocutory *adj* diffuse.
circumnavigate *vt* to sail round.
circumscribe *vt* to enclose; to limit.
circumspect *adj* wary.
circumspection *n* caution.
circumstance *n* an event; (*pl*) state of affairs; condition.
circumstantial *adj* indirect; incidental.
circumvent *v;* to avoid by going round; to evade; to outwit.
circus *n* (*pl* **circuses**) an enclosed area or place for games etc.; a travelling show of entertainers and animals.
cirrus *n* (*pl* **cirri**) a thin, trailing cloud.
cistern *n* a water tank.
citation *n* quotation; summons.
cite *vt* to summon; to quote.
citizen *n* an inhabitant of a city.
citizenship *n* the rights of a citizen.
citrus *n* a type of tree including the orange and lemon; the fruit.
city *n* a large town.
civet *n* a civet cat; the perfume obtained from it.
civic *adj* pertaining to a city or citizen.
civil *adj* municipal; non-military; of the state; polite; internal.
civilian *n* one engaged in civil, not military pursuits.
civility *n* courtesy.
civilization *n* culture; social development; the modern world.
civilize *vt* to convert from a savage or wild state; to refine.
clad *pp* of clothe.
claim *vt* to demand as due; to assert outright to; to state one's ownership of. * *n* a formal demand; the thing claimed.
claimant *n* one who claims.
clairvoyance *n* the supposed power of seeing things not present to the senses.
clamber *vi* to scramble over.
clammy *adj* sticky; damp; moist.
clamorous *adj* noisy.
clamour *n* shouting; uproar. * *vi* to demand with shouts.
clamp *n* a gripping appliance. * vi to fasten or grip.
clan *n* a family; a tribe.
clandestine *adj* secret; underhand.
clang *n* a ringing noise.
clank *n* a dull metallic ring as of chains.
clannish *adj* united; belonging to a group and excluding others.
clap *vt* to strike together noisily, especially the hands; to pat. * *n* explosive sound as of thunder.
clapper *n* the tongue of a bell.
claret *n* a red wine. * *adj* claret-coloured.
clarify *vti* to make clear; to purefy by heating.
clarinet *n* a reed instrument.
clarion *n* a shrill trumpet. * *adj* rousing.
clash *vi* to make a noise by collision; to be antagonistic to or incompatible. * *n* noisy collision; jarring.
clasp *n* an embrace; a hook. * *vt* to fasten; to embrace.
clasp knife *n* a knife with blades that fold into the handle.
class *n* a rank; a group; a body of students learning together, a standard or grade of worth. * *vt* to arrange in classes.
classic *adj* of the first rank. * *n* a work of the first rank in any of the arts.

classical *adj* refined; standard; pertaining to or in keeping with the great masterpieces of Greece and Rome; traditional.
classification *n* organization into classes or categories.
classify *vt* to arrange; to categorize; to restrict, especially information, to an inner group for security reasons.
clatter *vi* to make rattling noises; to talk noisily. * *n* a rattling noise.
clause *n* a part of a sentence; a single item of a treaty, contract, bill, etc.
claustrophobia *n* a morbid fear of confined spaces or being shut in.
clavicle *n* the collarbone.
claw *n* a hooked nail; a crab's pincer. * vt to scratch or dig with claws or nails.
clay *n* heavy soil.
claymore *n* a large two-edged sword; a basket-hilted sword.
clean *adj* free from dirt; pure. * *vt* to purify; to cleanse.
cleanliness *n* state of being clean.
cleanse *vt* to make clean or pure.
clear adj bright; shining; limpid; fair; plain; shrill. * *adv* manifestly. * *vt* to make clear; to free from suspicion.
clearance *n* a setting free; an emptying; a discharge.
clearing *n* the act of making clear; a settling up; land cleared of trees.
cleavage *n* a splitting or tendency to split.
cleave *vi* to stick; to adhere.
cleave *vt* to split; to sever.
cleaver *n* a butcher's axe or knife.
clef *n* a mark to show the key in music.
cleft *n* a crevice; a fissure.
clemency *n* mercy.
clench vt to hold tight; to close (teeth) tightly.
clergy *npl* the ministers of the Christian religion.
cleric *n* a clergyman.
clerical *n* pertaining to the clergy, or to a clerk.
clerk *n* an office employee; an official who looks after records.
clever *adj* adroit; talented.
cleverness *n* ability.
click *vi* to clink; to make a faint sharp sound.
client *n* a customer.
clientele *n* clients collectively.
cliff *n* a steep rock face.
climacteric *n* a critical period in life; the menopause.
climate *n* weather characteristics or conditions; a prevailing atmosphere, mood or feeling.
climax *n* the highest point; an ascending scale.
climb *vi, vt* to ascend; to mount.
clinch *vt* to settle finally (a deal, an argument); to fasten; to grasp. * n a grip hindering the use of the arms; a tight embrace.
cling *vi* to adhere; to cleave.
clinic *n* a place for the care of out patients; a private hospital; doctors practising in a group.
clinical *adj* of or pertaining to the treatment, progress and medical observation of patients; objective; detatched.
clink *vt* to jingle.
clinker *n* burnt brick, or hard cinders.
clip *vt* to shear; to trim with scissors; to shorten or cut off words when speaking; to grip or fasten with a clip or clasp. * *n* a clasp to hold or fasten or hook together; an excerpt or extract from a film.
clique *n* a party; a set; an exclusive group.
cloak *n* a loose outer garment; a pretext. * *vt* to hide; to veil.
clock *n* a timepiece.
clockwork *n* the machinery of a clock; unfailing regularity.
clod *n* a lump of earth; a stupid fellow.
clog *n* a shoe with a wooden sole.
cloister *n* a monastery or convent; a covered walk there or in a college.
close *vt* to shut; to finish. * *vi* to end. * *n* the end.
close *adj* shut fast; tight; dense; near; stingy; secretive. * *n* an enclosed place; a courtyard or its entrance; the precincts of a cathedral.
close-fisted *adj* niggardly.
closet *n* a small room or recess. * *vt* to shut up.
closure *n* a stoppage; a closing.
clot *n* a curdled or coagulated mass (of blood). * *vi* to become thick.

cloth *n* a woven fabric.
clothe *vt* to attire.
clothes *n* dress; coverings.
cloud *n* a mass of visible water vapour high in the air; a crowd; gloom. * vt to darken; to obscure; to hide.
cloudless *adj* clear.
cloudy *adj* overcast; indistinct; muddy.
clove *n* a spice; one segment of a bulb of garlic.
clover *n* a three-leaved plant used as fodder.
clown *n* a lout; a jester; a circus entertainer.
clownish *adj* boorish.
cloy *vt* to glut; to surfeit with sweetness.
club *n* a cudgel; a golf stick; a society of people; their meeting place; a suit at cards; an association for some common object. * *vt* to beat with a club. * *vi* to join together.
clue *n* a guide or help to solve a puzzle.
clump *n* a thick cluster; the sound made by heavy or clumsy footsteps.
clumsy *adj* awkward; graceless; tactless; a collection of eggs hatched at the one time; a brood of chickens.
cluster *n* a bunch. * *vi* to keep close together.
clutch *vt* to seize; to grasp. * *n* the lever that puts an engine in or out of action.
coach n a four-wheeled close vehicle; a long-distance bus; a sports trainer.
coagulate *vti* to curdle; to clot; of liquid, to thicken to a semisolid state.
coal *n* a black mineral used as fuel.
coalesce *vi* to unite; to fuse; to muge.
coalition *n* a party union; an alliance.
coal mine *n* a mine containing coal.
coal tar *n* a black liquid got by distilling coal.
coarse *adj* rude; gross; crude.
coast *n* the seashore. * vi to sail along a shore; to travel without mechanical power, especially downhill.
coaster *n* a vessel which trades along the coast; a protective mat to place under a glass or bottle.
coastguard *n* a coast police force.
coasting *adj* a brakeless downhill ride.
coat *n* an outer garment; a covering; a layer. * *vt* to cover.
coax *vt* to wheedle; to pursuade by gentleness or flattery.
cobble *vt* to mend coarsely. * *npl* a road surfaced with rounded stones.
cobbler *n* a mender of shoes.
cobweb *n* a spider's web.
cocaine *n* a drug injected to deaden pain.
cochineal *n* an insect; the scarlet dye got from it.
cock *n* a male bird; a tap; the hammer of a gun. * *vt* to set erect.
cockney *n* a native of London. * *adj* pertaining to a cockney.
cockpit *n* a pit where game cocks fight; a pilot's compartment in an aeroplane.
cocktail *n* an alcoholic drink composed of a mixture of spirits and other ingredients.
cocoa *n* cacao seeds; the beverage made from them.
coconut *n* the fruit of the coco palm.
cocoon *n* the case spun by the silkworm.
coddle *vt* to be overprotective; to cook in water below boiling point.
code *n* a collection of laws, rules, or signals; letters, numbers, symblos arranged to transmit secret messages.
codicil *n* a supplement to a will.
codification *n* reducing laws to a code.
codify *vt* to systematize laws, rules etc.
coefficient *adj* cooperating. * *n* a factor in an expression.
coerce *vt* to force; to compel.
coercion *n* the act of compulsion; government by force.
coexecutor *n* a joint executor.
coexist *vi* to live together, especially peacefully; at the same time.
coffee *n* a drink made from the seeds of the coffee tree.
coffer *n* a chest for holding valuables.
coffin *n* the coffer or chest for holding a corpse.
cog *n* the tooth of a wheel.**cogency** *n* force.
cogent *adj* convincing.
cogitate *vi* to ponder.
cognac *n* French brandy.
cognition *n* perception.
cognizable *adj* capable of being known or perceived.
cognizance *n* knowledge; judicial notice.

cognizant *adj* having knowledge of.
cohabit *vi* to dwell together.
cohere *vi* to stick together.
coherent *adj* connected; intelligible, of speech; logical and consistent.
cohesion *n* the force keeping the particles of bodies together.
cohort *n* a company of soldiers.
coiffure *n* a hairstyle.
coil *vt* to wind into a ring. * *n* a ring or rings into which a rope, etc, is wound, or a spiral of a thing wound, esp. a wire for electric current.
coin *n* a piece of money. * *vt* to mint; to invent a new word or phrase.
coinage *n* coined money.
coincide *vi* to correspond in space or time; to agree exactly.
coincidence *n* concurrence; the occurrence by chance of two events at the same time.
coincident *adj* corresponding.
colander *n* a strainer for food.
cold *adj* not hot; chill; indifferent. * *n* absence of heat; an illness due to cold.
coleslaw *n* raw cabbage shredded and mixed in a dressing as a salad.
colic *n* a griping pain.
collaborator *n* an associate in literary or scientific labour; one who works against one's country in wartime.
collage *n* a picture or piece of artwork composed of random scraps of paper, material etc. pasted on a surface.
collapse *n* a breakdown; a fall; a failure. * *vi* to fall; to break down.
collar *n* a band worn round the neck; the neckband of a garment.
collate *vt* to examine and compare, as books, etc.
collateral *adj* side by side; indirect.
collation *n* the collating of texts etc.
colleague *n* an associate in office, a fellow worker.
collect *vti* to bring together; to infer; to arrange; to accumulate things as a hobby.
collect *n* a short prayer.
collected *adj* self-possessed.
collection *n* act of collecting; that which is collected; an accumulation of things of value or interest; money gathered for a purpose.
collective *adj* taken as a whole.
collectivism *n* the doctrine of the state ownership of land and all means of production.
college *n* an institution of scholars; a centre of higher learning.
collide *vi* to strike against each other.
collier *n* a coal miner; a coal ship.
colliery *n* a coal mine.
collision *n* act of striking together; conflict.
colloquial *adj* conversational; informal and non-literary of talk.
collude *vi* to connive.
collusion *n* fraud by agreement; conspiracy.
collusive *adj* fraudulently concerted.
colon *n* a mark of punctuation, thus (:); the large intestine.
colonel *n* the commander of a regiment.
colonial *adj* pertaining to a colony. * n a person belonging to a colony.
colonist *n* an inhabitant of a colony.
colonization *n* act of colonizing.
colonize *vt* to found a colony.
colonnade *n* a range of columns.
colony *n* a settlement in a new country.
colophon *n* the device or emblem of a publisher on a book.
colossal *adj* huge.
colour *n* the hue or appearance of a body to the eye; a pigment; complexion; pretence; (*pl*) a flag. * *vt* to tinge; to varnish; to embellish. * *vi* to blush.
colouring *n* act of giving a colour; colour applied; a false appearance.
colourist *n* a painter who excels in use of colour.
colt *n* a young horse.
column *n* a pillar; a body of troops; a section of a page; a line of figures; an article or feature appearing regularly in a newspaper etc.
coma *n* a stupor; a lengthy period of unconsciousness.
comatose *adj* torpid; deathlike.
comb *n* a toothed appliance for dressing hair, wool. etc. * *vt* to arrange hair with a comb; to search for thoroughly.
combat *vi* to fight * *vt* to oppose. * *n* a

fight; a contest.
combatant *adj* contending. * *n* a fighter.
combative *adj* disposed to fight.
combination *n* a union; an alliance of persons; numbers arranged to open the combination lock of a safe.
combine *vt* to join. * *vi* to league together. * *n* a machine that cuts and threshes crops.
combustible *adj* inflammable.
combustion *n* a burning.
come *vi* to move forward; to draw near; to arrive; to happen.
comedian *n* an actor of comic roles; one who entertains by telling jokes.
comedy *n* drama written to amuse.
comely *adj* good-looking; becoming.
comestible *n* an eatable.
comet *n* a heavenly body having a luminous tail.
comfort *vt* to console; to gladden. * *n* consolation.
comfortable *adj* contented; at ease; having adequate money to live well.
comic *adj* relating to comedy; amusing.
comical *adj* funny.
comma *n* a mark of punctuation, thus (,).
command *vt* to order; to govern; to have at one's disposal. * *vi* to have chief power. * *n* order; authority.
commandant *n* the military officer in charge of men or an establishment.
commandeer *vt* to appropriate.
commander *n* one who commands.
commanding *adj* dominating; authoritative.
commandment *n* a precept of the moral law.
commando *n* a soldier belonging to a special attacking force.
commemorate *vt* to celebrate the memory of someone or something.
commemoration *n* a solemn celebration as a memorial to.
commence *vi, vt* to take the first step; to begin.
commend *vt* to praise; to recommend.
commendable *adj* worthy of praise.
commendation *n* praise.
commensurate *adj* proportional.
comment *vi* to make remarks or criticisms. * *vt* to annotate. * *n* an explanatory note.
commentary *n* a book of comments or notes; a spoken explanation of events as they take place.
commentator *n* one who reports and explains events as on TV.
commerce *n* exchange of goods, trade.
commercial *adj* trading; pertaining to commerce; intended to be profit-making. * *n* an advertisement shown on TV.
commingle *vt* to blend.
commiserate *vt* to pity; to condole with.
commiseration *n* pity; sympathy.
commissariat *n* the stores department of an army; the supplies themselves.
commission *n* trust; warrant; a percentage; a body of commissioners; the appointment of a soldier to officer's rank; a business or task given or entrusted to someone. * *vt* to require the services of.
commissionaire *n* a porter or messenger.
commissioner *n* one appointed to perform some office.
commit *vt* to entrust; to consign especially to custody; to perpetrate.
commitment *n* a pledge; imprisonment.
committal *n* the act of committing.
committee *n* a body appointed to manage any matter on behalf of a larger body.
commodious *adj* spacious and suitable.
commodity *n* any article of commerce.
commodore *n* the commander of a squadron.
common *adj* general; usual; of no rank; of little value. * *n* an open public ground.
commonly *adv* usually.
commonplace *adj* ordinary; trite.
common sense *n* sound judgment.
commonwealth *n* the public good; the state; a republic; a federation of states.
commotion *n* tumult; disorder.
communal *adj* belonging to a community or commune; shared; common to.
commune *vi* to confer with privately or spiritually.
commune *n* a group of people living together and sharing everything.
communicable *adj* capable of being imparted to another.
communicant *n* a partaker of the Lord's

supper.

communicate *vti* to impart.

communication *n* news; a message; (*pl*) the passing and exchange of information, ideas etc. by means of speech, telecommunications, the media etc.

communicative *adj* candid; talkative.

communion *n* intercourse; celebration of the Lord's Supper.

communism *n* the doctrine of a community of property.

communist *n* an advocate of communism.

community *n* the body of the people; a body of people living in the same locality.

commutable *adj* exchangeable.

commutation *n* exchange; change; lessening.

commute *vt, vi* to travel a distance daily between home and work; to exchange; to lessen; to reduce the length of a prison sentence.

compact *adj* solid; dense. * *vt* to consolidate. * *n* an agreement.

compact disc *n* a disc playing recordings read by a laser beam.

companion *n* a comrade; a friend.

companionable *adj* sociable.

company *n* a body of guests, of traders, or of soldiers; a business; a ship's crew.

comparable *adj* similar.

comparative *adj* relative.

compare *vt* to examine side by side; to liken; to form degrees of comparison.

comparison *n* relation; simile; illustration; inflection in an adjective.

compartment *n* spaces divided off (in drawers, etc); one of the several divisions of a railway carriage carrying passengers; something separate; a category.

compass *n* a circuit; limit; range; an instrument with a magnetic needle pointing to the north; an instrument for describing circles.

compassion *n* sympathy.

compatible *adj* consistent; in keeping; able to live with agreeably; of like mind.

compatriot *n* one of the same country.

compel *vt* to drive; to urge; to force.

compendium *n* a summary.

compensate *vt* to make amends for; to requite. * *vi* to atone.

compensation *n* recompense.

compete *vi* to strive (as rival); to contend.

competence n sufficiency, ability.

competent *adj* well qualified; fit.

competently *adv* adequately.

competition *n* rivalry; a contest; a, match.

competitor *n* a rival.

compilation *n* the act of compiling; the thing compiled.

compile *vt* to collect (facts, figures, etc).

complacence, complacency *n* satisfaction; self-satisfaction.

complacent *adj* pleased, with oneself.

complain *vi* to grumble at; to be dissatisfied with; to lament; to make a charge; to feel unwell.

complainant *n* a plaintiff.

complaint *n* a grumble; an accusation; an ailment.

complement *n* the full quota, allowance or number.

complementary *adj* completing.

complete *adj* finished. * *vt* to finish; to fulfil.

completion *n* the fulfilment; the finishing.

complex *adj* involved; difficult. * n a whole composed of many parts e.g. buildings or units.

complexion *n* the colour of the face; aspect.

complexity *n* intricacy.

compliance *n* concurrence; acquiescence.

compliant *adj* yielding; docile.

complicate *vt* to make complex or difficult.

complication *n* a complex situation; something that worsens or adds to a difficulty; a medical condition following on and arising from the original malady.

complicity *n* state of being an accomplice.

compliment *n* an expression of praise or admiration. * *vt* to praise; to congratulate.

comply *vi* to acquiesce.

component *adj* constituent. * n a constituent part.

compose *vt* to write, especially music; to calm.

composed *adj* calm; serene.

composer *n* awriter of music.
composite *adj* compound.
composition *n* a putting together; the thing composed, as a piece of music or literature; the make-up of something.
compositor *n* one who sets types.
composure *n* calmness.
compound *vt, vi* to put together; to mix; to adjust. * *adj* composed of two or more parts. * *n* a mass composed of two or more elements; an enclosure.
comprehend *vt* to understand.
comprehensible *adj* intelligible.
comprehension *n* understanding.
comprehensive *adj* inclusive; of wide scope. * *n* a secondary school accepting pupils of all abilities.
compress *vt* to press together. * *n* a soft pad to apply to a wound.
compressed *adj* flattened; condensed.
compression *n* a condensing; the increasing of pressure in an engine to compress the gases so that they explode.
comprise *vt* to contain; to consist of.
compromise *n* a settlement by agreement. * *vt* to settle by mutual concessions; to endanger.
comptroller *n* a controller.
compulsion *n* force; an overpowering urge.
compulsive *adj* compelling; acting as if forced.
compulsory *adj* obligatory.
compunction *n* remorse.
computation *n* reckoning.
compute *vt* to count; estimate.
computer *n* an electronic device that processes data according to instructions fed into it.
comrade *n* a mate; companion.
concave *adj* curving inwards.
conceal *vt* to hide.
concealment *n* a hiding place.
concede *vt* to yield; to grant.
conceit *n* vanity; an exaggerated opinion of oneself.
conceited *adj* vain.
conceivable *adj* thinkable; imaginable.
conceive *vti* to comprehend; to think; to become pregnant.
concentrate *vt* to collect to one point; to direct the mind solely to one aim or object; to condense in order to increase the strength of something.
concentric *adj* having a common centre.
concept *n* a general idea; an abstract idea.
conception *n* act of conceiving; an idea.
concern *vt* to interest oneself in; to apply to; to cause anxiety to. * *n* anxiety.
concert *n* agreement; harmony; a musical performance.
concerted *adj* planned; combined.
concertina *n* a musical instrument.
concerto *n* a musical composition for solo instrument and orchestra.
concession *n* a grant; the act of yielding.
conch *n* a marine shell.
conciliate *vt* to reconcile; to propitiate.
conciliatory *adj* persuasive.
concise *adj* brief; pointed.
conclave *n* the assembly of cardinals for the election of a pope; a close assembly.
conclude *vti* to end; to deduce.
conclusion *n* inference; the end; a final judgement or opinion.
concoct *vt* to devise; to plot; to produce from a mixture of ingredients; to fabricate.
concoction *n* a mixture; an invention.
concomitant *adj* accompanying. * n a connected circumstance.
concord *n* union; harmony.
concordance *n* agreement; a complete index.
concourse *n* a gathering; a crowd; a large area where crowds can gather.
concrete *adj* solid; real, not abstract. * n a mass of stones and mortar.
concretion *n* a compacted mass.
concur *vi* to unite; to agree.
concurrence *n* agreement; association; joint action.
concurrent *adj* happening at the same time; agreeing; attendant.
concussion *n* a violent shock especially of an explosion or heavy blow; unconseiousness due to a heavy blow to the head.
condemn *vt* to censure; to sentence.
condemnatory *adj* condemning.
condensation *n* act of condensing; state of being condensed; an abridgement.

condense *vt* to compress; to liquefy; to reduce by cutting especially of text or speech.
condenser *n* a chamber in which steam is condensed; a vessel for condensing or accumulating electricity.
condescend *vi* to stoop; to deign; to be patronizing.
condescension *n* graciousness; patronizing behaviour.
condiment *n* seasoning or spice.
condition *n* state; case; stipulation; illness.
conditioned *adj* depending; relative; displaying learned behaviour.
condole *vi* to sympathize.
condolence *n* expression of sympathy.
condone *vt* to pardon.
conducive *adj* leading to; contributing to.
conduct *n* behaviour; management; escort. * *vt* to lead; to manage; to behave; to direct an orchestra; to transmit e.g. heat or electricity.
conduction *n* property by which bodies transmit heat or electricity.
conductor *n* a leader; a director of an orchestra; one who is in charge of a train.
conduit *n* a channel; a subway for pipes.
cone *n* a pointed figure with a circular base; the fruit of firs, etc.
confection *n* a mixture; a sweetmeat.
confectioner *n* a maker of sweetmeats.
confederacy *n* a league.
confederate *adj* allied. * *n* an ally; a fellow conspirator. * *vti* to unite.
confederation *n* a league of states.
confer *vi* to consult together. * *vt* to give or bestow.
conference *n* a meeting for consultation.
confess *vt* to own; to admit. * *vi* to make a confession.
confessedly *adv* avowedly.
confession *n* the act of confessing; a creed.
confessional *n* the place where a priest hears confessions.
confessor *n* a priest who hears confession.
confidant *nm* **confidante** *nf* a trusted friend.
confide *vi, vt* to trust wholly; to entrust.
confidence *n* trust; assurance.
confidential *adj* private; privy to secrets.
confidently *adv* with assurance.
confiding *adj* trusting.
configuration *n* shape brought about by arranging of parts.
confine *n* a boundary. * *vt* to restrain; to shut up.
confinement *n* imprisonment; childbirth.
confirm *vt* to ratify; to coroborate; to admit to comminion in church.
confirmation *n* proof; the receiving into full communion.
confirmatory *adj* corroborative.
confirmed *adj* fixed; settled.
confiscable *adj* liable to forfeiture.
confiscate *vt* to seize as forfeit.
conflagration *n* a great fire.
conflict *n* a struggle; a fight; strife; an emotional upset. * *vi* to be at variance.
conflicting *adj* contradictory.
confluence *n* a flowing together; the meeting of streams.
confluent *adj* mingling.
conform *vti* to adapt; to comply.
conformation *n* structure.
conformity *n* agreement; likeness; keeping to established rules.
confound *vt* to confuse; to astound; to overthrow.
confront *vt* to face; to oppose; to challenge face to face.
confuse *vt* to mix together; to derange; to perplex; to embarass.
confusion *n* disorder.
confute *vt* to disprove.
congeal *vt* to coagulate; to thicken.
congenial *adj* kindred; having like natures or tastes; compatible.
congenital *adj* hereditary.
congested *adj* overcrowded; clogged with blood etc; blocked.
congestion *n* undue fullness (esp. of blood); overcrowding; a blockage of traffic.
conglomerate *adj* stuck together in a mass.
conglomeration *n* a mixed mass.
congratulate *vt* to compliment; to felicitate.
congratulatory *adj* complimentary.
congregate *vti* to meet together.
congregation *n* an assembly.
Congregationalism *n* the form of church

government where each separate church managing its own affairs.
congress *n* an assembly; the legislature of the United States.
congressional *adj* pertaining to a congress.
congruence, congruency *n* agreement; suitability.
congruent *adj* suitable; agreeing; corresponding.
congruous *adj* accordant; corresponding; appropriate.
conic, conical *adj* cone-like; cone-shaped.
coniferous *adj* bearing cones.
conjectural *adj* reading an opion by guesswork.
conjecture *n* supposition. * *vt* to surmise.
conjoin *vt* to unite.
conjoint *adj* united.
conjugal *adj* pertaining to marriage.
conjugate *vt* to inflect (a verb). * *adj* joined in pairs.
conjugation *n* the inflection of verbs.
conjunction *n* connexion; a connecting word.
conjunctive *adj* uniting
conjuncture *n* a crisis.
conjure *vt* to summon up by magic. * *vi* to juggle.
conjurer, conjuror *n* one who entertains with magic tricks and juggling.
connect *vt* to join; to associate; to link by telephone; to transfer from one vehicle to another to continue journey.
connective *adj* binding together. * *n* a conjunction.
connection, connexion *n* a relation by blood or marriage; relationship; the vehicle timed to connect with another.
connive *vi* to concur in a wrong.
connoisseur *n* an expert; a judge of fine arts.
connotation *n* the implied meaning; the resultant meaning.
conquer *vt* to gain by force; to vanquish. * *vi* to overcome.
conqueror *n* a victor.
conquest *n* subjugation; that which is conquered.
conscience *n* the sense of right and wrong.
conscientious *adj* high principled; regulated by conscience; thorough; diligent.
conscious *adj* aware; sensible of.
consciousness *n* awareness.
conscript *n* one compulsorily enrolled to serve in the army or navy.
conscription *n* a compulsory enrolment for military or naval service.
consecrate *vt* to set apart for sacred use; to dedicate.
consecutive *adj* following in order.
consent *n* concurrence; agreement; permission. * *vi* to assent; to acquiesce; to permit.
consequence *n* result; inference; importance.
consequent *adj* following; resulting.
consequential *adj* pompous.
conservancy *n* a board controlling a port, fishery, countryside, etc.
conservation *n* preservation especially of the environment and natural resources.
conservative *adj* averse to change. * *n* one opposed to political changes; a Tory.
conservatory *n* a greenhouse.
conserve *vt* to keep in a sound state; to keep safe; to preserve or pickle food.
consider *vti* to think on; to ponder; to weigh up; to examine.
considerable *adj* worth considering; fairly large.
considerate *adj* thoughtful of others.
consideration *n* serious deliberation.
considering *prep* in view of; allowing for; seeing that.
consign *vt* to hand over to another.
consignee *n* the person to whom goods are consigned.
consigner *n* one who consigns.
consignment *n* goods consigned.
consist *vi* to be composed of.
consistency *n* a degree of density or firmness; harmony; being true to one's previous ideas, behaviour etc.
consistent *adj* fixed; compatible; reliably unchanging in deed or thought.
consolation *n* solace; a comfort.
consolatory *adj* giving consolation.
console *vt* to comfort.
consolidate *vt* to make solid; to strengthen.
consonance *n* concord; agreement.

consonant *adj* accordant; consistent. * *n* a letter or sound that is not a vowel.
consort *n* a partner; a wife or husband; a companion. * *vi* to associate with unsuitable people; to agree; to accord.
consortium *n* a combining for a special purpose.
conspicuous *adj* outstanding; noticable.
conspiracy *n* a plot.
conspire *vi* to plot together.
constable *n* a policeman or woman of the lowest rank.
constabulary *n* the body of constables.
constancy *n* steadfastness.
constant *adj* steadfast; faithful. * *n* a fixed quantity.
constellation *n* a group of stars.
consternation *n* dismay.
constipation *n* difficulty in moving the bowels.
constituency *n* the body of voters; the voters of an area.
constituent *adj* component; being a part of a whole. * *n* an elector; one essential part of a whole.
constitute *vt* to set up; to compose; to appoint.
constitution *n* the condition of the body; a system of government.
constitutional *adj* of, pertaining to a constitution; legal. * *n* a walk taken for one's health.
constrain *vt* to force; to necessitate; to restrain; to imprison.
constrained *adj* forced; embarassed.
constraint *n* necessity; embarassment; inhibition; confinement.
constrict *vt* to contract; to compress; to limit free movement.
constriction *n* contraction; a feeling of tightness; compression.
construct *vt* to build; to devise.
construction *n* a structure; meaning; interpretation.
constructive *adj* having ability to construct; develop; improve.
construe *vt* to arrange words so as to discover the sense of a sentence; to interpret.
consul *n* a state agent in foreign towns.
consulate *n* the office or residence of a consul.
consult *vi, vt* to take counsel; to consider; to seek advice.
consultant *n* a consulting physician.
consultation *n* a seeking of advice from a doctor or lawyer.
consume *vt, vi* to eat or drink; to destroy; to use up; to squander.
consumer *n* one who buys goods and uses services.
consummate *vt* to finish, to perfect. * *adj* complete; perfect.
consummation *n* end; perfection.
consumption *n* expenditure.
contact *n* a touching together; close union; a business aquaintance; one who has been close to a person with a contagious disease. * *vt* to get in touch with.
contagious *adj* infectious, spread by touch.
contain *vt* to hold; to restrain.
contaminate *vt* to corrupt; to pollute.
contamination *n* pollution.
contemplate *vt* to meditate on; to intend.
contemplation *n* meditation.
contemplative *adj* thoughtful.
contemporaneous *adj* concurrent.
contemporary *adj* belonging to the same time. * *n* one who lives at the same time; a person of the same age.
contempt *n* scorn; disregard.
contemptible *adj* mean; worthy of contempt.
contemptuous *adj* scornful.
contend *vi* to strive; to vie; to dispute.
content *adj* satisfied. * vt to please; to satisfy. * *n* satisfaction; capacity; (*pl*) the things held by a container.
contented *adj* satisfied.
contention *n* a struggle; a quarrel.
contentious *adj* quarrelsome.
contest *vt, vi* to call in question; to strive; to contend; to emulate. * *n* a competition.
context *n* the setting (of a passage).
contiguity *n* the nearness.
contiguous *adj* touching; adjacent.
continent *adj* chaste; moderate; able to control urination and defecation.
continent *n* a large mass of land; the mainland of Europe.

contingency *n* a possible event; accident.
contingent *adj* incidental; conditional; that may happen. * *n* a quota; a detachment of troops; a possible happening.
continual *adj* incessant.
continuance *n* duration.
continue *vi* to remain; to persevere. * *vt* to prolong; to extend.
continuity *n* unbroken sequence; the whole script and scenario of a film.
continuous *adj* uninterrupted.
contort *vt* to twist; to pull out of shape.
contortion *n* a twisting out of shape.
contortionist *n* an entertainer who twists his body into unnatural positions.
contour *n* outline; form; a line on a map joining all points at the same height above sea level.
contraband *n* smuggled goods.
contract *vt* to reduce; to incur; to shorten (a word); to be affected by a disease. * *vi* to shrink; to make a mutual agreement. * *n* an agreement; abond.
contraction *n* shrinking; a shortening; tensing of a muscle.
contractor *n* a firm that arranges sale of materials or goods or manpower.
contradict *vt* to deny; to say the contrary.
contradictory *adj* inconsistent.
contralto *n* the lowest voice of a woman.
contraption *n* a devise; a gadget; an improvised or complicated contrivance.
contrary *adj* opposite; adverse; opposed; perverse. * *n* the opposite.
contrast *vt* to set in opposition; to show up the differences in. * *vi* to stand in contrast to * *n* opposition; difference.
contravene *vt* to oppose; to transgress.
contravention *n* violation.
contribute *vt* to give; to write magazine articles; to make suggestions.
contribution *n* something given; a gift.
contributor *n* one who contributes; a writer to a periodical.
contributory *adj* aiding; partly responsible for.
contrite *adj* penitent.
contrition *n* sorrow for sin; repentance.
contrivance *n* a scheme; a plan; an invention, often mechanical.
contrive *vt* to invent; to devise; to achieve, often by unusual means.
control *n* restraint; authority; a standard to compare with and check against. * *vt* to regulate; to be in command.
controller *n* a supervisor of public accounts.
controversial *adj* disputable.
controversy *n* a dispute.
contusion *n* a severe bruise.
conundrum *n* a riddle.
convalesce *vi* to recover health.
convalescence *n* gradual recovery after illness.
convalescent *n* one recovering from sickness.
convene *vi* to assemble; to call a meeting. * *vt* to convoke.
convenience *n* ease; comfort; something useful and labour saving; a public lavatory.
convenient *adj* suitable.
convent *n* a monastery; a nunnery.
convention *n* an assembly; an agreement; a recognized social custom.
conventional *adj* customary; unoriginal; following accepted rules.
converge *vi* to tend to the same point.
convergent *adj* approaching; meeting; arriving at the same point or result.
conversant *adj* familiar with; versed in.
conversation *n* easy talk.
conversationalist *n* a good talker.
conversazione *n* a social meeting.
converse *vi* to talk familiarly. * *n* conversation; the very opposite.
conversion *n* a change of religion, party, etc.; an alteration to a building.
convert *vti* to transform; to change. * *n* one who has changed his opinion, practice, or religion.
convertible *adj* transformable * *n* a car with a folding or detachable roof.
convex *adj* curved outwards.
convey *vt* to transport; to carry; to transfer especially the title of a property; to make known.
conveyance *n* any means of transport; a transference of property by deed.
convict *vt* to prove to be guilty. * *n* a criminal undergoing sentence.
conviction *n* a proving guilty; a strong

belief.

convince *vt* to persuade; to satisfy.

convincing *adj* conclusive; believable beyond doubt.

convivial *adj* festive; jovial; sociable.

convolute, convoluted *adj* rolled, coiled on itself; invloved; difficult to follow.

convolution *n* a winding; a spiral.

convoy *vt* to escort. * *n* a protecting force of ships or vehicles.

convulse *vt* to agitate violently * vi to cause spasms of helpless laughter.

convulsion *n* a shaking fit; a disturbance.

convulsive *adj* spasmodic.

cook *vt* to prepare food; to concoct. * *n* one who prepares food.

cookery *n* the art of preparing food.

cool *adj* moderately cold; self-possessed. * *vt* to make cool.

coolly *adv* with assurance.

coolness *n* calm assurance.

coop *n* a cage or pen for poultry.

cooper *n* one who makes barrels.

cooperage *n* the work or workshop of a cooper.

cooperate *vi* to act, work together with another.

cooperation *n* copartnership.

cooperative *adj* operating jointly; helpful.

coopt *vt* to elect into a body, committee etc. by vote of its members.

coordinate *adj* equal in rank. * *vt* to arrange in the same order; to integrate.

coordination *n* act of coordinating; harmonious movement of parts of the body.

cope *vt* to cover; to grapple (with); to manage something successfully.

copestone *n* the topmost stone.

copier, copyist *n* a transcriber; a machine that makes copies; an imitator.

coping *n* the topmost course of a wall, etc.

copious *adj* abundant.

copper *n* a reddish metal.

copperplate *n* an engraver's plate; the print from it; perfect handwriting.

coppersmith *n* one who works in copper.

coppice, copse *n* a thicket.

copulate *vi* to have sexual intercourse.

copulative *adj* that unites. * *n* a conjunction.

copy *n* an imitation; matter to be set up in type. * *vt* to imitate; to transcribe.

copyright *n* the sole right to publish (a book, etc).

coquetry *n* flirtation.

coracle *n* a boat made of skin-covered wickerwork.

coral *n* a sea rock built up from the skeletons of minute organisms.

cord *n* a thin rope; a band.

cordial *adj* hearty. * *n* a refreshing drink.

cordiality *n* heartiness.

cordon *n* a line or chain of police or soldiers barring entry to an area; a knight's ribbon.

corduroy *n* a thick cotton stuff corded or ribbed.

core *n* the heart; the essence; the seed-bearing centre of fruit; the centre of the earth below the mantle.

co-respondent *n* a joint respondent in divorce proceedings.

cork *n* a tree or its bark; a stopper. * *vt* to stop with a cork.

corm *n* a bulb-shaped root.

corn *n* grain (as wheat, oats, etc); a horny growth on the foot.

cornea *n* the transparent membrane over the eye.

corned *adj* salted.

corner *n* an angle; the place where two lines, sides, streets etc. meet; a difficult or dangerous position; a free kick from the corner of the pitch in football, hockey; a nook.

cornerstone *n* the indispensable stone, part, or basis.

cornet *n* a brass instrument of the trumpet family; a cone-shaped wafer for ice cream.

cornice *n* the upper moulding of a column, a room, a wall, etc.

cornucopia *n* the horn plenty full of fruit and vegetables.

corolla *n* the inner envelope; the petals of a flower.

corollary *n* an additional inference from a proved proposition.

corona *n* the halo round the sun in total eclipse; a circle of florets.

coronation *n* the ceremony of crowning.

coroner *n* an officer who holds an inquest in a case of sudden death.
corporal *n* the lowest noncommissioned officer. * *adj* pertaining to the body; physical; material.
corporate *adj* formed into a legal body; united; joint.
corporately *adv* in a corporate capacity.
corporation *n* a body corporate, empowered to act as an individual.
corporeal *adj* material; not spiritual.
corps *n* a body of troops.
corpse *n* the dead body of a human being.
corpulence *n* excessive fatness.
corpulent *adj* portly; fat.
corpuscle *n* a red or white blood cell in the body.
corpuscular *adj* pertaining to corpuscles.
corral *n* a pen for cattle; an enclosure or stockade.
correct *adj* right. * *vt* to make right; to chastise.
corrective *adj* intended to correct * *n* that which corrects; restriction.
correlate *vi* to be reciprocally related. * *vt* to determine the relations between.
correlation *n* reciprocal relation.
correlative *adj* having a mutual relation, as father and son. * *n* a word that relates to another word, as: either and or.
correspond *vi* to be like or similar; to agree; to write to.
correspondence *n* agreement; exchange or writing of (letters, etc).
corridor *n* a passage in a building or train linking rooms, compartments, etc.
corroborate *vt* to strengthen; to confirm.
corroboration *n* confirmation.
corrode *vt* to eat or wear away by degrees; to rust.
corrosion *n* wearing away through chemical action.
corrosive *adj* gnawing; blighting. * *n* a corroding agent.
corrugate *vt* to wrinkle; to fold into parallel ridges.
corrugated *adj* wrinkled; ridged.
corrupt *vt* to taint morally; to infect; to bribe. * *vi* to become debased or vitiated. * *adj* tainted; depraved.
corruptible *adj* subject to decay, destruction, debasement.
corruption *n* act or process of corrupting; depravity; bribery.
corset *n* a close-fitting undergarment supporting the lower body.
cortége *n* a train of attendants; a funeral procession.
cortex *n* the bark of a tree; a membrane.
coruscate *vi* to flash; to glitter.
corvette *n* a escort ship of war.
cosy *adj* snug. * *n* a teapot cover.
cosmetic *n* a skin beautifier. * *adj* beautifying; correcting; improving.
cosmic *adj* relating to the universe.
cosmography *n* a description of the world.
cosmology *n* the science of the world or the universe.
cosmonaut *n* a Russian astronaut.
cosmopolitan, cosmopolite *n* a citizen of the world; a much travelled person; someone without national prejudices. * *adj* unprejudiced.
cosmos *n* the universe and its system.
cost *vt* to be bought for; to set a price on; to cause. * *n* charge; price; trouble.
costal *adj* pertaining to the ribs.
costive *adj* constipated.
costume *n* an established mode of dress; garb; attire; clothing worn by actors.
costumier *n* a dealer in costumes.
cot *n* a small house; a small bed.
coterie *n* a small social group of people with like interests; a clique.
cottage *n* a small house.
cotton *n* a soft substance in the pods of several plants; cloth made of cotton.
cotton wool *n* cotton in the raw state bleached and sterilized.
couch *vt* to express in specific language or mode of speech. * *n* a bed; a sofa.
couchant *adj* lying down.
cough *n* a noisy explosion of air from the lungs. * *vt, vi* to make a violent effort to expel the air from the lungs.
could past tense of **can** was able.
council *n* an assembly; a governing or advisory body elected or appointed.
councillor *n* a member of a council.
counsel *n* deliberation; advice; design; a

barrister. * *vt* to advise; to recommend.

counsellor *n* an adviser; a barrister.

count *vt* to number; to judge. * *vi* to reckon; to rely on; to matter or be of importance; to mark time. * *n* reckoning.

countenance *n* the face; air; aspect; favour. * *vt* to favour.

counter *n* a shop table; (*pl*) tokens for card games. * *vt* to parry. * *adj* rival; opposite.

counteract *vt* to act in opposition to; to hinder; to check; to neutralize.

counterbalance *vt* to weigh against with an equal weight or power.

counterfeit *vt, vi* to forge; to copy; to feign. * *adj* fraudulent. * *n* a forgery.

counterfoil *n* a part of a cheque, etc, kept for reference.

countermand *vt* to annul a former command. * *n* a contrary order.

counterpane *n* a bedcover.

counterpart *n* a corresponding part or person; a duplicate.

counterpoint *n* the art of musical composition; the sounding or playing of two or several melodies or parts at the same time.

countersign *vt* to sign with an additional signature. * *n* a password.

countess *n* the wife of an earl or count.

countless *adj* innumerable.

country *n* a large tract of land; a region; a kingdom or state; the public; rural parts. * *adj* rural.

country dance *n* a folk dance usually with partners facing each other in line.

county *n* a shire or division of a country.

coup *n* a stroke or blow; a masterstroke.

coupé *n* a four seater closed car with two doors and a sloped back.

couple *n* a pair; a brace; a man and his wife. * *vt, vi* to unite; to copulate.

couplet *n* two lines that rhyme.

coupling *n* the links connecting railway carriages or machine parts.

coupon *n* a ticket entitling holder to some money, service, or privilege.

courage *n* bravery.

courageous *adj* bold; fearless.

courier *n* an express messenger.

course *n* a running; a passage; a route; career; ground run over; line of conduct; a track; a series of lectures, etc; range of subjects taught; a layer of stones in masonry; part of a meal served at one time.

court *n* an enclosed area; the retinue of a sovereign; judges in session; flattery. * *vt* to woo; to flatter; to seek.

courteous *adj* polite.

courtesy *n* politeness.

courtier *n* an attendant at a royal court.

courtliness *n* dignity mingled with graciousness.

courtly *adj* dignified.

court martial *n* (*pl* **courts martial**) a court to try military or naval offences.

courtship *n* wooing.

cousin *n* the child of an uncle or aunt.

cove *n* a small inlet.

covenant *n* a contract; a compact. * *vi, vt* to enter into a formal agreement.

cover *vt* to overspread; to cloak; to shelter; to defend; to wrap up; to brood on; to include; to understudy; to write a newspaper report. * *n* a cloak; disguise; shelter; insurance against loss etc.

coverlet *n* the cover of a bed.

covert *adj* secret; private. * *n* a shelter.

covet *vt* to desire eagerly; to envy.

covetous *adj* grasping; greedy.

cow *n* a female of domestic cattle, whale, elephant etc. * *vt* to terrorise; to dishearten; to intimidate.

coward *n* one who is not brave.

cowardice *n* timidity.

cower *vi* to crouch; to waver or tremble through fear.

cowl *n* a monk's hood; a covering over a chmney to aid ventilation.

cowpox *n* an eruption on the teats of cows from which the smallpox vaccine is obtained.

coxcomb *n* a fop; a vain fellow.

coxswain *n* the person who steers a boat or has charge of a ship's boat.

coy *adj* shy; reserved.

crab *n* a crustacean; a sign of the zodiac.

crabbed *adj* perverse.

crack *n* a chink; a sudden sharp sound; a sounding blow; a chat. * *vt, vi* to split; to break; to open a safe forcibly; to open a bottle; to make a joke; to decipher a code; to chat; to give in under pressure.

cracker *n* a small firework; a hard biscuit.

crackle *vi* to make small sharp noises.

cradle *n* an infant's bed on rockers; a framework under a ship for launching or suppporting it; a frame for a broken limb. * *vt* to lay or rock in a cradle.

craft *n* ability; guile; manual art; trade; a ship or aircraft.

craftily *adv* artfully; cunningly.

craftsman *n* an skilled worker.

crafty *adj* cunning.

crag *n* a steep rugged rock.

cram *vti* to stuff; to coach for an examination.

cramp *n* a spasmodic contraction of a muscle; a clamp. * *vt* to affect with spasms; to restrain; to hamper.

cramped *adj* restrained; restricted; of handwriting, small and hard to read.

crane *n* a long-legged, long-necked bird; a machine for raising heavy weights. * *vi* to stretch out one's neck.

cranial *adj* relating to the skull.

cranium *n* the skull.

crank *n* a contrivance for producing a horizontal or perpendicular motion by means of a rotary motion, or the contrary; a bend or turn; a fadist. * *adj* liable to be overset; loose. * *vt* to wind.

cranny *n* a chink.

crash *vi* to fall with a clatter; to collide with or fall violently; to gatecrash. * n a noise of breakage; a collapse esp. financial; a failure; a violent impact or descent.

crass *adj* gross; dense; stupid.

crate *n* a wooden packing case.

crater *n* the bowl-shaped mouth of a volcano; a hole or depression caused by a bomb or meteor explosion.

cravat *n* a neckcloth.

crave *vt* to ask earnestly; to have an intensely strong desire for.

craven *n* a coward. * *adj* cowardly.

craving *n* a morbid desire.

craw *n* the crop of fowls.

crawl *vi* to creep on hands and knees; to be servile towards. * *n* a crawling motion; slow motion; a swimming stroke.

crayon *n* a pencil of coloured chalk; a coloured drawing.

craze *vt* to shatter; to derange. * *vi* to become crazy. * *n* an inordinate desire or enthusiasm; a passing fashion.

crazy *adj* deranged.

creak *vi* to make a grating sound. * *n* a sharp, grating sound.

cream *n* the oily part of milk from which butter is made; the best of anything. * *vt* to take off cream from.

creamery *n* a place where milk is made into butter and cheese.

crease *n* a mark made by folding; the lines marking the batman's stance (in cricket). * *vt* to make creases in.

create *vt* to make out of nothing; to cause to be; to shape; to invent; to appoint.

creation *n* the universe; an original work of any kind.

creative *adj* original; imaginative.

creator *n* the Supreme Being; a producer.

creature *n* a human being; a mere tool.

crèche *n* a public nursery for children.

credence *n* credit; trust.

credential *n* warrant; voucher (*pl*) testimonials.

credibility *n* reliability.

credible *adj* worthy of belief.

credit *n* belief; reputed integrity; transfer of goods on trust; side of an account in which payment is entered; money possessed or at one's disposal; distinction given to an examinee for good marks. * *vt* to trust; to believe; to sell or lend in trust.

creditable *adj* estimable; praiseworthy.

creditor *n* one to whom a debt is due.

credulity *n* simplicity; overtrustfulness.

credulous *adj* easily imposed on.

creed *n* belief.

creek *n* a small bay.

creel *n* a fisherman's basket.

creep *vi* to crawl; to move stealthily; to be servile; to shiver.

creeper *n* a creeping plant.

cremate *vt* to consume by burning.

creosote *n* an oily liquid, antiseptic and wood preservative.

crepuscular *adj* pertaining to twilight.

crescent *n* a figure shaped like the new moon. * *adj* increasing.
crest *n* a tuft on the head of certain birds; the plume of feathers on a helmet; a device or symbol of a family or office; the top of a hill.
crestfallen *adj* dejected.
cretaceous *adj* chalky.
cretin *n* one afflicted with deficiency of thyroid hormone resulting in mental retardation.
crevice *n* a cleft; a fissure.
crew *n* a company; a gang; the personnel of a ship or aircraft.
crib *n* a child's bed; a small habitation; a rack; a stall for cattle; a literal translation or list of answers often used illicitly by students in examinations. * *vt* to confine; to pilfer; to copy illicitly.
crick *n* a cramp in the neck.
cricket *n* a chirping insect; a game played with bat and ball at a wicket.
crime *n* a breach of law.
criminal *adj* guilty; wicked. * *n* a malefactor; one who has broken the law.
crimp *vt* to curl; to seize; to pinch or fold together.
crimson *n* a deep red colour. * *adj* of a deep red. * vt to dye a deep red colour. * *vi* to blush.
cringe *vi* to fawn; to crouch.
crinkle *vi* to wrinkle. * *vt* to be corrugated or crimped. * n a wrinkle.
cripple *n* a lame person. * *vt* to lame; to disable.
crisis *n* (*pl* **crises**) a turning point; a critical moment; an emergency.
crisp *adj* brittle; friable; fresh and bracing. * *n* a thin potato chip.
criterion *n* (*pl* **criteria**) a standard; a rule regarded as a measure of judgment.
critic *n* a judge; a reviewer; a censor.
critical *adj* skilled in judging; crucial; exacting.
criticism *n* the art or act of judging or the exposition of it.
criticize *vi, vt* to judge critically; to censure.
critique *n* a review.
croak *vi* to make a low hoarse noise in the throat. * *n* the cry of raven or frog.
crochet *n* a type of knitting, some with a hooked needle.
crock *n* an earthen vessel; a pot.
crockery *n* china dishes; earthenware pots.
croft *n* a small plot of land with a farmhouse.
crone *n* an old woman.
crony *n* a familiar friend.
crook *n* a bend; a hooked staff; a shepherd's staff; a pastoral staff; a dishonest person; a swindler.
crooked *adj* bent; deceitful.
crop *n* the stomach or craw of birds; grain while growing; a riding whip. * *vt* to clip or cut short; to browse; to cultivate; (with **up**) to appear unexpectedly.
crop-eared *adj* having the ears cut short.
croquet *n* an open-air game played with mallets, balls and hoops.
croquette *n* a ball of mashed potato, meat or fish fried until brown.
cross *n* two straight lines crossing each other; a monument in the form of a cross; the symbol of the Christian religion; the meeting place of roads, the town centre; adversity. * *vt* to mark with a cross; to pass over; to intersect; to cancel; to vex or thwart. * *adj* peevish.
crossbow *n* a bow fixed crosswise on a stock.
crossbreed *n* a mixed breed.
cross-examination *n* the examination of a witness by the opposing lawyer.
cross-purpose *n* a contrary purpose or aim; a misunderstanding.
cross-question *vt* to cross-examine.
crossroad *n* a road that crosses another; (*pl*) the point where two roads cross.
cross section *n* a surface exposed after cutting a solid at right angles to its length; a representative group (of people) chosen at random.
crosswise *adv* transversely.
crossword *n* a word puzzle on a grid with clues in which words reading down must fir in with those reading across.
crotch *n* the part of the body where the legs fork; the area of the genitals.
crotchet *n* a note in music; a half a minim.
crotchety *adj* perverse; bad-tempered.

crouch *vi* to bend low; to squat.
croupier *n* the dealer at a gaming table.
crow *n* a large black bird with croaking voice; the cock's cry. * *vi* to make the cry of a cock; to exult.
crowbar *n* a bar of iron used as a lever.
crowd *n* a throng. * *vt* to press together. * *vi* to throng.
crown *n* royal headgear; a king's power and symbol of office; the completion; the top of the head; a wreath or garland; a reward; the centre of a road; the upper part of a tooth. * vt to invest with a crown; to adorn; to perfect.
crowning *adj* highest; final.
crow's-feet *npl* the wrinkles about the eyes.
crucial *adj* decisive; critical.
crucible *n* a vessel or pot for heating substances to high temperatures.
crucifix *n* a figure of Christ upon the cross.
Crucifixion *n* the death of Christ.
cruciform *adj* cross-shaped.
crucify *vt* to put to death by nailing to a cross.
crude *adj* raw; unripe; rough; vulgar.
cruel *adj* unmerciful; harsh; fierce.
cruelty *n* severity; barbarity.
cruet *n* a small bottle for holding oil, vinegar etc.
cruise *vi* to sail hither and thither; to travel at a moderate speed. * *n* a sailing to and fro; a pleasure voyage.
cruiser *n* a swift armed warship.
crumb *n* a fragment; a small piece.
crumble *vti.* to break into small fragments; to pulverize; to decay.
crumple *vt, vi* to press into wrinkles; to crease; to collapse.
crunch *vt* to crush between the teeth.
crusade *n* an enterprise or serious activity to further a cause.
crush *vt* to squeeze; to bruise; to overpower; to stamp out. * vi to press forward. * *n* a crowding; an infatuation.
crushing *pa* overwhelming.
crust *n* the hard outer coating of anything. * *vt, vi* to cover with a crust.
crustacea *npl* a general name for jointed shellfish.
crusty *adj* covered with a crust; surly.
crutch *n* a stick with armpit or arm rests to support the body and allow mobility to a lame person; the crotch.
crux *n* the crucial or deciding point.
cry *vi* to utter the loud shrill sounds of weeping, joy, etc; to weep. * *vt* to proclaim. * *n* a shriek or scream; weeping; an appeal for help; a catchword.
crypt *n* an underground vault used as chapel or burial place.
cryptic *adj* hidden; secret; mysterious.
cryptogram *n* secret characters or cipher.
crystal *n* pure transparent quartz; articles made of this; the geometrical form assumed by certain bodies in solidifying.
crystallize *vti* to form into crystals.
cub *n* the young of the bear, fox, etc; a junior boy scout.
cube *n* a regular solid body, with six equal square sides; the third power of a number. * *vt* to raise to the third power.
cubic, cubical *adj* cube-shaped.
cubicle *n* a compartment with a bed partitioned off in a dormitory.
cubism *n* a style of painting representing subjects from different viewpoints at the same time using geometrical shapes, cubes etc.
cud *n* the food which ruminants bring up to chew again.
cuddle *vt* to hug closely; to curl up comfortably.
cudgel *n* a short thick stick.
cue *n* the last words of an actor's speech as a sign to a following actor; catchword; hint; the straight rod used in billiards.
cuff *n* a blow; a slap; part of a sleeve near the hand. * *vt* to beat with the fist or open hand.
cuisine *n* style of cooking.
cul-de-sac *n* a blind alley.
culinary *adj* relating to cookery.
cull *vt* to gather; to reduce numbers of certain animals by killing.
culminate *vi* to reach the highest point.
culmination *n* the highest point; acme
culpability *n* blame; guilt.
culpable *adj* blameworthy.
culprit *n* an accused person; a criminal.
cult *n* a system of worship often with special or secret rites.

cultivate *vt* to till; to refine; to civilize.
culture *n* refinement; appreciation of the arts; the whole range of skills of a people at a certain period; artificial rearing of bees, bacteria, etc.
cultured *adj* educated; refined.
culvert *n* an arched waterway or drain.
cumbersome *adj* burdensome; awkward; heavy.
cumin, cummin *n* an aromatic plant.
cummerbund *n* a girdle or waistband.
cumulate *vt* to heap together.
cumulative *adj* growing by additions.
cumulus *n* (*pl* **cumuli**) a cloud formation resembling snowy mountains.
cuneiform *adj* wedge-shaped
cunning *adj* astute; crafty. * *n* craftiness.
cup *n* a small drinking vessel with a handle; its contents; a cup-shaped trophy often silver or ornamental.
cupboard *n* a shelved cabinet for crockery, food, etc.
cupidity *n* a longing to posess; avarice.
cur *n* a mongrel dog; a low fellow.
curate *n* an assistant clergyman.
curative *adj* tending to cure.
curator *n* a superintendent; a custodian.
curb *vt* to control; to check. * *n* a check; part of a bridle; the edge of the pavement; the kerb.
curd *n* coagulated milk. * *vt, vi* to curdle; to congeal.
curdle *vti* to change into curds; to thicken.
cure *n* healing; a remedy. * vt to heal; to preserve food by salting, pickling etc.
curfew *n* an evening bell rung as a signal to put out lights.
curio *n* a curiosity.
curious *adj* inquisitive; strange; singular.
curl *vt* to form into ringlets. * *vi* to go into coils; to play at the game of curling. * *n* a ringlet of hair; a twist.
curling *n* a game played on ice with large, heavy, smooth stones.
currency *n* circulation; circulating medium; the time when a thing is currect or prevalent; the money used in a particular country.
current *adj* running; circulating. * *n* a running; a stream; progressive motion of water, electricity, etc.
curriculum *n* a course of study (at school, university, etc).
curriculum vitae *n* a (written) statement or summary of a person's career.
curry *n* a highly spiced sauce; a dish spiced with this. * *vt* to flavour with curry; to comb a horse; to seek (favour).
curse *vt* to call down evil on; to blight; to torment. * *vi* to swear. * *n* an oath.
cursed *adj* execrable; detestable.
cursive *adj* running; flowing. * *n* running script.
cursory *adj* hasty; careless; superficial.
curt *adj* short; rude; abrupt.
curtail *vt* to cut short; to cut down e.g. privileges.
curtain *n* a screen for a window, etc; the moving screen of a theatre stage; (*pl*) the end; death. * *vt* to enclose with curtains.
curtsy, curtsey *n* an obeisance or bow.
curvature *n* a curving.
curve *n* a bent line; an arch. * *vt, vi* to bend.
cushion *n* a pillow for a seat; the padded rim of a snooker table; any buffer against shock. * *vt* to furnish with cushions; to protect against; to lessen shock or impact.
cusp *n* a point or sharp horn, as of moon.
custard *n* a mixture of milk, eggs, and sugar prepared as a pudding or sauce.
custodian *n* a guardian; a keeper.
custody *n* care; security; imprisonment.
custom *n* habit; fashion; business patronage; (*pl*) duties on merchandise imported or exported.
customary *adj* habitual; usual.
customer *n* a regular purchaser at a shop or from a business.
cut *vt* to divide into pieces; to mow; to clip; to reduce prices etc. * *vi* to make an incision; to stop filming. * *adj* gashed. * *n* a wound; act of dividing a pack of cards; form; fashion or shape of a garment; a reduction in price; a share of gains etc.
cutaneous *adj* pertaining to the skin.
cuticle *n* the skin at the base of fingernails and toenails; epidermis.
cutlass *n* a broad, curving sword.

cutlery *n* instruments used for eating; forks, knives and spoons.
cutlet *n* a piece of meat cut off the ribs, leg or neck; a chop.
cutter *n* a light sailing vessel; a ship's boat; one who cuts cloth.
cutting *n* a piece cut off; an incision; a passage; a piece cut off a plant for propagating; an excerpt cut from a newspaper; film editing.
cyanide *n* a poisonous compound of cyanogen and a metal.
cycle *n* a period of time; a series; a bicycle. * *vi* to ride a bicycle.
cyclic, cyclical *adj* recurring in series.
cyclist *n* one who rides a bicycle.
cyclone *n* a storm moving in a circle; a hurricane.
cylinder *n* a solid or hollow roller-shaped body.
cymbal *n* a musical instrument of two brass plates which are clashed together.
cynic *n* a sneering, censorious person.
cynic, cynical *adj* sceptical; surly; sneering; captious.
cynicism *n* surliness; heartlessness.
cypher *n see* **cipher**.
cyst *n* a sac in animal bodies containing morbid matter.
czar, tsar *n* the former emperor of Russia.
Czech *n* a native of Czech Lands; the language.

D

dab *vt* to hit lightly with something soft or moist. * *n* a gentle blow; a small mass of anything soft or moist; an adept.
dabble *vt* to wet; to sprinkle; to move hands or feet in water. * *vi* to trifle.
dado *n* the decorative border round the lower part of the walls of a room.
dagger *n* a short sharp-pointed sword.
daily *adj* happening every day. * *adv* day by day. * *n* a newspaper published every weekday
dainty *adj* nice; delicate; elegant. * *n* a delicacy.
dairy *n* a place where milk is sold, or converted into butter or cheese.
dais *n* the high table where principal guests or speakers are seated; a raised platform.
dale *n* a valley.
dalliance *n* lovemaking; trifling.
dally *vi* to trifle; to delay; to lose time by idleness.
dam *n* a mother (of a four-footed animal.); a barrier to confine water. * *vt* to confine by a dam.
damage *n* hurt; injury; money; compensation. * *vt* to injure; to harm.
damask *n* a figured cloth, usually of silk or linen. * *adj* pink or rosy colour of the **damask rose**.
dame *n* a lady.
damn *vt* to condemn; to curse; to consign to eternal punishment.
damnation *n* condemnation.
damned *adj* hateful; detestable; consigned to hell.
damp *adj* moist; humid. * *n* moist air. * *vt* to moisten; to dispirit; to stifle.
dampness *n* moisture.
damsel *n* a girl.
dance *vi* to move in time to music; to skip or leap lightly. * *n* a party for dancing; a dance performance of an artistic nature; music for dancing.
dandruff *n* scurf on the head under the hair.
dandy *n* a fop; a coxcomb.
danger *n* risk; hazard; peril.
dangle *vi* to hang loose. * *vt* to swing.
dank *adj* damp; moist.
dapper *adj* small and neat.
dappled *adj* spotted.
dare *vti* to be bold; to defy; to venture on; to challenge. * *n* a challenge.
daredevil *n* a reckless fellow. * *adj* daring; bold.
daring *adj* bold; fearless. * *n* courage.
dark *adj* without light; gloomy; secret; ignorant; having brown or black skin or hair. * *n* darkness; ignorance.
darkness *n* absence of light; gloom.
darling *adj* dearly beloved. * *n* one much beloved.
darn *vt* to mend holes in clothes.

dart *n* a pointed missile thrown by the hand; a sudden bound. * *vt* to shoot. * *vi* to move rapidly; (*pl*) an indoor game in which darts are thrown at a target.

dash *vti* to shatter; to rush; to frustrate. * *n* a violent striking; a rushing or onset; a mark in writing (—); a small quantity of something added to food; a tinge.

dashboard *n* an instrument panel in a car.

dashing *adj* spirited; showy; stylish.

data *see* **datum**.

data processing *n* the analysis of information stored in a computer for various uses.

date *n* the time when any event happened; an appoitment esp. with one of the opposite sex; era; age. * *vt, vi* to note the time of; to have origin to affix a date to.

dative *adj, n.* a grammatical case.

datum *n* (*pl* **data**) a fact granted as basis for further inference.

daub *vt* to smear; to paint without skill. * *n* poor painting; a smear.

daughter *n* a female child.

daughter-in-law *n* a son's wife.

daunt *vt* to intimidate; to scare; to cow.

dauntless *adj* fearless.

dawdle *vi* to waste time; to saunter.

dawn *vi* to grow light. * *n* the break of day; first appearance.

day *n* the time between the rising and setting of the sun; light; time; a particular period of success or influence.

daybreak *n* the dawn.

daydream *n* a reverie.

daylight *n* the light of the sun; dawn; a visible gap; a sudden realization or understanding.

daytime *n* the time of daylight.

daze *vt* to stupefy; to stun; to perplex. * *n* confusion; bewilderment esp. produced by a blow or a shock.

dazzle *vt* to overpower with light or splendour. * *vi* to be intensely bright.

deacon *n* a church official.

dead *adj* without life; perfectly still; cold; unerring; exact. * *n* stillness; gloom.

deadbeat *adj* quite exhausted.

deaden *vt* to make numb; to muffle.

dead-end *n* a cul-de-sac; a hopeless situation; a job without prospects.

dead heat *n* a race in which the competitors finish at the same time.

deadline *n* the time or date by which a thing must be done.

deadlock *n* a complete standstill; a clash of interests making progress inpossible.

deadly *adj* mortal; implacable.

deadpan *adj* deliberately expressionless.

dead weight *n* a heavy or oppressive burden; weight of a body without its load.

deaf *adj* unable to hear; inattentive.

deafen *vt* to stun with noise.

deaf-mute *n* a deaf and dumb person.

deal *n* an indefinite quantity; a business transaction; the distribution of playing cards. * *vt* to distribute; to behave; to do business with; to solve.

dealer *n* a trader; one who deals cards; a seller of illegal drugs.

dealing *n* conduct; behaviour; business.

dean *n* the head of the chapter of a cathedral; an officer in a university.

dear *adj* costly; valuable; beloved.

dearth *n* scarcity; want.

death *n* extinction of life; decease; the destruction of something.

deathless *adj* immortal.

death rate *n* the proportion of deaths in a town, country, etc.

debacle *n* a sudden break-up; a crash; a rout.

debar *vt* to shut out from something.

debase *vt* to lower; to degrade.

debate *n* a discussion; a formal argument; controversy. * *vt, vi* to dispute; to deliberate.

debauch *vt* to corrupt. * vi to revel. * *n* excess in eating or drinking.

debauched *pa* profligate.

debauchery *n* intemperance; depraved over-indulgence; corruption; lewdness.

debenture *n* interest-bearing bonds in return for a loan.

debilitate *vt* to enfeeble.

debility *n* weakness.

debit *n* a recorded item of debt; the left-hand page or debtor side of a ledger.

debonair *adj* sauve; carefree; sprightly.

debris *n* (*sing or pl*) fragments; rubbish; wreckage.

debt *n* what is owing; an obligation.

debtor *n* one who owes.
début *n* a first appearance in public.
decade *n* a period of ten years.
decadence *n* a falling off; decay; deterioration esp. of morality.
decamp *vi* to leave without notice.
decant *vt* to pour from one vessel into another.
decanter *n* a stoppered bottle in which wine is brought to table.
decapitate *vt* to behead.
decay *vi* to fall away; to waste; to wither; to fail. * *n* decline; putrefaction.
decease *n* death. * *vi* to die.
deceased *adj* dead.
deceit *n* fraud; guile; treachery.
deceive *vt* to mislead; to cheat.
December *n* the twelfth and last month of the year.
decency *n* propriety.
decent *adj* quite good; kind; generous.
decentralize *vt* to transfer power from the central to the local authority.
deception *n* the act or state of being deceived; fraud.
deceptive *adj* misleading; ambiguous.
decide *vti* to determine; to settle; to resolve; to give a judgment on.
deciduous *adj* (of trees) shedding all leaves annually.
decimal *adj* by tens; having 10 as the basis of numeration.
decimate *vt* to destroy a large number.
decipher *vt* to decode; to solve.
decision *n* determination of a judgment; verdict; firmness of character.
decisive *adj* conclusive; absolute.
deck *vt* to clothe; to adorn. * *n* the floor of a ship, aircraft, bus or bridge; a pack of playing cards; the turntable of a record-player; the ground.
declaim *vi* to make a formal speech; to harangue.
declamatory *adj* grandiloquent.
declaration *n* assertion; affirmation.
declare *vti* to make known; to assert; to admit possession of (dutiable goods).
declared *adj* avowed.
declension *n* a falling off; a downcome; the variation in form that nouns, etc, undergo.
decline *vi* to bend downwards; to swerve; to fail. * *vt* to refuse; to inflect a noun, etc.; to diminish; to draw to an end; to deviate. * *n* a falling off; decay; consumption.
declivity *n* a downward slope.
decode *vt* to decipher.
decompose *vt* to resolve into original elements. * *vi* to decay.
decomposition *n* analysis; decay.
décor *n* a general decorative effect or appearance esp. of a room.
decorate *vt* to adorn; to deck.
decoration *n* ornamentation; a mark or badge of honour.
decorative *adj* ornamental.
decorator *n* one who paints houses.
decorous *adj* seemly; becoming.
decorum *n* propriety; seemliness.
decoy *n* an animal or bird trained to lure others into a snare; one who lures others into a trap. * *vt* to lure into a snare.
decrease *vi, vt* to become or make less. * *n* a diminution; a reduction.
decree *n* an edict; an order or law. * *vt* to enact; to award.
decrepit *adj* broken down with age.
decry *vt* to cry down; to disparage.
dedicate *vt* to consecrate; to devote (*often refl*); to inscribe to a friend.
dedication *n* consecration; inscription or address.
deduce *vt* to infer; to arrive at by reasoning.
deduct *vt* to subtract from.
deduction *n* inference; discount.
deductive *adj* that is or may be deduced from premises.
deed *n* an act; feat; a written agreement.
deem *vt* to judge. * *vi* to be of opinion.
deep *adj* being far below the surface; involved; engrossed; profound; intense; secret; artful. * *n* the sea.
deepfreeze *n* a refrigerator in which food is frozen and stored.
deeply *adv* at a great depth; profoundly.
deer *n* (*pl* **deer**) a quadruped with antlers on the males.
deerstalking *n* the hunting of deer.
deface *vt* to disfigure; to erase.
defalcation *n* misappropriation of funds.
defamation *n* slander.

defame *vt* to slander.
default *n* an omission; neglect; absence; lapse. * *vi* to fail to meet payment or keep contract.
defaulter *n* one who fails to answer a summons or to make payment due.
defeat *n* overthrow; loss of battle; frustration of one's plans; loss of a game, race etc. * *vt* to frustrate; to conquer.
defect *n* a want; a blemish.
defection *n* abandonment of a person or cause.
defective *adj* faulty; incomplete.
defence *n* a protection; fortification; vindication; apology; plea; defending the goal etc. against attacks from the opposing side; the defending players in a team.
defenceless *adj* unprotected.
defend *vt* to guard; to support; to act as defendant.
defendant *n* one sued at law.
defensible *adj* justifiable.
defer *vt* to postpone. * *vi* to yield to another's opinion, wishes, judgment.
deference *n* regard; respect.
deferential *adj* respectful.
defiance *n* wilful disobedience; a challenge to fight; contempt of danger.
defiant *adj* bold; insolent; challenging.
deficiency *n* want; defect; deficit.
deficient *adj* defective; lacking.
deficit *n* shortage; the amount by which a sum falls short of what is needed; an excess of expenditure over income.
defile *vt* to pollute. * *n* a narrow pass.
define *vt* to limit; to explain exactly.
definite *adj* precise; exact.
definition *n* an explanation or description.
definitive *adj* limiting; positive; final.
deflate *vt* to release gas or air from; to reduce in size or importance; to reduce inflation in the economy.
deflect *vi* to deviate. * *vt* to turn aside.
deflection n deviation.
deflower *vt* to strip of flowers; to ravish.
defoliation *n* the shedding of leaves.
deform *vt* to disfigure.
deformed *adj* misshapen.
defraud *vt* to cheat.
defray *vt* to bear the charges of.
deft *adj* apt; clever; nimble.
defunct *adj* deceased; no longer functioning. * *n* a dead person.
defuse *vt* to disarm an explosive by removing its fuse; to decrease tension in a crisis or other situation
defy *vt* to dare; to challenge; to set at nought; to resist attempts at; to elude.
degeneracy *n* decline in good qualities.
degenerate *vi* to decline in good qualities. * *adj* depraved; base. * *n* a degenerate or immoral person.
degradation *n* a depriving of rank; disgrace; humiliation.
degrade *vt* to depose; to dishonour.
degraded *adj* debased; dishonoured.
degree *n* a step; rank; grade; measure; the 360th part of the circumference of a circle; a university distinction.
dehydrate *vt* to remove water from. * *vi* to lose water esp. from body tissue.
deify *vt* to make a god of; to idolize.
deign *vi* to condescend to give or do something.
deity *n* a god.
deject *vt* to dispirit; to depress.
dejected *adj* cast down; discouraged.
dejection *n* lowness of spirits.
delay *vti* to defer; to retard; to stop; to linger. * *n* a stay; a hindrance.
delectable *adj* delightful.
delegate *vt* to send as a representative; to depute. * *n* a representative; an agent.
delegation *n* a body of delegates.
delete *vt* to erase; to efface.
deleterious *adj* hurtful.
deliberate *vi, vt* to weigh well; to consider; to debate. * *adj* cautious; well advised; intentional.
deliberation *n* thoughtful consideration.
delicacy *n* refinement of taste; tenderness; a luxurious food.
delicate *adj* pleasing; fine; minute; tender; not robust.
delicious *adj* highly delightful esp. to the taste.
delight *n* great joy or pleasure. * *vt, vi* to charm; to take great pleasure.
delightful *adj* charming; giving pleasure.
delineate *vt* to draw in outline; to sketch.
delinquency *n* a fault; wrongdoing; a crime.

delinquent *adj* neglecting duty. * *n* culprit; an offender, esp. a young law breaker.
delirious *adj* raving; frenzied.
delirium *n* temporary disorder of the mind.
deliver *vt* to set free; to rescue; to hand over; to carry and distribute regularly; to give birth; to launch or throw.
deliverance *n* release; rescue; a legal judgment.
delivery *n* childbirth; rescue; distribution (of letters); manner of speaking; the act of giving birth; the bowling of a ball in cricket.
dell *n* a small valley.
delta *n* the space between diverging mouths of a river; the fourth letter of the Greek alphabet.
delude *vt* to deceive; to trick.
deluge *n* a flood; the flood; heavy rain. * *vt* to inundate; to drown.
delusion *n* a mistaken idea; a fallacy.
delusive *adj* deceptive.
delve *vti* to dig.
demagogue *n* a voluble political orator deriving power from appealing to popular prejudices.
demand *vt* to claim by right; to question. * *n* a claim, often urgent; a challenging; the desire shown by consumers for particular goods or services.
demarcation *n* a boundary; a fixed limit.
demean *vt* to lower in dignity; to debase.
demeanour *n* behaviour.
demented *adj* insane; infatuated.
demise *n* death; termination.
demit *vt* to resign (an office).
demobilize *vt* to discharge from the armed forces; to disband.
democracy *n* government by the people through elected representatives; political, social or legal equality.
democrat *n* a friend to popular government.
demolish *vt* to pull down; to defeat.
demon *n* an evil spirit.
demonstrable *adj* that may be demonstrated or proved.
demonstrate *vt* to prove beyond doubt; to exhibit * *vi* to show support for a cause by public protest and parades.
demonstration *n* proof; show of feeling; a display of feeling by public protest, mass meetings etc.
demonstrative *adj* open; unreserved.
demoralization *n* corruption; loss of morale.
demoralize *vt* to corrupt; to dispirit.
demur *vi* to hesitate; to object. * *n* pause; objection.
demure *adj* affectedly modest.
demy *n* a size of paper, generally 22 x 17 inches.
den *n* a cave; a dell; a lair of a wild beast.
denial *n* contradiction; refusal of a request; reluctance to admit the truth of something.
denim *n* a hard-wearing cloth esp. for jeans. (*pl*) trousers of this.
denomination *n* class; religious sect.
denominator *n* the divisor in a vulgar fraction.
denote *vt* to indicate; to imply; to mean.
dénouement *n* the unfolding, the final outcome of the plot in a play; the issue.
denounce *vt* to threaten; to condemn; to accuse publicly.
dense *adj* thick; close.
density *n* compactness; stupidity; the ratio of mass to volume.
dent *n* a mark made by a blow or pressure. * *vt* to mark.
dental *adj* pertaining to the teeth.
dentist *n* one qualified to treat disorders of the teeth.
denude *vt* to make bare; to strip.
denunciation *n* the utterance of a threat, censure or menace.
deny *vt* to contradict; to disavow.
deodorant *n* a preparation that masks unpleasant smells.
deodorize *vt* to rid of smell.
deoxidize *vt* to deprive of oxygen.
depart *vi* to go away; to deviate; to die.
department *n* a separate part; a division; a branch; a place of activity.
department store *n* a large shop with many departments each selling different types of goods.
departure *n* act of going away; withdrawal, death.

depend *vi* to hang from; to be reliant on; to trust.
dependant *n* one who depends on another; a retainer.
dependence *n* reliance; trust; subordination.
dependency *n* a subject territory.
dependent *adj* relying on; contingent.
depict *vt* to portray; to describe.
depilate *vt* to strip of hair.
deplete *vt* to empty; to exhaust.
deplorable *adj* shocking; pitiable.
deplore *vt* to regret deeply; to deprecate.
deploy *vt* to open out; to distribute and position strategically (soldiers etc).
depopulate *vt* to reduce the population of.
deport *vt* to expel (an undesirable person) from a country; to conduct (one's self).
deportation *n* banishment from a country.
deportment *n* carriage; behaviour.
depose *vt* to dethrone; to divest of office.
deposit *vt* to lay down; to lodge in a place. * *n* something deposited; money left in a bank; money left in security.
deposition *n* affidavit; testimony; displacement.
depot *n* a storehouse; a warehouse; a place for storing military supplies; a military training centre; a railway or bus station.
deprave *vt* to corrupt.
depraved *adj* profligate; perverted.
deprecate *vt* to disapprove of.
deprecation n disapproval.
depreciate *vt* to lower the value of; to undervalue. * *vi* to fall in value.
depreciation *n* a fall in value, esp. of an asset through wear and tear.
depress *vt* to press down; to deject.
depression *n* dejection; an economis phase characterized by stagnation, unemployment etc.; a lowering of atmospheric pressure; a hollow.
deprivation *n* want; bereavement.
deprive *vt* to take from; to dispossess.
deprived *adj* lacking the essentials of life, e.g. food, housing, education.
depth *n* deepness; a deep place; intensity; profoundness.
deputation *n* persons sent to act for others.
depute *vt* to appoint as a substitute.
deputy *n* a substitute; a representative.
derange *vt* to displace; to disorder; to unbalance; to make insane.
deranged *adj* distracted.
derelict *adj* abandoned. * *n* the thing or person abandoned.
dereliction *n* failure; wilful neglect.
deride *vt* to ridicule; to jeer.
derision *n* mockery.
derisive *adj* mocking.
derivation *adj* source or origin.
derivative *adj* derived. * *n* a derivative word; an offshoot.
derive *vti* to obtain; to draw; to trace to its origin; to come from.
dermatology *n* the study of skin and its diseases.
derogatory *adj* disparaging.
descant *n* a discourse; a melody. * vi to sing; to discourse.
descend *vi, vt* to climb down; to invade; to be derived; to sink morally.
descendant *n* an heir; offspring.
descent *n* act of descending; declivity; invasion; lineage.
describe *vt* to portray; to relate.
description *n* a verbal account; relation; kind; sort.
descriptive *adj* graphic.
desecrate *vt* to violate a sacred place.
desecration *n* profanation.
desert *adj* waste. * *n* a sandy barren region.
desert *vi* to leave; to quit. * *vi* to run away esp. from the armed forces. * *n* virtue; merit.
deserter *n* a runaway.
deserve *vti* to merit.
deservedly *adv* justly.
desiccate *vt* to dry.
design *vt* to plan; to propose; to make working drawings for. * *vi* to intend. * *n* a drawing or sketch; purpose; aim.
designate *vt* to point out; to name; to mark; to appoint or nominate for a position.
designation *n* name; title; nomination.
designedly *adv* purposely.
designer *n* one who designs; a creator of high-class fashion clothes. * *adj* of the

latest fashion or trend.
designing *adj* artful; scheming.
desirable *adj* longed for; advisable.
desire *n* longing; craving; love. * *vt* to wish for; to covet.
desist *vi* to stop; to leave off.
desk *n* a (sloping) table designed for writer's or reader's use; the section of a newspaper responsible for a particular topic.
desolate *adj* forlorn; forsaken; waste. * *vt* to lay waste.
desolation *n* ruin; gloom; loneliness.
despair *n* hopelessness. * *vi* to give up all hope.
despatch, dispatch *vt* to send away in haste; to kill; to perform quickly. * *n* an official message; speed.
desperate *adj* reckless; hopeless; urgently needing money; extreme; dangerous.
despicable *adj* contemptible.
despise *vt* to scorn; to disdain.
despite *prep* not withstanding; in spite of.
despoil *vt* to rob; to rifle; to plunder.
despondent *adj* dejected; hopeless.
despondency *n* dejection.
despot *n* a tyrant.
despotic *adj* autocratic.
dessert *n* the fruit or sweet course at the end of a meal.
destination *n* a goal; the place to which one is going.
destiny *n* fate; a predetermined course of events.
destitute *adj* in want; forlorn.
destitution *n* want.
destroy *vt* to pull down; to overthrow; to kill.
destroyer *n* a small swift warship to destroy submarines.
destruction *n* ruin; death; slaughter.
destructive *adj* ruinous causing destruction; negative or adverse (of criticism).
desultory *adj* casual; rambling.
detach *vt* to separate; to release.
detached *adj* separate; (of a house) not joined to another; aloof; unbiassed.
detachment *n* separation; a body of troops away from the main army.
detail *vt* to recount; to particularize; to set apart. * *n* an individual fact; an item; a small part of a picture, statue etc.; a small detachment for special duties.
detailed *adj* minute; thorough.
detain *vt* to keep back; to arrest; to place in confinement.
detect *vt* to discover; to notice.
detective *n* a police officer whose duty is to detect criminals.
detention *n* act of detaining; confinement; being kept in (school) after hours.
deter *vt* to hinder; to discourage.
detergent *adj* cleansing; purging. * *n* a cleaning agent.
deteriorate *vi* to grow worse. * *vt* to depreciate.
determination *n* firm resolution; conclusion.
determine *vt* to bound; to fix permanently; to resolve; to bring to an end.
deterrent *n* a warning; a curb; a nuclear weapon to deter attack through fear of retaliation. * *adj* detering.
detest *vt* to abhor; to loathe.
detestable *adj* odious.
dethrone *vt* to depose.
detonate *vti* to explode.
detonation *n* an explosion.
detour *n* a roundabout way.
detract *vti* to disparage; to defame.
detractor *n* a slanderer; a muscle which detracts.
detriment *n* loss; damage.
devastate *vt* to lay waste; to overwhelm.
develop *vt* to unfold; to make visible; to make to grow; to treat a photographic film or plate to reveal an image. * *vi* to grow or expand.
development *n* growth; land or property that has been improved.
deviate *vi* to stray; to wander; to diverge.
device *n* a contrivance; an emblem.
devil *n* an evil spirit; Satan; a wicked person; a difficulty. * *vt* to pepper and broil. vi. to drudge for another, especially a barrister.
devilment *n* mischief.
devilry *n* extreme wickedness.
devious *adj* circuitous; deceitful; underhand.
devise *vt* to plan; to contrive; to invent.
devoid *adj* destitute; free from.

devolution *n* the transfer of duties or business to another.
devolve *vt* to transfer; to depute.
devote *vt* to dedicate; to give or use for a particular activity or purpose.
devoted *adj* zealous; attached; loyal.
devotion *n* consecration; attachment; strong affection; piety.
devour *vt* to eat ravenously; to swallow up; to absorb eagerly.
devout *adj* pious; sincere.
dew *n* atmospheric vapour deposited on cool surfaces at night.
dexterity *n* adroitness; skill.
dexterous *adj* skilful; expert.
dhow *n* an Arab trading vessel.
diabolic, diabolical *adj* fiendish.
diagnose *vt* to identify a disease from symptoms.
diagnosis *n* the identification of an illness from symptoms.
diagonal *adj* applied to a line drawn from corner to corner.
diagram *n* an illustrative figure in outline.
dial *n* a time recorder; the face of a clock; the numbered disc on some telephones for connecting some calls.
dialect *n* the form of a language peculiar to a province.
dialectic, dialectical *adj* relating to dialectics; pertaining to a dialect.
dialectics *npl* the art of reasoning; logical skill.
dialogue *n* a conversation between two or more.
diameter *n* the line passing through or across the centre (esp. of a circle).
diamond *n* the most valuable of gems; a suit of playing cards; the playing field in baseball.
diaphragm *n* the midriff, a muscle separating thorax and abdomen; a disc or plate closing partly or wholly a tube; a contraceptive cap.
diarrhoea *n* looseness of the bowels.
diary *n* a daily record of events.
diastole *n* dilation of the heart in beating.
diatribe *n* a tirade.
dice *see* **die**.
dictaphone *n* an instrument for recording and reproducing speech.
dictate *vt* to read for reproduction by another person or by a recording machine; to prescribe; to order.
dictation *n* act, art, or practice of dictating; command.
dictator *n* one invested with absolute authority.
diction *n* a way of speaking or enunciating; a choice of words.
dictionary *n* a book with the words of a language arranged alphabetically, with their meanings, pronunciations etc.
didactic *adj* instructive.
diddle *vt* to trick.
die *vi* to cease to live; to expire.
die[1] *n* (*pl* **dice**) a cube with sides marked 1, 2, 3, 4, 5, 6, used in games of chance.
die[2] *n* (*pl* **dice**) a stamp.
diesel *n* a vehicle driven by a diesel engine.
diesel engine *n* an internal combustion engine where ignition is produced by the heat of highly compressed air alone.
diet *n* food; a course of feeding. * *vt, vi* to eat or cause to eat according to special guidelines.
differ *vi* to be unlike; to disagree.
difference *n* dissimilarity; a dispute; a disagreement; remainder (in subtraction).
different *adj* distinct; dissimilar.
differential *adj* discriminating; variable; relating to increments in given functions. * *n* an infinitesimal difference between two states of a variable quantity; the difference in wage rates for different types of labour esp. within an industry.
differentiate *vt* to mark or distinguish by a difference.
difficult *adj* arduous; perplexing; hard to please; hard to understand.
diffidence *n* want of confidence; reserve.
diffident *adj* wanting confidence; bashful.
diffuse *vt* to pour out and spread; to proclaim. * adj widely spread; not concise.
diffusion *n* dispersion; circulation.
dig *vt* to turn up with a spade. * vi to work with a spade; to excavate; to investigate; to nudge; to understand; to approve.

digest *vt* to assimilate; to think out; to dissolve in the stomach. * *n* a summary.
digestible *adj* capable of being digested.
digestion *n* process of making food assimilable.
digit *n* a finger; any of the figures 0 to 9.
digital *adj* of, using digits e.g. a clock.
dignified *adj* stately; grave.
dignify *vt* to ennoble; to grace; to exalt.
dignitary *n* one holding high rank.
dignity *n* honour; rank; formality in manner and appearance.
digress *vi* to depart from main subject; to deviate.
dike, dyke *n* a ditch; an embankment.
dilapidated *adj* in a ruinous condition.
dilapidation *n* decay; ruin.
dilation *n* expansion; enlargement.
dilate *vti* to expand; to distend.
dilatory *adj* tardy; putting off.
dilemma *n* a fix; a quandary.
diligence *n* application.
diligent *adj* industrious; persevering.
dilute *vt* to reduce in strength by adding water or some qualifying matter. * *adj* weak; diluted.
dilution *n* reduction in strength.
dim *adj* obscure; faint. * *vt* to dull; to make dark.
dimension *n* the measure of a thing, size, extent, capacity.
diminish *vti* to lessen; to decrease.
diminutive *adj* small. * *n* a word denoting smallness.
dimple *n* a small hollow on the cheek or chin.
din *n* a loud sound long continued. * vt to stun with noise; to teach with constant repetition.
dine *vi* to eat dinner.
dinghy *n* a small ship's boat.
dingy *adj* dull; faded.
dinner *n* the principal meal of the day.
diocese *n* the see of a bishop.
dip *vt* to plunge quickly in and out of a liquid; to immerse. * *vi* to incline. * *n* a bathe; downward slope; a mixture in which to dip something.
diphtheria *n* an infectious throat disease.
dipthong *n* the blending of two vowel sounds.
diploma *n* a document conferring a degree of honour.
diplomacy *n* the art of negotiating esp. between nations; tact.
diplomat *n* a diplomatist.
diplomatic *adj* prudent, tactful.
dire *adj* dreadful; urgent.
direct *adj* straight; express; sincere. * *vt* to point or aim at; to show; to conduct; to order; to instruct; to address a letter.
direction *n* course; guidance; command; management; address on a letter; the way in which one is pointing.
directly *adv* without delay; expressly.
director *n* a superintendent; a counsellor; one who directs the production of a stage or screen show.
directory *n* a book with lists of names, addresses, telephone numbers etc.
dirge *n* a lament.
dirt *n* any filthy substance; scandal.
dirty *adj* soiled with dirt; mean; dishonest; obscene. * *vt* to soil; to sully.
disable *vt* to deprive of power; to injure.
disabled *adj* handicapped physically.
disabuse *vt* to undeceive.
disadvantage *n* inconvenience; loss.
disaffect *vt* to estrange; to make discontented.
disaffection *n* disloyalty.
disagree *vi* to differ; to fall out; to dissent.
disagreeable *adj* offensive; displeasing.
disagreement *n* difference; discord.
disappear *vi* to vanish from sight.
disappearance *n* removal from sight.
disappoint *vt* to fail to fulfil the hopes of a person; to frustrate; to foil.
disapprobation *n* disapproval; censure.
disapproval *n* dislike; blame.
disapprove *vt* to censure as wrong; to blame.
disarm *vt, vi* to deprive of arms; to disband.
disarmament *n* the laying down of arms.
disarrange *vt* to derange; to upset.
disarray *vt* to throw into disorder. * n disorder.
disaster *n* a calamity; a failure.
disavowal *n* denial.
disband *vt* to disperse. * *vi* to break up.

disbelief *n* want of belief; distrust.
disbelieve *vt* to refuse to credit.
disburse *vt* to pay out.
disc, disk *n* the flat face of a thin, round body (e.g. coin, sun, counter, gramophone record, etc).
discard *vt* to throw away.
discern *vti* to perceive; to judge.
discerning *adj* sharp-sighted; acute.
discharge *vt* to unload; to fire; to dismiss; to perform; to acquit. * *n* a dismissal; release; matter coming from a sore or wound.
disciple *n* a learner; a follower.
disciplinarian *n* one who enforces discipline; a martinet.
disciplinary *adj* intended for discipline.
discipline *n* training; order; subjection to laws; punishment; correction. * *vt* to train; to punish to enforce discipline; tobring under control.
disclaim *vt* to disown, reject.
disclaimer *n* disavowal; denial.
disclose *vt* to open; to uncover; to reveal.
discoloration *n* stain.
discolour *vt* to change the colour; to stain.
discomfiture *n* rout; disappointment.
discomfort *n* uneasiness; its cause; lack of comfort.
disconcert *vt* to embarrass.
disconnect *vt* to disunite; to separate.
disconsolate *adj* comfortless.
discontentment *n* dissatisfaction.
discontinue *vti* to leave off; to cease.
discord *n* want of harmony; strife.
discordant *adj* harsh sounding.
discotheque *n* a gathering for dancing to recorded music; a club or party for this.
discount *n* a sum deducted from the cost. * vt to cash a bill at present worth; to take away from.
discourage *vt* to dishearten; to dissuade.
discourse *n* a speech; a treatise; a sermon. * *vi* to talk.
discourteous *adj* rude.
discover *vt* to lay open to view; to detect; to find or learn about for the first time.
discredit *n* want of credit; distrust. * *vt* to damage the reputation of.
discreditable *adj* dishonourable.
discreet *adj* prudent.
discrepancy *n* variance; a disagreement as between firgures in a total.
discretion *n* prudence; judgment.
discretionary *adj* left to one's discretion.
discriminate *vt* to distinguish; to select.
discrimination *n* discernment.
discursive *adj* rambling.
discus *n* a quoit; a disc.
discuss *vt* to debate; to examine by argument.
discussion *n* a debate.
disdain *vt* to scorn. * *n* contempt.
disdainful *adj* contemptuous.
disease *n* an ailment.
disembark *vti* to put or go ashore.
disembody *vt* to divest of the body.
disenchant *vt* to disillusion.
disengage *vt* to detach; to release; to extricate.
disentangle *vt* to extricate.
disfavour *n* want of favour.
disfiguration *n* defacement.
disfigure *vt* to mar the appearance of.
disfigurement *n* a blemish.
disgorge *vt* to vomit; to discharge; to surrender.
disgrace *n* shame; dishonour.
disgraceful *adj* shameful.
disguise *vt* to conceal; to dissemble; to change the appearance of. * *n* a make up; a pretence; a false appearance.
disgust *n* loathing; repugnance. * *vt* to offend; to sicken.
disgusting *adj* repulsive; sickening.
dish *n* an open vessel for serving food; the meat served. * *vt* to put in a dish.
dishearten *vt* to discourage.
dishevelled *adj* disarranged; untidy.
dishonest *adj* fraudulent; untrustworthy.
dishonesty *n* fraudulence.
dishonour *n* disgrace. * *vt* to bring shame on; to refuse payment of.
dishonourable *adj* base; vile.
disinclined *adj* unwilling.
disinfect *vt* to cleanse from infection.
disinfectant *n* a substance that destroys infectious germs.
disingenuous *adj* crafty; cunning.
disinherit *vt* to cut off from inheriting.
disintegrate *vt* to break up into parts.
disinter *vt* to take out of a grave.

disinterested *adj* impartial.
disjointed *adj* unconnected; incoherent.
disk *n* see disc.
dislike *n* aversion; distaste. * *vt* to feel aversion to.
dislocate *vt* to displace a joint; to upset the working of.
dislodge *vt* to remove; to oust.
disloyal *adj* faithless; untrustworthy
dismal *adj* dark; gloomy.
dismantle *vt* to strip; to take apart.
dismay *vt* to terrify; to appal. * *n* terror; consternation.
dismember *vt* to sever limb from limb.
dismiss *vt* to send away.
dismissal *n* discharge.
dismount *vi* to descend from a horse.
disobedience *n* neglect or refusal to obey.
disobedient *adj* failing, refusing to obey; unruly.
disobey *vt* to neglect or refuse to obey.
disobliging *adj* unaccommodating.
disorder *n* confusion; disease. * *vt* to disarrange.
disorganize *vt* to throw into confusion.
disown *vt* to repudiate; to refuse to acknowledge as one's own.
disparage *vt* to depreciate; to belittle.
disparate *adj* unlike.
disparity *n* inequality.
dispassionate *adj* cool; impartial.
dispel *vt* to scatter; to banish.
dispensary *n* a place where medicines are made up and dispensed.
dispensation *n* distribution; exemption.
dispense *vt* to deal out; to administer; to exempt.
disperse *vti* to scatter; to diffuse; to vanish.
dispirited *adj* dejected.
displace *vt* to derange; to supersede.
displacement *n* quantity of water displaced by a floating body.
display *vt* to unfold; to show; to parade. * *vi* to make a show. * *n* exhibition; parade; a computer monitor for presenting visual information.
displease *vt* to offend; to disgust.
displeased *adj* annoyed.
displeasing *adj* unpleasant.
displeasure *n* annoyance.
disport *n* pastime. * *vi* to sport; to gambol.
disposable *adj* designed to be discarded after use; available.
disposal *n* control; arrangement.
dispose *vti* to arrange; to incline; to regulate; to give, sell or transfer to another; to throw away.
disposed *adj* inclined.
disposition *n* order; character; inclination; arrangement.
dispossess *vt* to deprive of possession.
disproportion *n* inequality.
disproval *n* disproof.
disprove *vt* to prove to be wrong; to confute.
dispute *vi* to argue; to debate. * *vt* to impugn. * *n* controversy; strife.
disqualify *vt* to make ineligible through violation of rules; to incapacitate.
disquiet *n* unrest; anxiety.
disregard *n* neglect. * *vt* to slight; to ignore.
disrepair *n* neglect.
disreputable *adj* of bad character.
disrepute *n* disgrace.
disrespect *n* discourtesy.
disrobe *vt* to undress; to uncover.
disruption *n* disorder; confusion.
dissatisfaction *n* discontent.
dissatisfied *adj* discontented.
dissect *vt* to cut up; to examine minutely.
dissemble *vt, vi* to hide; to disguise.
disseminate *vt* to spread abroad esp. ideas, information etc.
dissemination *n* propagation.
dissension *n* discord.
dissent *vi* to disagree; to separate from an established church. * *n* disagreement.
dissenting *adj* disagreeing.
dissertation *n* a formal discourse or treatise.
disservice *n* an ill-service.
dissident *adj* dissenting. * *n* one who disagrees with government policies so strongly as to suffer imprisonment.
dissimilar *adj* unlike.
dissimulate *vti* to dissemble.
dissipate *vti* to scatter; to squander.
dissipated *adj* dissolute.
dissociate *vt* to disunite; to repudiate a

connection with.
dissolute *adj* profligate.
dissolution *n* melting; break up (of a parliament); death.
dissolve *vti* to liquefy; to break up legally; to annul; to be overcome with emotion.
dissuade *vt* to exhort against; to deter by argument.
distance *n* remoteness in place or time; space between two points or places; reserve. * vt to outstrip.
distant *adj* far off; cold; shy.
distaste *n* dislike.
distemper *n* a disordered state of mind or body; a dog disease; a method of painting on plaster without oil.
distend *vti* to stretch; to swell.
distention *n* inflation.
distil *vi, vt* to extract the essence of; to fall in drops; to rectify or purify.
distiller *n* a maker of alcoholic spirit.
distillery *n* a distilling factory.
distinct *adj* separate; clear; definite.
distinction *n* difference; eminence; honour.
distinctive *adj* distinguishing.
distinctness *n* clearness; precision.
distinguish *vti* to mark a difference; to perceive; to differentiate; to honour.
distinguished *adj* eminent; of elegant appearance.
distort *vt* to twist; to misrepresent.
distract *vt* to draw the attention aside; to bewilder; to confuse.
distracted *adj* frantic; maddened.
distraction *n* derangement; diversion; an amusement; extreme agitation.
distrain *vt* to seize, as goods, for debt.
distraught *adj* distracted; agitated.
distress *n* anguish; destitution. * *vt* to afflict with pain.
distressed *adj* afflicted; extremely agitated, pained or poor.
distressing *adj* grievous.
distribute *vt* to deal out; to apportion; to classify.
distribution *n* division; sharing.
district *n* a region marked off for some special purpose.
distrust *vt* to doubt; to suspect. * *n* doubt; suspicion.
distrustful *adj* suspicious.
disturb *vt* to throw into disorder; to agitate.
disuse *n* neglect. * *vt* to cease to use.
ditch *n* a long narrow trench.
divan *n* a sofa or bed without back or sides.
dive *vi* to plunge into water head foremost; to descend steeply (of aircraft); to submerge; to dash headlong.
diverge *vi* to deviate; to digress
divergent *adj* diverging; dissimilar.
diverse *adj* different; unlike.
diversified *adj* varied.
diversify *vt* to vary; to invest in a broad range or securities, or in a variety of commercial operations to reduce risk or risk of loss.
diversion *n* amusement; a feigned attack.
diversity *n* variety.
divert *vt* to turn aside; to amuse.
diverting *adj* amusing.
divest *vt* to strip; to unclothe.
divide *vt* to separate into parts; to share; to sever; to estrange * *vi* to part; to vote.
dividend *n* a number to be divided; share of profit.
divider *n* a distributor; (*pl*) compasses.
divination *n* prediction.
divine *adj* of or belonging to God. * *n* a clergyman. * *vti* to foretell; to guess; to dowse.
divining rod *n* a wand used by diviners to locate underground water.
divinity *n* the science of divine things.
divisible *adj* capable of division.
division *n* act of dividing; separation; a separation into two opposing sides to vote; disunion; portion; a process in arithmetic.
divisive *adj* creating division or discord.
divisor *n* the number by which the dividend is divided.
divorce *n* a dissolution of marriage; a separation. * *vt* to dissolve a marriage.
divulge *vt* to disclose.
dizzy *adj* giddy.
do *vt, aux* to perform; to bring about; to prepare. * *vi* to act or behave; to fare in health; to cheat; to rob. * *n* a party.
docile *adj* easily taught; tractable.

dock *n* an enclosed basin for ships; an enclosure in court for prisoners. * *vt* to cut off; to put a ship in dock.
docket *n* a summary; a bill tied to goods. * vt to make or attach an abstract of.
dockyard *n* an area with docks and facilities for repairing and refitting ships.
doctor *n* a learned person; a physician.
doctorate *n* the degree of a doctor.
doctrine *n* a principle or belief; the teaching of a person, school, or church.
document *n* written evidence or proof.
dodge *vt, vi* to move nimbly aside; to evade a duty; to quibble. * *n* a trick.
dog *n* a domestic quadruped. * *vt* to follow closely.
dogged *adj* obstinate; relentless.
doggerel *n* worthless verse.
dogma *n* a body of opinion; authoritative belief.
dogmatic, dogmatical *adj* positive; overbearing.
dogmatism *n* assertion without proof.
doldrums *npl* the dumps; equatorial region of calms.
dole *n* money reeived from the state while unemployed; what is dealt out. * *vt* to deal out in small quantites.
doleful *adj* woeful; gloomy; sad.
doll *n* a child's toy in human form.
dollar *n* an American unit of money.
dolmen *n* a table-shaped ancient stone structure.
dolorous *adj* mournful.
dolt *n* a blockhead.
domain *n* an estate; a province; a sphere of activity etc.
dome *n* an arched roof; a large cupola.
domestic *adj* belonging to the home; tame. * *n* a household servant.
domesticate *vt* to make domestic or tame.
domicile *n* a habitation.
dominant *adj* ruling; prevailing over others; overlooking from a superior height.
dominate *vt* to rule.
domineer *vi* to lord over others.
domineering *adj* overbearing.
dominion *n* territory with one ruler or government; authority.
domino *n* (*pl* **dominoes**) a masquerade dress; a half-mask; (*pl*), a game played with dotted ivory or bone rectangles.
don *n* a fellow of a college. * *vt* to put on.
donate *vt* to bestow.
donation *n* a gift.
donor *n* one who gives something; one who donates blood, organs etc. for medical purposes..
doom *n* fate; ruin. * *vt* to condemn to failure or ruin.
door *n* the entrance of a house, room, carriage, etc; the frame closing it.
doric *adj* an order of architecture; a rustic dialect.
dormant *adj* sleeping; inactive.
dormitory *n* a sleeping room with many beds.
dorsal *adj* pertaining to the back.
dose *n* the quantity of medicine given at one time.
dot *n* a small point, as made with a pen, etc. * *vt* to mark with a dot.
dotage *n* the feeble-mindedness of old age.
dote *vi* to be excessively fond of.
double *adj* twice as large, as strong etc.; designed or intended for two; made of two similar parts; having two meanings, characters, etc. * *adv* twice; in twos. * *n* a number or amount that is twice as much; a person or thing identical to another. * *vti* to make or become twice as much or as many; to fold, to bend; to bend sharply backwards; to have an additional purpose.
double bass *n* the lowest-toned instrument of violin class.
double-dealing *n* duplicity.
double-cross *vt* to betray an associate; to cheat.
doubt *vi* to waver; to question; to suspect. * *vt* to believe to be uncertain. * n uncertainty; suspicion.
doubtful *adj* feeling doubt; uncertain; suspicious.
doubtless *adv* unquestionably.
douche *n* a jet of water applied to the body.
dough *n* flour moistened with water or milk and kneaded to make bread.
douse, dowse *vti* to plunge into water.
dovetail *n* a wedge-shaped joint resembling a dove's tail used in woodwork.

* *vt, vi* to join as above; to fit exactly.

dowager *n* a title given to the widow of a nobleman.

dowdy *adj* ill-dressed; not stylish.

down *n* the fine soft feathers of birds; a hill. * *adv* toward or in a lower physical position; toward or to the ground, floor, or bottom; or in a lower status or in a worse condition; in cash; to or in a state of less activity. * *adj* occupying a low position, esp. lying on the ground; depressed, dejected. * *n* a low period (as in activity, emotional life, or fortunes); (*inf*) prejudice. * *vti* to defeat; to swallow.

downcast *adj* dejected.

downfall *n* ruin.

downpour *n* a heavy fall of rain.

downright *adj* plain; blunt; utter.

downtrodden *adj* oppressed.

downward, downwards *adv* in a descending course. * *adj* descending.

dowry *n* a wife's marriage portion.

doze *vi* to be half asleep. * *n* a light sleep.

dozen *n* twelve.

drab *adj* of a dull brown colour; dull; uninteresting.

draconian *adj* very severe.

draft *n* a detachment of men or things; an order for money; the first sketch or outline of speech or other writing; conscription in U.S. * *vt* to sketch; to select.

draftsman *n see* **draughtsman**.

drag *vt* to draw along slowly and with force; to search with a dragnet or a hook. * *vi* to protract. * *n* a brake; a check.

dragnet *n* a net to be drawn along the bottom.

dragon *n* a fabulous winged monster.

dragoon *n* a cavalry man. * *vt* to harass; to persecute.

drain *vt, vi* to draw off; to filter; to flow off; to drink the entire contents of. * *n* a sewer; a channel for liquids.

drainage *n* a system of drains.

dram *n* a unit of weight; a small draught of spirits.

drama *n* a stage, radio or television play.

dramatic, dramatical *adj* pertaining to the drama; theatrical.

dramatize *vt* to turn into a drama.

drape *vt* to cover or hang with cloth.

drastic *adj* acting with strength or violence.

draught *n* the quantity drunk at once; a sketch; the depth a ship sinks in water; a current of air; (*pl*) a game on a squared board using 24 round pieces.

draughtsman *n* a designer.

draw *vt, vi* to pull along or towards; to cause to come; to attract; to sketch; to infer; to end a game with equal scores; to shrink. * *n* the act of drawing; a drawn game.

drawback *n* a defect; a hindrance or handicap.

drawbridge *n* a movable (up and down or sideways) bridge.

drawer *n* one who draws a cheque; a sliding box in a table, chest or desk; (*pl*) an undergarment.

drawing *n* a pencil sketch.

drawing room *n* a reception or living room.

drawl *vi, vt* to speak slowly with drawn-out vowel sounds. * *n* affected slowness of speech.

dread *n* fear; terror. * *adj* exciting great fear; terrible. * vt to fear greatly.

dreadful *adj* terrible.

dream *n* a vision in sleep; an idle fancy; an ambition. * *vt, vi* to have dreams; to fancy.

dreary *adj* cheerless.

dredge *n* a dragnet. * *vt* to scoop up, esp from the bottom of a river etc.

dredger *n* a floating vessel for dredging and deepening.

dregs *npl* lees; grounds.

drench *vt* to soak.

dress *vt* to clothe; to set in order; to decorate; to wash and bandage; to prepare food for cooking. * *n* clothes; a woman's one-piece garment; style or manner of clothing.

dresser *n* a kitchen sideboard; a surgeon's assistant.

dressing *n* a bandage, oitment etc. applied to a wound; a sauce.

dribble *vi* to trickle. * *vt* (in games) to move the ball little by little with the foot, hand, stick etc.

drift *n* a heap of snow, sand, etc. deposited by the wind; natural course, tendency; the general meaning or intention (of what is said); an aimless course. * *vt* to cause to drift. * *vi* to be driven or carried along by water or air currents.

drill *vti* to pierce a hole with a drill; to train (soldiers); to furrow; to sow in rows. * *n* a hole borer; a furrow; exercise; procedure; routine.

drill *n* a cotton cloth.

drink *vi* to swallow liquid. * *n* a beverage; alcoholic liquor.

drip *vi* to fall in drops. * *n* a liquid that falls in drops; its sound; a device for injecting a fluid slowly and continuously into a vein.

dripping *n* the fat from roasting meat.

drive *vb* (*pt* **drove**, *pp* **driven**) vt to urge, push or force onward; to convey in a vehicle; to carry through strongly; to propel (a ball) with hard blow. * *vi* to be forced along; to be conveyed in a vehicle. * *n* a trip in a vehicle; a stroke to drive a ball (in golf, etc.); a driveway; an intensive campaign; the transmission of power to machinery.

driver *n* one who drives; a golf club.

drizzle *vi* to rain in small fine drops. * *n* a fine rain.

droll *adj* comic; amusing; whimsical.

drone *n* the male or nonworking bee; a humming sound; monotonous speech. * *vi* to hum; to speak in a monotonous tone.

droop *vi* to hang down; to languish.

drop *n* a globule of any liquid; a distance to fall. * *vt, vi* to pour or let fall in drops; to fall; to let fall; to sink; to set down from a vehicle; to mention in passing; to give up (an idea etc.).

dropsy *n* an unnatural collection of water in the body.

dross *n* the scum of metals; refuse; rubbish.

drought *n* a period of very dry weather.

drove *n* a herd or flock in motion.

drown *vt, vi* to suffocate or be suffocated in water.

drowse *vi* to doze.

drowsy *adj* sleepy, heavy.

drudge *vi* to toil; to slave. * *n* a menial servant.

drudgery *n* distasteful toil.

drug *n* any substance used in medicine. * *vt* to dose with drugs.

drum *n* a sound percussion instrument; a stretched membrane in the ear. * *vi, vt* to beat a drum; to teach or instruct by constant repetition.

drunk *adj* intoxicated.

drunkard *n* one given to drink.

drunkenness *n* intoxication.

dry *adj* free from moisture; thirsty. * *vt, vi* to free from moisture; thirsty; marked by a matter-of-fact, ironic or terse manner of speech; uninteresting.

dry rot *n* a timber disease.

dual *adj* consisting of two; twofold.

dub *vt* to confer a knighthood on by touching with a sword.

dubiety *n* doubtfulness.

dubious *adj* wavering; uncertain; untrustworthy.

duchess *n* a duke's wife.

duchy *n* a country ruled by a duke.

duck *vti* to plunge in water; to bow. * *n* a waterfowl; a kind of canvas.

duct *n* a narrow tube in the body; a channel or pipe for fluids, electric cables etc.

due *adj* owed; owing; proper. * *adv* directly. * *n* a fee; a right; a just title.

duel *n* a set fight between two persons; any conflict between two people, sides, ideas etc.

duet *n* a piece of music for two performers.

duke *n* one of the highest order of nobility.

dukedom *n* the lands or title of a duke.

dulcet *adj* sweet; melodious.

dull *adj* stupid; drowsy; cheerless. * *vt* to make dull; to stupefy; to blunt; to sully.

dulse *n* an edible seaweed.

duly *adv* properly; suitably.

dumb *adj* mute; silent.

dumbbells *n* weights used for developing the muscles of the arm.

dumbfound, dumfound *vt* to astonish; to confuse.

dummy *n* a stupid person; a figure used to display clothes; the exposed hand in

a game of bridge; a sham.
dump *n* a place for refuse; a temporary store; a thud; a dirty, dilapidated place; (*pl*) low spirits.
dunce *n* a stupid person.
dune *n* a sand hill on the sea coast.
dung *n* the excrement of animals. * *vt* to manure.
dungeon *n* an underground prison.
duodenum *n* the first portion of the small intestines.
dupe *n* one easily cheated. * *vt* to impose on; to deceive; to trick.
duplex *adj* double; twofold.
duplicate *adj* double. * *n* a copy. * *vt* to double; to make an exact copy.
duplicity *n* guile; trickery.
durable *adj* lasting; permanent.
duration *n* continuance; the period in which an event continues.
duress *n* constraint; imprisonment.
during *prep* for the time of; throughout.
dusk *n* twilight.
dusky *adj* darkish.
dust *n* fine dry particles of earth, etc; earth as symbolic of mortality. * *vt* to free from dust; to sprinkle.
duster *n* a cloth, etc, for removing dust.
duty *n* what one is bound to do; service; a tax on goods.
dux *n* the head of a class in a school.
dwarf *n* one noticeably undersized. * *vt* to make (or make seem) small.
dwell *vi* to live in a place; to continue; to focus the attention on; to think, talk, write at length about.
dwelling *n* habitation; abode.
dwindle *vi* to diminish gradually.
dye *vt* to stain; to give a new colour to. * *n* a colouring matter; tinge; hue.
dynamic *adj* relating to force that produces motion; forceful; energetic
dynamics *n* the science of force or power.
dynamite *n* a powerful explosive.
dynamo *n* a machine for producing an electric current.
dynasty *n* a line of rulers of the same powerful family.
dysentery *n* a disorder of the intestines.
dyspepsia, dyspepsy *n* indigestion.

E

each *adj, pron* everyone separately.
eager *adj* keen; ardent earnest.
ear *n* the organ of hearing; the power of appreciating musical sounds; heed; a spike of corn.
earache *n* a pain in the ear.
early *adv, adj* before the expected time; of or occurring in the first part of a period or series; timely, soon.
earn *vt* to gain by labour; to deserve.
earnest *adj* ardent; eager; serious.
earnings *npl* wages.
earring *n* an ornament worn in the ear.
earth *n* the globe we inhabit; dry land; the ground; the burrow of a badger, fox etc. * *vt* to cover with earth.
earthenware *n* ware made of clay; pottery.
earthquake *n* a shaking or trembling of the earth.
earthwork *n* a rampart of earth.
earthy *adj* consisting of or resembling earth; crude.
earwig *n* an insect with a pineen-like apendage at the end of the body.
ease *n* freedom from toil, pain, etc; rest; comfort. * *vt* to calm; to alleviate; to shift a little.
easel *n* a stand to support pictures while they are being painted.
east *n* that part of the sky where the sun rises; the countries east of Europe. * *adj* in or towards the east.
Easter *n* the festival commemorating Christ's Resurrection.
easterly *adj* coming from the east, as winds; moving towards the east.
eastern *adj* belonging to the east; oriental.
easy *adj* free from pain or anxiety; simple; relaxed in manner; lenient; compliant; unhurried.
eat *vt* to chew and swallow, as food; to wear away; to corrode.
eaves *npl* that part of the roof overhanging the walls.
eavesdrop *vi* to try to hear or to listen in to a private conversation.

ebb *n* the flowing back of the tide; decline. * *vi* to flow back; to decline.
ebony *n* a hard, heavy, dark wood.
ebullient *adj* enthusiastic; exuberant; boiling.
eccentric *adj* not conforming to the usual pattern; unconventional; odd; whimsical.
eccentricity *n* oddity of conduct, dress, etc.
ecclesiastic, ecclesiastical *adj* belonging to the church or clergy. * *n* a clergyman.
echo *n* the repetition of sound by reflection of sound waves; imitation. * *vl;vi* to repeat; to resound; to imitate.
eclectic *adj* selecting the best of everything (esp. in philosophy and the arts).
eclipse *n* an obscuring of the light of the sun, moon etc, by some other body; an overshadowing. * *vt* to darken; to surpass.
economic, economical *adj* pertaining to economics or the economy; showing a profit; frugal; careful.
economics *n* the science of the application of wealth and concerned with the production, and consumption and distribution of goods and services.
economize *vti* to manage money with prudence to save.
economy *n* thrift; prudent management; the management of finances and resources of a business, industry etc; the economic system of a country.
ecstasy *n* rapture; enthusiasm.
ecstatic, ecstatical *adj* entrancing; transporting.
ecumenic, ecumenical *adj* of the whole christian church; seeking christian unity worldwide
eczema *n* a skin disease.
eddy *n* a whirling current of water or air. * *vi* to move round and round.
edge *n* the sharp side; an abrupt border or margin; keenness; force; effectiveness. * *vt* to put an edge or fringe on; to move gradually.
edged *adj* sharp; keen.
edgeways *adv* sideways.
edible *adj* eatable.
edict *n* a decree; a manifesto.
edifice *n* a large building.
edify *vt* to improve morally or mentally.
edit *vt* to prepare a text for publication; to prepare a final version of a film by selecting, cutting and arranging sequences.
edition *n* the number of copies of a book printed at one time.
editor *n* one who is responsible for the issue of a book or newspaper.
editorial *n* a leading article in a newspaper expressing the opinions of its editor or owner.
educate *vt* to train and instruct; to provide schooling.
education *n* instruction and training, as imparted in schools, colleges and universities; the theory and practice of teaching.
eerie *adj* awesome; weird.
efface *vt* to blot out; to erase; to make oneself inconspicuous through shyness, humility or false modesty.
effect *n* a result; an impression; (*pl*) belongings. * *vt* to bring about; to accomplish.
effective *adj* efficient; making a striking impression; forceful; fruitful.
effectual *adj* producing the desired result.
effeminacy *n* a display or impression of feminine qualities in a man; weakness; timidity.
effeminate *adj* womanish; unmanly.
effervesce *vi* to bubble or sparkle.
effervescent *adj* bubbling; sparkling.
effete *adj* worn out; feeble; decadent.
efficacious *adj* achieving the desired result.
efficiency *n* competence
efficient *adj* capable; competent.
effigy *n* a portrait; a sculpture or figure of a person esp. one crudely executed to ridicule or show contempt.
effluent *adj* flowing out. * *n* a stream from a river or lake; liquid waste discharged from a sewer, an industrial plant, a nuclear station etc.
effluvium *n* (*pl* **effluvia**) noisome vapour.
effort *n* exertion; strenuous endeavour.
effrontery *n* brazen impudence.
effusion *n* a pouring out; copious utterance.

effusive *adj* profuse; gushing.
egg *n* the shell-covered embryo laid by birds, snakes, insects, etc. * *vt* to urge on.
ego *n* the 'I'; the self, self-image; conceit.
egoist *n* a self-centred person.
egotism *n* self-importance; self-centredness.
egotist *n* one always talking of him or herself.
egregious *adj* conspicuously bad or flagrant.
egress *n* exit.
egret *n* a species of heron.
eiderdown *n* the down or soft feathers of the eider duck used for stuffing quilts etc.
eight *adj n* a cardinal number and its symbol (8); the crew of an eight-oared rowing boat.
eighteen *adj, n* eight and ten (18).
eighteenth *adj, n* the ordinal number of 18.
eighth *adj, n* the ordinal number of 8.
eightieth *adj, n* the ordinal number of 80.
eighty *adj* eight times ten (80).
either *adj, pron* one or the other; one of two. * *conj* used as correlative to or.
ejaculate *vt* to exclaim.
eject *vt* to throw out; to expel. * *vi* to escape from an aircraft or spacecraft using an ejecetion seat.
ejection seat *h* an escape seat, esp. in combat aircraft, that can be ejected with its occupant in an emergancy by means of explosive bolts.
eke *vt* (with **out**) supplement; to use frugally; to make a living with difficulty.
elaborate *vt* to workout; to explain in detail. * *adj* highly detailed.
elapse *vi* to by, of time.
elastic *adj* springy; rebounding; flexible.
elated *adj* exultant.
elation *n* joy; exultation.
elbow *n* the joint between the forearm and upper arm; a sharp turn or bend. * *vt* to push away with the elbow.
elder *adj* older. * *n* an older person; an office bearer in the Presbyterian Church.
elderly *adj* quite old
eldest *adj* oldest.
elect *vt* to choose by voting to select. * *adj* chosen.
election *n* the act of choosing by vote; the choice made esp.
electioneering *n* the arts used to secure the election of a candidate.
elector *n* one who has a vote in an election.
electorate *n* the body of electors.
electric, electrical *adj* containing, conveying, worked or produced by electricity.
electricity *n* the force that is developed by friction, and by chemical, thermal, or magnetic action.
electrify *vt* to charge with electricity; to thrill; to astonish.
electrocute *vt* to kill by electricity.
electrode *n* a conductor through which an electric current enters or leaves a gas discharge tube etc.
electrodynamics *n* the science which treats of electric currents.
electrolysis *n* chemical decomposition by electricity.
electromagnetic *adj* having electric and magnetic properties. * *n* electromagnetism
electron *n* a negativley charged elementary particle that forms the part of the atom outside the nucleus.
electronic *adj* of or worked by streams of electrons flowing through devices, vacuum or gas. * *adv* electronically.
electronics *n* (*sing*) the study, developemant and application of electronic devices; as (*pl*) electronic circuits.
elegance *n* beauty; refinement; grace.
elegant *adj* graceful; refined; dignified.
elegy *n* a lament.
element *n* a constitiuent part; a favourable environment for a plant or animal; a wire that produces heat in a electric cooker, kettle, etc; (*pl*) atmospheric conditions (wind, rain, etc,); (*pl*) the basic principles, rudiments.
elementary *adj* basic, simple.
elevate *vt* to lift up; to raise in rank; to improve in intellectual or moral stature.
elevation *n* a raised place; the height above the earth's surface or above sea

level; the angle to which a gun is raised above the horizon; a drawing that shows the front, the rear, the front view of something.

elevator *n* a cage or platform for moving something from one level to another; a moveable surface on the tailplane of an aircraft to produce motion up or down; a lift; a building for storing grain.

eleven *adj* one more than ten (11).

eleventh *adj, n* the ordinal number of 11..

elicit *vt* to draw out by inquiry.

elide *vt* to omit a letter or syllable at the beginning or end of a word.

eligible *adj* qualified; suitable.

eliminate *vt* to get rid of; to eradicate; to exclude a competitor froma competition by defeat.

elite *n* the pick; the best.

elixir *n* the specific sought after by alchemists to prolong life or transmute metals.

ellipse *n* an oval figure; a closed plane figure found by the plane section of a right-angled cone.

elocution *n* the art of effective speaking.

elongate *vt* to lengthen.

elope *vi* to run away secretly esp. of lovers to be married.

eloquence *n* skill in speaking and the use of words; persuasive speech.

else *adj, adv* other; besides.

elsewhere *adv* in some other place.

elucidate *vt* to make clear.

elude *vt* to avoid by artifice; to baffle.

elusive *adj* evasive; deceptive; difficult to contact.

emaciate *vi, vt* to become or make lean.

emanate *vi* to flow out; to issue.

emanation *n* outflowing; effluvium.

emancipate *vt* to free from restraint; to liberate esp. form slavery.

emasculate *vt* to castrate; to enfeeble.

embalm *vt* to preserve (corpse) with drugs, chemicals etc.

embankment *n* a protecting mound to hold back water or to carry a roadway.

embargo *n* prohibition on ships from sailing; restraint; a restriction of commerce by law; a prohibtion

embark *vti* to go or put on board; to begin an activity or enterprise.

embarrass *vt* to confuse; to harass; to burden; to make a person uncomfortable.

embarrassment *n* confusion; entanglement; trouble; abashment.

embassy *n* the office or residence of an ambassador.

embellish *vt* to adorn.

embellishment *n* decoration; ornament.

embers *n* live remains of a fire.

embezzle *vt* to misapply funds.

embezzlement *n* fraudulent use of funds.

embitter *vt* to make bitter.

emblem *n* a symbol; a heraldic device.

emblematic, emblematical *adj* symbolic.

embody *vt* to give concrete form to; to incorporate in a single book, law, system etc..

emboss *vt* to mould or adorn in relief.

embrace *vt* to clasp in the arms; to accept an idea etc. eagerly.

embroider *vt* to adorn with patterned needlework.

embroidery *n* decorative needlework.

embroil *vt* to involve a person in trouble.

embryo *n* unborn or unhatched offspring.

embryonic *adj* rudimentary; imperfect.

emendation *n* correction (in texts, etc).

emerald *n* a bright green precious stone, its colour. * *adj* bright green.

emerge *vi* to come forth; to issue; to be revealed as the result of investigation.

emergency *n* a crisis requiring immediate attention.

emetic *n* a medicine that induces vomiting.

emigrant *n* one who leaves one's country to settle in another.

emigrate *vi* to go to reside in another country.

eminence *n* a height; fame; a title for a cardinal.

eminent *adj* exalted; prominent.

emissary *n* an agent sent on a mission; a messenger.

emit *vt* to send or throw out; to utter.

emollient *adj* soothing; softening.

emolument *n* salary; remuneration.

emotion *n* a strong feeling of joy, sadness, anger, fear etc..

emperor *n* the sovereign of an empire.
emphasis *n* a particular stress placed on anything; force, vigour.
emphasize *vt* to lay stress on.
emphatic, emphatical *adj* impressive; decisive.
empire *n* dominion; sway; states ruled by an emperor.
empirical *adj* based on observation, experiment or experience.
employ *vt* to give work to; to keep at work
employee *n* one who works for an employer.
employment *n* occupation or profession.
emporium *n* (*pl* **emporia, emporiums**) a commercial centre; a large shop selling goods of all types.
empower *vt* to authorize.
empress *n* the consort of an emperor; a female ruler of an empire.
empty *adj* void; vacant; lacking in substance, value or reality; hungry. * *vt* to take everything out of.
emulate *vt* to strive to equal; to vie with.
emulsion *n* a mixture of mutually insoluble liquids in which one is dispersed in droplets throughout the other; a lightsenstive substance on photographic paper or film.
enable *vt* to empower; to authorize.
enact *vt* to establish by law; to decree; to act.
enactment *n* a decree; an act.
enamel *n* an ornamental or preservative glass-like coating on metals, etc.; the hard outer layer of a tooth. * *vt* to cover with enamel.
enamour *vt* to inspire with love.
encampment *n* a camp.
enchant *vt* to charm; to fascinate.
enchanter *n* a sorcerer; a bewitching person.
enchanting *adj* charming.
enchantment *n* magic; fascination.
encircle *vt* to encompass; to embrace.
enclosure *n* a space fenced in; something enclosed with a letter on a parcel or envelope.
encompass *vt* to encircle; to sail round.
encore *adv* again; once more. * *n* a call for a performance to be repeated.
encounter *n* an unexpected meeting; a conflict. * *vt,vi* to confront; to fight against.
encourage *vt* to inspire with hope; to urge on; to promote the development of.
encroach *vi* to trespass on rights, lands, etc, of others.
encroachment *n* trespass; intrusion.
encrust *vt* to cover with a crust.
encumber *vt* to burden; to hamper.
encumbrance *n* a burden; a mortgage.
encyclopaedia, encyclopedia *n* a book or books of general knowledge.
end *n* the extreme point; the close; the stopping place; death; result; aim. * *vt* to bring to an end. * *vi* to come to an end; to result in.
endanger *vt* to imperil.
endear *vt* to make dear or more loved.
endeavour *n* effort; attempt. * *vi* to try; to strive; to aim.
endemic *adj* peculiar to a people or region.
endorse *vt* to write one's name on the back of (cheques, etc); to ratify; to support; to record an offence on a driving licence.
endorsement *n* a docket; signature; approval.
endow *vt* to settle money or property on; to enrich; to provide with special power.
endurance *n* fortitude; patience.
endure *vi, vt* to bear patiently; to tolerate; to last; to continue in existence.
enemy *n* one who is unfriendly; an antagonist; a hostile army; something harmful.
energetic adj forceful; vigorous; lively.
energy *n* power; force; vigour; capacity to do work.
enervate *vt* to enfeeble.
enforce *vt* to urge with energy; to impose; to compel compliance with threats.
enfranchise *vt* to give the right of voting to.
engage *vt* to bind by pledge; to attach; to promise to marry; to attract; to enter into; to attack. * *vi* to bind one's self.
engagement *n* a contract; a betrothal; an appointment arranged with someone; a fight.
engaging *adj* winning; attractive.

engender *vt* to breed; to occasion.
engine *n* a power machine; a locomotive; a contrivance.
engineer *n* a maker or designer or operator of machinery. * *vt* to plan or construct; to contrive; to plan.
engineering *n* the art or business of an engineer.
engrave *vt* to cut or carve on metal; to imprint.
engraving *n* a print from an engraved plate.
engross *vt* to absorb.
engulf vt to swallow up.
enhance *vt* to increase in value, importance, attractiveness.
enigma *n* a puzzle; a mystery.
enigmatic, enigmatical *adj* puzzling; obscure; mysterious.
enjoin *vt* to command; prescribe.
enjoy *vi* to take delight in; to experience.
enjoyment *n* pleasure; satisfaction.
enlarge *vti* to make large; to grow large; to speak or write.
enlighten *vt* to make clear; to instruct.
enlightened *adj* instructed; cultured.
enlist *vi* to enter on a list; to enrol (in army). * *vt* to ensure support of.
enliven *vt* to brighten; to gladden.
enmity *n* hostility; ill-will.
ennoble *vt* to exalt; to dignify.
enormity *n* great wickedness, a serious crime.
enormous *adj* huge.
enough *adj* adequate, sufficient. * *n* a sufficiency. * *adv* tolerably.
enrage *vt* to make very angry.
enrapture *vt* to fill with delight.
enrich *vt* to make rich; to fertilize.
enrol *vt* to write in a roll; to record; to admit as a member of a society.
enrolment *n* act of enrolling; a register; a record.
enshrine *vt* to enclose; to cherish.
ensign *n* a badge; an emblem; a flag.
enslave *vt* to make a slave of; to subjugate.
ensnare *vt* to entrap.
ensue *vi* to result from.
entail *vt* to involve as a result; to settle lands on individuals in succession so that all are really only life-renters. * *n* this mode of settlement.
entanglement *n* disorder; a relationship between a man and a woman considered to be unsuitable.
enter *vi* to go or come in or into; to come on stage; to begin, start; (*with* **for**) to register as an entrant. * *vt* to come or go into; to pierce, penetrate; (*organization*) to join; to insert; (*proposal etc.*) to submit; to record (*an item*) in a diary etc.
enteric *adj* belonging to the intestines. * *n* enteric fever, same as typhoid fever.
enterprise *n* a venture; boldness.
entertain *vti* to receive as a guest; to please; to amuse; to consider; to have in mind.
entertaining *adj* pleasing; amusing.
entertainment *n* entertaining; amusement; an act or show intended to amuse and interest.
enthral *vt* to enslave; to charm; to captivate.
enthusiasm *n* ardent feeling; fervent zeal; keen interest.
enthusiast *n* a person full of enthusiasm for something.
entice *vt* to tempt; to allure; to lure away by promise of reward.
enticing *adj* attractive; tempting; fascinating.
entire *adj* whole; complete.
entitle *vt* to give a title to; to empower.
entity *n* being; existence.
entomology *n* the science of insect life.
entrails *npl* the intestines.
entrance *n* coming or going in; the place of entry; the power or authority to enter; an admission fea.
entrance *vt* to enrapture; to fill with delight.
entreat *vt* to beg earnestly; to implore.
entreaty *n* urgent prayers or plea.
entrench *vt* to dig in; to establish oneself in a strong defensive position.
entry *n* act of entering; entrance; an item recorded in a diary, account or dictionary.
enumerate *vt* to count one by one; to list.
enunciate *vt* to utter; to pronounce (clearly)..

enunciation *n* clear utterance; statement; expression; declaration; public attestation.

envelop *vt* to wrap up.

envelope *n* a cover (of letter, etc).

enviable *adj* exciting envy.

environment *n* conditions and surroundings that influence our development and that of plants and animals.

environs *npl* neighbourhood.

envisage *vt* to picture to one's self.

envoy *n* one sent on a mission.

envy *n* jealousy; discontent caused by another's possessions, achievements etc. * *vt* to begrudge.

enzyme *n* a complex protein produced by living cells that induces or speeds chemical reactions inplants and animals.

ephemeral *adj* short-lived.

epic *adj* heroic; in the grand style. * *n* a heroic poem.

epidemic *adj* a disease affecting a whole community. * *n* a disease which attacks many people at the same period.

epidermis *n* the outer skin.

epiglottis *n* the valve covering larynx during swallowing.

epigram *n* a pointed, witty, or sarcastic saying.

epilepsy *n* a disorder of the nervous system marked by convulsions and loss of consiousness.

epilogue *n* a speech addressed to audience at the close of a play; the concluding section of a book.

episcopacy *n* Church government by bishops; bishops collectively.

episcopal *adj* relating to bishops.

episode *n* an incident in a sequence of events; a piece of action in a book or drama.

epistle *n* a letter.

epitaph *n* an inscription on a tomb.

epithet *n* a descriptive adjective.

epitome *n* a typical example; personification; a brief summary.

epoch *n* a period of time.

equable *adj* uniform; even; hot extreme; even tempered.

equal *adj* the same in all respects. * *n* one not inferior or superior to another. * *vt* to make or be equal to ; to do something equal to.

equality *n* sameness; evenness.

equalize *vt* to make equal.

equanimity *n* evenness of temper.

equate *vt* to make equal; to make, treat or regard as compatible

equation *n* an act of equalling; the state of being equal; (*chem*) an expression representing a reaction in symbols.

equator *n* an imaginary circle passing round the globe, equidistant from the poles.

equestrian *adj* on horseback. * *n* a horseman.

equidistant *adj* equally distant.

equilateral *adj* equal sided.

equilibrium *n* a state of balance, weight, power, force etc.

equine *adj* pertaining to a horse.

equinox *n* the two times at which the sun crosses the equator and day and night are equal.

equip *vt* to furnish; to provide with all necessary tools, supplies etc.

equipment *n* everything needed for a particular task, expedition etc.

equitable *adj* fair; just.

equity *n* fairness; just dealing; (*pl*) ordinary shares in a company.

equivalent *adj, n* equal in value amount, force, meaning etc; virtually identical, esp. in function as effect. * *n* an equivalent thing.

equivocal *adj* ambiguous; questionable.

equivocate *vi* to quibble.

era *n* a fixed reckoning date; a period of time.

eradicate *vt* to root out; to obliterate.

erase *vt* to rub out; to remove a recording from magnetic tape; to remove data froma computer memory or storage medium.

erect *adj* upright;sex organs, rigid from sexual stimulation. * *vt* to build.

erection *n* act of erecting; formation; anything erected; structure; a swelling and rigidity of the penis due to sexual excitement.

erode *vt* to eat or wear away gradually.

erosion *n* a wearing away (as of sea cliffs).

erotic *adj* of sexual love; amatory.
err *vi* to wander; to stray.
errand *n* a message; a short journey to carry out a task.
errant *adj* roving; wandering.
erratic *adj* irregular; eccentric; unreliable.
erratum *n* (*pl* **errata**) an error in printing, etc.
erroneous *adj* wrong; mistaken.
error *n* a mistake; a fault.
erudite *adj* deeply read; learned.
erupt *vi* to burst out; to break out into a rash; to explode ejecting ash and lava from a volcano.
eruption *n* a bursting forth; a breaking out.
escapade *n* a mad prank.
escape *vti* to get out of the way of; to avoid; to be free. * *n* a getting away by flight; a leakage e.g. of gas etc.; a temporary respite.
escarpment *n* the steep side of a hill, rock, or rampart.
eschew *vt* to shun; to avoid.
escort *n* a guard; an attendant. * *vt* to attend and guard.
esoteric *adj* private; select; understood only by elite minority.
especial *adj* distinct; chief.
espionage *n* spying.
esplanade *n* a seaside terrace or promenade.
espouse *vt* to marry; to adopt a cause etc.
espy *vt* to catch sight of.
essay *vt* to try. * *n* an endeavour or experiment; a short literary composition.
essence *n* the nature or being of anything; a substance extracted from another without the loss of the qualities of the origional; perfume.
essential *adj* vital; indispensable; volatile (oil).
establish *vt* to fix firmly; to institute; to set up (a business etc.) permanently to settle a person in a position; to have generally accepted; to place beyond doubt.
established *adj* legally confirmed (church); assured.
establishment *n* household staff; a place of business; (cap) those in power whose aim is to preserve the status quo.
estate *n* landed property; a large area of residential or industrial developement; a person's total possessions, esp. at their death; a social or political class.
estate agent *n* a person whose business is selling and leasing property.
esteem *vt* to value on; to regard highly; to prize. * *n* judgment; estimation; regard.
estimable *adj* worthy; respected.
estimate *vt* to calculate; to appraise. * *n* valuation; an approximate calculation; a judgement or opinion.
estrangement *n* withdrawal of friendship.
estuary *n* the mouth of a river; a firth.
etch *vt* to portray on metal plates by use of acids.
etching *n* the impression taken from an etched plate.
eternal *adj* everlasting.
eternity *n* infinite time; future life.
ether *n* a volatile liquid used as an anaesthetic or solvent.
ethereal *adj* airy; heavenly; aerial; intangible.
ethic, ethical *adj* moral.
ethics *n* the science of morals; principles.
ethnic, ethnical *adj* of races or large groups of people classed accordingly to common traits and customs.
etiquette *n* code of manners; decorum.
etymology *n* the study of the history and development of words.
eugenics *n* the science which treats of racial improvement.
eulogize *vt* to praise; to extol.
eulogy *n* praise; panegyric.
euphemism *n* the use of a mild for a harsh term ('fairy tale' for 'lie'.)
euphonic *adj* pleasing to the ear.
euthanasia *n* the act or practice of killing painlessly, esp. to relieve incurable suffering.
evacuate *vt* to make empty; to quit; to move people from a danger to a safe area; to discharge wastes from the body.
evade *vt* to avoid; to escape from.
evaluate *vt* to assess; to determine the value carefully.
evangelist *n* a preacher of the gospel.
evaporate *vi* to change into vapour; to remove water from; to disappear.
evasion *n* avoidance; an equivocal reply

or excuse.
evasive *adj* shuffling; equivocating.
eve, even *n* evening; the evening before as (Christmas Eve).
even *adj* level; smooth; equal; divisible by 2. * *vt* to equalize; to make even; to balance (debts etc.) * *adv* just; exactly; fully; quite; at the very time..
evening *n* the close of the day.
event *n* an incident; a happening; contingency; an item or contest; an itenm or contect in a sports programme.
eventful *adj* memorable.
eventuality *n* a possible result.
ever *adv* always; at any time; in any case.
evergreen *n* a tree or plant always in leaf. * *adj* always green.
everlasting *adj* eternal; never ending.
every *adj* each of all.
everybody *n* every person.
everyday *adj* happening daily; commonplace; worn or used every day.
everything *pnon* all things; all; of the greatest inportance.
everywhere *adv* in every place.
evict *vt* to dispossess by law; to expel.
eviction *n* expulsion (of tenant).
evidence *n* testimony; proof.
evident *adj* clear; plain; understandable.
evil *adj* wicked; bad. * *n* sin; harm.
evince *vt* to show; to prove.
eviscerate *vt* to disembowel.
evoke *vt* to call forth.
evolution *n* a process of change in a particular direction; the process by which something attains its distinctive characteristics; a theory thta existing types of plants and animals have developed from earlier forms. * *adj* evolutionary.
evolve *vti* to unfold; to open out; to develop.
exacerbate *vt* to aggravate; to make something worse.
exact *adj* accurate; precise. * *vt* to compel payment.
exacting *adj* severe; greatly demanding; requiring close attention and precision.
exactly *adv* in an exact manner; precisely. * *interj* quite so! indeed!
exaggerate *vt* to overstate.
exalt *vt* to raise in power, rank, etc; to extol.
examination *n* an interrogation; a testing by set questions.
examine *vt* to scrutinize; to inquire into; to question (witness); to test.
example *n* a sample; pattern; model; a warning to others.
exasperate *vt* to enrage; to annoy intensely.
excavate *vt* to hollow out by digging; to unearth; to expose to view (remains etc.) by digging.
exceed *vt* to surpass; to overstep (the limit).
excel *vt* to surpass. * *vi* to be preeminent.
excellent *adj* of high quality; choice.
except *vt* to omit; to exclude. * *vi* to object. * *prep* without.
excepting *prep* excluding; except.
exceptional *adj* unusual; rare; superior.
excerpt *n* an extract. * *vt* to extract from a book, etc.
excess *n* surplus; intemperance.
excessive *adj* undue; extreme.
exchange *vt* to give and take (one thing in return for another). * *n* the conversion of money from one currency to another; a place where things and services are exchanged, esp. a marketplace for securities; a centre or device in which telephone lines are interconnected
excision *n* a cutting out.
excitable *adj* easily agitated.
excite *vt* to arouse the feelings of, esp. to generate feelings of pleasurable anticipation; to cause to experience strong emotion; to rouse to activity; to stimulate a response, eg. in a bodily organ.
excitement *n* strong pleasurable emotion; agitation; commotion.
exclaim *vi, vt* to call out; to declare loudly, suddenly and with emotion.
exclamation *n* a loud outcry; an emotional utterance; an interjection.
exclude *vt* to shut out.
exclusion *n* a shutting out; a ban; omission.
exclusive *adj* excluding all else; reserved for particular persons; snobbishly aloof; fashionable; high-class, expensive; unobtainable or unpublished elsewhere; sole, undivided.

excommunicate *vt* to bar from church privileges and rites.
excrement *n* waste matter discharged from the body.
excretion *n* ejection of waste matter.
excruciating *adj* intensley painful or distressful.
excursion *n* a pleasure trip.
excuse *vt* to let off; to forgive; to overlook. * *n* an apology; that which excuses; a reason or explanation of.
execrable *adj* hateful; detestable.
execute *vt* to perform; to carry out; to put to death; to make valid.
execution *n* the act or manner of performing; skill in music; capital punishment.
executive *n* a person or group concerned with administration or management of a business or organization. * *adj* having the power to execute decisions, laws, decrees etc.
executor *n* one who carries out provisions of will.
exemplary *adj* model; worthy of imitation.
exemplify *vt* to show by example.
exempt *vt* to free from; excuse. * *adj* free; immune.
exemption *n* release; immunity.
exercise *n* the use or application of a power or right; regular physical or mental exertion; something performed to develope or test a specific ability or skill. * *vt* to use, exert,employ; to engage in regular physical activity; to engage the attention of; to perplex.
exert *vt* to put forth strength etc; to strive.
exertion *n* effort.
exhale *vti* to breathe out.
exhaust *vt* to use up; to make empty; to use up; tire out; (subject) to deal with or develope completely. * the escape of waste gas or steam from an engine.
exhaustion *n* extreme weariness.
exhaustive *adj* full; thorough.
exhibit *vt* to display, esp in public; to present to a court in legal form. * *n* an act or instance of exhibiting, something exhibited; something produced and identified in court for use as evidence.
exhibition *n* display; any public show.
exhilarate *vt* to elate; to enliven.
exhort *vt* to encourage; to warn.
exhume *vt* to disinter.
exigence *n* pressing necessity; urgency.
exile *n* banishment; the person banished. * *vt* to banish from one's country.
exist *vi* to be; to live; to manage one's life with difficulty.
existent *adj* being; existing.
exit *n* a going out; a way out.
exonerate *vt* to free from blame.
exorbitant *adj* excessive esp. of prices.
exorcise *vi* to drive out evil spirits.
exotic *adj* foreign; excitingly different or unusual.
expand *vt,vi* to spread out; to swell; to describe in fuller detail; to become more friendly and genial.
expanse *n* a wide area.
expansion *n* enlargement; increase.
expansive *adj* wide; genial.
expatiate *vi* to speak or write about at lenght.
expatriate *vt* to exile oneself or banish another. * n (a person) living in another country, or self-exiled or banished.
expect *vt* to anticipate, to regard as likely to arrive or happen; to consider necessary, reasonable or due; to suppose.
expectancy *n* hope; expectation.
expectant *adj* awaiting; anxious; hopeful.
expectation *n* something that is expected to happen; (*pl*) prospects for the future, esp of inheritance.
expectorate *vt* to spit or cough out.
expediency *n* fitness; suitability under the circumstances.
expedient *adj* suitable for the present time or circumstances. * *n* device; a means to an end; a means used for want of a better.
expedite *vt* to accelerate.
expedition *n* promptness; an enterprise or those who undertake it.
expeditious *adj* speedy; prompt.
expel *vt* to drive out; to banish.
expend *vt* to spend; to use up; to consume.
expenditure *n* outlay; cost.
expense *n* cost; charge; price.
expensive *adj* costly; lavish.
experience *n* personal trial; knowledge

gained from contact with life or work; an effecting event. * *vt* to try; meet with.

experiment *n* a trial; a practical test; a controlled procedure carried out to disciver, test or demonstrate something.* *vi* to carry out experiments.

experimental *adj* of, derived from, or proceeding by experiment; provisional.

expert *adj* skilful; knowledgeable throughtraining and experience. * *n* a specialist.

expertise *n* expert knowledge or skill.

expiate *vt* to atone for.

expire *vt* to breathe out; to exhale. * *vi* to die; to end.

explain *vt* to make clear; to expound. * *vi* to account for.

explanation *n* interpretation; reason.

explanatory *adj* serving to explain.

expletive *n* an oath.

explicable *adj* explainable.

explicit *adj* definite; expressly or frankly stated.

explode *vti* to burst with a loud noise; to expose; discredit.

exploit *n* a brilliant deed; a bold achievement. * *vt* to make use of; to take unfair advantage of.

exploitation *n* successful application of industry to any object, as land, mines, etc.

explore *vt* to search; to examine closely; to travel through for the purpose of discovery.

explorer *n* a traveller in unknown regions.

explosion *n* a violent detonation; an outburst (of feeling).

explosive *adj* liable to explode. * *n* material that explodes.

exponent *n* a person who explains or interprets something.

export *vt* to send goods abroad for sale. * *n* the commodity exported.

expose *vt* to deprive of protection or shelter; to uncover; to display; to endanger.

exposed *adj* unmasked; unsheltered.

exposition *n* explanation; exhibition.

exposure *n* a laying open to view or weather or danger; the time during which light reaches and acts on a photographic film, paper or plate; publicity.

expound *vt* to explain.

express *vt* to declare; to utter; to make known; to squeeze out. * *adj* swift, special; explicit; plain. * *n* a swift messenger, service, or conveyance; an express train. * *adv* with haste; at high speed; by express service.

expression *n* a phrase or mode of speech; facial look; taste and feeling (music); terms or collection saving to express something in mathematics.

expressive *adj* striking; full of expression.

expressly *adv* of set purpose; explicity.

expulsion *n* ejection; discharge.

expunge *vt* to blot out; to erase.

expurgate *vt* to purify (from sin, etc); cut out offensive passages from (books, etc).

exquisite *adj* beautiful; incomparable; acutely felt, as pain or pleasure.

extend *vti* to stretch out; to prolong in time; to spread; to accord; to reach; to hold out, eg the hand.

extension *n* extent, scope; an added part, eg to a building; an extra period; a programme of extramural teaching provided by a college, etc; an additional telephone connected to the principal line.

extensive *adj* far-reaching; large.

extent *n* compass; size; range; scope.

extenuate *vt* to make excuses for.

extenuation *n* mitigation.

exterior *adj* external; outside.

exterminate *vt* to destroy utterly.

external *adj* on the outside; visible.

extinct *adj* dead; extinguished; no longer existing or active.

extinction *n* destruction.

extinguish *vt* to put out; quench.

extinguisher *n* a device for putting out a fire.

extol *vt* to exalt; glorify.

extort *vt* to exact by force, eg money, promises.

extortionate *adj* exorbitant; harsh.

extra *adj, adv* additional. * something additional; a specialedition of a newspaper; one who plays a non-speaking part in a film.

extract *vt* to take or pull out by force; to withdraw by chemical or physical

means; to abstract. * *n* the essence of a substance obtained by extraction; a passage taken from a book, play, film etc.
extraction *n* lineage; a drawing out.
extradite *vt* to give up foreign criminals to police of their own country.
extradition *n* the handing over of fugitive foreign criminals.
extramural *adj* connected with a university but not as regular students.
extraneous *adj* foreign; irrelevant; inessential.
extraordinary *adj* unusual; remarkable.
extravagance *n* excess; over-spending; flamboyance; wastefulness.
extravagant *adj* lavish in spending; excessively, high of prices; unrestrained; wasteful; profuse.
extravaganza *n* a fantastic literary or musical composition.
extreme *adj* of the highest degree or intensity; excessive, immoderate, unwarrented; very severe, stringent; outermost. * *n* the highest or furthest limit or degree.
extremely *adv* in the utmost degree.
extremist *n* a supporter of extreme measures.
extremity *n* the farthest point; the utmost need (*pl*) the hands or feet..
extricate *vt* to set free; to disentangle.
exuberance *n* high spirits.
exuberant *adj* high-spirited; lively.
exude *vti* to ooze out.
exult *vi* to rejoice exceedingly; to triumph.
exultant *adj* jubilant.
eye *n* the organ of vision; mind; perception; a small hole; a catch; a shoot. * *vt* to regard closely.
eyebrow *n* the hairy arch above the eye.
eyelash *n* the hair that edges the eyelid.
eyelid *n* the cover of the eye.
eyesight *n* power of sight.
eyesore *n* something offensive to the sight.
eye-witness *n* a person who sees an event.
eyrie *n* an eagle's nest.

F

fable *n* a short story with a moral; a falsehood.
fabled *adj* legendary.
fabric *n* frame of anything; a building; texture; cloth.
fabricate *vt* to fashion; to invent.
fabrication *n* construction; forgery.
fabulous *adj* incredible; mythical.
façade *n* front view of an edifice.
face *n* the front part of the head; the countenance; aspect; assurance; dial of a watch. * *vt* to front; to oppose.
facet *n* one of many sides (of gems).
facetious *adj* humorous.
facilitate *vt* to make easy.
facility *n* ease; dexterity.
facsimile *n* an exact copy.
fact *n* a deed; event; truth.
faction *n* an unscrupulous and self-interested party; discord.
factor *n* an agent; a land steward; an essential element; a measure of a number.
factory *n* a building where goods are made.
faculty *n* capacity; power; special aptitude; a department of a university.
fad *n* personal habit on idiosyncrasy.
fade *vt, vi* to (cause to) lose vigour or brightness or intensity gradually; to vanish gradually.
fail *vi* to weaken; to fade away; to stop operating; to become bankrupt; not to succeed; to miss; *vt* to disappoint the expectations on hope.
failure *n* failing, non-performance, lack of success; an unsuccessful person or thing.
faint *vi* to become feeble; to swoon. * *adj* dim., indistinct; weak; feeble. * *n* a swoon.
fair *adj* pleasing to the eye; light in colour; just; favourable (weather); moderately good or large; average * *adv* justly. * *n* a regular market or gathering for sale of goods
fairly *adv* honestly, justly; moderately.
fairy *n* an elf; a sprite.
faith *n* belief; trust; religious conviction;

system of beliefs; fidelity to one's promises.

faithful *adj* loyal; trusty; accurate.

faithless *adj* false; unfaithful.

fake *vt* to disguise and so cheat; to pretend; to simulate.* *n* a faked article; a forgery; an impostor.

fall *vi* to drop down; to descend; to collapse; to sin; to lose power, status, office; to be injured or die in battle; to happen. * *n* a drop; a decrease; a decline in status or position; overthrow.

fallacious *adj* deceitful; misleading.

fallacy *n* a false argument or idea.

fallible *adj* liable to err; make mistakes.

fall-out *n* a deposit of radioactive dust from a nuclear explosion; a by-product.

fallow *adj* left uncultivated for one or more seasons; yellowish-brown.

false *adj* not true; forged; treacherous; deceitful; artificial.

falsehood *n* untruth; a lie.

falsetto *n* an unnaturally high-pitched voice.

falsification *n* wilful misrepresentation.

falsify *vt* to make false by altering in order to deceive.

falter *vi* to hesitate; to waver; to move unsteadily.

fame *n* reputation; renown.

familiar *adj* well-acquainted; friendly; common; well-known; presumptuous. * *n* an intimate; a spirit supposed to assist a witch.

familiarity *n* intimacy; presumptuous.

family *n* parents and their children; a set of relatives; the descendants of a common ancestor; a group of related plants or animals.

famine *n* extreme scarcity of food.

famish *vt,vi* to starve; to suffer extreme hunger.

famous *adj* renowned.

fan[1] *n* an instrument or device for creating a current of air; to cool by moving; to ventilate; to stir up or excite; to spread out like a fan.* *vt* the air.

fan[2] *n* an enthusiastic follower of a person, a sport or a hobby .

fanatic *adj* frenzied, bigoted. * *n* a zealot; an over enthusiastic person.

fancy *n* imagination; caprice; whim; delusion. * *vt, ti* to imagine; to like. * *adj* elegant; unreal.

fancy dress *n*

fanfare *n* a flourish of trumpets.

fang *n* a long, sharp, pointed tooth.

fanlight *n* a window over a door.

fantastic *adj* unrealistic; fanciful; unbelievable; imaginative.

fantasy *n* imagination; a product of this; an imaginative poem, play or novel.

far *adj* remote; extreme in political views. * *adv* very distant in space, time or degree; very much.

farce *n* a ludicrous situation.

farcical *adj* droll; ludicrous.

fare *vi* to be in a specified condition. * *n* food; the cost of a journey.

farewell *interj, n* goodbye.

farinaceous *adj* starchy; mealy.

farm *n* land (with buildings) on which crops and animals are raised. * *vt,vi* to cultivate; to lease out; to subcontract.

farmer *n* one who manages and operates a farm.

farther *adj, comp* more remote. * *adv* to a greater degree.

farthest *adj super* most distant. * *adv* at the greatest distance.

fascia *n* the instrument panel of a motor vehicle, the dash-board; the flat surface above a shop front with the name etc.

fascinate *vt* to charm; to captivate.

fascination *n* charm; spell.

fashion *n* a current style of dress, conduct, speech etc; the manner of form of appearance or action. * *vt* to make in a particular form; to suit or adapt.

fashionable *adj* stylish; in keeping with the prevailing fashion.

fast *adj* firm; fixed; steadfast; swift; lasting. * *vt* to abstain from food. * *n* a period of doing without food.

fasten *vt,vi* to fix firmly; to become fixed.

fastidious *adj* hard to please; over-refined.

fat *adj* plump; oily; rich; fertile. * *n* oily substance in animal bodies; the richest or best point of anything.

fatal *adj* deadly; disastrous.

fatalist *n* one who holds all things are predetermined.

fatality *n* a fatal occurrence; a death caused by disaster or accident; a person so killed.
fate *n* destiny; necessity; death; doom; lot.
fateful *adj* having important, often unpleasant, consequences.
father *n* a male parent; an ancestor; name given to R.C. priests. * *vt* to adopt; to found; to originate.
fatherhood *n* state of being a father.
father-in-law *n* the father of one's husband or wife.
fatherland *n* one's native country.
fathom *n* a nautical measure of length (6 ft/1.83m) * *vt* to try the depth of; to sound; to comprehend.
fatigue *n* tiredness from physical or mental effort; the tendency of a material to break under repeated stress. **vt, vi* to make or become tired.
fatten *vt* to make fat.
fatuous *adj* foolish; idiotic.
fault *n* a slight offence; a flaw; a break of strata; an incorrect stroke in tennis.
faulty *adj* defective; imperfect.
fauna *n* a collective term for the animals of a region or specific environment.
favour *n* goodwill; kindness; leave; a token of goodwill; a gift presented at a party. * *vt* to befriend; to show support for; to oblige with; to facilitate.
favourable *adj* kindly disposed; propitious; conductive to.
favoured *adj* regarded with favour.
favourite *n* a person habitually preferred; a darling; a competitor expected to win; a minion. * *adj* preferred; beloved.
favouritism *n* showing undue partiality.
fawn *n* a young deer. * *vi* to cringe or flatter to gain favour. * *adj* light brown.
fax see **facsimile**.
fear *n* dread; terror; awe; anxiety. * *vt,vi* to dread; to hesitate; to reverence.
feasibility *n* practicability.
feasible *adj* practicable; possible.
feast *n* a sumptuous meal; a periodic religious celebration. * *vi, vt* to have or take part in a feast; to entertain with a feast.
feat *n* an exploit; a notable act.
feather *n* any of the light outgrowths forming the covering of a bird, a hollow central shaft with a vane of fine barbs on each side. * *vt* to ornament with feathers.
feature *n* any of the part of the face; a characteristic trait of something; a special attraction or distinctive quality of something; a prominent newspaper article etc. * *vt, vi* to make or be a feature of (something).
February *n* the second month in the year.
fecund *adj* fruitful; prolific.
federal *adj* united in a league for national purposes, but each partner having independent powers in local affairs.
federation *n* a union of independent bodies or states to take common action on certain matters.
fee *n* a reward for services; a payment; charge. * *vt* to pay a fee to.
feeble *adj* weak; infirm.
feed *vt* to give food to; to fatten. * *vi* to take food; to eat; to graze. * *n* food for animals; material fed into a machine.
feedback *n* a return to the input of part of the output of a system; information about a product, service etc. returned to the supplier for evaluation.
feel *n* the sense of touch; feeling; a quality as revealed by touch. * *vt, vi* to perceive or explore by the touch; to find one's way by cautious trail; to be conscious of, experience; to be affected by; to convey a certain sensation when touched.
feeler *n* an organ of touch in insects, &c.; remark, &c., made to probe a situation.
feeling *adj* sensitive; sympathetic. * *n* the sense of touch; emotion; sympathy; a belief; an opinion arising from emotion (*pl*) emotions; sensibilities.
feign *vt, vi* to pretend; to invent.
feint *n* a pretence (of doing); a sham blow.
felicitate *vt* to congratulate.
felicitous *adj* happy; apt.
felicity *n* happiness; aptness.
feline *adj* cat-like.
fell *adj* cruel; savage. * *n* a skin; a stony hill. * *vt* to strike down.
fellow *n* a partner; one of a pair; a man; a member of the governing body in some colleges and universities; a member of

a learned society.

fellowship *n* companionship; an association; the status of a college fellow.

felon *n* a criminal.

felony *n* a serious crime.

felt *n* a fabric made of wool.

female *n* a girl or woman. **adj* of the sex that produces young.

feminine *adj* womanly; womanish.

feminism *n* the movement to win political, economic and social equality for women.

femoral *adj* belonging to the thigh.

femur *n* the thigh bone.

fen *n* a marsh; a bog.

fence *n* a barrier put round land to mark a boundary, or prevent animals, etc from escaping; a receiver of stolen goods. * *vt, vi* to surround a fence; to keep (out) as by a fence; to make evasive answers; to act as a fence for stolen goods.

fencing *n* the practice of sword play; material for fences.

fend *vt* to keep or ward off; (with **for**) to provide a livelihood for.

fender *n* a hearth guard; a buffer along a ship's side; the part of a car body over the wheel.

ferment *n* that which causes fermentation, as yeast; tumult; agitation. * *vt, vi* to cause or subject to fermentation; to cause agitation or excitement.

fermentation *n* the breakdown of complex molecules in organic components caused by the influence of yeast or other substances.

ferocious *adj* fierce; savage.

ferocity *n* savagery; fury.

ferret *n* a species of weasel. * *vt* to drive out (rabbits); to search out (secrets).

ferry *n* a boat used for ferrying; a ferrying service; the location of a ferry. * *vt* to convey (passengers etc) over a stretch of water; to transport from one place to another, esp along a regular route.

fertile *adj* fruitful; inventive.

fertilize *vt* to enrich (soil) by adding nutrients; to impregnate.

fertilizer *n* natural organic or artificial substances used to enrich the soil.

fervent *adj* burning; ardent; passionate.

fervid *adj* zealous; eager.

fervour *n* zeal; earnestness.

fester *vi* to suppurate; to rankle.

festival *n* a feast; a gala day; performances of music, plays etc. Given periodically.

festive *adj* joyous; merry.

festivity *n* festive gaiety.

fetch *vt* to go and bring back; to heave.

fête *n* a festival. * *vt* to honour; to make much of.

fetid *adj* stinking; offensive.

fetish *n* anything excessively reverenced.

fetter *n* a shackle for feet; restraint. * *vt* to hobble; to restrict.

feu *n* land held in fee.

feud *n* a quarrel esp. between individuals, families, clans.

feudalism *n* the holding of land in return for military service.

fever *n* a disease marked by high temperature; restless excitement.

few *adj* not many; a small number.

fiancé, fiancée *n* a man, woman engaged to be married.

fiasco *n* an ignominious failure.

fibre *n* a natural or synthetic thread, e.g. from cotton, nylon, which is spun into yarn; a material composed of such yarn; texture; strength or character; roughage.

fibreglass *n* a glass composed of fibres often bonded with plastic used in making various products.

fickle *adj* vacillating; inconstant.

fickleness *n* inconstancy.

fiction *n* a made-up story; novels; plays collectively.

fictitious *adj* imaginary; false.

fiddle *n* a violin. **vt* to play the violin; to swindle.

fidelity *n* faithfulness; loyalty.

fidget *vi* to be restless. * *n* a restless person.

field *n* land suitable for tillage or pasture; range; sports ground; an area affected by electrical, magnetic or gravitational influence etc; the area visible through an optical lens; all competitors in a contest; in a computer; a section of a record in a database. * *vt, vi* to catch and return the ball in cricket etc; to handle (e.g. questions) successfully.

field marshal *n* an army officer of the highest rank.
fiend *n* a demon; a cruel person; an avid fan.
fiendish *adj* like a fiend.
fierce *adj* wild; savage; violent; intense.
fiery *adj* burning; passionate; irascible.
fight *vi, vt* to contend; to strive for victory. * *n* a struggle; a battle.
fighter *n* a person who fights; a person who does not yield easily; an aircraft designed to destroy enemy aircraft.
figment *n* a fiction; a falsehood.
figuration *n* shape; form.
figurative *adj* using figures of speech; metaphorical.
figure *n* form; outline; diagram; pattern; person; statue; symbol; price; digit; a set of steps on movements (*pl*) arithmetic. * *vt, vi* to represent in a diagram or outline to imagine; to estimate; to appear.
figurehead *n* the carved figure on the bow of ships; a nominal head or leader.
filament *n* a slender thread; the fine wire in a light bulb.
filch *vt* to pilfer; to steal.
file *n* a container for holding papers; an orderly arrangement of papers; a line of persons or things; in computer, a collection of related data under a specific name; a smoothing or polishing or grinding tool. * *vt, vi* to put on public records, to march in file; to wear down.
filial *adj* of or relating to a son or daughter.
filigree *n* delicate tracery in gold or silver.
filings *npl* particles rubbed off by a file.
fill *vt, vi* to make or become full; to pervade; to hold; to satisfy.
fillet *n* a thin boneless strip of fish or meat. * *vt* to bone meat, &c.
filling *n* a substance used to fill a tooth cavity; the contents of a sandwich, pie etc. **adj* substantial (of a meal).
filly *n* a female colt.
film *n* a fine, thin skin, coating etc; a flexible cellulose material covered with a light-sensitive substance used in photography; a haze or blur; a motion picture.
filter *n* a device or substance straining out solid particles, impurities etc; a traffic signal that allows cars to turn left or right while the main lights are red. * *vt, vi* to pass through or as through a filter, to remove with a filter.
filth *n* dirt; pollution; obscenity.
filthy *adj* dirty; foul; obscene.
filtrate *vt* to filter.
fin *n* an organ by which a fish etc. steers itself and swims; any fin-shaped object used as a stabilizer, as on an aircraft or rocket.
final *adj* last; conclusive. **n* (often *pl*) the last of a series of contests; a final examination.
finale *n* the last piece; end, esp. of any public performance; the last section in a musical composition.
finance *n* the management of money. * *vt* to supply or raise money for.
financier *n* one skilled in finance.
find *vt* to come upon; to discover; to have; to supply; to declare. * *n* a discovery.
finding *n* a verdict; a discovery.
fine *adj* slender; minute; keen; delicate. * *n* a money penalty. * *vt* to punish by a fine.
finery *n* showy apparel or jewellery.
finesse *n* delicacy or subtlety of performance; skilfulness, diplomacy in handling a situation. * *vt* to achieve by finesse.
finger *n* one of the five digits of the hand usually excluding the thumb; anything finger-shaped. * *vt* to touch.
fingerprint *n* the impression of the ridges on a fingertip, esp as used for purposes of identification.
finish *n* the last part, the end; anything used to finish a surface; the finished effect; means or manner of completion or perfecting; polished manners, speech etc. **vt, vi* to bring to an end, to come to the end of; to consume entirely; to perfect; to give a desired surface effect to.
finite *adj* limited; bounded.
fiord, fjord *n* an inlet of the sea.
fire *n* the flame, heat and light of combustion
fire alarm *n* a device that uses a bell, hooter etc, to warn of a fire.

firearm *n* a gun or rifle.

firebrand *n* a flaming piece of wood; one who causes mischief or disturbance.

fire brigade *n* an organisation of men and women trained to extinguish fires.

fire escape *n* a means of exit from a building, esp. a stairway, for use in case of fire.

fireplace *n* a place for a fire, esp a recess in a wall; the surrounding area.

fireproof *adj* incombustible.

fireside *n* the hearth; home.

firework *n* a device packed with explosive and combustible material used to produce noisy and colourful displays.

firing squad *n* a detachment with the task of firing a salute at a military funeral or carrying out an execution.

firm *adj* steady; strong; hard; resolute. * *n* a business partnership.

firmament *n* the sky or heavens.

first *n* an person or thing that is first; the beginning; the winning place, as in a race; the highest award in a university degree. **adj* before all others in a series; foremost, as in rank, equality etc. * *adv* before anyone or anything else.

first aid *n* emergency treatment for an injury etc., before regular medical aid is available.

first-class *adj, n* of the highest quality, as in accommodation, travel.

firsthand *adj* obtained directly.

first-rate *adj, adv* of the best quality; (*inf*) excellent.

firth *n* a wide river mouth.

fiscal *adj* relating to public finance. * *n* a public prosecutor.

fish *n* a cold-blooded animal living in water, having backbones, gills and fins. **vi* to catch or try to catch fish.

fisherman *n* one who fishes for a living or for sport.

fishery *n* the business of fishing; fishing ground.

fishing *n* the art of catching fish.

fishmonger *n* a dealer in fish; his shop.

fishy *adj* like a fish in odour, taste etc; creating doubt or suspicion.

fission *n* a split or cleavage; the splitting of the atomic nucleus resulting in the release of energy, nuclear fission.

fissure *n* a cleft; a chasm.

fist *n* the hand clenched.

fit *n* a spasm; convulsion; right size; caprice. * *adj* suitable; proper; healthy. * *vt, vi* to make fit; to suit; to adapt; to equip.

fitful *adj* spasmodic; uncertain.

fitment *n* a piece of equipment, esp fixed furniture.

fitter *n* one who fits; one who puts the parts of machinery together.

fitting *adj* becoming; appropriate. * *npl* fixtures.

five *adj, n* one more than four; the symbol for this (5, V,v).

fix *vt, vi* to make fast or firm; to settle; to appoint; to direct one's eyes steadily at something; to repair; to arrange or influence a result. * *n* a dilemma.

fixed *adj* firm; fast.

fixture *n* what is fixed to anything, as to land or to a house; a fixed article of furniture; a firmly established person or thing; a fixed or appointed time or event.

fizz *vi* to make a hissing sound.

flabby *adj* soft; limp.

flaccid *adj* flabby.

flag *n* a standard; ensign; a flat paving stone. * *vi* to droop; to languish.

flagellate *vt* to whip.

flagellation *n* a scourging.

flagon *n* a jug-shaped metal or pottery vessel.

flagrant *adj* glaring; shameful; notorious.

flail *n* a hand-threshing implement.

flair *n* natural ability; aptitude; discernment; stylishness.

flake *n* a scale; a fleecy particle (snow). * *vi* to peel off. * *vt* to form into flakes.

flamboyant *adj* florid; flaming; strikingly elaborate; dashing; exuberant.

flame *n* a sheet of fire; a blaze; passion. * *vi* to blaze; to become red in the face with emotion.

flan *n* an open case of pastry or sponge cake with a sweet or savoury filling.

flange *n* a raised edge on wheel.

flank *n* the fleshy part of the side; from the ribs to the hip; the side of (army, mountain, &c.). * *vt* to be at the side of;

to menace on the side.
flannel *n* a soft woollen cloth, a small cloth for washing the face; nonsense; equivocation. (*pl*) flannel trousers.
flap *n* the beat of wings or a similar sound; anything hanging loose (esp. part of a garment); *vi, vt* to move like wings; to flutter; agitation; panic, to panic.
flare *n* a sudden flash; a bright light used as a signal or illumination; a widened part or shape. * *vi* to burn with a sudden, bright, unsteady flame; to widen our gradually.
flash *n* a sudden gleam; a brief moment, display, news item. * *vi, vt* to shine out suddenly; to signal.
flashback *n* an interruption in the continuity of a story etc, by telling or showing an earlier episode.
flashbulb *n* a small bulb giving an intense light used in photography.
flashlight *n* a torch.
flash point *n* the ignition point.
flashy *adj* gaudy; showy.
flask *n* a kind of bottle; a vacuum flask.
flat *adj* level; prostrate; tasteless; below pitch; deflated; dull; tedious; (of battery) drained of electric current. * *n* a storey or set of rooms in a house.
flatten *vt* to make flat.
flatter *vt* to praise unduly or insincerely.
flattery *n* undeserved praise.
flatulence *n* wind in the stomach.
flaunt *vi, vt* to show off.
flavour *n* distinctive taste. * *vt* to season; to give flavour to.
flaw *n* a crack; a defect.
flax *n* a plant cultivated for its fibres.
flaxen *adj* of or like flax; fair; pale yellow.
flay *vt* to strip off (skin).
flea *n* a jumping, bloodsucking insect.
fleck *n* a spot; a streak. * *vt* to streak.
fledgling *n* a young bird; a trainee.
flee *vi* to run away from danger etc; to disappear.
fleece *n* a sheep's coat. * *vt* to shear the wool from; to rob; to defraud.
fleet *n* a squadron of ships; navy; a group of cars, ships, buses under one management. * *adj* swift; nimble.
fleeting *adj* transient; passing.
flesh *n* the soft part of the body; the pulpy part of fruits and vegetables; meat; the body and its appetites.
fleshy *adj* plump; fat.
flex *vt* to bend.
flexible *adj* pliable; supple; adaptable.
flick *n* a touch with a whip; a flip. * *vt* to flip; to strike with a flick.
flicker *vi* to burn unsteadily. * *n* an unsteady light; a flickering movement.
flight[1] *n* the act, manner, or power of flying; distance flown; an aircraft scheduled to fly a certain trip; a set of stairs, as between landings.
flight[1] *n* an act or instance of fleeing.
flighty *adj* fickle; giddy.
flimsy *adj* thin; slight; weak; light and thin; unconvincing * *n* copying paper.
flinch *vi* to shrink; to quail; to drawback.
fling *vt* to hurl; to scatter. * *vi* to kick out violently; to move quickly or impetuously. * *n* a throw; a Highland dance.
flint *n* a hard stone; a pebble.
flinty *adj* hard; cruel.
flip *n* a flick. * *vt* to flick; to flick with the thumb.
flippancy *n* undue levity; frivolity.
flippant *adj* saucy; heedless; frivolous.
flirt *vt, vi* to throw or jerk; to make insincere amorous approaches; to trifle or toy e.g. with an idea. * *n* one who toys amorously with the opposite sex.
flit *vi* to fly or dart ; to vacate premises.
float *n* a cork or other device used on a fishing line to signal that the bait has been taken; a low flat vehicle decorated for exhibit in a parade; a small sum of money available for cash expenditures. * *vt, vi* to rest on the surface of or be suspended in liquid; to put into circulation.
floe *n* floating ice.
flog *vt* to whip; to thrash.
flood *n* a deluge; a river; abundance. * *vt* to overflow; to deluge.
floodgate *n* a gate or lock in a waterway.
floodlight *n* a strongbeam of light used to illuminate a stage, sports field, stadium etc. * *vt* (*pt* **floodlit**) to illuminate with floodlights.

floodmark *n* high-water mark.

floodtide *n* the rising tide.

floor *n* the inside bottom surface of a room; the bottom surface of anything; as the ocean; a storey in a building; the lower limit, the base. * *vt* to provide with a floor; (*inf*) to defeat; (*inf*) to shock, to confuse.

flop *vi (pt* **flopped**) to sway or bounce loosely; to move in a heavy, clumsy or relaxed manner; (*inf*) to fail. * *n* a flopping movement; a collapse; (*inf*) a complete failure.

floppy *adj* limp; hanging loosely.

floppy disk *n* a disk of flexible material for storing data in a computer.

flora *n* the plant life of a region or district.

floral *adj* pertaining to flowers.

florid *adj* flowery; ruddy of complexion.

florist *n* a cultivator or seller of flowers.

flotation *n* the act or process of floating; a launching of a business venture.

flotilla *n* a small fleet.

flotsam *n* floating wreckage.

flounce[1] *vi,* to move in an emphatic or impatient manner.

flounce[2] *n* a frill of material sewn to the skirt of a dress. * *vt* to add flounces to.

flounder *n* a flat fish. * *vi* to move awkwardly and with difficulty; to be clumsy in thinking in speaking.

flour *n* the meal of grain.

flourish *vi* to grow luxuriantly; to thrive; to live and work at a specified period. * *vt* to brandish. * *n* showy expression; fanciful stroke of the pen; brandishing.

flout *vt* to disobey openly; to treat with contempt.

flow *vi* to move, as water; to issue; to glide smoothly; to hang loose; to circulate; to be plentiful. * *n* a stream; current.

flow chart *n* a diagram representing the sequence of and relationships between different steps or procedures in a complex process, e.g. manufacturing.

flower *n* the blossom of plants; youth; the prime. * *vi* to blossom; to bloom.

flowery *adj* full of or decorated with flowers; figurative; elaborate of language.

fluctuate *vi* (of prices) to be continually varying in an irregular way; to waver; to be unstable.

fluctuating *adj* varying.

flu *u* influenza.

flue *n* a smoke vent.

fluent *adj* flowing; voluble; able to speak and write a foreign language with ease; articulate; graceful.

fluff *n* light down or nap; a mistake.

fluid *adj* capable of flowing. * *n* that which flows, as water or air.

fluke *n* the barb of an anchor; a lucky stroke; a flat fish; a flattened parasitic worm.

fluoride *n* any of various compounds of fluoride.

flurry *n* a sudden gust of wind, rain or snow; bustle; hurry. *vt, vi* to (cause to) become flustered.

flush[1] *n* a rapid flow, as of water; sudden, vigorous growth; a sudden excitement; a blush. **vt, vi* to cause to blush; to excite; to flow rapidly.

flush[2] *vt* to make game birds fly away suddenly.

flush[3] *n* (poker, etc) a hand of cards all of the same suit.

fluster *vt* to agitate; to confuse.

flute *n* an orchestral woodwind instrument with finger holes and keys held horizontally and played through a hole located near one end; a decorative groove. * *vi* to play or make sounds like a flute.

flutist, flautist *n* a flute player.

flutter *vi* to flap; to quiver; to beat irregularly or spasmodically (of the heart) * *n* a tremor; stir; nervous excitement; commotion; a small bet.

fly[1] *n* a two-winged insect; a natural or imitation fly attached to a fish-hook as bait.

fly[2] *vb* (*pt* **flew**, *pp* **flown**) *vi, vt* to move through the air, esp on wings; to travel in an aircraft; to control an aircraft; to take flight, as a kite; to escape, flee from; to pass quickly; (*inf*) to depart quickly). * *n* a flap that hides buttons.

fly[3] *adj (inf)* sly, astute.

flying *adj* capable of flight; fleeing; fast-moving. * *n* the act of flying an aircraft.

flying start *n* a start in a race when the

competitor is already moving at the starting line; a promising start.

flyleaf *n* (*pl* **flyleaves**) a blank leaf at the beginning or end of a book.

flyover *n* a bridge that carries a road or railway over another; a fly-past.

fly-past *n* a processional flight of aircraft.

foal *n* young of horse, ass.

foam *n* froth or fine bubbles on the surface of liquid. * *vi* to cause or emit foam.

fob *n* a watch pocket in a trouser waistband. **vt* (with **off**) to cheat; to put off; to palm off.

focal *adj* belonging to a focus.

focus *n* point in which reflected rays converge; correct adjustment of the eye or lens to form a clear image; a centre of activity or interest. * *vt* to concentrate; the centre.

fodder *n* food for cattle.

foe *n* an enemy.

foetus *n* the unborn young of an animal, esp. in later stages; in humans, the offspring in the womb from the fourth month until birth.

fog *n* a thick mist; cloudiness on a developed photograph.

foible *n* a weakness or failing; an idiosyncrasy.

foil *vt* to frustrate; to baffle. * *n* defeat; a sword used in fencing; a leaf of metal; a background to set things off.

foist *vt* to palm off.

fold[1] *vt, vi* to cover by bending or doubling over so that one part covers another; to interlace (one's arms); to incorporate (an ingredient) into a food mixture by gentle overturning. * *n* something folded, as a piece of cloth; a crease or hollow made by folding.

fold[2] *n* a pen for sheep. * *vt* to pen in a fold.

foliage *n* leaves.

folio *n* a sheet once folded; a leaf in a ledger; a book of largest size.

folk *n* people in general; folk music.

folklore *n* popular tales, songs, &c. of a people.

follow *vt, vi* to go or come after; to pursue; to accompany; to succeed; to result from; to understand; to practise; to be occupied with.

follower *n* a disciple or adherent; a person who imitates another.

following *n* a body of followers, adherents or believers. * *adj* succeeding; next after; now to be stated.

folly *n* foolishness; madness; an extravagant or fanciful building serving no practical purpose.

foment *vt* to stir up strife or agitation.

fond *adj* tender; loving; doting.

fondle *vt* to caress.

font *n* the receptacle for baptismal on holy water; set of type.

food *n* nourishment; provisions.

fool *n* a simpleton; a clown; a jester; a cold pudding of whipped cream and fruit purée. * *vi* to trifle. * *vt* to deceive.

foolhardy *adj* rash; venturesome.

foolproof *adj* proof against failure; easy to understand; easy to use.

foolscap *n* a size of paper.

foot *n* (*pl* **feet**) that upon which anything stands; the lower end of the leg; the lower part or edge of something; the bottom; a measure of 12 inches, a group of syllables serving as a unit of metre in verse. * *vt* to pay; to walk; to dance.

football *n* a large ball; game played with it by two teams.

foothold *n* a ledge etc, for placing the foot when climbing etc; a place from which further progress may be made.

footing *n* foothold; basis; status.

footlights *n* a row of lights in front of the stage floor.

foot-path *n* a narrow path for pedestrians.

footprint *n* impression of the foot.

footsore *adj* having painful feet from excessive walking.

footstep *n* a track; a footprint.

for *prep,* because of, as a result of; as the price of, or recompense of; in order to be, to serve as; to quest of; in the direction of; on behalf of; in place of; in favour of; with respect to; in spite of; to the extent of; throughout the space of; during. * *conj* because.

forage *n* fodder. * *vt* to collect or go in search of provisions.

foray *vt* to pillage. * *n* a sudden raid.
forbear *vi* to endure; to avoid. * *vt* to hold oneself back from.
forbearance *n* patience; restraint.
forbid *vt* to prohibit; to oppose.
forbidding *adj* unfriendly; solemn; strict; repulsive.
force *n* strength, power, effort; (*physics*) (the intensity of) an influence that causes movement of a body or other effects; a body of soldiers, police etc. prepared for action; effectiveness; violence, compulsion. * *vt* to compel by physical effort, superior strength etc; to achieve by force; to press or drive against resistance; to produce with effort; to break open; to impose, inflict.
forced *adj* affected; overstrained.
forceful *adj* powerful, effective.
forceps *n* an instrument for grasping and holding firmly, or exerting traction upon objects, esp by jewellers and surgeons.
ford *n* a crossing place in a river. * *vt* to wade across.
fore *adj* in front of; prior. * *adv* before.
forearm *n* the arm from elbow to wrist.
forearm *vt* to arm beforehand.
forebode *vt* to foretell; to portend.
forecast *vt* to foresee; to predict events, weather etc. through national analysis. * *n* a prediction.
foreclose *vt* to preclude; to stop.
forecourt *n* an enclosed space in front of a building, as in a filling station.
forefathers *pl n* ancestors.
forefront *n* the foremost part.
foregoing *adj* preceding.
foregone *adj* past; inevitable; preceding.
foreground *n* the front part of a picture.
forehead *n* the brow.
foreign *adj* alien; native belonging to another country; introduces from outside.
foreman *n* an overseer; the spokesman in a jury.
foremost *adj* first; chief; most advanced.
forensic *adj* belonging to or used in courts of law.
forensic medicine *n* the application of medical expertise to legal and criminal investigations.
forerunner *n* a herald; precursor.
foresee *vt* (*pt* **foresaw**, *pp* **foreseen**) to be aware of beforehand.
foreshadow *vt* to prophesy; to augur.
foreshore *n* the shore between high- and low-water marks.
foresight *n* forethought; provision for the future.
forest *n* an extensive wood.
forestall *vt* to anticipate.
forestry *n* the science of planting and cultivating forests.
foretaste *n* a taste beforehand.
forever *adv* always; eternally.
foreword *n* a preface to a book.
forfeit *vt* to lose by fault; to be penalized by forfeit. * *n* a penalty.
forge *n* a furnace; a smithy. * *vt, vi* to shape by heating and hammering; to falsify; to counterfeit a signature etc.
forgery *n* fraudulently copying; a forged copy.
forget *vt* to cease to remember.
forgetful *adj* apt to forget; inattentive.
forget-me-not *n* a small blue flower.
forgive *vt* to pardon; to stop feeling resentment. * *vi* to be merciful or forgiving.
forgiving *adj* compassionate.
forgo *vt* to go without; to abstain from.
fork *n* a small, usu metal, instrument with two or more thin prongs set in a handle, used in eating and cooking; anything that divides into prongs or branches; the point of separation. (* *vt, vi* to divide into branches; to follow a branch of a fork in the road etc.
fork-lift truck *n* a vehicle with power-operated prongs for raising and lowering loads.
forlorn *adj* deserted; hopeless.
form *n* general structure; the figure of a person or animal; arrangement; a printed document with blanks to be filled in; a class in school; condition of mind or body; changed appearance of a word to show inflection. * *vt, vi* to shape; to train; to develop (habits); to constitute; to be formed.
formal *adj* in conformity with established rules or habits; regular; relating to outward appearance only; ceremonial;

punctilious; stiff.
formality *n* accordance with custom.
format *n* the size, form, shape in which books, etc are issued; the general style or presentation of something; (*comput*) the arrangement of data on magnetic disk etc of access and storage. * *vt* to arrange in a particular form, esp for a computer.
formative *adj* pertaining to formation and development; shaping.
former *adj comp deg* past; preceding.
formidable *adj* terrifying; difficult.
formula *n* (*pl* **formulas, formulae**) a set of symbols expressing the composition of a substance; a general expression in algebraic form for solving a problem; a prescribed form; a fixed method according to which something is to be done.
formulate *vt* to express clearly or in a formula.
forsake *vt* to abandon; to renounce.
fort *n* a fortress.
forte *adv* loudly (*mus*). * *n* a person's strong point.
forth *adv* forward; abroad.
forthcoming *adj* about to appear.
forthright *adv* frank; straightforward; outspoken.
forthwith *adv* without delay.
fortification *n* the act of fortifying; defensive works.
fortify *vt* to strengthen; to erect defences; to add alcohol to.
fortitude *n* endurance; courage; patience.
fortnight *n* two weeks.
fortress *n* a stronghold; a castle.
fortuitous *adj* chance; accidental.
fortunate *adj* lucky; prosperous.
fortune *n* chance; luck; fate; vast wealth; prosperity.
fortune-teller *n* a person who claims to foretell a person's future.
forum *n* an assembly or meeting to discuss topics of public concern; a medium for public debate, as a magazine.
forward *adv* towards the front. * *adj* in advance, ready; bold; pert. * *n* a first-line player. * *vt* to hasten; to advance; to send on .
fossil *adj* petrified and preserved in rocks. * *n* petrified remains of plants and animals; an out-of-date person or thing.
foster *vt* to nourish; to promote; to bring up a child not one's own.
foul *adj* dirty; filthy; stormy; impure; obscene; contrary to rules. * *vt, vi* to defile; to dirty; to strike against. * *n* unfair play.
found *vt* to lay the base of; to establish; to institute; to cast (in a mould). * *vi* to rest on.
foundation *n* an endowment for an institution; such an institution; the base of a house, wall etc; an underlying principle etc.
founder *n* an originator; an endower; a moulder of metals. * *vi, vt* to fill with water and sink; to fall ; to collapse.
foundry *n* a workshop for casting metal.
fount *n* a set of printing type on characters of one style and size; a source.
fountain *n* a spring; an artificial jet; source.
fowl *n* a bird; poultry.
fox *n* a dog-like animal, red-furred and bushy-tailed; a sly person. **vt* to deceive by cunning.
fracas *n* an uproar.
fraction *n* a small part, amount etc; (*math*) a quantity less than a whole, expressed as a decimal or with a numerator and denominator. * *adj* **fractional**. * *adv* **fractionally**.
fractious *adj* snappish; peevish.
fracture *n* a break; breaking of a bone. * *vt* to break.
fragile *adj* easily broken; frail; delicate.
fragment *n* a part broken off. **vt, vi* to break or cause to break into fragments.
fragmentary *adj* disjointed.
fragrance, fragrancy *n* a perfume.
fragrant *adj* sweet-smelling.
frail *adj* easily broken; weak; fragile.
frame *vt* to form according to a pattern; to construct; to put into words; to enclose (a picture) in a border; (*sl*) to falsify evidence against (an innocent person). * *n* something composed of parts fitted together and united; the physical make-up of an animal esp a human body; the case enclosing a window, door etc;

an ornamental border, as round a picture; (*snooker*) a single game. *n* **framer**.

franc *n* a French coin.

franchise *n* the right to vote in public elections; authorization to sell the goods of a manufacturer in a particular area. * *vt* to grant a franchise.

frank *adj* free and direct in expressing oneself; honest, open. * *vt* to mark letters etc with a mark denoting free postage. * *n* a mark indicating free postage. *n* **frankness.**

frankincense *n* incense; perfume.

frantic *adj* mad; distracted; furious; wild.

fraternal *adj* of or belong to a brother or a fraternity; brotherly; friendly.

fraternity *n* brotherly feeling; a society of people with common interests.

fraternize *vi* to associate as brothers.

fratricide *n* murder of a brother.

fraud *n* criminal deception; a deceitful person; an impostor.

fraudulent *adj* dishonest.

fraught *adj* full of; loaded with.

fray *n* an affray; a fight. * *vt, vi* to wear away or become worn.

freak *n* an unusual happening; (*inf*) a person who dresses or acts in a notably unconventional manner. * *adj* **freakish**.

freakish *adj* grotesque.

freckle *n* a brownish spot on the skin.

free *adj* (**freer, freest**) not under the control or power of another; having social and political liberty; independent; able to move in any direction; not exact; generous; frank; with no cost or charge; clear of obstruction. * *adj* without cost; in a free manner. * *vt* (*pt* **freed**) to set free.

freedom *n* liberty; privilege; frankness; undue familiarity.

freehand *adj* drawn by hand.

freehanded *adj* generous.

freehold *n* land with no burdens except taxes.

freelance *n* a person who pursues a profession without long-term commitment to any employer * *vt* to work as a freelance. also **freelancer**.

Freemason *n* a member of the secretive fraternity dedicated to mutual aid.

free trade *n* trade based on the unrestricted international exchange of goods with tariffs used only as a source of revenue. *n* **freetrader**.

freeway *n* in North America, a fast road, a motorway.

freewheel *vi* to ride a bicycle with the gear disconnected; to drive a car with the gear in neutral. * *n* **freewheeler**.

free will *n* freedom of human beings to make choices that are not determined by prior causes or by divine intervention.

freeze *vi, vt* to be formed into, or become covered by ice; to become motionless; to be made speechless by strong emotion; to become formal and unfriendly; to convert from a liquid to a solid with cold.

freezer *n* a container that freezes and preserves food for long periods.

freezing point *n* the temperature at which a liquid solidifies.

freight *n* cargo (ship); load (train); the cost of transport.

freighter *n* a ship or aircraft carrying freight.

French fries, french fries *npl* thin strips of potato fried in oil etc, chips.

French windows, French doors *npl* a pair of floor-length casement windows in an outside wall, opening on to a patio, garden etc.

frenzied *adj* distracted; maddened.

frenzy *n* madness; passion; wild excitement.

frequent *adj* coming, happening often; numerous; common. * *vt* to visit often.

frequency *n* repeated occurrence; the number of occurrences, cycles etc, in a given period.

fresco *n* a painting on plaster while wet or fresh.

fresh *adj* new; brisk; unfaded; not salt; not stale; pure; cool.

freshen *vt* to make fresh. * *vi* to grow fresh.

freshman *n* a novice; newcomer; a student in the first year at a university etc.

fret *vt* to eat into; to vex. * *vi* to be vexed. * *n* irritation; peevishness; one of a series of ridges along the fingerboard of a guitar, banjo etc. used as a guide for depressing the strings.

fretful *adj* peevish; petulant.

fretwork *n* ornamental and perforated woodwork.

friable *adj* easily crumbled.

friar *n* a member of certain RC religious orders.

fricassé *n* a dish of white meat highly seasoned.

friction *n* a rubbing together; resistance offered to moving bodies; unpleasantness; conflict between differing opinions, ideas etc.

Friday *n* the sixth day of the week.

fridge *n* a refrigerator.

friend *n* a close companion; one warmly attached to another; a Quaker.

friendly *adj* kind; well-disposed; favourable. * *n* a sporting game played for fun, not in a competition.

friendship *n* mutual attachment.

frieze *n* a decorative band round the upper part of room walls.

frigate *n* a warship smaller than a destroyer used for escort, anti-submarine, and patrol duties.

fright *n* sudden fear; a shock; something unsightly or ridiculous in appearance.

frighten *vt* to strike with fear; to terrify.

frightful *adj* dreadful; fearful; very bad.

frigid *adj* cold; stiff; formal.

frill *n* a ruffle; a fringe; an affectation.

fringe *n* a decorative border of hanging threads; an outer edge; a marginal or minor part. * *vt* to be or make a fringe fore. * *adj* at the outer edge; additional; minor; unconventional.

frisk *vi* to dance, skip, gambol. * *vt* to search (a person) by feeling or looking for concealed weapons etc.

frisky *adj* jumping with gaiety; lively.

fritter *n* fried batter with fruit; a pancake. * *vt* to trifle away; to waste.

frivolity *n* levity; trifling act, thought or action.

frivolous *adj* trivial; trifling; irresponsible.

frizzle *vi* to curl; to grill with hissing noise.

fro *adv* from; back; backward.

frock *n* an outer garment; dress.

frogman *n* a person who wears a rubber suit, flippers, oxygen supply etc and is trained in working underwater.

frolic *adj* joyous; frisky. * *n* a lively party or game; merriment; a merry prank. * *vi* to gambol.

frolicsome *adj* given to pranks.

from *prep* beginning at, starting with; out of; originating with; out of the possibility or use of.

frond *n* the leaf of a fern.

front *n* a outward behaviour; (*inf*) an appearance of social standing etc; the part facing forward; the first part; the promenade of a seaside resort; the advanced battle area in warfare; a person or group used to hid another's activity

frontage *n* the front of a building.

frontal *adj* of or belonging to the front; of the forehead. * *n* a decorative covering for the front of an altar.

frontier *n* the border between two countries; the limit of existing knowledge of a subject.

frontispiece *n* picture facing the title page of a book.

frost *n* a temperature at or below freezing point; a coating of powdery ice particles; coldness of manner. * *vt* to cover (as if) with frost or frosting; to give a frost-like opaque surface to (glass).

frostbite *n* injury or deadening of sensation to a part of the body by excessive cold.

froth *n* foam; bubbles; empty talk; frivolity.

frown *vi* to scowl; to concentrate or look displeased by contracting the brow. * *n* a stern look.

frozen *see* **freeze**.

frugal *adj* careful; thrifty; meagre.

frugality *n* thrift.

fruit *n* the produce of plants; offspring; the outcome or result of any action.

fruitful *adj* producing much fruit; very productive.

fruition *n* fulfilment; realization.

frump *n* a dowdy woman.

frustrate *vt* to balk; to foil; to prevent from achieving a goal or gratifying a desire.

frustration *n* disappointment.

fry *vt* to cook over direct heat in hot fat * *n* young fish.

fuddle *vt* to stupefy with drink.

fudge *n* a soft sweet made of butter, milk, sugar, flavouring etc. * *vt, vi* to fake; to fail to come to grips with; to refuse to commit oneself; to cheat.

fuel *n* material burned to supply heat and power, or as a source of nuclear energy; anything that serves to intensify strong feelings. * *vt, vi* (*pt* **fuelled**) to supply with fuel.

fugitive *adj* fleeting; transient. * *n* a runaway; a refugee.

fugue *n* a piece of music in which the theme is taken up by the parts in succession.

fulcrum *n* (*pl* **fulcra, fulcrums**) the point of support of a lever.

fulfil *vt* to carry into effect; to carry out a promise; to satisfy; to bring to an end; complete.

fulfilment *n* accomplishment.

full *adj* having or holding all that can be contained; having eaten all one wants; having a great number (of); complete; having reached to greatness size, extent etc. **adj* completely, directly, exactly.

full-blown *adj* fully developed or expanded.

full stop *n* the punctuation mark (.) at the end of a sentence.

full time *n* the finish of a match.

full-time *adj* working or lasting the whole time.

fulminate *vi, vt* to thunder; to explode.

fulsome *adj* insincere; excessively, flattering.

fumble *vi* to grope; to handle clumsily.

fume *n* (often *pl*) smoke; vapour; rage. * *vi* to emit smoke; to rage.

fumigate *vt* to purify, disinfect by fumes.

fun *n* merriment; sport; amusement.

function *n* office; duty; work; occupation; an official ceremony or social entertainment. * *vi* to perform work; to act; to operate.

functional *adj* of a function or functions; practical, not ornamental.

fund *n* a stock; money set apart for a special object; a supply. * (*pl*) ready money. * *vt* to provide money for; to invest.

fundamental *adj* basic; essential. * *n* an essential part.

funeral *n* the ceremony associated with the burial or cremation of the dead; a procession accompanying a coffin to a burial.

funereal *adj* dark; dismal.

fungus *n* (*pl* **fungi, funguses**) any of a major group of lower plants, as mildews, mushrooms, yeasts etc, that lack chlorophyll and reproduce by spores.

funicular *adj* made of ropes. * *n* a cable railway.

funnel *n* a utensil for conveying liquids into bottles; an air or smoke shaft; a metal chimney for the escape of smoke, steam etc. * *vt, vi* to (cause to) pour through a funnel.

funny *adj* droll; comical; puzzling; unwell.

fur *n* the short soft hair of certain animals; a coating.

furious *adj* full of rage; violent.

furl *vt* to roll up a sail.

furlong *n* the eighth of a mile.

furlough *n* leave of absence esp. for military personnel.

furnace *n* a fire chamber where powerful heat can be raised.

furnish *vt* to provide a room with furniture; to supply; to equip.

furnishing *n pl* furniture, carpets etc.

furniture *n* household effects.

furore *n* excitement; stir.

furrow *n* a trench made by a plough; a wrinkle. * *vt* to groove; to wrinkle.

further *adv* besides; farther; in addition. * *adj* more distant; additional. * *vt* to advance; to promote.

furthermore *adv* moreover; besides.

furthermost *adj* most remote.

furthest *adj, adv* farthest.

furtive *adj* sly; stealthy.

fury *n* rage; frenzy.

fuse *n* a tube or wick filled with combustible material for setting off an explosive charge; a piece of thin wire that melts and breaks when an electric current exceeds a certain level. * *vt* to join or become joined by melting.

fuselage *n* the body of an aircraft.
fusilade *n* a general discharg of rifles.
fusion *n* act of melting; a blending; union; partnership; nuclear fusion.
fuss *n* excited activity; bustle; anxious state. * *vt* to worry over.
fusty *n* musty; mildewed.
futile *adj* serving no useful end; ineffective.
futility *n* uselessness.
future *adj* forthcoming. * *n* time to come; future events; likelihood of eventual success.
futuristic *adj* forward-looking in design, appearance, intention etc.
fuzz *n* fluff.
fuzzy *adj* like fuzz; fluffy; blurred.

G

gab *vi* to chatter. * *n* idle talk.
gabble *vt, vi* to talk or utter rapidly or incoherently; to utter inarticulate or animal sounds. * *n* **gabbler**.
gable *n* the top of end wall of a house.
gadfly *n* a cattle-biting fly.
gadget *n* a small, often ingenious, mechanical or electronic tool or device.
gag *vt* to stop the mouth; to silence. **vi* to retch; to tell jokes * *n* something thrust into mouth, any restraint.
gaiety *n* mirth; high spirits, liveliness.
gain *vti* to obtain, earn, esp by effort; to win in a contest; to attract; to get as an addition (esp profit or advantage); to make an increase in; to reach. * *vi* to make progress, to increase in weight. * *n* an increase esp in profit or advantage; an acquisition.
gainful *adj* profitable. * *adv* **gainfully**.
gainsay *vt* to contradict; to deny; to dispute.
gait *n* a manner of walking.
gala *n* a celebration; a festival; a festive season.
galaxy *n* any of the systems of stars in the universe; any splendid assemblage; the Milky Way.
gale *n* a strong wind; an outburst.
gall *n* bile; rancour; spite; nut-like growth on oaks. * *vt* to fret; annoy intensely.
gallant *adj* brave; courteous; dignified.
gallantry *n* bravery; courtesy.
gall bladder *n* a membranous sac attached to the liver in which bile is stored.
galleon *n* a Spanish warship.
gallery *n* a long, usu low, ship of ancient or medieval times, propelled by oars; the kitchen of a sip, aircraft; (print) a shallow tray for holding type; proofs printed from such type. Also **galley proof**.
galley *n* a long, low vessel with sails and oars; a shallow tray for type; a proof sheet printed from such type; a ship's kitchen.
galling *adj* bitter; provoking.
gallon *n* measure holding 2,77.42 cubic inches.
gallop *vi* to go at full speed. * *n* a horse's fastest pace.
gallows *n sing* (*pl* **gallows**) a wooden frame for hanging criminals.
gallstone *n* a small solid mass in the gall bladder.
galore *n* abundance; plenty.
galvanize *vt* to electrify; to electroplate; to stimulate into action.
galvanometer *n* an instrument for measuring electric force.
gambit *n* any action to gain an advantage.
gamble *vi* to play games of chance for money.
gambol *vi* to skip; to frisk. * *n* a frolic.
game *n* sport of any kind; a contest; a scheme; animals and birds hunted for sport or food. * *adj* brave; plucky; willing.
gamekeeper *n* a person who breeds and takes car of game birds and animals, as on an estate.
gaming *n* gambling.
gammon *n* a lower part of cured or smoked ham; flitch of bacon; nonsense.
gamut *n* the musical scale; the entire range of emotions etc.
gang *n*.a group of persons, esp labourers, working together; a group of person acting or associating together, esp for illegal purposes. * *vt, vi* to form into or act as a gang.

ganglion *n* an enlargement in the course of a nerve; any centre of activity or energy.

gangrene *n* death of body tissue when the blood supply is obstructed.

gangster *n* a member of a criminal gang.

gangway *n* a passageway, esp an opening in a ship's side for loading etc; a gangplank.

gaol *see* **jail**.

gap *n* an opening; a breach in a wall, fence etc; an interruption in continuity; an interval; a mountain pass; divergence.

gape *vi* to open the mouth wide; to stare wide-eyed and open-mouthed in astonishment; to yawn.

garage *n* an enclosed shelter for motor vehicles; a place where motor vehicles are repaired and services, and fuel sold. * *vt* to put or keep in a garage.

garb *n* dress; clothes.

garbage *n* waste matter; offal; rubbish

garble *vt* to tell a confused or jumbled story; to tell only part of truth.

garden *n* an area of ground for growing herbs, fruits, flowers, or vegetables, usu attached to a house; a public park or recreation area, usu laid-out with plants and trees. * *vi* to make, or work in, a garden. *n* **gardener, gardening.**

gargle *vt, vi* to rinse the throat by breathing air from the lungs through liquid held in the mouth. * *n* a liquid for this purpose; the sound made by gargling.

gargoyle *n* a grotesquely carved face as a gutter spout.

garish *adj* gaudy; showy.

garland *n* a wreath of flowers.

garlic *n* a bulbous strong-smelling herb.

garment *n* any article of clothing.

garner *vt* to store up.

garnet *n* a precious stone.

garnish *vt* to adorn; to decorate (food).

garret *n* an attic.

garrison *n* the soldiers in a fortress. * *vt* to man with troops.

garrotte, garrote *vt* to throttle or strangle.

garrulous *adj* very talkative.

garter *n* an elasticated band to hold up a stocking or sock.

gas *n* (*pl* **gases**) an air-like substance with the capacity to expand indefinitely and not liquefy or solidify at ordinary temperatures; (*inf*) empty talk; gasoline. * *vt* (*pt* **gassed**) to poison or disable with gas; (*inf*) to talk idly.

gash *vt* to slash; to cut. * *n* a deep cut.

gasket *n* a piece or ring of rubber, metal etc sandwiched between metal surfaces to act as a seal.

gasp *vi* to labour for breath; to pant. * *vt* to utter breathlessly.

gastric *adj* belonging to the stomach.

gastronomy *n* the art of good eating.

gate *n* a movable structure controlling passage through an opening in a fence or wall; a device (as in a computer) that outputs a signal when specified input conditions are met. * *vt* to supply with a gate.

gate-crash *vt* to arrive at a party etc. uninvited.

gather *vt, vi* to bring together in one place or group; to collect (as taxes); to harvest; to draw (parts) together; to come together in a body; to cluster around a focus of attention.

gathering *n* an assembly; folds made in a garment by gathering; an abscess.

gauche *adj* socially inept; graceless; tackless.

gaudy *adj* showy; flashy.

gauge *vt* to measure. * *n* a measuring rod; a measure; distance between rails of a railway; calibre.

gaunt *adj* emaciated; lean.

gauze *n* a light transparent cloth; a surgical dressing.

gavotte *n* a sprightly dance.

gay *adj* merry; frolicsome; colourful; homosexual.

gaze *vi* to stare; to contemplate. * *n* a fixed look.

gazette *n* a newspaper, especially an official one.

gazetteer *n* a geographical dictionary.

gazump *vt, vi* to force up a price (esp of a house) after a price has been agreed. *n* **gazumper**.

gear *n* clothing; equipment, esp for some task or activity; a toothed wheel for meshing with another; a specific adjustment of such a system. * *vt* to connect by or furnish with gears; to adapt (one thing) to confirm with another.

gearbox *n* a metal case enclosing a system of gears.

gear lever *n* a lever used to engage or change gear, esp in a motor vehicle.

gelatine *n* a tasteless, odourless substance extracted by boiling bones, hoofs etc and used in food, medicines etc.

gelding *n* a castrated male horse.

gem *n* a precious stone.

gemini *npl* the Twins, a sign of the zodiac.

gender *n* sex, male or female; words, masculine or feminine.

genealogy *n* family descent; lineage.

general *adj* not local, special, or specialized; of or for a whole genus, relating to or covering all instances or individuals of a class or group; widespread, common to many; not specific or precise; holding superior rank, chief.

general election *n* a national election to choose parliamentary representatives in every constituency.

generalize *vt, vi* to form general conclusions from specific instances; to talk (about something) in general terms. * *n* **generalization**.

generally *adv* in general; popularly; usually.

general practitioner *n* a non-specialist doctor who treats all types of illnesses in the community.

generate *vt* to beget; to produce.

generation *n* the act or process of generating; a single succession in natural descent; people of the same period.

generator *n* one who or that which generates; a machine that changes mechanical energy to electrical energy.

generic *adj* pertaining to a genus.

generosity *n* liberality.

generous *adj* noble; bountiful.

genesis *n* origin.

genetic *adj* relating to origin, development or production; of relating to genes.

genial *adj* cordial; cheerful; pleasing; warm.

genitals, genitalia *npl* the external sexual organs.

genius *n* (*pl* **geniuses**) outstanding capacity; disposition; one gifted with extraordinary mental power.

genius *n* (*pl* **genii**) demon; spirit of place.

genre *n* portrayal of scenes from ordinary life; a sort or category of work esp. literary or autistic.

genteel *adj* affectedly refined or polite.

gentility *n* refinement; gentle birth.

gentle *adj* well-born; refined, mild; hot rough or rude.

gentleman *n* a man of good birth; a courteous, honourable man.

gentry *n* well-born people.

genuflection, genuflexion *n* a bending of the knee.

genuine *adj* real; true; sincere.

genus *n* (*pl* **genera**) a kind; race; class containing several species.

geography *n* the science of the physical nature of the earth, such as land and sea masses, climate, vegetation etc, and their interaction with the human population; the physical features of a region. * *n* **geographer, geographic, geographical**.

geology *n* the science relating to the history and the structure of the earth.

geometric, geometrical *adj* pertaining to geometry.

geometry *n* the branch of mathematics dealing with the properties, measurement, and relationships of points, lines, planes and solids.

germ *n* any microscopic, disease-causing organism; an origin or foundation capable of growing and developing.

germane *adj* closely allied; relevant.

germinate *vi* to sprout; to start developing.

gerrymander *vt* to manipulate in one's own or party interests.

gerund *n* a verbal noun.

gestate *vt* to carry (young) in the womb during pregnancy; to develop (a plan, etc) gradually in the mind. * *n* **gestation**.

gesticulate *vi, vt* to make gestures when speaking.

gesture *n* an expressive movement of the body or limbs.
get *vt, vi* to obtain: to gain; to reach; to become; to catch; to persuade; to cause to be; to prepare; to kill; to understand; to come; to go; to arrive; to manage.
geyser *n* a hot-water spring; a water heater.
ghastly *adj* deathlike; hideous.
ghetto *n* (*pl* **ghettos**) a section of a city in which members of a minority group live, esp because of social, legal or economic pressure.
ghost *n* a spirit; an apparition; a faint trace or suggestion. * *vt* to ghost write; to write on behalf of another who then gets the credit.
ghoul *n* a spirit said to prey on corpses.
giant *n* a huge legendary being of great strength; a person or thing of great size, strength, intellect etc. * *adj* incredibly large.
gibberish *n* inarticulate talk; nonsense..
gibe *vt* to taunt; to sneer. * *n* a taunt.
giddy *adj* dizzy; fickle; frivolous; flightly.
gift *n* a present; talent; natural ability. * *vt* to endow; to present.
gifted *adj* talented.
gigantic *adj* huge; colossal; immense.
giggle *n* to snigger.
gild *vt* to cover with gold; to illuminate.
gill, gil *n* the organ of respiration in fishes.
gill *n* a quarter of a pint.
gilt *pp of* **gild** overlaid with gold.
gimlet *n* a boring tool with screw point.
gimmick *n* a trick or device for attracting notice, advertising or promoting a person, product or service. * *n* **gimmickry**.
gin *n* a spirit flavoured with juniper berries; a pile-driving machine; a snare.
ginger *n* a hot spice; vigour; a reddish-brown.
gingerbread *n* a cake flavoured with ginger.
gingerly *adv* cautiously.
gingham *n* a striped or checked cotton cloth.
gipsy *see* **gypsy**
girder *n* a large steel beam for supporting joists, the framework of a building etc.
girdle *n* a belt. * *vt* to encompass.
girl *n* a female child.
girlfriend *n* a female friend, esp with whom one is romantically involved.
girth *n* a saddle strap; the thickness round the waist etc.
gist *n* the essence; the substance of anything.
give *vt* to bestow; to hand over; to deliver; to yield; to utter; to pledge; to act as host.
gizzard *n* the muscular stomach of a bird.
glacial *adj* icy, frozen.
glacier *n* a slowly moving mass of ice on a mountain side.
glad *adj* pleased; cheerful.
gladden *vti* to make or become glad.
glade *n* a clear space in wood.
gladiator *n* a combatant in Roman arenas.
glamour *n* charm; allure; attractiveness; beauty.
glance *vi* to strike obliquely and go off at an angle; to flash; to look quickly.
gland *n* an organ that separates substances from the blood and synthesizes them for further use in, or for elimination from, the body. * *adj* **glandular**.
glare *n* a dazzling light; a fixed , fierce stare. * *vi* to shine brightly; to look fiercely and angrily.
glass *n* a hard brittle substance, usu transparent; glassware; a glass article, as a drinking vessel; (*pl*) spectacles or binoculars.
glasshouse *n* a large greenhouse for the commercial cultivation of plants.
glassware *n* objects made of glass, esp drinking vessels.
glassy *adj* smooth; expressionless, lifeless.
glaucoma *n* an eye disease.
glaze *vt, vi* to provide (windows etc) with glass; to give a hard glossy finish to (pottery etc); to cover (foods, etc) with a glossy surface.
glazier *n* one whose business is to set window glass.
gleam *n* a ray. * *vi* to flash.
glean *vt, vi* to gather (after reapers); to pick up.
glee *n* joy and gaiety; a song in parts for three or more male voices.
glen *n* a narrow valley.
glib *adj* speaking or spoken smoothly, to

the point of insincerity.

glide *vt,vi* to move smoothly and effortlessly; to descend in an aircraft or glider with little or no engine power.

glider *n* an engineless aircraft carried along by air currents.

glimmer *vi* to give a faint, flickering light; to appear faintly.

glimpse *n a b*rief, momentary view. * *vt* to catch a glimpse of.

glint *n* a brief flash of light; a brief indication. * *vt, vi* to (cause to) gleam brightly.

glisten *vi* to shine, as light reflected from a wet surface.

glitter *vi* to sparkle; (*usu with* **with**) to be brilliantly attractive. * *n* a sparkle; showiness, glamour; tiny pieces of sparkling material used for decoration.

gloaming *n* twilight.

gloat *vi* to feast one's eyes on with evil feelings of satisfaction.

globe *n* a sphere; a planet; a star; the earth.

globule *n* a small globe-like particle; a droplet of liquid.

gloom *n* darkness; deep sadness.

gloomy *adj* dark; dismal; depressed.

glorify *vt* to extol; to magnify the worth or importance.

glory *n* praise; honour; renown; splendour. * *vi* to rejoice; to exult.

gloss *n* the lustre of a polished surface; a superficially attractive appearance. * *vt* to give a shiny surface; (*with* **over**) to hide (an error etc) or make seem right or inconsequential.

glossary *n* a list of specialized or technical words and their definitions.

glossy *adj* smooth and shining; highly polished; superficial; lavishly produced (of magazines).

glove *n* a cover for the hand.

glow *vi* to shine (as if) with an intense heat; to emit a steady light without flames; to be full of life and enthusiasm. * *n* a light emitted due to intense heat; a steady, even light without flames.

glower *vi* to scowl; to stare sullenly or angrily.

glowworm *n* a beetle that units a greenish luminous light.

glucose *n* a crystalline sugar occurring naturally in fruits, honey etc.

glue *n* a sticky substance used as an adhesive. * *vt* to join with glue.

glum *adj* sullen; moody.

glut *vt* to over supply (the market); to stuff; to gorge. * *n* over abundance.

glutinous *adj* gluey; viscous.

glutton *n* a voracious eater; a person with a great capacity for e.g. work.

gluttony *n* excess in eating.

glycerine *n* a colourless sweet liquid obtained from fats.

gnarl *n* a knot in wood.

gnarled *adj* full of knots; rough and weather-beaten (of hands).

gnash *vt* to grind (the teeth).

gnat *n* a biting insect.

gnaw *vt, vi* to nibble; to bite away bit by bit; to torment as by pain or guilt.

gnome *n* a sprite; a dwarf dwelling in the earth.

go *vi, vt* to move on a course; to proceed; to work properly; to act, sound, as specified; to result; to become; to be accepted or valid; to leave, to depart; to die; to be allotted or sold; to be able to pass (through); to fit (into); to be capable of being divided (into); to undertake (duties etc); to fall asleep; to take place as planned.

goad *n* a spiked stick to prick cattle; a spur; a stimulus to action.

goal *n* the winning post; an objective; an aim.

gobble *vt* to gulp; to bolt; to read eagerly.

go-between *n* a messenger, an intermediary.

goblet *n* a drinking cup without handle; a saucepan.

goblin *n* a mischievous or evil sprite.

god *n* any of various beings conceived of as supernatural and immortal, esp a male deity; an idol; a person or thing deified. (*with cap*) in monotheistic religions, the creator and ruler of the universe.

goddess *n* a female deity.

godfather *n* a male sponsor for a child at baptism. (Also **godmother, -son, -daughter**.)

god-forsaken *adj* desolate, wretched.

godliness *n* piety.
godsend *n* anything that comes unexpectedly when needed or desired.
goggle *vi* to roll the eyes; to stare with bulging eyes. * *adj* bulging. * *npl* large spectacles.
gold *n* a precious yellow metal; coins; jewellery made of this, money; wealth.
golden *adj* made of or relating to fold; bright yellow; priceless; flourishing.
gold leaf *n* gold beaten out thin.
goldsmith *n* a worker in gold.
golf *n* an outdoor game in which the player attempts to hit a small ball with clubs around a turfed course into a succession of holes in the smallest number of strokes.
golf course, links *n* a tract of land laid out for playing golf.
gondola *n* a long narrow, black boat used on the canals of Venice; an enclosed car suspended from a cable used to transport passengers, esp skiers up a mountain.
gondolier *n* a person who rows a gondola.
gong *n* a disk-shaped percussion instrument struck with a usu padded hammer; (*sl*) a medal.
good *adj* having the right or proper qualities; valid; healthy or sound; virtuous, honourable; enjoyable, pleasant etc. * *n* something good; benefit; something that has economic utility.
goodness *n* quality of being good.
good sense *n* sound judgment.
good-tempered *adj* good-natured.
goodwill *n* benevolence; the established custom and reputation of a business.
gore *n* (clotted) blood; a gusset in material to shape a garment. * *vt* to wound with tusk or horn.
gorge *n* the throat; a very narrow pass. * *vt* to eat greedily and overmuch.
gorgeous *adj* splendid; strikingly attractive; brightly coloured.
gory *adj* bloody.
gospel *n* one who chatters idly about others; such talk. * *vi* to take part in or spread gossip.
gossamer *n* cobweb-like threads in the air or on bushes; any very flimsy material.
gossip *n* a tattler; idle talk about others. * *vt* to tattle.
Gothic *adj* in the pointed-arch style of architecture of the Middle Ages; dark, supernatural, grotesque of a certain style of literature.
gouge *n* a chisel with a grooved blade. * *vt* to scoop out.
gourd *n* a general name for melon-like plants; a drinking vessel.
gourmand *n* a glutton.
gourmet *n* a fastidious eater.
gout *n* a disease affecting joints, esp. the big toe.
govern *vt* to rule; to regulate; to influence the action of.
government *n* the exercise of authority over a state, organization etc; a system of ruling, political administration etc; those who direct the affairs of a state etc.
governor *n* a person appointed to govern a province etc; the elected head of any state of the US.
gown *n* a loose outer garment, specifically a woman's formal dress, a nightgown, a long, flowing robe worn by clergymen, judges, university teachers etc; a type of overall worn int he operating room.
grab *vt* to seize; to snatch; to catch the interest or attention.
grace *n* favour; kindness; divine influence; mercy; a title; beauty of form or movement; ease of manner; short prayer before meals. * *vt* to adorn; to dignify.
graceful *adj* elegant.
gracious *adj* having or showing kindness, courtesy etc; compassionate; polite to supposed inferiors.
gradation *n* arrangement step by step.
grade *n* a stage or step in a progression; a group of people of the same rank, merit etc; the degree of slope; a sloping part; a mark or rating in an examination.
gradient *n* degree of ascent or descent, in a road; a sloping road or railway.
gradual *adj* slow and regular.
graduate *vt, vi* to mark off into degrees; to receive a university degree. * *n* a recipient of a degree.
graduation *n* act of marking with degrees;

the conferring or receiving of university degrees.

graft *n* a shoot inserted in another plant; the transplanting of skin, bone etc. * *vt* to insert such a shoot; to join organically.

grain *n* the seed of any cereal plant, as wheat, corn etc; cereal plants; a tiny, solid particle, as of salt or sand; the arrangement of fibres, layers etc of wood, leather etc.

grammar *n* the study of the correct use of language; the rules for speaking and writing a language; a grammar textbook.

gramme *n* the French unit of weight.

gramophone *n* an instrument that recorded and reproduced sounds; forerunner of the record player.

granary *n* a storehouse for grain.

grand *adj* noble; magnificent; imposing; important; illustrious; comprehensive.

grandeur *n* greatness; splendour.

grandfather *n* a father's or mother's father.

grandiloquence *n* pompous language.

grandiose *adj* imposing; bombastic.

grandmother *n* a mother's or father's mother.

grand piano *n* a large piano with a horizontal harp-shaped case.

granite *n* a hard igneous rock; firmness and endurance.

grant *vt* to bestow; to confer on; to admit as true; to cede. * *n* a gift; money or a gift granted for a particular purpose; a conveyance in writing.

granular *adj* consisting of grains.

granulate *vti* to form into grains.

granule *n* a little grain.

grape *n* the juicy purple or green berry fruit of the vine growing in clusters.

graph *n* a diagram representing successive changes int he value of a variable quantity of quantities.

graphic, graphical *adj* described in realistic detail; pertaining to a graph, lettering, drawing, painting etc.

grapple *vt, vi* to seize; to wrestle.

grasp *vt, vi* to grip; to lay hold of; to understand. * *n* a grip; reach; comprehension.

grasping *adj* avaricious; greedy.

grass *n* any of a large family of plants with jointed stems and long narrow leaves including cereals, bamboo etc; such plants grown as lawn; pasture.

grate *n* a frame of metal bars for holding fuel in a fireplace; a grating * *vt* to grind into particles by scraping; to rub against (an object) or grind (the teeth) together with a harsh sound; to irritate.

grateful *adj* pleasing; gratifying; appreciative.

grater *n* a grinding-down utensil.

gratification *n* pleasure; enjoyment.

gratify *vt* to please; delight; to indulge.

grating *n* a frame of bars. * *adj* harsh; irritating.

gratis *adv* without charge.

gratitude *n* thankfulness for favours, gifts received.

gratuitous *adj* free of charge; unjustified.

gratuity *n* a free gift; a tip.

grave *vt* to engrave; to impress deeply. * *n* a tomb. * *adj* weighty; serious; solemn; sombre.

gravel *n* small pebble; a disease of the kidneys.

gravitate *vt, vi* to tend towards the centre.

gravity *n* the force drawing bodies towards the centre of the earth; seriousness.

gravy *n* meat juice.

graze *vti* to rub lightly; to scrape (the skin) slightly; to scratch; to eat grass; to supply grass.

grease *n* fat in a soft state. * *vt* to smear with grease; to lubricate.

great *adj* large; eminent; noble; chief; intense; excellent; skilful.

greatness *n* eminence; grandeur.

greed *n* avarice; excessive hunger or desire for food, money etc.

greedy *adj* ravenous; grasping; voracious.

green *adj* grass-coloured; fresh; not ripe; in experienced; naive; environmentally conscious; jealous. * *n* a grassy plot; the colour of grass; a mixture of blue and yellow.

greengrocer *n* a dealer in vegetables and fruit.

greenhouse *n* a glass house for rearing plants.

greenroom *n* a theatre retiring room.
greet *vt* to salute; to welcome; to address in a friendly way.
gregarious *adj* living in flocks; sociable; fond of company.
grenade *n* a small bomb thrown manually or projected (as by a rifle or special launcher).
grey *n* a neutral colour between black and white; something, esp. an animal of a grey colour. * *adj* of a grey colour; grey-haired; dreary; vague; indeterminate.
grid *n* a gridiron, a grating; an electrode for controlling the flow of electrons in an electron tube; a network of squares on a map used for easy reference; a national network of transmission lines, pipes etc for electricity, water, gas etc.
griddle *n* a flat iron plate for baking scones etc.
grief *n* sorrow; deep distress.
grievance *n* injustice; hardship; a cause for complaint.
grieve *vti* to deplore; to mourn.
grievous *adj* heavy; distressing.
grill *vt* to cook by direct heat using a grill or gridiron (*inf*) to question relentlessly. * *n* a device on a cooker that radiates heat downward for grilling; a gridiron; grilled food; a grille; a grillroom.
grille,grill *n* an open grate forming a screen.
grillroom *n* a restaurant that specializes in grilled food.
grim *adj* stern; unyielding; forbidding.
grimace *n* a contortion of the face.
grime *n* soot, dirt. * *vt* to dirty; to soil or befoul.
grimy *adj* foul; dirty.
grin *vi* to laugh through the teeth. * *n* a broad, friendly smile.
grind *vb* (*pt* **ground**) *vt* to reduce to powder or fragments by crushing; to wear down, sharpen, or smooth by friction.
grip *n* a grasp; a handle. * *vti* to grasp, clutch.
gripe *vt, vi* to grasp; to pinch; to complain. * *n* a clutch.
grisly *adj* dreadful; terrifying.
gristle *n* cartilage esp. in meat.
grit *n* coarse particles of sand; stubborn or resolute courage or firmness. * *vt* to clench or grind the teeth; to spread grit esp. on icy roads.
grizzled *adj* greyish.
groan *vi* to moan. * *n* a deep moan.
grocer *n* a merchant who deals in food and household supplies.
grog *n* a mixture of spirits and cold water.
groggy *adj* dazed and unsteady.
groin *n* the junction of the trunk and thighs in front.
groom *n* one who tends horses; a bridegroom. * *vt* to clean and care for animals; to make heat and tidy; to train someone for a specific purpose.
groove *n* a long hollow; a rut, a spiral track in a gramophone record for the stylus; a settle routine. * *vt* to furrow or to make a groove in.
grope *vi* to search about blindly as in the dark; to search uncertainly for a solution to a problem. * *vt* to find by feeling; (*sl*) to fondle sexually.
gross *adj* thick; coarse; obscene; shameful; whole. * *n* twelve dozen; the whole; the total without deduction.
grotesque *adj* distorted or fantastic in appearance, shape etc; absurdly incongruous.
grotto *n* a picturesque cave.
ground *n* the solid surface of the earth; soil; the connection of an electrical conductor with the earth.
grounding *n* basic general knowledge of a subject.
groundwork *n* basis; foundation.
group *n* a number of persons or things considered as a collective unit; two or more figures forming one artistic design.
grouse *n* a gamebird. * *vt* to complain.
grout *n* coarse meal; mortar.
grove *n* a small wood.
grovel *vi* to crawl; to prostrate or abase oneself.
groveller *n* an abject wretch.
grow *vi* to increase; to make progress; to become; to develop; to accrue. * *vt* to produce; to raise; to cultivate.
growl *vi* to snarl; to make a rumbling noise as an angry animal. * *vt* to speak in a growling voice. * *n* a growling sound; a grumble.

grown-up *adj* adult.

growth *n* the act or process of growing; progressive increase, development; something that grows or has grown; an abnormal formation of tissue, as a tumour.

grub *vi, vt* to dig; to root out; to work hard. * *n* the larva of an insect.

grubby *adj* dirty, soiled.

grudge *vi, vt* to envy; to give unwillingly. * *n* ill-will; envy; resentment.

gruel *n* food made by boiling meal in water.

gruelling *adj* severely testing; exhausting.

gruesome *adj* repulsive; causing horror.

gruff *adj* surly; harsh; hoarse.

grumble *vi* to mutter with discontent.

grumpy *adj* surly; gruff; bad-tempered.

grunt *vi* to make a noise like a hog.

guarantee *n* a pledge or security for another's debt or obligation; a pledge to replace something substandard etc; an assurance that something will be done as specified.

guarantor *n* a person who gives a guaranty or guarantee.

guard *vti* to watch over; to defend. * *n* defence; protector; sentinel; attention.

guarded *adj* circumspect; discreet.

guardian *n* a custodian; a person legally in charge of a minor or someone incapable of taking care of their own affairs.

guerrilla *n* a member of a force of irregular soldiers, usually biased politically, in conflict with regulars on police etc.

guess *vt* to form an opinion of or state with little or no factual knowledge; to judge correctly by doing this; to think or suppose. * *n* an estimate based on guessing.

guest *n* a person entertained at the home, club etc of another; any paying customer of a hotel, restaurant; a performer appearing by special invitation.

guesthouse *n* a private home or boardinghouse offering accommodation.

guide *vt* to point out the way for; to lead; to direct the course of; to control. * *n* a person who leads or directs others.

guidebook *n* a book containing directions and information for tourists.

guided missile *n* a military missile whose course is controlled by radar or internal instruments etc.

guide dog *n* a dog trained to guide people who are blind.

guild, gild *n* a society for mutual aid.

guile *n* wiliness; deceit.

guillotine *n* an instrument for beheading persons; a machine for cutting paper.

guilt *n* the fact of having done a wrong or committed an offence; a feeling of self-reproach from believing one has done a wrong.

guilty *adj* criminal; wicked; feeling guilt.

guinea pig *n* a person or thing subject to an experiment.

guise *n* an external appearance, aspect; an assumed appearance, pretence.

guitar *n* a musical instrument having six strings and is plucked with the fingers.

gulf *n* an arm of the sea; a bay; a chasm.

gull *n* a long-winged sea bird.

gullet *n* the throat; the food passage from the mouth.

gully *n* watercourse cut out by heavy rain.

gulp *vt* to swallow eagerly. * *n* a mouthful.

gum *n* the firm tissue surrounding the teeth; the sticky substance found in some trees.

gumption *n* shrewd good sense.

gun *n* a weapon with a metal tube from which a projectile is discharged by an explosive.

gunman *n* an armed gangster; a hired killer.

gunmetal *n* an alloy of copper and tin formerly used for cannon.

gunner *n* a soldier etc, who helps fire artillery; a naval warrant officer in charge of a ship's gun.

gunpowder *n* an explosive mixture used for blasting etc.

gunwale, gunnel *n* the upper edge of a ship's side.

gurgle *vi* to flow with a bubbling sound; to utter this sound.

gush *vi* to rush out; to be effusively sentimental in speech or writing.

gushing *adj* rushing forth; effusive.

gusset *n* a triangular piece of cloth inserted

in a garment to strengthen or widen.
gust *n* a sudden blast fo wind; an outburst.
gut *n* the intestine; (*pl*) entrails.; courage; daring * *vt* to remove entrails.
gutter *n* a water channel below eaves or at the roadside. * (candle) to melt unevenly.
gutter press *n* news-papers that concentrate on the sensational in their coverage.
guttural *adj* throaty. * *n* a throat sound, as g.
guy *n* a rope to steady anything; an effigy of Guy Fawkes; a man or boy.
guzzle *vi, vt* to swallow greedily.
gymnasium *n* (*pl* **gymnasia, gymnasiums**) a place for athletic exercises.
gymnast *n* a gymnastic expert.
gymnastics *npl* athletic exercises; training in these.
gynaecology *n* the branch of medicine dealing with disorders of the female reproductive system.
gypsy *n* (*with cap*) a member of a travelling people, orig from India.
gyrate *vi* to rotate, to whirl.
gyration *n* a whirling round.
gyroscope, gyrostat *n* an apparatus for illustrating laws of rotation.

H

haberdasher *n* a draper.
habit *n* usage; custom; a distinctive costume or dress.
habitable *adj* that may be inhabited.
habitat *n* the natural abode.
habitation *n* abode; residence.
habitual *adj* customary; usual.
habituate *vt* to accustom; to inure.
habitué *n* a regular frequenter.
hack *n* a hired horse; a worn-out horse; a mediocre writer; a coach for hire. * *vt* to gash; to kick; to ride a horse cross-country. * *adj* banal; hackneyed.
hackneyed *adj* much used; trite.
haemorrhage *n* the escape of blood from a blood vessel; heavy bleeding. * *vi* to bleed heavily.
haemorrhoids *npl* piles.
haft *n* the handle of an axe etc.
hag *n* an ugly old woman.
haggard *adj* wild-looking; gaunt.
haggis *n* a dish of heart, liver, etc, of sheep minced and boiled in the stomach sac.
haggle *vt* to drive a hard bargain; to barter.
hail *n* frozen rain; a call. * *vi, vt* to rain hail; to call to; to greet or welcome with approval; to acclaim; to originate from.
hair *n* a thread-like covering on the skin of mammals; a mass of hair growing on the human head etc.
hairdresser *n* a person who cuts, styles, colours, etc hair.
hairpiece *n* an additional piece of hair attached to a person's real hair.
hairpin bend *n* a sharply curving bend in a road etc.
hair-raising *adj* terrifying, shocking.
hair's-breadth *n* a minute distance.
hairsplitting *n* making fine distinctions.
hairstyle *n* an arrangement of the hair in a certain way.
hairy *adj* covered in hair; difficult; dangerous.
halcyon *adj* calm; peaceful.
hale *adj* sound; robust. * *vt* to drag by force.
half *n* (*pl* **halves**) one of two equal parts.
half-brother *n* a brother by one parent only.
half-caste *n* one born of parents of different races.
half-hearted *adj* lukewarm.
half-sister *n* a sister by one parent only.
hall *n* a large public room; the entrance passage of house.
hallmark *n* a mark used on gold, silver or platinum articles to signify a standard of purity; a characteristic feature. * *vt* to stamp with a hallmark.
hallucination *n* the apparent perception of sights, sounds etc that are not actually present; something perceived in this manner.
halo *n* circle of light round sun or moon; a symbolic disc round the head of a saint.
halt *vi, vt* to hesitate; to stop; to cease marching. * *n* a limp; stoppage on a

march; a minor station on a railway line.

halter *n* a rope or headgear for a horse.

halve *vt* to divide into two equal parts.

halyard *n* a line for handling sails.

ham *n* the thigh of a pig salted and dried; an actor who overacts; a licensed amateur radio operator.

hamburger *n* ground beef; a cooked patty of such meat, often in a bread roll.

hamlet *n* a small village.

hammer *n* a tool for driving nails, etc. * *vt,v i* to beat or forge; to defeat utterly.

hammock *n* a swinging bed of cloth or netting suspended by the ends.

hamper *n* a large basket. * *vt* to hinder; to interfere; to encumber.

hand *n* the part of the arm below the wrist, used for grasping; a side or direction; control; applause; help; a hired worker; a pointer on a clock; the breadth of a hand, four inches when measuring the height of a horse.

handbook *n* a textbook; a manual.

handcuff *n* a fetter; a manacle.

handful *n* as much as the hand will hold; a small quantity or number; a person difficult to control.

handicap *n* an allowance in sporting contests to make the chances more equal for the competitors; a mental or physical impairment.

handicraft *n* manual skill.

handiwork *n* product of one's own labour.

handkerchief *n* a cloth for blowing the nose.

handle *vt* to feel, use, or hold with the hand; to deal with; to manage; to buy and sell goods. * *n* the part of anything designed to be held by the hand.

handsome *adj* good-looking; dignified; genius.

handwriting *n* manner of writing.

handy *adj* expert; convenient; ready; near.

hang *vt, vi* to suspend; to attach by hinges to allow to swing freely; to execute.

hangar *n* a shelter for aircraft.

hanger *n* a device on which something is hung, e.g. clothes.

hanger-on *n* a dependent; a parasite.

hangman *n* a public executioner.

hangover *n* the unpleasant after-effects of excessive consumption of alcohol.

hang-up *n* an emotional preoccupation with something.

hanker *vi* to desire longingly.

haphazard *adj* chance; random.

hapless *adj* unlucky; unhappy.

happen *vi* to take place; to occur.

happy *adj* pleased; lucky; joyous.

harangue *n* a speech; a tirade.

harass *vt* to plague; to vex; to imitate.

harbour *n* a shelter; a haven; an inlet for anchoring ships. * *vt* to shelter; to nurse in the mind secretly.

hard *adj* firm; solid; difficult to understand, accomplish, bear; painful; unfeeling; harsh; grasping; alcoholic (of drink). * *adv* fast; with difficulty; earnestly.

hardboard *n* a stiff board made of compressed wood chips.

hard cash *n* payment in coins and notes as opposed to cheque etc.

harden *vt, vi* to make hard; to inure; to be unfeeling.

hardhearted *adj* pitiless.

hardly *adv* scarcely; barely; with difficulty; not to be expected.

hard sell *n* an aggressive selling technique.

hardship *n* privation; injustice.

hardware *n* common metal articles, e.g. tools etc; the mechanical and electronic components that make up a computer system.

hardy *adj* bold; intrepid; able to withstand exposure or emotional hardship.

harebrained *adj* giddy; heedless.

harelip *n* a deformity of the upper lip in the form of a vertical fissure.

hark *vi* to listen.

harlequin *n* a well-known comic pantomime figure; a comic; a buffoon.

harlot *n* a prostitute.

harm *n* hurt; damage; evil. * *vt* to injure.

harmful *adj* hurtful.

harmless *adj* not likely to cause harm.

harmonic, harmonical *adj* pertaining to harmony; musical. * *n* a secondary tone.

harmonica *n* a small wind instrument.

harmonious *adj* melodious; friendly.

harmonize *vi, vt* to be in, or bring into, or sing in harmony.

harmony *n* musical concord; accord; agreement in action, ideas etc.
harness *n* device by which a horse is fastened to a vehicle, plough etc. * *vt* to put a harness on; to control so as to use the power of.
harp *n* a stringed musical instrument.
harpoon *n* a barbed whaling spear.
harpsichord *n* a stringed instrument with keyboard resembling a grand piano.
harridan *n* a bad-tempered hag; a nag.
harrow *n* a large rake for breaking ploughed ground * *vt* to draw a harrow over; to cause mental distress to.
harrowing *adj* distressing.
harry *vt* to harass; to worry; pillage; to plunder.
harsh *adj* grating; rough; jarring on the senses or feeling; rigourous,cruel.
harvest *n* the reaping season; the crop reaped; the fruit of labour.
hash *vt* to chop; to mince. * *n* a dish of minced meat.
hashish *n* resin derived from the leaves and shoots of the hemp plant, smoked or chewed as an intoxicant.
hasp *n* a clasp for a staple.
hassock *n* a footstool.
haste *n* speed; hurry. * *vt* to hurry.
hasten *vt, vi* to haste; to accelerate.
hasty *adj* speedy; rash; precipitate.
hat *n* a head covering.
hatch *vt* to produce (young) from eggs; to contrive; to devise. * *n* a brood; a trap door; a door or opening on an aircraft.
hatchback *n* a sloping rear end on a car with a door; a car of this design.
hatchet *n* a small axe.
hatchway *n* an opening in a ship's deck.
hate *vt* to detest; to abhor. * *n* great dislike; the person or thing hated.
hateful *adj* odious.
hatred *n* great dislike.
haughty *adj* proud and disdainful; arrogant.
haul *vt* to pull; to drag. * *n* a catch (of fish, etc); the distance over which something is transported.
haulage *n* the transport of commodities; the charge for hauling.
haunch *n* the hip; the thigh.
haunt *vt* to frequent; to recur repeatedly to; to appear habitually as a ghost. * *n* a resort; a place often visited.
haunted *adj* visited by apparitions.
have *vt* (*pres t* **has**, *pr p* **having**, *pt* **had**) to have in one's possession; to possess as an attribute; to experience; to allow, or tolerate; to engage in; to cause, compel, or require to be; to be obliged.
haven *n* a harbour; a shelter.
havoc *n* widespread destruction or disorder; devastation.
hawk *n* a bird of prey; an aggressive or ruthless person. * *vt* to hunt with hawks.
hawser *n* a small cable.
hay *n* grass cut and dried for fodder.
hazard *n* risk; venture; obstacle on the golf course. * *vt* to risk.
hazardous *adj* perilous; risky.
haze *n* vapour; mist; smoke; slight vagueness.
hazy *adj* obscure; dim; vague.
he *pron* of the third person. * *n* a male person.
head *n* the part of an animal or human body containing the brain, eyes, ears, nose and mouth; the top part of anything; the chief person; (*pl*) mind; pressure of water, steam etc; the source of a river etc; froth, as on beer.
headache *n* pain in the head.
headgear *n* covering for the head.
heading *n* something forming the head, top or front; the title, topic etc of a chapter etc; the direction in which a vehicle is moving.
headlight *n* a light at the front of a vehicle.
headline *n* printed lines at the top of a newspaper article giving the topic.
headlong *adj* with the head first; with uncontrolled speed or force; rashly.
head-on *adj* with the head or front foremost; without compromise.
headquarters *n* the centre of operations of one in command, as in an army; the main office in any organization.
headstrong *adj* obstinate; determined to do as one pleases.
headway *n* progress or success.
heady *adj* rash; hasty.

heal *vt* to make sound or healthy; to cure..
health *n* a sound state of body or mind.
healthy *adj* hale; sound; beneficial.
heap *n* a mass; a pile. * *vt* to amass.
hear *vt, vi* to perceive by the ear; to listen; to learn; to conduct a legal hearing.
hearing *n* one of the five senses; attention; opportunity to be heard.
hearing aid *n* an electronic amplifier worn behind the ear to improve hearing.
hearsay *n* report; rumour.
hearse *n* a car for conveying a coffin.
heart *n* the organ which propels the blood; the centre of life; spirit; strength; courage; (*pl*) a suit of playing cards marked with a heart-shaped symbol.
heartache *n* sorrow; anguish.
heartbeat *n* the rhythmic contraction and dilation of the heart.
heartbreak *n* overwhelming sorrow or grief.
heartburn *n* a burning sensation in the lower chest.
hearten *vt* to encourage.
hearth *n* the floor of the fireplace; the fireside; home.
heartless *adj* unfeeling.
hearty *adj* warm; cordial; keen; unrestrained, as laughter; healthy; plentiful.
heat *n* energy produced by molecular agitation; the quality of being hot; hot weather or climate; strong feeling, esp anger etc; the period of sexual excitement and readiness for mating in female animals.
heath *n* a waste or shrub-covered tract of land; heather.
heathen *n* a pagan an irreligious or uncivilized person.
heating *n* a system of providing heat.
heatwave *n* a prolonged period of hot weather.
heave *vt, vi* to lift; to move upward; to utter; to swell; to come to a stop (of ship).
heaven *n* the sky; bliss.
heaviness *n* weight; gloom.
heavy *adj* weighty; sad; drowsy; hard to do; clumsy; dull; serious; grievous.
heavyweight *n* a professional boxer weighing more than 175 pounds (29 kg); (*inf*) a very influential or important individual.
heckle *n vt* to harass a speaker with questions or taunts.
hectic *adj vt, vi* feverish.
hector *n* a bully; involving intense excitement on activity; to bluster; to bully.
hedge *n* a fence consisting of a dense line of bushes or small trees; an evasive or non-committal answer or statement. * *vt* to surround or enclose with a hedge; to place secondary bets as a precaution.
hedonism *n* the doctrine that pleasure is the chief good.
heed *vt* to attend to; to notice. * *n* care; attention.
heedless *adj* inattentive; negligent.
heel *n* the hind part of the foot; the part of a sock or shoe covering the heel. * *vt* to add a heel to; to list or tilt (of ships).
hefty *adj* heavy; large and strong; big.
height *n* the distance from top to bottom.
heighten *vt* to raise higher or more intense.
heinous *adj* flagrant.
heir *n* one who inherits.
heiress *n* a female heir.
heirloom *n* any possession which descends from generation to generation.
helicopter *n* a kind of aircraft lifted and moved, or kept hovering, by large rotary blades mounted horizontally.
helium *n* a gaseous element.
helix *n* (*pl* **helices**) a wire coil.
hell *n* the abode of the wicked after death; any place or state of extreme misery or pain.
hello *interj* an expression of greeting. * *n* the act of saying 'hello'.
helm *n* a rudder, the steering wheel on a ship; management; authority.
helmet *n* head armour.
helmsman *n* the man who steers a ship.
help *vt* to make things better or easier for; to aid; to assist; to remedy; to keep from; to serve or wait on. * *n* the action of helping; aid; assistance; a remedy.
helpful *adj* giving help; useful.
helpless *adj* unable to manage alone, dependent on others; weak and defenceless.
hem *n* the border of a garment. * *vt* to form a hem; (with **in**) to enclose; to confine.

hemisphere *n* a half sphere; half the earth.
hen *n* a female bird.
hence *adv* from this place; time, reason.
henceforth *adv* from now on.
henchman *n* a trusted supporter.
heptagon *n* a seven-sided figure.
her *pron* the possessive and objective case of **she.**
herald *n* a person who conveys news or messages; a forerunner. * *vt* to proclaim.
heraldry *n* the study of genealogies and coats of arms; ceremony; pomp.
herb *n* any plant used medicinally or as seasoning.
herbaceous *adj* descriptive of fleshy as opposed to woody plants.
herbal *n* a book treating of herbs.
herbalist *n* one skilled in herbs.
herbarium *n* (*pl* **herbariums, herbaria**) a collection of dried plants.
herbivorous *adj* herb-eating.
herd *n* a large number of animals, esp cattle, living and feeding together. * *vt, vi* to assemble or move animals together.
here *adv* in this place; now; on earth.
hereabout *adv* about this place.
hereafter *adv* after this time. * *n* (with the) the future; life after death.
hereby *adv* by this means; near.
hereditary *adj* transmitted to offspring.
heredity *n* the transmission of genetic material that determines physical and mental characteristics from one generation on to another.
heresy *n* a belief contrary to accepted beliefs or doctrines.
heretic *n* one guilty of heresy.
heritable *adj* transmissible.
heritage *n* something inherited at birth; anything deriving from the past.
hermaphrodite *adj* being of both sexes.
hermetic, hermetical *adj* airtight.
hermit *n* a recluse.
hernia *n* a rupture esp. of part of the intestine.
hero *n* a brave man; the chief character in a play or novel or film.
heroine *n* a woman with the attributes of a hero; the leading female character in a play, novel etc.
heroism *n* the qualities or conduct of a hero; magnanimity; bravery; valour.
hers *pron possessive* used only when no noun follows; belonging to her.
herself *pron* emphatic and reflexive form of she and her.
hesitancy *n* a hesitating.
hesitate *vi* to pause; to be uncertain or undecided; to falter; to stammer.
hew *vi* to cut; chop; hack; to shape.
hexagon *n* a rectilinear figure of six sides.
heyday *n* a period of greatest success or happiness; bloom; prime.
hiatus *n* a gap; a break.
hibernate *vt* to pass the winter in sleep; to be inactive.
hide *vt, vi* to conceal; to screen; to lie hidden. * *n* the skin of an animal; camouflaged place of concealment used by hunters, bird-watchers etc.
hidebound *adj* bigoted; narrow-minded.
hideous *adj* frightful; ugly; horrifying.
hiding *n* concealment; a thrashing.
hierarchy *n* a group of people or things arranged in order of rank, grade etc.
hieroglyph, hieroglyphic *n* picture writing; writing hard to decipher.
high *adj* elevated; dear; (of price); not fresh (of food); intoxicated. * *adv* greatly; in on to a high degree, rank etc. * *n* a high level, place etc; a euphoric state induced by drugs or alcohol.
highborn *adj* of noble birth.
highbrow *n, adj* an intellectual.
high-flyer *n* an ambitious person; a person of great ability in any profession.
high-handed *adj* overbearing.
highland *n* a mountainous region; (*pl*)
highlight *n* the lightest area of a painting etc; the most interesting or important feature; (*pl*) lightening of areas of the hair using a bleach. * *vt* to bring to special attention; to give highlights to.
high-minded *adj* proud; having honourable pride.
highness *n* a title of honour given to royalty; the state or quality of being high.
high-rise *adj, n* (a building) with multiple storeys.
highroad *n* main road.
high school *n* a secondary school.
highway *n* a public road; a major road.

hike *vi* to take a long walk. * *vt* to pull up. * *n* a long walk; a tramp.
hilarious *adj* very amusing.
hilarity *n* laughter; jollity.
hill *n* a rise in the land lower than a mountain; a slope in a road.
hillock *n* a small hill.
hilt *n* a handle, particularly of a sword.
him *pron* the objective case of **he**.
himself *pron* the emphatic and reflexive form of **he** and **him**.
hind *n* a female stag; a rustic. * *adj* situated at the back.
hinder *vt* to prevent; to thwart.
hindmost *adj* farthest behind; last.
hindrance *n* a check; an obstruction; an obstacle.
hinge *n* a joint or flexible part on which a door, lid, etc turns; a natural joint, as of a clam. * *vt, vi* to attach or hang by a hinge; to depend.
hint *vt, vi* to suggest indirectly; to insinuate. * *n* an indirect or subtle suggestion; a slight mention; a little piece of advice.
hip *n* the joint of the thigh; the fruit of dog the rose. * *adj* stylish; up-to-date.
hire *vt* to engage for wages; to lease out. * *n* wages; payment for the temporary use of something.
hirsute *adj* hairy; shaggy.
his *pron* possessive case of **he.**
hiss *vt* to make a sound like that of letters.
histology *n* the study of tissues, animal or vegetable.
historian *n* a writer of history.
history *n* a record or account of past events; the study, analysis of past events.
histrionic, histrionical *adj* theatrical.
histrionics *n* theatricals; exaggerated behaviour.
hit *vt, vi* to strike; not to miss; to reach; to affect strongly. * *n* a stroke; a blow; a collision; a successful and popular song.
hitch *vt, vi* to move, pull etc with jerks; to fasten with a hook, knot etc; to obtain a ride by hitchhiking.
hitchhike *vct* to travel by asking for free lifts from motorists along the way.
hive *n* a shelter for a colony of bees; a beehive; a scene of great activity.
hoard *n* a hidden stock or accumulation of money stored away for future use. * *vt, vi* to collect; to store secretly.
hoarding *n* a large board for pasting advertisements on.
hoarse *adj* rough-voiced; grating.
hoary *adj* white or grey with age.
hoax *n* a practical joke. * *vt* to deceive; to trick.
hob *n* a flat surface on a cooker with hot plates or burners.
hobble *vi* to limp; to shackle (a horse).
hobby *n* a favourite spare time pursuit.
hobbyhorse *n* a wooden horse for children; a favourite or obsessive subject.
hobgoblin *n* a goblin; an imp.
hobnob *vi* to socialize.
hockey *n* game played with a ball and curved stick between two teams of eleven players each.
hod *n* a trough on a pole for carrying mortar and bricks.
hoe *n* a garden tool with a long handle.
hog *n* a castrated male pig raised for its meat; a selfish, greedy or dirty person. * *vt* to take more than one's share; to hoard greedily.
hoist *vt* to heave up. * *n* an elevator; lift.
hold *vt, vi* to have one's grasp; to confine; to keep; to maintain; to contain; to possess; to occupy; to support; to regard; to believe; to consider. * *n* a grasp; possession; a dominance over; lowermost inside part of a ship.
holding *n* a small rented farm with land; (often *pl*) property, esp. land, stocks and bonds.
hole *n* a hollow place; an aperture; cavity; a den; a small dirty place; a difficult situation; a small bound hollow to receive a golf ball; a fairway plus tee in golf.
holiday *n* a day or period away from work etc; a time for rest or amusement.
holiday-maker *n* a person on holiday.
holiness *n* sanctity.
hollow *adj* not solid; empty; false. * *n* a depression; a cavity; a valley. * *vt* to excavate.
holocaust *n* the mass murder of Jews in Europe by Nazis.
holograph *n* a document in one's own

handwriting.
holster *n* a pistol case attached to a belt.
holy *adj* sinless; consecrated.
homage *n* duty; fealty; a demonstration of respect or honour.
home *n* one's own abode; residence; native place; a household; an institution.
homeland *n* the country where a person was born.
homely *adj* simple; plain; everyday.
home-made *adj* made or looking as if made at home.
homesick *adj* affected with homesickness; longing for home.
homespun *adj* coarse; rough; unsophisticated. * *n* a home-made cloth.
homestead *n* a house with the grounds and buildings attached; native seat.
homeward *adv* towards home.
homework *n* work, esp piecework, done at home; schoolwork to be done outside the classroom; preliminary study for a project.
homicidal *adj* murderous.
homicide *n* manslaughter; a person who kills.
homily *n* a sermon; sound advice.
homoeopathy, homeopathy *n* curing disease by producing similar symptoms, 'like curing like'.
homogeneous *adj* of the same kind; of uniform structure.
homonym *n* a word alike in form or sound, but not in meaning, as here, hear.
honest *adj* free from fraud; upright; truthful; trustworthy; frank.
honesty *n* uprightness; truth.
honey *n* a sweet sticky yellowish substance juice collected by bees from flowers and made into a food.
honeycomb *n* the waxy storage cells of bees.
honeymoon *n* the holiday spent together by a newly married couple.
honeysuckle *n* a sweet-smelling climbing plant.
honorary *adj* unpaid; conferring honour; voluntary.
honour *n* glory; good name; fame; integrity; distinction; a title of respect; (*pl*) university distinctions. * *vt* to esteem; exalt; pay (bill) when due.
honourable *adj* worthy of honour; distinguished; just.
hood *n* a cowl; a head covering.
hoof *n* the horny part of an animal's foot.
hook *n* a piece of metal bent so as to catch or hold; a sickle. * *vt* to catch with a hook; to ensnare; to drive a ball to the left (golf). * *vi* to bend; to be curving.
hoop *n* the band of a cask; a ring; anything so shaped.
hoot *vi* to shout in contempt; to cry as an owl; to blow a whistle etc.
hooter *n* something that makes a hooting sound e.g. a car horn; a nose.
hop *n* a leap on one leg; a spring; a short trip by air. * *vi* to leap; to skip.
hope *vt* to desire and expect. * *vi* to trust. * *n* expectation and desire; the object of this.
hopeful *adj* filled with hope; inspiring hope or promise of success.
hopeless *adj* without hope; despondent.
hopper *n* a contrivance for passing grain into a mill; a barge for dredgings.
horde *n* a crowd; a throng; a rabble.
horizon *n* the apparent junction of the earth and sky; the limit of a person's knowledge; interest etc.
horizontal *adj* level; parallel to the plane of the horizon.
hormone *n* a product of living cells formed in one part of the organism and carried to another part, where it takes effect; a synthetic compound having the same purpose.
horn *n* a hard pointed growth on the heads of some animals; anything horn-like; a wind instrument esp. the French horn; a device blown or sounded as a warning.
horology *n* the science of clockmaking.
horoscope *n* a chart of the signs and positions of planets etc, by which astrologers profess to predict future events.
horrible *adj* dreadful; frightful; very unpleasant.
horrid *adj* shocking; hideous.
horrify *vt* to shock; to appal.
horror *n* dread; intense fear; a person or thing inspiring horror.
horse *n* four-legged, solid-hoofed her-

bivorous mammal with a flowing mane and a tail.

horseman *n* a skilful rider.

horseplay *n* rough, rude conduct.

horseshoe *n* a flat, U-shaped plate nailed to a horse's hoof.

horticulture *n* the art or science of growing flowers, fruit and vegetables.

hose *n sing or pl* stockings; breeches; a flexible tube for conveying water etc.

hosiery *n* stockings and socks.

hospice *n* a nursing home for the care of the terminally ill.

hospitable *adj* generous and welcoming; kind.

hospital *n* an institution for the care of the sick.

hospitality *n* kindness, generosity to guests and strangers.

host[1] *n* a person who receives or entertains; an animal or plant on or in which another lives; a compere.

hostage *n* a person kept as a pledge to secure the performance of conditions.

hostel *n* a lodging house.

hostess *n* a female host.

hostile *adj* unfriendly.

hostility *n* enmity; (*pl*) warfare.

hot *adj* (**hotter, hottest**) of high temperature; very warm; giving or feeling heat; causing a burning sensation on the tongue; following closely.

hot *adj* having heat; burning; passionate; pungent; eager.

hot-blooded *adj* high-spirited.

hotel *n* a commercial establishment providing lodging and meals for travellers etc.

hotelier *n* the owner or manager of a hotel.

hothead *n* an impetuous person. * *adj* **hotheaded**.

hothouse *n* a heated greenhouse for raising plants; an environment that encourages rapid growth.

hound *n* a hunting dog. * *vt* to urge on.

hour *n* a period of 60 minutes, a 24th part of a day; the time.

hourly *adj* occuring every hour; done during an hour; frequent. * *adj* at every hour; frequently.

house *n* a building to live in, esp by one person or family; a household; the audience in a theatre; a legislative assembly.

house arrest *n* detention in one's own house, as opposed to prison.

housebreaker *n* a burglar; one employed to demolish buildings.

household *n* inmates of a house. * *adj* domestic; pertaining to house and family.

housekeeper *n* a person who runs a home, esp one hired to do so.

housekeeping *n* the daily running of a household.

house warming *n* a party given to celebrate moving into a new house.

housing *n* houses collectively; the provision of accommodation; a casing enclosing a piece of machinery etc.

hovel *n* a small mean dwelling.

hover *vi* to hang in the air; to linger.

hovercraft *n* a land or water vehicle that travels supported on a cushion of air.

how *adv* in what manner.

however *adv* in whatever manner. * *conj* yet; though.

howl *vt, vi* to utter the long, wailing cry of wolves, dogs etc; to shout or laugh in pain, amusement etc.

hub *n* the centre part of a wheel; a centre of activity.

hubbub *n* tumult; noise.

huddle *vi, vt* to crowd together.

hue *n* colour; tint; an outcry.

huff *n* a state of smouldering resentment. * *vi* to blow; to puff.

hug *vt* to embrace; to keep close to; to squeeze tightly. * *n* a close embrace.

huge *adj* immense; enormous.

hulk *n* the body of an old ship; a large, clumsy person.

hulking *adj* unwieldly; bulky.

hull *n* the outer covering of anything, as nut, grain; the framework of a ship. * *vt* to strip off covering.

hum *vb* (*pt* **hugged**) *vt, vi* to make a low continuous vibrating sound.

human *adj* of or relating to human beings.

humane *adj* merciful; compassionate.

humanity *n* the human race; philanthropy;

kindness.

humble *adj* lowly; modest; meek; servile. * *vt* to lower in condition or rank; to humiliate.

humdrum *adj* commonplace; dull.

humid *adj* moist; damp (of air).

humidity *n* moisture; (a measure of) the dampness in the air.

humiliate *vt* to humble; to mortify; to lower the pride or dignity.

humility *n* modesty; meekness.

hummock *n* a rounded knoll.

humorist *n* a wit; a humorous writer.

humorous *adj* jocular; funny; amusing.

humour *n* disposition; mood; caprice; jocularity; temperament; state of mind. * *vt* to gratify; to indulge.

hump *n* a protuberance.

humpback *n* a species of whale.

humus *n* vegetable mould.

hunch *n* a hump; an intuitive feeling. **vt* to arch into a hump. * *vt* to move forward jerkily.

hundred *adj* ten times ten.

hundredweight *n* 112 lb.; 1/20 ton.

hunger *n* a craving for food; any strong desire.

hungry *adj* longing for food; craving something.

hunt *vt, vi* to chase; to search for; to drive away. * *n* hunting; the chase; a party organised for hunting.

hurdle *n* a portable frame of bars for temporary fences or for jumping over.

hurl *vt* to throw with force.

hurrah *interj* an exclamation of joy.

hurricane *n* a violent tropical storm.

hurried *adj* hasty; performed quickly.

hurry *vt, vi* to act; move; drive with haste. * *n* rush; urgency; haste.

hurt *n* a wound; an injury; harm. * *vt* to pain; bruise; harm; injure; damage.

hurtful *adj* harmful.

hurtle *vi* to move or throw with great speed and force.

husband *n* a man who has a wife. * *vt* to manage frugally; to conserve.

hush *n* stillness. * *vt, vi* to silence.

husk *n* the outer dry covering of certain fruits and seeds.

husky *adj* dry; hoarse; harsh; hefty; strong. * *n* an Arctic sled dog.

hussy *n* a shameless girl.

hustle *vt, vi* to jostle; to push or force hurriedly; to obtain by rough means.

hut *n* a small crude house or cabin..

hutch *n* a pen or coop for small animals.

hybrid *n* the offspring of two plants or animals of different species; a mongrel. * *adj* crossbred.

hydrant *n* a large pipe with a valve for drawing water from a main.

hydraulic *adj* operated by water or other liquid.

hydraulics *n* the science dealing with the mechanical properties of liquids.

hydrogen *n* a flammable, colourless, odourless, tasteless, gaseous chemical element, the lightest substance known.

hydrometer *n* an instrument for finding specific gravity of liquids.

hydrophobia *n* a disease caused by the bite of an infected animal and marked by dread of water; rabies.

hydrostatic *adj* relating to hydrostatics.

hydrostatics *n* the science which treats of the reactions of fluids at rest.

hygiene *n* principles and practice of health and cleanliness.

hymn *n* a song of praise.

hyperbole *n* an exaggeration for effect or emphasis.

hypercritical *adj* overcritical.

hyphen *n* a mark (-) joining syllables or words.

hypnosis *n (pl hypnoses)* a relaxed state resembling sleep in which the mind responds to external suggestion.

hypnotism *n* the act of inducing hypnosis; the study and use of hypnosis.

hypnotize *vt* to put in a state of hypnosis; to fascinate.

hypochondria *n* needless and anxiety about one's health.

hypocrisy *n* a falsely pretending to possess virtues, beliefs etc; an example of this. * *n* **hypocritical**.

hypodermic *adj* introduced beneath the skin (injection).

hypotenuse *n* the side opposite the right angle of a right-angled triangle.

hypothesis *n (pl* **hypotheses**) something

assumed for the purpose of argument.
hysteria *n* a mental disorder marked by excitability, anxiety, imaginary organic disorders etc; frenzied emotion.
hysteric *n* a hysterical person.
hysterical *adj* caused by hysteria; suffering from hysteria; (*inf*) extremely funny.

I

I *pron* pronoun, the first person who is speaking or writing used in referring to himself or herself.
ice *n* frozen water; ice cream or water ice. **vt, vi* to freeze; to cool with ice; to cover with icing.
iceberg *n* a floating mass of ice.
icebound *adj* surrounded with ice.
ice cream *n* a sweet frozen food.
ice floe *n* a sheet of floating ice.
icicle *n* a hanging taper of ice formed by frozen dripping water.
icy *adj* like ice; chilling.
idea *n* a mental impression or notion; an opinion or belief.
ideal *adj* perfect. * *n* perfect type; a standard for attainment or imitation; an aim or principle.
idealism *n* the doctrine that ideas are the sole reality.
idealist *n* a visionary.
idealize *vt* to represent as ideal.
identical *adj* exactly the same.
identification *n* act of identifying.
identify *vt* to consider to be the same; to establish the identity of; to associate closely.
identity *n* the state of being exactly alike; the distinguishing characteristics of a person, personality; the state of being the same as a specified person or thing.
ideology *n* the doctrines, opinions or beliefs of an individual, social class, political party etc.
idiocy *n* mental deficiency; stupidity.
idiom *n* an accepted expression with a different meaning from the literal.
idiosyncrasy *n* a personal peculiarity; a quirk; eccentricity.
idiot *n* (*inf*) a foolish person.
idiotic *adj* stupid; senseless.
idle *adj* doing nothing; lazy; not occupied; out of work; useless; worthless **vt* to waste or spend time uselessly **vi* to move aimlessly; (*of an engine*) to operate without transmitting power.
idleness *n* inaction; sloth.
idly *adv* lazily; carelessly.
idol *n* a graven image or anything worshipped.
idolatry *n* the worship of idols.
idolize *vt* to love excessively.
idyl, idyll *n* a romantic or a pastoral poem.
idyllic *adj* describing an idyll; charmingly picturesque.
if *conj* on condition that; in the event that; supposing that; even though; whenever.
igneous *adj* descriptive of rocks formed from solidified magma or lava.
ignite *vt, vi* to kindle; to set fire to; to burn or cause to burn.
ignition *n* an act or instance of igniting; the starting of an internal combustion engine.
ignoble *adj* mean; base.
ignominious *adj* shameful; base.
ignominy *n* public disgrace; shame.
ignoramus *n* (*pl* **ignoramuses**) an ignorant person.
ignorance *n* want of knowledge.
ignorant *adj* uninformed; uneducated.
ignore *vt* to disregard.
ill *adj* bad or evil; crabbed; sick; ugly. * *n* evil; pain. * *adv* not well; badly.
ill-bred *adj* not polite; rude.
illegal *adj* contrary to law.
illegible *adj* unreadable.
illegitimate *adj* born out of wedlock.
illicit *adj* improper; unlawful.
illiterate *adj* not able to read or write; ignorant.
ill-judged *adj* injudicious; unwise.
ill-mannered *adj* rude; boorish.
ill-natured *adj* bad-tempered; spiteful.
illness *n* sickness.
illogical *adj* not logical.
ill-tempered *adj* cross; morose.
ill-treat *vt* to treat unkindly, unfairly etc.
illuminate *vt* to light up; to adorn; to enlighten.

illumination *n* a brightening up with colours or lights.
illuminative *adj* enlightening.
illusion *n* a false notion; an unreal or misleading image or appearance; deception.
illusionist *n* a conjuror; a magician.
illusive *adj* deceptive.
illusory *adj* fallacious.
illustrate *vt* to make clear by explanation or drawing.
illustration *n* an example, a picture, or drawing; esp in a book.
illustrative *adj* explanatory.
illustrious *adj* renowned; distinguished.
ill-will *n* hatred; malice.
image *n* a likeness; an idol; a mental picture; the visual impression of something in a lens, mirror etc.
imagery *n* picturesque language.
imaginary *adj* not real; visionary.
imagination *n* fancy; the creative faculty.
imagine *vt,vi* to fancy; to conceive; to believe falsely.
imbecile *adj* weak-minded; foolish.**n* an adult with a mental age of a three to eight-year-old child; a silly person.
imbibe *vt* to drink in; to absorb.
imitate *vt* to copy; to mimic; to impersonate.
imitation *n* a counterfeit; a copy; an act of impersonation or mimicking.
imitative *adj* given to imitation.
immaculate *adj* spotless; pure; morally unblemished.*adj* inherent; all pervading.
immaterial *adj* unimportant.
immature *adj* unripe; not mature.
immeasureable *adj* immense.
immediate *adj* acting or occuring without delay; next, nearest, without intervening agency; next in relationship; in close proximity, near to.
immediately *adv* instantly; directly; near.
immemorial *adj* ancient beyond memory.
immense *adj* immeasurable; huge; vast.
immensity *n* infinity; vastness.
immerse *vt* to plunge into (esp. water).
immersion heater *n* an electric element for heating liquids.
immigrant *n* one who settles in a country not his own.
immigrate *vi* to enter a country as a settler.
imminent *adj* impending; about to happen; threatening.
immobile *adj* fixed; stable.
immoderate *adj* excessive; intemperate.
immodest *adj* indelicate.
immoral *adj* depraved; wicked; corrupt.
immortal *adj* eternal; living forever; having lasting fame **n* an immortal being or person.
immortality *n* endless life or fame.
immortalize *vt* to make famous for ever.
immovable *adj* steadfast; unalterable.
immune *adj* not susceptible to a specified disease through innoculation or natural resistance; confering immunity.
immunity *n* freedom from (disease, service, &c); exemption.
immunize *vt* to make immune, esp against infection.
immutable *adj* unchangeable.
imp *n* a mischievous child.
impact *n* a collision; a blow.
impair *vt* to make worse; to weaken.
impale *vt* to transfix with a sharp pointed instrument.
impalpable *adj* intangible; not easily understood.
impart *vt* to give; to bestow; to confer.
impartial *adj* just; fair; unbiased.
impartiality *n* freedom from bias.
impassable *adj* incapable of being travelled over or through.
impasse *n* a deadlock.
impassioned *adj* moved by passion.
impassive *adj* unmoved; apathetic.
impatience *n* intolerance of delay; restlessness; short temper.
impatient *adj* fretful; intolerant; restless.
impeach *vt* to question a person's honesty; to charge with a crime.
impeachment *n* an indictment.
impeccable *adj* faultless.
impecunious *adj* penniless.
impede *vt* to hamper; to obstruct.
impediment *n* an obstruction; a physical defect, e.g. a stammer.
impel *vt* to drive or urge forward.
impend *vi* to hang over; to threaten.
impenetrable *adj* impervious; unable to be passed through.

impenitent *adj* unrepentant; obdurate.
imperative *adj* commanding; obligatory; designating or of the mood of a verb that expresses a command, entreaty etc.
imperceptible *adj* minute; not easily grasped or detected by the senses.
imperfect *adj* incomplete; faulty; designating a verb tense that indicates a past action or state as incomplete or continuous.
imperfection *n* the state or quality of being imperfect; a defect, fault.
imperial *adj* pertaining to an empire.
imperil *vt* to endanger.
imperious *adj* commanding; arrogant.
imperishable *adj* indestructible.
impermeable *adj* impervious; impenetrable by liquids.
impersonal *adj* without reference to a particular person; cold; unfeeling; (of a verb) occuring only in the third person singular
impersonate *vt* to assume the character of another for entertainment or for fraud.
impertinence *n* insolence; irrelevance; rudeness.
impertinent *adj* saucy; pert; rude; irelevant.
imperturbable *adj* serene; unmoved.
impervious *adj* impassable; not receptive to or affected by.
impetuous *adj* hasty; thoughtless.
impetus *n* the force with which a body moves against resistance; driving force or motive.
impinge *vi* to collide; to clash; to encroach.
impious *adj* profane; irreverent.
impish *adj* mischievous.
implacability *n* pitilessness; relentlessness.
implacable *adj* not to be appeased; inexorable; unrelenting.
implant *vt* to plant; to instil.
implement *n* a tool, utensil, or instrument. * *vt* to fulfil; to carry out.
implicate *vt* to involve; to incriminate.
implication *n* entanglement; inference; deduction.
implicit *adj* implied; not stated; unquestioning.
implore *vti* to beseech, to entreat.
imply *vt* to suggest; to suggest indirectly.
impolite *adj* rude; uncivil.
impolitic *adj* inexpedient.
imponderable *adj* without weight; **n* something difficult to measure or assess.
import *vt* to bring from abroad; to signify; to imply.
importance *n* significance; a high place in public estimation; high self-esteem.
important *adj* momentous; serious; powerful and authoritative.
importunate *adj* urgent; persistent.
importune *vt* to press urgently; to crave.
impose *vt* to lay on as a tax; to inflict oneself on others; to cheat; to lay pages of type or film and secure them.
imposing *adj* impressive; stately.
imposition *vt, vi* an unfair obligation.
impossibility *n* state or character of being impossible; that which cannot be, or cannot be done.
impossible *adj* not possible; inconceivable; unendurable.
impostor, imposter *n* a deceiver.
impotence, impotency *n* powerlessness; inability to engage in sexual intercourse.
impotent *adj* feeble; incompetent; sexually impotent.
impound *vt* to confine; to seize legally.
impoverish *vt* to make poor; to exhaust.
impracticable *adj* not feasible; unmanageable; unattainable.
impractical *adj* not practical; not competent in practical skills.
impregnable *adj* invincible; secure against attack.
impregnate *vt* to cause to become prgnant; to fertilize; to saturate; to pervade.
impresario *n* the manager of an opera, concert series, etc.
impress *vt* to press into; to stamp; to fix deeply and favourably (on the mind).
impression *n* the effect produced in the mind by an experience; a mark produced by imprinting; a vague idea, notion; the number of copies of a book printed at one time; an impersonation.
impressionable *adj* susceptible; easily influenced.

impressionism *n* a movement in art giving more attention to general effect and impressions than to details.
impressionist *n* an artist who aims at broad effects; a mimic or impersonator.
impressive *adj* imposing; striking; arousing admiration.
imprint *vt* to impress; to stamp. * *n* a printer's and publisher's name, address etc.
imprison *vt* to confine in prison.
improbability *n* unlikelihood.
improbable *adj* unlikely to be true or to happen.
impromptu *n* an unprepared remark, poem, etc; a short, unrehearsed musical composition* *adj* extempore.
improper *adj* lacking propriety; indecent; erroneous; unsuitable.
impropriety *n* an unbecoming act.
improve *vt, vi* to better; to grow better; to use to good purpose.
improvement *n* advance; betterment; an alteration that enhances the value of something.
improvidence *n* wastefulness.
improvident *adj* thriftless; careless.
improvise *vt* to compose and recite, etc, without preparation. to do or use whatever is at hand.
imprudence *n* rashness, indiscretion.
imprudent *adj* indiscreet; heedless.
impudent *adj* impertinent; saucy.
impugn *vt* to challenge; to contradict.
impulse *n* a thrust; a motive; a sudden determination to act.
impulsive *adj* impetuous; hasty.
impunity *n* freedom from punishment.
impure *adj* foul; obscene; adulterated.
impurity *n* pollution; adulteration.
impute *vt* to attribute; ascribe.
in *prep, adv* within; not out; during; being a member of; wearing.
inability *n* lack of ability.
inaccessible *adj* unattainable.
inaccuracy *n* uncorrectness; error.
inaccurate *adj* incorrect; not exact.
inaction *n* idleness; rest.
inactive *adj* idle; indolent.
inadequacy *n* insufficiency.
inadequate *adj* defective; not capable.
inadmissible *adj* not allowable.
inadvertent *adj* heedless; careless.
inadvisable *adj* not advisable; inexpedient.
inalienable *adj* incapable of being transferred.
inane *adj* silly; senseless.
inanimate *adj* lifeless; spiritless.
inanity *n* silliness.
inapplicable *adj* inappropriate.
inapposite *adj* not to the point.
inappropriate *adj* unsuitable.
inapt *adj* unapt; unfit.
inaptitude *n* unfitness.
inarticulate *adj* not expressed in words; incapable of coherent or effective expression of ideas, feelings, etc.
inattention *n* want of attention; neglect.
inattentive *adj* not attending; thoughtless.
inaudible *adj* unable to be heard.
inaugural *adj* introductory.
inaugurate *vt* to introduce, to install into office; to open a building etc. formally to the public; to initiate.
inauguration *n* a formal opening or start.
inauspicious *adj* ill-omened.
inborn *adj* innate; inherent.
inbred *adj* innate; produced by inbreeding
inbreed *vt,vi* to breed by continual mating of individuals or closely related stocks.
incalculable *adj* numberless; very great; uncertain.
incandescent *adj* white or glowing with heat.
incantation *n* recital of words containing a magic spell.
incapable *adj* unfit to perform an activity.
incapacitate *vt* to render unfit; to disable.
incapacity *n* unfitness; disqualification.
incarceration *n* imprisonment.
incarnate *vt* to embody in flesh. * *adj* endowed with a human body.
incarnation *n* embodiment in human form.
incautious *adj* unwary; imprudent.
incendiary *n* one who wilfully sets fire to property; an arsonist **adj* inflammatory; seditious; (of bomb) design to start

fires.

incense *n* perfume of spices burnt in religious rites.

incense *vt* to inflame; to provoke.

incentive *adj* inciting. * *n* an inducement.

inception *n* the initial stage.

incessant *adj* unceasing; constant.

incessantly *adv* continually.

incest *n* intercourse between close blood relations.

incestuous *adj* guilty of incest.

inch *n* the twelfth part of a foot in length; * *vt,vi* to move very slowly or by degrees.

incidence *n* the degree or range of occurence or effect.

incident *n* a distinct event; a minor event.

incidental *adj* casual; occasional; happening by the way; (*pl*) miscellaneous items.

incidentally *adv* in passing; as an aside.

incinerate *vt* to burn to ashes.

incinerator *n* a furnace for burning.

incipient *adj* beginning to be or appear.

incise *vt* to cut in or into; to carve.

incision *n* a cut, esp by a surgeon into a body.

incisive *adj* sharp; biting; trenchant.

incisor *n* a front cutting tooth.

incite *vt* to urge on; to stir up.

incitement *n* a motive; encouragement.

inclemency *n* harshness, severity (of the weather).

inclement *adj* not clement; stormy.

inclination *n* a propensity or disposition, esp a liking; a deviation from the horizontal or vertical; a slope.

incline *vi* to lean, to slope; to be disposed towards an opinion or action. * *vt* to cause to bend forwards; to cause to deviate. * *n* a slope

inclined *adj* sloping; disposed.

include *vt* to enclose; to comprise; to contain.

inclusive *adj* including; comprising.

incoherence *n* rambling, inarticulate speech or thought; unconnected.

incoherent *adj* confused; unintelligible.

incombustible *adj* not able to be burned.

income *n* all moneys coming in for work or investments etc.

incoming *adj* coming; accruing; **n* the act of coming in; that which comes in; income.

incommunicative *adj* reserved; unsocial.

incomparable *adj* matchless.

incompatible *adj* irreconcilable; unable to exist together in harmony.

incompetence, incompetency *n* unfitness; incapacity; lack of skill or ability.

incompetent *adj* not competent; incapable; unskilful; an incompetent person.

incomplete *adj* imperfect; defective; unfinished.

incomprehensible *adj* unintelligible; inconceivable.

inconceivable *adj* unimaginable.

inconclusive *adj* indecisive; uncertain as to result or outcome.

incongruity *n* inconsistency; absurdity.

incongruous *adj* discordant; inconsistent; lacking harmony or agreement of parts.

inconsequential, inconsequent *adj* not following logically; irrelevant.

inconsiderable *adj* unimportant; insignificant.

inconsiderate *adj* thoughtless; unkind.

inconsistency *n* incongruity; want of agreement; irregularity; fickleness.

inconsistent *adj* not consistent; variable.

inconsolable *adj* grieved beyond measure.

inconspicuous *adj* not easily noticed; undistinguished.

incontestable *adj* unquestionable.

incontinence *n* lack of self-restraint; inability to control excretion of bodily wastes.

incontinent *adj* suffering from incontinence; unrestrained.

incontrovertible *adj* certain; indisputable.

inconvenience *n* annoyance; awkwardness; that which incommodes.

inconvenient *adj* awkward.

incorporate *vt* to unite in one body.

incorporation *n* a union.

incorrect *adj* faulty; untrue; improper.

incorrigible *adj* incurable; hopeless.

incorruptible *adj* incapable of physical corruption, decay or dissolution; incapable of being bribed.

increase *vi* to become greater; to augment. * *vt* to add to. * *n* a growing larger; ad-

dition; profit; interest.
incredible *adj* unbelievable.
incredulity *n* doubt; scepticism.
incredulous *adj* sceptical; doubting.
increment *n* the amount of an increase.
incriminate *vt* to involve in an accusation; to accuse.
incubate *vi* to sit on eggs; to hatch.
incubator *n* an apparatus in which eggs are hatched by artificial heat; an apparatus for nurturing premature babies.
inculcate *vt* to teach; to implant.
incumbent *n* holder of a church living.
incumbrance *see* **encumbrance**.
incur *vt* to bring upon oneself.
incurable *adj* hopeless; past cure.
incursion *n* a raid; an inroad.
indebted *n* beholden; obliged; owing.
indebtedness *n* amount of debt owed.
indecency *n* immodesty; impurity.
indecent *adj* unseemly; obscene.
indecipherable *adj* incapable of being deciphered.
indecision *n* inability to take a decision.
indecisive *adj* wavering; vacillating.
indecorous *adj* unseemly; improper.
indeed *adv* truly; certainly **interj* expressing irony, disbelief, surprise, etc.
indefatigable *adj* untiring; unremitting.
indefensible *adj* untenable; inexcusable.
indefinable *adj* vague; difficult to explain clearly.
indefinite *adj* uncertain; unlimited; vague.
indelible *adj* not able to be erased.
indelicacy *n* immodesty; coarseness.
indelicate *adj* improper; coarse.
indemnify *vt* to make good a loss; to insure against loss, damage, etc.
indemnity *n* compensation for loss.
indent *vt* to notch; to indicate a paragraph by leaving a space at the margin. * *n* an order for supplies.
indentation *n* a notch; a small bay.
indenture *n* a written contract between two parties.
independence *n* the state of being independent.
independent *adj* free; unrestrained.
indescribable *adj* unutterable; inexpressible; too beautiful, etc for words.
indestructible *adj* imperishable.
indeterminate *adj* uncertain.
index *n* an alphabetical list of names, subjects, items, etc mentioned in a printed book, usually listed alphabetically at the end of the text; any indication or sign.
index finger *n* the forefinger.
index-linked *adj* anything linked directly to changes in the cost of living index.
indicate *vt* to point out; to show; to be a sign or symptom of; to state briefly; to suggest.
indicative *adj* pointing out; affirming; serving as a sign of.
indicator *n* a thing that indicates or points; an instument showing the operating condition of a piece of machinery.
indict *vt* to charge with a crime.
indictment *n* a formal charge or accusation of a crime.
indifference *n* unconcern; apathy.
indifferent *adj* unconcerned; heedless; uninterested; average; mediocre.
indigenous *adj* native; existing naturally in a particular country, region or enviroment.
indigestible *adj* not easily digested.
indigestion *n* pain caused by difficulty in digesting food.
indignant *adj* angry; scornful.
indignation *n* wrath and scorn; annoyance; esp at an injustice.
indignity *n* humiliation; an insult.
indigo *n* a blue vegetable dye.
indirect *adj* roundabout.
indiscreet *adj* tactless; imprudent.
indiscretion *n* imprudence; a thoughtless act; rashness.
indiscriminate *adj* not making any distinction; general; confused; random.
indispensable *adj* necessary; vital.
indisposed *adj* disinclined; unwell.
indisposition *n* a slight ailment.
indisputable *adj* unquestionable.
indistinct *adj* faint; confused.
indistinguishable *adj* incapable of being distinguished.
individual *adj* existing as a seperate thing or being; of, by, for, or relating to a single person. * *n* a single thing or being.
individualist *n* a person who thinks or behaves with marked independence.

individuality *n* seperate or distinct existence; personality.
individually *adv* separately.
indivisible *adj* not able to be divided.
indoctrinate *vt* to instruct systematically in a doctrine, idea or belief.
indolence *n* laziness; idleness.
indolent *adj* lazy; idle.
indomitable *adj* unyielding; invincible.
indoors *adv* within house.
indorse, etc *see* endorse, etc.
indubitable *adj* certain; evident.
induce *vt* to persuade; to draw(a conclusion) from particular facts; to bring on.
inducement *n* an incentive; a motive.
induct *vt* to install; to introduce.
induction *n* introduction to office; a prologue; magnetic influence.
indulge *vt* to gratify; to humour. * *vi* to give way to one's desire.
indulgence *n* favour; intemperance; tolerance.
indulgent *adj* forbearing; yielding; lenient.
industrial *adj* pertaining to industry.
industrialist*n* a person who owns or manages an industrial enterprise.
industrious *adj* diligent; active.
industry *n* organised production or manufacture of goods.
inebriated *adj* drunken.
inedible *adj* not fit to be eaten.
ineffable *adj* indescribable.
ineffective *adj* useless; impotent.
ineffectual *adj* fruitless; futile.
inefficacy *n* failure to produce effect.
inefficient *adj* incapable; ineffective.
inelegant *adj* plain; ungraceful; uncouth.
ineligibility *n* state or quality of being ineligible.
ineligible *adj* not qualified; unsuitable.
inept *adj* unsuitable; awkward; clumsy.
ineptitude *n* unfitness; silliness.
inequality *n* lack of equality; unevenness of surface.
inequitable *adj* unfair; unjust.
inert *adj* lifeless; sluggish; inactive; dull with few or no properties.
inertia *n* inactivity; tendency of matter to remain in existing state of rest (or continue in a fixed direction) unless acted on by an outside force.
inestimable *adj* invaluable; priceless.
inevitable *adj* unavoidable.
inexact *adj* not exactly true or correct.
inexcusable *adj* indefensible.
inexhaustible *adj* unfailing.
inexorable *adj* inflexible; relentless.
inexpedient *adj* not advisable; injudicious.
inexpensive *adj* cheap.
inexperienced *adj* unskilled; raw.
inexplicable *adj* unaccountable.
inexpressible *adj* unspeakable.
inextricable *adj* that cannot be disentangled, solved, or escaped from.
infallibility *n* freedom from liability to error; perfection.
infallible *adj* incapable of errors; reliable.
infamous *adj* scandalous; notorious.
infamy *n* public disgrace; ignominy.
infancy *n* early childhood; the early stages of anything.
infant *n* a very young child.
infanticide *n* child murder.
infantile *adj* childish; weak.
infantry *n* foot soldiers.
infatuate *vt*to inspire with foolish or short-lived passion.
infatuated *adj* besotted.
infect *vt* to taint with disease; to corrupt.
infection *n* an infecting or being infected; an infectious disease; a diseased condition.
infectious *adj* able to be transmitted.
infer *vt* to conclude, to deduce.
inference *n* conclusion; deduction.
inferior *adj* subordinate. * *n* a person lower in rank, degree, quality.
inferno *n* hell; intense heat; a devastating fire.
infernal *adj* diabolical; fiendish; extremely irritating.
infertility *n* barrenness.
infest *vt* to overrun in large numbers, usu to be harmful; to be parasitic in or on.
infidelity *n* want of faith; dishonesty; unfaithfulness esp in marriage.
infighting *n* intense competition within an organisation.
infiltrate *vt, vi* to filter or pass gradualy through or into; to permeate; to penetrate

gradually or stealthily, e.g. as spies.
infinite *adj* limitless; vast.
infinitesimal *adj* microscopic; minute.
infinitive *n* the form of a verb without reference to person, number or tense.
infinitude *n* infinity.
infinity *n* immensity; a countless number, quantity or time period.
infirm *adj* weak; sickly.
infirmary *n* a hospital.
infirmity *n* physical weakness; fault; disease.
inflame *vt* to kindle; to excite; to incense. * *vt* to grow hot.
inflammable *adj* combustible.
inflammation *n* a condition of the body marked by heat, swelling, and pain.
inflammatory *adj* tending to excite passion.
inflate *vt* to fill up with air or gas; distend; to increase beyond what is normal, esp the supply of money or credit.
inflated *adj* puffed up; elated.
inflation *n* an increase in the currency in circulation or a marked expansion of credit, resulting in a fall in currency value and a sharp rise in prices.
inflection *n* modulation of voice; changes in word forms.
inflexible *adj* unbending; rigid.
inflict *vt* to impose as a penalty.
inflorescence *n* a flowering.
influence *n* moving or directing power; sway; effect. * *vt* to move; to persuade.
influential *adj* exerting influence; possessing power.
influenza *n* contagious, feverish viral disease marked by muscular pain and inflamation of the respitory system.
influx *n* a flowing in of people or things to a place.
inform *vt* to tell; to enlighten; to teach; to give information to the police etc, in accusing another.
informal *adj* without ceremony; unofficial; casual.
information *n* intelligence; news; data stored in, or retrieved from a computer.
informative *adj* instructive.
informer *n* one who informs; a spy.
infraction *n* a violation; a breach.
infrequent *adj* uncommon; rare.
infringe *vt* to break; to transgress.
infringement *n* a breach, esp of the law.
infuriate *vt* to madden; to enrage.
infuse *vt* to pour in; to instil; to steep.
infusion *n* process of infusion; liquor (as tea) so obtained.
ingenious *adj* inventive, original; resourceful.
ingenuity *n* inventiveness.
ingenuous *adj* open, original or candid.
inglorious *adj* unhonoured; humiliating.
ingot *n* a bar of metal got from a mould.
ingrate *n* an ungrateful person.
ingratiate *vt* to get into another's favour.
ingratitude *n* thanklessnes.
ingredient *n* something included with others in a mixture; a component.
ingress *n* entrance.
inhabit *vt,vi* to live in; to dwell; to reside.
inhabitable *adj* habitable.
inhabitant *n* a resident.
inhale *vt* to draw into the lungs.
inhaler *n* a respirator; an apparatus for inhaling vapours.
inharmonious *adj* discordant.
inherent *adj* inborn; ingrained.
inherit *vt,vi* to come into possession of as an heir.
inheritance *n* a heritage; something inherited.
inhibit *vt* to restrain; to forbid.
inhibition *n* restraint; embargo.
inhospitable *adj* unfriendly and ungenerous to strangers; barren.
inhuman *adj* cruel; merciless.
inhumanity *n* cruelty.
inimical *adj* unfriendly; hostile.
inimitable *adj* matchless; peerless.
iniquitous *adj* wicked; criminal.
iniquity *n* wickedness; injustice.
initial *adj* primary; of or at the beginning. * *n* the first letters of a person's name (*pl.*) * *vt* to mark or sign with initials.
initiate *vt* to begin; to originate; to admit as a member of a club etc.
initiation *n* formal introduction or admittance.
initiative *n* first step; lead; power of originating.
inject *vt* to force (fluid into the body) esp

with a syringe.

injudicious *adj* unwise; indiscreet.

injunction *n* a command; exhortation; advice; a legal writ restraining or ordering.

injure *vt* to hurt; to damage.

injurious *adj* harmful; wrongful.

injury *n* physical damage; harm.

injustice *n* wrong; unfairness.

ink *n* a coloured liquid used for writing, printing etc. **vt* to cover, mark, or colour with ink.

inkling *n* a vague notion; a hint.

inland *adj* interior; remote from the sea; domestic; **n* an inland region.

inlay *vt* to decorate a surface by inserting pieces of metal, wood, etc.

inlet *n* a narrow strip of water extending into a body of land; an opening.

inmate *n* a resident; an occupant, esp of a prison or other institution.

inn *n* a small hotel; a public house.

innate *adj* inborn; natural; instinctive.

inner *adj* interior. * *n* the part of a target adjoining the bull's eye.

innings *n sing* (*pl* innings) the batting period of each side (cricket).

innocence *n* purity; simplicity; without guilt or guile.

innocent *adj* not guilty of a particular crime; free from sin; blameless.

innocuous *adj* harmless.

innovate *vi* to introduce new methods, ideas, etc; to make changes.

innovation *n* novelty; change.

innuendo *n* an indirect hint; a sly remark, often derogatory.

innumerable *adj* countless.

inoculate *vt* to inject a serum or a vaccine into, esp in order to create an immunity; to protect as if by inoculation.

inopportune *adj* untimely; inconvenient.

inordinate *adj* excessive; extravagant.

inorganic *adj* not having the structure or characteristics of living organisms.

inpatient *n* a patient being treated while remaining in hospital.

inquest *n* a judicial inquiry held by a coroner; esp into a case of violent or unexplained death.

inquire *vi* to ask about; to question; to investigate.

inquiring *adj* questioning; curious.

inquiry, enquiry *n* research; a question; an investigation.

inquisition *n* an inquiry; a formal search; a tribunal for trial.

inquisitive *adj* prying; inquiring; curious.

inroad *n* a raid; a foray; an encroachment or advance.

insane *adj* not sane; mentally ill.

insanity *n* lunacy; derangement of the mind; mania.

insatiable *adj* rapacious; greedy.

inscribe *vt* to mark or engrave on a surface; to add (a person's name) to a list; to dedicate (a book) to someone.

inscription *n* words engraved on stone or metal.

inscrutable *adj* hard to understand; incomprehensible; enigmatic.

insect *n* any of a class of small anthropods with three pairs of legs, a head, thorax, and abdomen and two or four wings.

insecticide *n* an insect killer.

insectivorous *adj* insect-eating.

insecure *adj* unsafe; risky; feel anxiety; not dependable.

insecurity *n* unsteadiness; peril; risk; lack of confidence; instability; something insecure.

insensibility *n* want of feeling; apathy.

insensible *adj* unconscious; unaware; indifferent; imperceptible.

insensitive *adj* not sensitive; callous.

inseparable *adj* never apart; closely attached, as romantically.

insert *vt* to put, fit, or set in.

insertion *n* a thing inserted (as advertisement); lace, etc, worked into cloth.

inset *vt* to set in; to implant. * *n* an insertion.

inshore *adj, adv.* near or towards the shore.

inside *n* the inner side, surface, or part; internal; known only to insiders; secret. * *adv* on or in the inside; within; indoors; (*prep*) in or within.

insider *n* a person within a place or group; a person with access to confidential information.

insidious *adj* treacherous; stealthy.

insight *n* discernment; penetration.
insignia *npl* badges of office or honour.
insignificance *n* littleness; triviality.
insignificant *adj* trifling; mean.
insincere *adj* faithless; deceitful.
insincerity *n* hypocrisy.
insinuate *vt* to introduce slowly, by degrees, etc.; to hint.
insipid *adj* tasteless; flat; uninteresting.
insist *vi* to urge or press strongly.
insistence *n* urgency.
insobriety *n* intemperance.
insolence *n* rudeness; impudence.
insolent *adj* overbearing; insulting.
insoluble *adj* incapable of being dissolved; impossible to solve or explain.
insolvency *n* bankruptcy.
insolvent *adj* not able to pay debts.
insomnia *n* abnormal sleeplessness.
inspect *vt* to examine; to scan carefully.
inspection *n* careful survey; examination.
inspector *n* an official who inspects in order to ensure compliance with regulations, etc.
inspectorate *n* a body of examiners.
inspiration *n* an inspiring; any stimulus to creative thought.
inspire *vt* to stimulate, as to some creative effort; to motivate by divine influence; to arouse (a thought or feeling) in (someone); to cause.
instability *n* inconstancy; fickleness.
install *vt* to invest with office; to settle in a position or state.
installation *n* machinery, equipment, etc that has been installed.
instalment *n* a sum of money to be paid at regular specified times.
instance *n* an example; a step in proceeding. * *vt* to give as an example
instant *adj* immediate; (food) concentrated or precooked for quick preparation. * *n* a moment; a particular moment.
instantaneous *adj* done in an instant.
instead *adv* in place of.
instep *n* the upper part or arch of the foot.
instigate *vt* to spur on; to urge; to initiate.
instigation *n* incitement; prompting.
instil *vt* to put (an idea etc) in or into (the mind) gradually.
instinct *n* a natural impulse; a knack.
instinctive *adj* spontaneous.
institute *vt* to set up; to found; to begin; to originate. * *n* an organization for the promotion of science, art etc.
institution *n* an established law, custom etc; an organization having a social, educational, or religious purpose; the building housing it; (*inf*) a long-established person or thing.
instruct *vt* to teach; to advise; to give instruction.
instruction *n* information; education; knowledge imparted; (*pl*) orders, directions; detailed guidance.
instructive *adj* educational; informative.
instrument *n* a thing by means of which something is done; any of various devices for indicating, controlling, measuring etc; any of various devices producing musical sound; a formal document.
instrumental *adj* serving as a means of doing something; helpful; of, performed on, or written for a musical instrument or instruments.
instrumentalist *n* a person who plays a musical instrument.
insubordinate *adj* disobedient; mutinous.
insubordination *n* revolt; disobedience.
insufferable *adj* intolerable.
insufficiency *n* inadequacy; unfitness.
insufficient *adj* not enough; inadequate.
insular *adj* pertaining to an island; narrow-minded.
insulate *vt* to set apart; to isolate; to cover with a non-conducting material in order to prevent the escape of, heat, sound, etc.
insulin *n* a hormone that controls absorption of sugar by the body.
insult *n* a gross affront; indignity. * *vt, vi* to treat with insolence; to offend.
insuperable *adj* insurmountable.
insupportable *adj* intolerable.
insurance *n* a contract purchased to guarantee compensation for a specified loss by fire, death, etc.
insure *vt* to contract against loss, damage, etc.
insurgent *adj* rebellious. * *n* a rebel.
insurmountable *adj* insuperable.
insurrection *n* a revolt; a rebellion.

intact *adj* untouched; unimpaired; whole.

intangible *adj* that cannot be touched, incorporeal; indefinable. * *n* something that is intangible.

integer *n* a whole; a whole number.

integral *adj* necessary for completeness; whole or complete; made up of parts forming a whole.

integrate *vt* to make up a whole; to complete; to bring parts together into a whole.

integrity *n* uprightness; honesty.

intellect *n* the ability to reason or understand; high intelligence; a very intelligent person.

intellectual *adj* of, involving, or appealing to the intellect; requiring intelligence. * *n* an intellectual person.

intelligence *n* the ability to learn or understand; the ability to cope with information; those involved with gathering secret, esp military, information.

intelligent *adj* quick of mind; acute; well informed.

intelligible *adj* comprehensible; clear.

intemperance *n* excess of any kind.

intemperate *adj* immoderate; unrestrained; extreme (weather).

intend *vt* to design; to have in mind as an aim or purpose.

intense *adj* strained; extreme; severe; passionate; emotional.

intensely *adv* in a high degree.

intensify *vt* to deepen; to augment.

intensity *n* vehemence; keenness; ardour; strength; the force or energy of any physical agent.

intensive *adj* strained; concentrated; describing the special and extensive care give to patients after serious surgery.

intent *adj* set; bent. * *n* purpose.

intention *n* purpose; design.

intentionally *adv* on purpose.

inter *vt* to bury.

interact *vi* to act reciprocally.

interaction *n* mutual or reciprocal action.

intercede *vi* to mediate; to plead for.

intercept *vt* to take or stop in its course; to obstruct; to cut off.

interception *n* act of intercepting.

intercession *n* mediation.

interchange *vt* to give and receive one thing for another

intercom *n* (*inf*) a system of intercommunication, as in an aircraft.

intercommunication *n* interchange of ideas and means for securing it.

intercourse *n* communion; fellowship; sexual intercourse.

interdict *vt* to forbid; to veto.

interest *n* a feeling of concern about something; anything in which one has a share; benefit; money paid for the use of money; **vt* to excite the attention of; to cause to have a share in; to concern oneself with.

interested *adj* concerned; biased.

interesting *adj* engaging; intriguing; attractive.

interfere *vi* to clash; to interpose; to meddle; to obstruct.

interference *n* intermeddling; clashing; (radio,T.V) the interruption of reception by atmospherics or by unwanted signals.

interim *n* the meantime; an intervening period of time; * *adj* temporary.

interior *adj* internal; inland.

interject *vt* to throw in between; to insert; to interrupt

interjection *n* a word thrown in abruptly.

interlace *vti* to weave together.

interleave *vt* to insert blank leaves between other leaves.

interlock *vi, vt* to clasp together.

interloper *n* an intruder; a meddler.

interlude *n* an interval.

intermediary*n* a go-between; a mediator.

intermediate *adj* intervening; middle.

interment *n* burial.

interminable *adj* endless; boundless.

intermingle *vt* to mingle together.

intermission *n* a pause between parts of a performance; a rest.

intermittent *adj* coming and going; ebbing and flowing; periodic.

intern *vt* to confine prisoners, etc, in a prescribed area.

internal *adj* of or on the inside; inward.

international *adj* between or among nations; concerned with the relationship between nations; for the use of all nations; of or for people in various nations.

internecine *adj* deadly; bloody; mutually destructive.
interpolate *vt* to interrupt speech etc. with comments; to insert a passage into a text.
interpose *vt* to place between.
interpret *vt* to explain; to translate; to construe; to give one's own conception of; * *vi* to translate between speakers of different languages.
interpretation *n* an explanation.
interpreter *n* one who interprets; a translator.
interrogate *vt* to question.
interrogation *n* a questioning; a mark of questioning, (?).
interrogative *adj* denoting a question.
interrupt *vi* to break in upon.
interruption *n* a hindrance; a stoppage; a break in continuity, by passing through or crossing.
intersect *vt* to divide; to cross mutually.
intersection *n* a cutting; crossing of two lines; the point of crossing.
intersperse to scatter; to mingle.
interstellar *adj* among the stars.
intertwine *vt* to weave or twist together.
interval *n* time or distance between; the difference of pitch between two sounds.
intervene *vi* to interpose or interfere; to settle or hinder a matter etc.
intervention *n* a coming between; interference; mediation.
interview *n* a meeting in which a person is asked about his or her views, etc; a meeting at which a candidate for a job is questioned and assessed for a job.
interweave *vt* to intertwine.
intestate *adj* dying without having made a will.
intestinal *adj* pertaining to the intestines.
intestine *n* the part of the alimentary canal between the stomach and the anus.
intimacy *n* close friendship; familiarity; close friendship.
intimate *adj* most private or personal; very close or familiar, esp sexually. * *n* a close friend. * *vt* to make known.
intimation *n* a hint; an announcement.
intimidate *vt* to overawe; to cow.
into *prep* expressing motion towards the inside; to a particular condition.
intolerable *adj* insufferable; unbearable.
intolerance *n* bigotry; narrow-mindedness; inability to endure.
intolerant *adj* illiberal; bigoted.
intonation *n* a modulation of the voice.
intone *vi* to chant in a slow monotone.
intoxicant *n* an alcoholic drink etc.
intoxicate *vt* to make drunk; to stir up.
intoxication *n* drunkenness; frenzy; great excitement.
intractable*adj* ungovernable; headstrong; difficult to solve (of problem) or alleviate (of illness).
intransigent *adj* irreconcilable; unwilling to compromise.
intransitive *adj* of a verb whose action is limited to subject.
intrepid *adj* undaunted; fearless.
intricacy *n* entanglement; complexity.
intricate *adj* involved; detailed.
intrigue *n* an underhand plot. * *vi* to plot secretly; to rouse curiosity.
intriguing *adj* scheming; crafty; interesting; attractive.
intrinsic, intrinsical *adj* in itself; belonging to the real nature of a person or thing; inherent.
introduce *vt* to present; to insert; to begin; to make known; to bring into use.
introduction *n* an introducing or being introduced; the presentation of one person to another; preliminary statement; preface; presentation.
introductory *adj* prefatory; preliminary.
introspection *n* self-examination.
introvert *n* a person who is more interested in his or her own thoughts, feelings, etc than in external objects or events. **adj* characterized by introversion (*also* **introverted**)
intrude *vi* to trespass; meddle. * *vt* to thrust in; to force oneself on others.
intrusion *n* encroachment; trespass.
intrusive *adj* jutting in; forward.
intuition *n* insight; instinctive perception apprehension of the truth of something.
intuitive *adj* natural; apprehended instinctively.
inundate *vt* to flow over; to flood.
inundation *n* a flood; a deluge.
inure *vt* to harden by use.

invade *vt* to enter as an enemy; to attack; to encroach upon.
invalid[1] *adj* void; illegal.
invalid[2] *n* a person who is ill or disabled. * *vt* to cause to become an invalid; to disable; to cause to retire from the armed forces because of ill-health or injury.
invalidate *vt* to render of no effect; no legal use.
invalidity *n* ineffectiveness.
invaluable *adj* priceless.
invariable *adj* constant; unchangeable.
invasion *n* hostile entrance; encroachment; intrusion.
invective *n* a tirade; vituperation. * *adj* abusive.
inveigh *vi* to rail against.
inveigle *vt* to beguile; to decoy.
invent *vt* to originate; to devise; to concoct; to fabricate (a lie etc.).
invention *n* a new contrivance; ingenuity.
inventive *adj* ingenious; skilled in invention.
inventory *n* an itemized list of goods, property etc, as of a business. **vt* to make an inventory of; to enter in an inventory.
inverse *adj* opposite; reversed; contrary.
inversion *n* reversal; complete turn about.
invert *vt* to turn upside down; to reverse in order, position or relationship.
invertebrate *adj* without backbone; *n* an animal without a backbone..
inverted *adj*turned upside down etc.
invest *vt* to commit (money) to property, stocks and shares etc, for profit; to devote effort, time, etc on a particular activity; to install in office with ceremony; to furnish with power, authority, etc. **vi* to invest money.
investigate *vt* to search into; to examine; to inquire into.
investiture *n* the act or right of giving legal possession; the ceremony of investing a person with an office, robes, title, etc.
investment *n* the act of investing money productively; the amount invested; an activity in which time, effort or money has been invested.
inveteracy *n* confirmed obstinacy.
inveterate *adj* deep-rooted; confirmed.
invidious *adj* envious; causing ill-will.
invigorate *vt* to strengthen; to enliven; to refresh.
invincible *adj* unconquerable.
inviolable *adj* sacred; not to be broken.
inviolate *adj* virgin; stainless; intact.
invisible *adj* unseen; imperceptible.; hidden.
invitation *n* a bidding to come or do something.
invite *vt* to ask to come somewhere or do something; to ask for; to give reason for; to tempt; to entice.
inviting *pa* attractive; enticing.
invocation *n* a prayer to God for help; an appeal to muse for aid; a summons.
invoice *n* a list of goods supplied, with prices; a bill. * *vt* to make out a bill (for goods).
invoke *vt* to call upon (God etc.); to address in prayer; to resort to (law etc.) as pertinent; to implore.
involuntary *adj* done without power to choose; instinctive.
involve *vt* to roll up; include; to implicate; to complicate; to make busy.
invulnerable *adj* not able to be hurt; secure.
inward *adj* situated within or directed to the inside; relating to or in the mind or spirit. **adv* inwards.
inwardly *adv* within; in the mind or spirit; towards the inside or centre.
inwards *adv* towards the inside or interior; in the mind or spirit.
iodine *n* a nonmetallic element got from seaweed.
Ionic *adj* one of orders of Greek architecture.
iota *n* the ninth letter of the Greek alphabet; a jot; a very small quantity.
ipecacuanha *n* a medicinal plant and medicine got from it.
irascibility *n* anger; testiness.
irascible *adj* easily angered; irritable.
irate *adj* angry; enraged.
ire *n* anger; wrath; rage.
iridescence *n* display of colours like the rainbow.

iridescent *adj* shimmering with rainbow colours.

iris *n* (*pl* **irises, irides**) the round pigmented membrane surrounding the pupil of the eye; a perennial herbaceous plant with sword shaped leaves and brightly coloured flowers.

irk *vt* to weary; to vex; to annoy.

irksome *adj* wearisome; tedious.

iron *n* a metallic element, the most common of all metals; a tool, etc of this metal; a heavy implement with a heated flat undersurface for pressing cloth; (*pl*) shackles of iron; firm strength; power; any of certain golf clubs with angled metal heads. * *adj* of iron; like iron, strong and firm. * *vt, vi* to press with a hot iron.

ironic, ironical *adj* satirical; sarcastic.

ironmonger *n* a dealer in hardware; metal goods, tools etc.

irony *n* a form of sarcasm in which the sense is opposite to the words.

irradiate *vt* to illuminate; to enlighten.

irradiation *n* illumination.

irrational *adj* void of reason; senseless; absurd.

irreconcilable *adj* inconsistent; implacable; incompatible.

irredeemable *adj* hopelessly lost; inconvertible.

irrefutable *adj* unanswerable; unable to deny or disprove.

irregular *adj* not regular; crooked; not conforming to the rules; imperfect; not belonging to the regular armed forces.

irrelevance, irrelevancy *n* inaptness; lack of point.

irrelevant *adj* not to the point.

irreligious *adj* not religious; profane.

irremediable *adj* without remedy.

irreparable *adj* irremediable; not able to be repaired, rectified or made good.

irrespressible *adj* uncontrollable.

irreproachable *adj* faultless.

irresistible *adj* overwhelming; resistless; fascinating.

irresolute *adj* undecided; wavering.

irresolution *n* indecision.

irrespective *adj* making no exceptions; regardless of.

irresponsible *adj* lacking a sense of responsibility; flighty.

irretrievable *adj* irreparable; hopeless.

irreverence *n* disrespect; impiety.

irreverent *adj* not paying due respect.

irreversible *adj* irrevocable.

irrevocable *adj* unalterable.

irrigate *vt* to water land artificially; (medicine) to wash out a cavity, wound etc.

irrigation *n* supplying land with water.

irritability *n* hastiness of temper.

irritable *adj* short-tempered; touchy.

irritant *adj* irritating; galling. * *n* an irritating agent; a stimulant.

irritate *vt* to provoke; to inflame.

irritating *adj* annoying.

irritation *n* annoyance.

irruption *n* an invasion; inroad.

irruptive *adj* rushing in or upon.

is 3rd per. sing. pres. indic. verb to *be*.

Islam *n* the religion of Mohammed; the Moslem world.

island *n* land surrounded by water.

isle *n* an island.

islet *n* a little isle.

isobar *n* a line on a map joining places with equal atmospheric pressure.

isolate *vt* to cut off; to set apart from others; to quarantine; to seperate a constituent subject from a compound.

isolation *n* detachment; loneliness.

isometric *adj* pertaining to equality of measure or dimension.

isosceles *adj* having two sides equal.

isotherm *n* a line on a map joining places with equal temperature.

isotope *n* any of two or more forms of an element having the same atomic number but different atomic weights.

issue *n* an outgoing; an outlet; a result; offspring; a point under dispute; a sending or giving out; all that is put forth at one time (an issue of bonds, a priodical etc.)* *vi* to go or flow out; to result (from) or end (in); to be published. * *vt* to let out; to discharge; to give or deal out, as supplies; to publish.

isthmus *n* a narrow neck of land; connecting two larger bodies of land.

it *pron* 3rd. per. neuter.

italic *adj* the name of a printing type in

which the letters slant upwards to the right *pl* ; italic type (*italic*).

italicize *vt* to print in italics.

itch *n* an irritating sensation on the surface of the skin causing a need to scratch; an insistent desire;* *vt* to have or feel an irritating sensation in the skin; to feel a restless desire.

item *n* an article; a unit; a seperate thing; a bit of news or information; (*inf*) a couple having an affair.

itemize *vt* to specify the terms of; to set down by items.

iterate *vt* to repeat.

iteration *n* repetition.

itinerant *adj* travelling from place to place; **n* a traveller.

itinerary *n* a travel route; a record or detailed plan of a journey.

its *pron* 3rd per. possessive of it.

itself *n* the neuter reflexive pronoun.

ivory *n* a hard bony substance forming tusks of elephants, etc; a creamy white colour; * *adj* of or like ivory; creamy white.

ivy *n* a climbing or creeping plant with a woody stem and evergreen leaves.

J

jab *vt, vi* (*pt*) to poke or thrust roughly; to punch with short, straight blows.

jabber *vi* to gabble; to speak or say rapidly, incoherently, or foolishly.

jack *n* any of various mechanical or hydraulic devices used to lift something heavy. * *vt* to raise by means of a jack.

jacket *n* a short outer garment; an outer covering.

jackknife *n* a pocket-knife. * *vi* (articulated lorry) to lose control so that the cab and trailer swing against each other.

jackpot *n* the accumulated stakes in certain games, as poker.

jade *n* a hard, semiprecious stone; it's light green colour.

jaded *adj* tired, exhausted; satiated.

jag *vt* to notch; to prick. * *n* a point.

jagged *adj* ragged; notched.

jail *n* a prison; a gaol.

jam *n* a preserve made of boiled fruit and sugar; * *vt* to press into a confined space; to crowd full of people or things; to cause interference to a radio signal rendering it unintelligable.

jangle *vi* to make a harsh or discordant sound, as bells. * *vt* to cause to jangle.

janitor *n* a caretaker.

January *n* the first month of the year.

jar *vi* to clash; to grate. * *n* a harsh sound; a vase or jug; a jolt.

jargon *n* the specialised or technical vocabulary of a science, profession, etc; obscure and usu pretentious language.

jaundice *n* a disease marked by yellowness of the eyes and skin.

jaundiced *adj* disillusioned.

jaunt *vi* to go from place to place.

jauntily *adv* briskly; sprightly.

jaunty *adj* sprightly.

javelin *n* a spear for throwing.

jaw *n* one of the bones which hold the teeth.

jaywalk *vi* to walk across a street carelessly without obeying traffic rules.

jazz *n* a general term for American popular music, characterized by syncopated rhythms.

jealous *adj* suspicious of a rival; envious.

jealousy *n* suspicion; envy.

jeans *npl* trousers made from denim.

jeep *n* a small robust vehicle with heavy duty tyres and four-wheel drive.

jeer *vi* to laugh derisively; to mock.

jelly *n* the juice of fruit boiled with sugar to a glutinous state.

jemmy *n* a burglar's crowbar.

jeopardize *vt* to hazard.

jeopardy *n* hazard; risk.

jerk *vt, vi* to give a sudden pull, thrust, or push to. * *n* a sudden thrust; a quick pull.

jerky *adj* moving by jerks.

jersey *n* a knitted woollen garment; a sweater.

jest *n* a joke; pleasantry. * *vi* to joke.

jet *n* a spouting forth; a nozzle for emission of fluid or gas; a hard black mineral that when polished is used for jewellery.

jet-black *adj* of the deepest black.

jetsam, jetson *n* cargo thrown overboard

to lighten a ship; this cargo when washed ashore.
jettison *v.* to throw goods overboard.
jetty *n* a small pier.
jewel *n* a precious stone; highly prized.
jeweller *n* a dealer in jewels.
jewellery *n* jewels in general, e.g. rings, necklaces, brooches etc.
jib *n* the triangular foremost sail of a ship; the arm of a crane.
jib *vt, vi* to shift a sail; to turn aside.
jibe *vt* to taunt; to scoff at; gibe. * *n* a taunt; a sneer.
jig *n* a lively dance or tune. * *vi* to dance.
jigsaw *n* a picture on wood or board cut into irregular shapes for re-assembling for amusement.
jilt *vt* to discard a lover.
jingle *vi, vt* to clink, or tinkle. * *n* a tinkling sound, as of bells; a catchy verse.
jingoism *n* belligerent patriotism.
jinx *n* someone or something thought to bring bad luck.
jitter*vi* to feel nervous. **npl* a nervous feeling of panic.
job *n* a piece of work done for pay; a task; a duty; the thing or material being worked on; work; employment.
jobber *n* a carriage hirer; a stockjobber.
jockey *n* a professional racehorse rider. * *vt* to manoeuvre for a better position.
jocular *adj* joking; full of jokes.
jocularity *n* merriment.
jog *vt* to give a slight shake or nudge to; to rouse, as the memory. * *vi* to run at a slow pace for exercise. * *n* a slight shake or push; a nudge; a slow walk or trot.
join *vt, vi* to bring and come together (with); to connect; to unite; to unite; to become a part or member of (a club, etc.); to participate in; * *n* a joining; a place of joining.
joiner *n* a worker in wood.
joint *n* a place where, or way in which, two things are joined; the part where two bones move on one another in an animal. * *adj* common to two or more; sharing with another. * *vt* to connect by a joint or joints; to divide (an animal carcass) into parts for cooking.
jointly *adv* together; in common.
joist *n* a beam supporting floorboards.
joke *n* something said or done to cause laughter; a thing said or done merely in fun.
jolly *adj* merry; jovial; full of fun.
jolt *vi, vt* to shake with sudden jerks; to surprise or shock suddenly.
jostle *vti* to knock against; to hustle; to elbow for position.
jot *n* an iota. * *vt* to note down briefly.
jotter *n* a notebook.
jotting *n* a memorandum.
journal *n* a daily record of happenings, as a diary; a newspaper or periodical.
journalism*n* the work of gathering news for, or producing a newspaper, magazine or broadcast.
journalist *n* a newspaper contributor.
journey *n* a travelling; the distance travelled; a tour * *vi* to travel.
jovial *adj* gay; merry; jolly.
jowl *n* the jaw. *cheek by jowl*, side by side.
joy *n* delight; gladness.
joyful *adj* filled with, expressing, or causing joy.
joyous *adj* full of joy.
jubilant *adj* rejoicing greatly; triumphant.
jubilation *n* the joy of triumph.
jubilee *n* a 25th or 50th anniversary of an event.
Judaism *n* the religion of the Jews; Jewish modes of thought.
judge *n* a public official with authority to hear and decide cases in a court of law. * *vt,vi* to hear and pass judgement on the relative worth of anything.
judgment *n* act of judging; a legal decision; an opinion; good sense; discernment; censure.
judicial *adj* pertaining to judges or courts of justice; impartial.
judiciary *adj* relating to courts of justice * *n* judges collectively.
judicious *adj* possessing prudence; characterized by sound judgement.
jug *n* a vessel for holding and pouring liquids; a pitcher.
juggernaut *n* a terrible, irresistable force; a large heavy truck.
juggle *vi* to conjure; to manipulate.
juggler *n* a conjuror.

jugular *adj* pertaining to the throat.
juice *n* fluid of fruits, vegetables and meat.
July *n* the seventh month of the year.
jumble *vt,vi* to mix in a confused mass * *n* a muddle; articles for a jumble sale.
jumbo *n* something very large of its kind.
jump *vi* to spring or leap from the ground, a height, etc; to jerk; a sudden transition; an obstacle; a nervous start.
jumper *n* a knitted pullover.
junction *n* a point of union; a railway centre.
juncture *n* where lines meet; link or cross each other.
June *n* the sixth month of the year.
jungle *n* an area overgrown with dense tropical trees and other vegetation, etc.
junior *adj* younger in age; of more recent or lower status; of juniors.
junk *n* discarded rubbish or useless articles; any narcotic drug; Chinese floating vessel.
jurisdiction *n* judicial authority, its range or extent.
jurisprudence *n* the science or philosophy of law; a division of the law.
jurist *n* one versed in law.
juror *n* one who serves on a jury.
jury *n* a number of men and women sworn to hear evidence and deliver a verdict on a case; a panel.
just *adj* fair, impartial; deserved, merited; proper, exact; conforming strictly with the facts. **adv* exactly; nearly; only.
justice *n* justness, fairness; the use of authority to maintain what is just; the administration of law; a judge.
justiciary, justiciar *n* an administrator of justice.
justifiable *adj* that may be justified.
justification *n* a defence; vindication; remission of sin.
justify *vt* to prove right; to vindicate.
justly *adv* rightly; properly.
jut *vi* to project.
juvenile *adj* young; youthful; immature.
juxtaposition *n* a placing near or side by side.

K

kail, kale *n* a kind of cabbage.
kaleidoscope *n* a small tube containing bits of coloured glass reflected by mirrors to form symmetrical patterns as the tube is rotated.
keel *n* the backbone of a ship. * *vt, vi* to (cause to) turn over.
keen *adj* shrewd; sharp; eager; low (of prices) as to be competative.
keep *vt* to hold; to preserve; to guard; to detain; to continue any state, course, or action; to obey; to perform * *vi* to endure; not to perish or be impaired * *n* care; guard; a strong tower.
keeper *n* one who guards.
keeping *n* care, charge; observance.
keepsake *n* a gift treasured because of the giver.
keg *n* a small cask or barrel.
kennel *n* a small shelter for dogs; (*pl*) a place where dogs are bred or kept.
kerb *n* stone edging to pavement.
kernel *n* the core (esp. of nut).
kerosene *n* a fuel oil distilled from petrol.
kettle *n* a metal vessel with spout for boiling water.
kettledrum *n* a drum made of a hollow metal body with a parchment head.
key *n* a device for locking and unlocking something; a thing that explains or solves, as the legend of a map, a code etc.
keyboard *n* a set of levers on which the fingers press on a piano, computer, etc.
keynote *n* the basic note of a musical scale; the basic idea or ruling principle.
keystone *n* the top stone of an arch, keeping whole together.
khaki *adj* dull yellowish-brown.
kick *vt, vi* to strike with the foot; to recoil * *n* a blow with the foot or feet; recoil; a thrill; an intoxicating effect.
kidnap *vt* to carry off a person by force and hold to ransom.
kidney *n* one of two glands that secrete urine an animal's kidney as food.
kill *vt* to cause the death of; to destroy. * *n* the act of killing; an animal or animals

killed.

kiln *n* a stone furnace for baking or hardening lime, bricks, pottery etc.

kilogram, kilogramme *n* a measure of weight (2.204 lbs).

kilometre *n* a measure of length, 1000 metres or 0.62 mile.

kin *n* family; kindred; relatives.

kind *n* race; genus; variety; nature * *adj* humane; friendly; sympathetic.

kindle *vt, vi* to set on fire; to light; to arouse.

kindly *adj* friendly; genial; kind; gracious.

kindness *n* goodness; helpfulness; benevolence.

kindred *n* kinship; blood relations * *adj* related; akin; similar.

kinetic *adj* causing motion; of motion in relation to force.

kinetics *n* the science of motion in relation to force.

king *n* the man who rules a country and its people; a man with the title of ruler, but with limited power to rule.

kingdom *n* a state; a realm, a country headed by a king; any of the three divisions of the natural world: animal, vegetable, mineral.

kink *n* a tight twist or curl in a piece of string, rope, hair etc; a painful cramp in the neck, back, etc; an eccentricity of personality. * *vt, vi* to form or cause to form a kink or kinks.

kiosk *n* a light open structure for sale of papers, sweets, etc; a public telephone booth.

kipper *n* a herring split open, salted, and dried.

kirk *n* a church.

kiss *vt, vi* to touch with the lips as an expression of love, affection or in greeting. * *n* an act of kissing; a light, gentle touch.

kit *n* an outfit; equipment e.g. tools etc.; a set of parts for assembly.

kitchen *n* a place where food is prepared.

kite *n* a light paper-covered frame for flying in air.

kith *n* relatives and friends.

kleptomania *n* an irresistible impulse to steal.

knack *n* dexterity; a trick; a habit.

knapsack *n* a backpack.

knead *vt* to work dough; to squeeze and press with the hands.

knee *n* the joint between the thigh and the lower part of the human leg; anything shaped like a bent knee. * *vt* (*pt* **kneed**) to hit or touch with the knee.

kneel *vi* to go down and remain on the knees.

knell *n* the sound of a bell (esp. funeral bell). * *vi* to toll.

knickers *npl* an undergarment covering the lower body and having separate leg holes, worn by women and girls.

knife *n* a cutting instrument. * *vt* to cut or stab with a knife.

knight *n* a rank conferring title Sir; a chessman shaped like a horse's head.

knighthood *n* the rank or dignity of a knight.

knit *vb* (*pt* **knitted** *or* **knit**) *vt, vi* to form (fabric or a garment) by interlooping yarn using knitting needles or a machine.

knitting *n* the thing being knitted.

knob *n* a rounded lump or protuberance; a boss or stud or handle (of a door).

knock *vt, vi* to strike; to strike against; to rap on a door; to criticize. * *n* a blow; a rap.

knocker *n* the device hinged against a door for knocking.

knockout *n* a punch or blow that produces unconsciousness.

knoll *n* a little round hill.

knot *n* a lump in a thread, etc formed by a tightened loop or tangling; a fastening made by tying lengths of rope, etc. * *vt, vi* (*pt* **knotted**) to make or form a knot (in); to entangle or become entangled.

know *vt* to be aware that; to be sure that; to understand; to be acquainted with. * *vi* to have knowledge.

knowing *adj* well informed; shrewd; implying a secret understanding.

knowledge *n* acquaintance with; learning; information.

knuckle *n* the joint of a finger.

Koran *n* the sacred book of Muslims.

kudos *n* glory; fame; renown.

L

label *n* a slip of paper, cloth, metal etc attached to anything to provide information about its nature, contents.

laboratory *n* a building where scientific work and research is carried out.

laborious *adj* arduous; laboured; hardworking.

labour *n* exertion; toil; workers collectively; the process of childbirth * *vi* to work; to be burdened; to give unnecessary details.

labourer *n* a worker; esp doing heavy or manual work.

labyrinth *n* a place full of winding paths; a maze.

lac *n* a resin yielding shellac.

lace *n* a cord, etc used to draw together and fasten parts of a shoe, a corset etc.

lacerate *vt* to tear to torture.

lack *vt* to want; to need. * *vi* to be in want. * *n* want; failure deficiency.

lackadaisical *adj* languid; showing lack of energy or interest.

lackey *n* footman; flunkey.

laconic *adj* concise; brief; using few words.

lacquer *n* n varnish; lacquered ware * *vt* to varnish; to gloss.

lactic *adj* related to or procured from milk.

lad *n* a boy; a young man.

ladder *n* a portable metal or wooden framework for climbing up and down.

laden *adj* loaded; burdened.

lading *n* cargo; freight.

ladle *n* a large long-handled spoon.

lady *n* a woman of rank; a title.

lag * *vi* to loiter; to fall behind; to insulate pipes with insulating material.

lager *n* a light beer.

laggard *adj* slow * *n* a dawdler.

lagging *n* insulating material.

lagoon *n* a shallow saltwater lake cut off from the sea by a coral reef.

laisser faire *n* non-interference; freedom of action (esp. in commerce, etc).

laity *n* lay people, as distinguished from the clergy.

lake *n* water wholly surrounded by land; a purplish-red pigment.

lame *adj* crippled; limping.

lament *vi* to weep; to grieve * *vt* to bewail * *n* a mournful song or tune.

lamentable *adj* distressing; deplorable.

lamentation *n* mourning; sorrow.

lamp *n* any device producing light, either by electricity, gas or by burning oil etc.

lance *n* a long spear * *vt* to cut or pierce with a lancet.

land *n* the solid part of the earth's surface; ground, soil; a country and its people; property in land. * *vt,vi* to go ashore from a ship; to come to port; to arrive at a specified place; to come to rest.

landing *n* act or place of disembarking; a platform or flat area at the top of a flight of stairs; the floor between flights of stairs.

landlady *n* the mistress of an inn or boarding house; a woman who rents property.

landlocked *adj* enclosed by land.

landlord *n* owner of land or houses; owner or host of an inn, etc.

landlubber *n* one with little experience of the sea and sailing.

landmark *n* a prominent feature that serves as a guide or distinguishes a locality; an important event or turning point.

landowner *n* a person who owns land.

landscape *n* an expanse of natural scenery seen in one view; a picture of natural, inland scenery. * *vt* to make (a plot of ground) more attractive.

landslip, landslide *n* the sliding of a mass of soil or rocks down a slope; an overwhelming victory esp in an election.

lane *n* a narrow road, path etc; a path or strip specifically designated for ships, aircraft, cars etc.

language *n* human speech; speech peculiar to a nation.

languid *adj* faint; listless; weak.

languish *vi* to be or become faint; to droop; to pine.

languishing *pa* pining, spiritless.

languor *n* faintness; listlessness.

lank *adj* tall and thin; long an limp.

lanky *adj* **(lankier, lankiest)** lean, tall and ungainly.

lanoline *n* a soothing ointment.
lantern *n* a portable transparent case for holding a light.
lap *n* the seat formed by knees and thighs in sitting posture; one round of a course in a race.
lapel *n* the folded back part of coat etc. continuous with the cotton.
lapse *n* a small error; a decline or drop to a lower condition, degree, or state; a moral decline.
larceny *n* theft of goods.
lard *n* melted and clarified pig fat. * *vt* to embellish.
larder *n* a store cupboard for provisions.
large *adj* great in size, number; big, bulky.
largely *adv* widely; copiously; mainly.
largess *n* a present; bounty.
largo *a* adv slow (in music).
lark *n* a frolic; a prank.
larva *n* (*pl* **larvae**) an insect in grub state.
larynx *n* the upper part of the windpipe containing the vocal cords.
lascivious *adj* lewd; lecherous.
lash *n* the thong of a whip; a stroke with a whip * *vt* to whip; to bind.
lassitude *n* faintness; weariness.
last *adj* coming after all the others; latest; final. * *adv* the last time. * *vi* to endure; to continue. * *n* a shaped block on which shoes are made; a foot mould.
lasting *adj* durable; permanent.
latch *n* the catch of a door, gate etc. * *vt, vi* to fasten with a latch.
late *adj* behind time; long delayed; deceased * *adv* at a late time; recently.
latent *adj* not yet apparent; dormant.
lateral *adj* of, at, from, towards; on the side.
lath *n* a long narrow slip of wood to support plaster, etc.
lathe *n* a machine for shaping wood or iron.
lather *n* froth of soap and water; frothy.
Latin *adj* of ancient Rome, its people, their language etc.
latitude *n* breadth; width; scope; freedom from restriction on action or opinions; distance north or south of the equator.
latter *adj* later; coming after; modern; being the last mentioned of two.
lattice *n* a network of crossed laths; a trellis; a window so formed.
laudable *adj* praiseworthy.
laudatory *adj* expressing praise.
laugh *vi* to make the sound expressive of mirth; to be gay, mirthful * *n* the sound or act of laughing.
laughable *adj* amusing; comical.
laughing stock *n* an object of ridicule.
laughter *n* the act or sound of laughing.
launch *vt* to throw; to propel and slide (into water). * *vi* to initiate; to put into action. * *n* the act of launching; a large open motorboat.
launder *vt, vi* to wash and iron clothes.
launderette *n* an establishment equipped with coin-operated washing machines.
laundry *n* place where clothes are washed and ironed.
laureate *adj* decked with laurel leaves as a mark of honour. * a poet laureate, the official court poet.
lava *n* molten volcanic rocks.
lavatory *n* a place for washing hands, urinating etc.
lavish *adj* profuse; generous; abundant; extravagant * *vt* to give or spend generously.
law *n* all the rules of conduct in an organized community as upheld by authority.
law-abiding *adj* obeying the law.
lawbreaker *n* a person who violates the law.
lawful *adj* legal; rightful.
lawgiver *n* a legislator.
lawless *adj* not regulated by law; not in conformity with law, illegal.
lawn *n* a smooth level grass plot; a fine linen.
lawsuit *n* a suit between private parties in a law court.
lawyer *n* a person whose profession is advising others in matters of law or representing them in a court of law.
lax *adj* loose; slack; vague; not strict.
laxative *adj* purging * *n* a gentle purgative.
laxity *n* slackness; carelessness.
lay *vt* to cause to lie; to place; to impose; to allay, to bring forth eggs; to wager. * *n* a song; a poem. * *adj* not clerical, or

expert.

layer *n* a stratum; a single thickness; a coat, as of paint. * *vt* to separate into layers.

layman *n* one not a clergyman; a non-specialist or professional.

layout *n* the manner in which anything is laid out.

laziness *n* indolence; sloth.

lazy *adj* slothful; indolent.

lea *n* a meadow.

lead *n* a soft and heavy metal; a stick of graphite.

lead *vt, vi* to guide or conduct; to direct; to precede; to entice; to influence; to be first * *n* guidance; the role of a leader; the amount or distance ahead; a clue; the leading role in a play etc.

leaden *adj* heavy; dull; like lead; gloomy.

leader *n* a guide; a captain; an editorial article; the first violin in an orchestra.

leading *adj* chief; principal.

leaf *n* one of the thin parts of a plant growing from the skin; a sheet of paper or metal; two pages of a book.

leaflet *n* a little leaf; a sheet of printed information or advertising matter.

league *n* a union for mutual help; an alliance; a treaty; an association of sports club that organizes matches between members.

leak *n* a hole which admits water or gas; confidential information made public deliberately or accidentally * *vi* to let water in or out; to disclose.

leakage *n* a leaking.

lean *vi* to slope; to incline; to rest against; to rely on.

lean *adj* thin; barren; meagre.

leaning *n* inclination, tendency.

leap *vi, vt* to jump; to bound * *n* a spring.

learn *vt, vi* to gain knowledge or skill; to find out; to realize.

learning *n* knowledge; scholarship.

lease *n* a letting for a term of years * *vt* to let or lease.

leasehold *adj* held by lease * *n* tenure by lease.

leaseholder *n* a tenant under a lease.

leash *n* a thong or strap for leading animals. * *vt* to hold or restrain on a leash.

least *adj* smallest. * *adv* in the smallest degree. * *n* the smallest amount.

leather *n* tanned and dressed hide.

leave *n* permission; farewell; the period allowed for absence. * *vt* to let remain; to bequeath; to quit; to deposit.

lecherous *adj* lustful; lewd.

lectern *n* a reading desk in a church.

lecture *n* a discourse; a reprimand * *vi* to deliver a lecture * *vt* to reprove.

ledge *n* a narrow shelf; a ridge; a layer.

ledger *n* an account book.

leech *n* a bloodsucking worm; a person who clings to or uses another.

leer *n* a sly or lewd glance. * *vi* to give a leer.

lees *npl* dregs; sediment.

leeward *adj* pertaining to the lee. * *adv* towards the lee.

leeway *n* the drift of a ship to leeward * to make up leeway, to make up lost time.

left *adj* denoting opposite to the right; towards the west when facing north. * *n* the left side; the left hand; the left wing in politics.

left-wing *adj* of or relating to the liberal faction of a political party.

leg *n* one of the limbs on which humans and animals support themselves and walk; any of a series of games or matches in a competition.

legacy *n* money, property etc. left to someone in a will.

legal *adj* of or based on law; permitted by law; of or for lawyers. * *vt* to make lawful.

legality *n* conformity to law.

legalize *vt* to make lawful; to sanction.

legatee *n* one to whom a legacy is left.

legend *n* a story handed down from the past; a notable person or the stories of his or her exploits.

legendary *adj* fabulous; mythical.

leggings *npl* protective outer covering for the lower leg; a leg-hugging fashion garment for women.

legible *adj* able to be read.

legion *n* a great number.

legislate *vi* to make or pass laws.

legislative *adj* capable of enacting laws.

legislator *n* one who makes laws.

legislature *n* the lawmaking body in a state.
legitimate *adj* legal; born in wedlock; genuine; valid.
leguminous *adj* pertaining to pod-bearing plants, e.g. peas, pulse, beans, etc.
leisure *n* spare time; freedom from business; relaxation.
leisurely *adj* not hasty; relaxed. * *adv* slowly.
lend *vt* to grant use of a thing temporarily; to provide money at interest.
length *n* extent from end to end; duration; extension; a long expanse; a piece of specified length cut from a longer piece.
lengthen *vt* to make long; to extend.
lengthwise *adv* in the direction of the length.
lenience, leniency *n* quality of being lenient; mildness.
lenient *adj* merciful; forbearing; not harsh.
lens *n* (*pl* **lenses**) a curved piece of transparent glass, plastic etc used in optical instruments to form an image; a similar transparent part of the eye that focuses light rays on the retina.
Leo *n* the Lion, fifth sign of zodiac.
leotard *n* a skintight one-piece garment worn by dancers and others engaged in strenuous exercise.
leper *n* one affected with leprosy.
leprosy *n* disease of the skin.
lesbian *n* a female homosexual. * *adj* of or characteristic of lesbians.
lesion *n* an injury; a wound.
less *adj* smaller. * *adv* in a lower degree; to a smaller extent. * *n* a smaller quantity.
lessee *n* the holder of a lease.
lessen *vt, vi* to make or become less.
lesser *adj* less; smaller.
lesson *n* something to be learned or studied; an example.
lest *conj* for fear that.
let *vt* to permit; to allow; to lease; to rent.
let-down *n* a disappointment.
lethal *adj* deadly; fatal.
lethargic *adj* drowsy; dull.
lethargy *n* a drowsy state.
letter *n* a symbol representing a phonetic value in a written language; a character of the alphabet; a written or printed message.
letter box *n* a slit in the doorway of a house or building through which letters are delivered; a postbox.
lettering *n* the act or process of inscribing with letters; letters collectively; a title; an inscription.
lettuce *n* a leafy plant used in salads.
leukaemia, leukemia *n* a chronic disease characterized by an abnormal increase in the number of white blood cells.
level *n* an instrument for determining the horizontal; a horizontal line or surface; an even surface. * *adj* horizontal; even; flat * *vt, vi* to make level; to flatten.
level-headed *adj* having an even temper and sound judgment.
lever *n* a bar for raising weights; a means to an end; a device used to operate machinery.
leverage *n* power gained by use of a lever; power; influence.
levity *n* lightness; frivolity; lack of seriousness.
levy *vt* to collect (taxes) by the force or authority. * *n* the amount levied.
lewd *adj* lustful; sensual; obscene.
lexicographer *n* a dictionary compiler.
lexicon *n* a dictionary.
liability *n* an obligation; debt; a handicap; a disadvantage. *pl* debts; obligations.
liable *adj* responsible; subject to; likely to do.
liaison *n* intercommunication as between units of a military force; an illicit love affair.
liar *n* one who tells lies.
libel *n* a defamatory or damaging writing.
libellous *adj* slanderous; defamatory.
liberal *adj* generous; ample; profuse; not too strict; free; of education, contributing to a general broadening of the mind.
liberality *n* generosity; breadth of view.
liberate *vt* to free; to deliver.
liberator *n* one who liberates.
libertine *n* a profligate; a rake * *adj* licentious.
libertinism *n* depravity.
liberty *n* state of being free esp from slavery; captivity etc.; privilege; license;

undue familiarity; impertinence.
libidinous *adj* lustful.
Libra *n* the Balance, the seventh sign in zodiac.
librarian *n* the keeper of a library.
library *n* a collection of books or the place in which they are kept.
lice *npl of* **louse**.
licence *n* authority given to do something specified; a certificate or document giving permission; excess of liberty *
license *vt* to grant a licence to.
licensee *n* one to whom a licence is granted.
licentious *adj* profligate; morally unrestrained.
lichen *n* a kind of moss, alga or fungus.
licit *adj* lawful; legal.
lick *vt* to pass tongue over; to lap; to flicker round of flames; to thrash; to defeat.
lid *n* a removable cover of a box, vessel, etc., an eyelid.
lie *vi* to speak untruthfully. * *n* an untrue statement.
lie *vi* to stretch out or rest in a horizontal position; to be in a specified condition; to be situated; to exist. * *n* relative position of objects.
lieu *n* place; stead.
lieutenant *n* a deputy; a chief assistant; an army officer ranking below a captain.
life *n* the state of living or being alive; existence; spirit; vigour; vivacity.
lifeboat *n* a small rescue boat carried by a ship; a specially designed and equipped rescue vessel that helps those in distress along the coastline.
life buoy *n* a buoyant object for keeping persons afloat.
lifeguard *n* an expert swimmer employed to prevent drownings.
lifeless *adj* dead; dull; heavy.
lifelike *adj* true to life in appearance.
lifelong *adj* lasting through life.
lift *vt, vi* to raise up; to hoist; to cheer; to steal; to disperse (of fog); to rise * *n* a hoist; an elevation of mood; a ride in a vehicle.
liftoff *n* the vertical thrust of a space-craft etc, at launching; the time of this.
ligament *n* band of tough tissue joining bones at joints.
ligature *n* a tie for blood vessels in operations.
light *n* the agent by which objects are made visible to the eye; day; that which gives or admits light; illumination of mind. * *adj* bright; clear; not heavy; active; slight. * *vt* to give light to; to enlighten; to ignite. * *vi* to brighten; to alight.
lighten *vi* to shine; to flash * *vt* to illuminate; to make less heavy; to alleviate; to cheer.
lighter *n* a flat-bottomed boat for loading and unloading ships; a small device producing a flame to light cigarettes.
light-footed *adj* nimble; active.
light-headed *adj* giddy.
light-hearted *adj* merry; carefree.
lighthouse *n* a tower with a light to guide ships.
lightly *adv* easily; nimbly.
lightning *n* the vivid flash of electricity that precedes thunder.
lightweight *adj* of less than average weight; trivial, unimportant.
light year *n* the distance light travels in one year.
lignite *n* fossil wood.
like *adj* equal; similar; resembling * *adv, prep* similarly * *vt, vi* to be fond of; to be pleased; to approve. * *n* a like; a counterpart.
likelihood *n* probability.
likely *adj* probable; suitable.
liken *vt* to compare.
likewise *adv* in like manner; also.
liking *n* inclination; fondness; affection.
limb *n* the arm or leg; a large branch of a tree.
limber *adj* flexible * *n* the detachable front of a gun carriage.
limbo *n* a kind of purgatory; an intermediate stage between extremes.
lime *n* a substance got by heating limestone, and with sand and water forming cement.
limelight *n* intense publicity.
limerick *n* a humorous doggerel verse of five lines.
limestone *n* a rock composed mainly of

calcium carbonate of lime.

limit *n* boundary; utmost extent; restraint. * *vt* to bound; to restrict.

limited *adj* narrow; restricted; lacking imagination.

limp *vi* to walk lamely * *n* a lameness in walking. * *adj* not firm; flabby; lethargic.

limpid *adj* clear; crystal.

linchpin *n* a pin fastening a wheel to the axle; a person or thing vital to the success of an enterprise.

line *n* a length of cord, rope, or wire; a cord for measuring, making level; a system of conducting fluid, electricity etc; edge, limit, boundary; border, outline, contour, a row of persons or things, as printed letters across a page.

lineage *n* race; descent.

lineal *adj* straight; direct; hereditary.

lineament *n* a facial feature; form.

linear *adj* of, made of, or using a line or lines; narrow and long.

linen *n* cloth made of flax; household articles made of linen, e.g. sheets.

liner *n* a large passenger ship or aircraft.

linesman *n* an assistant referee.

linger *vi* to delay; to loiter; to remain in the mind.

linguist *n* one skilled in languages.

linguistics *adj* the science of language.

lining *n* an inner covering of a garment etc..

link *n* a single loop or ring of a chain; a person or thing acting as a connection, as in a communication system. * *vt, vi* to connect or become connected.

links *npl* flat sandy ground; a golf course, esp by the seaside.

linoleum *n* a floor covering of coarse fabric backing with a smooth, hard decorative coating.

linseed *n* flaxseed.

lint *n* linen specially prepared as a dressing for wounds; fluff.

lintel *n* the upper bar of a doorway or a window.

lion *n* a beast of prey; king of the beasts; sign in zodiac (Leo); a celebrity.

lion-hearted *adj* courageous.

lip *n* either of the front edges of the mouth; the edge or rim of a jug etc; insolent talk.

lipstick *n* a small stick of cosmetic for colouring the lips; the cosmetic itself.

liquefy *vt* to melt; to dissolve.

liqueur *n* a sweet, many-flavoured alcoholic drink..

liquid *adj* fluid; smooth. * *n* any fluid. *adj* in liquid form; clear; limpid; readily convertible into cash (of assets).

liquidate *vt* to settle the accounts of; to wind up a bankrupt business; to convert into cash; to kill; to eliminate.

liquidation *n* the winding up of a bankrupt estate.

liquor *n* a drink (esp alcoholic).

liquorice *n* a black extract from the root of a plant, used in medicine and confectionery; a liquorice flavoured sweet.

lisp *vi* to pronounce imperfectly (esp. 's'). * *n* lisping speech.

lissom, lissome *adj* supple.

list *n* a series of names, numbers written in order.

listen *vi* to try to hear; to give heed.

listener *n* a person who listens.

listless *adj* languid; weary; unenthusiastic.

litany *n* a series of petitions in a prayer book; any tedious recital.

literacy *n* the ability to read and write.

literal *adj* exact; word for word.

literary *adj* versed in letters and literature.

literate *adj* able to read and write; educated.

literature *n* the writings of a period or country.

lithe *adj* pliant; flexible.

lithesome *adj* supple; nimble.

lithograph *vt* to imprint on stone and transfer to paper.

litigant *n* one engaged in a lawsuit.

litigate *vt, vi* to go to law; to contest points of law.

litigious *adj* contentious.

litre *n* a unit of capacity in metric system, 1.76 pints.

litter *n* a portable bed; scattered rubbish; young produced at one birth. * *vt, vi* to strew carelessly; to make tidy.

little *adj* small; short * *adv* in a small degree; less; slightly; not in the least. * *n* small in amount, degree etc.

liturgy *n* a ritual for public worship.

live *vi* to exist; to dwell; to conduct one's self in life; to subsist; to gain a livelihood. * *vt* to lead; to spend; to pass.

live *adj* alive; having life; not exploded; carrying electric current.

livelihood *n* means of living.

lively *adj* vivacious; spirited.

liver *n* the organ which secretes bile; animal liver as food.

livestock *n* (farm) animals raised for use or sale.

livid *adj* of a leaden colour; very angry.

living *n* livelihood; benefice of a clergyman; a way of living.

living room *n* a room in a house used for general entertainment and relaxation.

load *vt* to charge with a load; to burden; to oppress; to put film in a camera; to install a program in a computer memory; to charge, as a gun. * *n* a burden; cargo; a large amount.

loading *n* a cargo; a burden.

loaf *n* a shaped mass of bread. * *vi* to idle about.

loam *n* a rich clayey soil.

loan *n* lending; something lent, esp money. * *vt, vi* to lend.

loath, loth *adj* reluctant.

loathe *vt, vi* to hate; abhor.

loathsome *adj* disgusting.

lob *n* a slow, high-pitched ball (cricket, etc). * *vt* to bowl slowly.

lobby *n* an entrance hall; a person or group who try to influence (legislators) to support a cause etc.

lobe *n* the lower part of the ear; a division of the brain, lungs, etc.

local *adj* pertaining to or serving the interests of a particular place; of or for a particular part of the body. * *n* an inhabitant of a specific place; a local pub.

locale *n* a locality.

locality *n* a place; a neighbourhood.

locate *vt* to place the position of something.

loch *n* a Scottish lake.

lock *n* a fastening device operated by a key; the part of a canal dock in which the level of the water can be changed by the operation of gates.

locker *n* a small cupboard, chest etc.

locket *n* a small gold case worn round the neck.

locksmith *n* a maker of locks.

locomotive *n* a railway engine.

locum (tenens) *n* a temporary deputy.

locust *n* a type of destructive grasshopper; a hardwood leguminous tree.

lode *n* a vein of mineral ore.

lodge *n* a small house at the entrance to a park or stately home. * *vt, vi* to live in a place for a time; to live as a paying guest.

lodger *n* a person who lives in a rented room in another's home.

lodging *n* a temporary abode; rented accommodation.

loft *n* the space or room under the rafters; a gallery. * *vt* to lift into the air.

lofty *adj* high; haughty; stately.

log *n* a section cut from a felled tree; a device for measuring the speed of ships; a written record, esp one kept on a ship's voyage or aircraft's flight.

logarithms *n* a mathematical system for facilitating calculations.

logbook *n* an official record of a ship's or aircraft's voyage or flight; an official document containing details of a vehicle's registration.

logic *n* the science of reasoning.

logical *adj* conforming to the rules of logic; capable of reasoning; consistent.

logistics *n* the planning and organization of any complex activity.

loin *n* the lower part of the back.

loiter *vi* to hang about; to linger.

loll *vi* to lean idly; to hang out (tongue).

lone *adj* solitary; single; isolated.

lonesome *adj* solitary.

long *adj* not short; protracted; late; tedious; slow; far-reaching; well supplied. * *vt* to desire earnestly. * *adv* for a long time; from start to finish.

long-distance *adj* travelling or communicating over long distances.

longevity *n* great length of life.

longhand *n* ordinary handwriting, as opposed to shorthand.

longing *n* an intense desire.

longitude *n* length; distance east or west of fixed meridian.

longitudinal *adj* running lengthwise.

long-suffering *adj* patient.

long-term *adj* of or extending over a long time.

long-winded *adj* tedious.

look *vi* to direct the eye so as to see; to gaze; to consider; to expect; to heed; to appear. * *n* gaze; a glance; aspect; appearance.

lookout *n* a watching for; a watching post; a watcher.

loom *n* a weaving machine. * *vi* to come into view indistinctly, large or threateningly.

loop *n* a figure made by a curved line crossing itself; an intra-uterine contraceptive device.

loophole *n* a narrow slit for outlook, etc; a way of escape or evading obligation etc.

loose *adj* untied; free; vague; careless; not firm, tight or compact. * *vt* to untie; to set free; to discharge a bullet.

loosen *vt* to make loose. * *vi* to become loose.

loot *n* booty; plunder; money.

lop *vt* to cut off.

lopsided *adj* leaning to one side.

loquacious *adj* talkative.

lord *n* a master; a ruler; a nobleman.

lordly *adj* proud; haughty.

lore *n* learning, esp of a traditional kind, e.g. folklore.

lose *vb* (*pt* **lost**) *vt, vi* to have taken from one by death, accident, removal, etc; to be unable to find.

loss *n* a losing or being lost; the damage, trouble caused by losing; the person, thing, or amount lost.

lot *n* a part or share; fate which falls to one; a considerable quantity; the thing drawn at random to decide something.

loth *adj see* **loath.**

lotion *n* a healing or cleansing or cosmetic liquid.

lottery *n* a system of raising money by selling numbered tickets that offer the chance of winning a prize.

lotus *n* a legendary plant causing forgetfulness to the eater; a kind of lily.

loud *adj* easily audible; noisy; showy; obtrusive.

lounge *vi* to loiter; to loll; to spend time idly. * *n* a comfortable room.

louse *n* (*pl* **lice**) a parasitic insect.

lousy *adj* infested with lice.

lout *n* an awkward, rude fellow.

love *vt* to regard with affection; to like; to delight in. * *vi* to be in love. * *n* warm affection; the passionate affection for another; a word of endearment.

lovely *adj* beautiful; charming.

lover *n* a person in love with another; a person having an extramarital sexual relationship.

loving *adj* fond; kind.

low *adj* situated below any given surface; not high; deep; mean.

lower *vt* to let down; to abase.

lower *vi* to frown; to threaten a storm.

lowering *adj* threatening a storm.

lowing *n* the bellowing of cattle.

lowland *n* comparatively low or level country.

lowly *adj* humble; meek.

loyal *adj* faithful; true.

loyalist *n* one who is true to his country.

loyalty *n* fidelity; constancy.

lubber *n* a clumsy fellow.

lubricant *n* a substance for oiling or greasing.

lubricate *vt* to smear with oil to lessen friction; to make smooth, slippery, greasy.

lucent *adj* shining; resplendent.

lucid *adj* easily understood; sane.

luck *n* chance; fortune; success.

lucky *adj* fortunate; auspicious.

lucrative *adj* paying; gainful.

ludicrous *adj* laughable; droll; absurd.

lug *vt* to haul. * *n* the ear.

luggage *n* a traveller's baggage.

lugubrious *adj* sad; doleful.

lukewarm *adj* moderately warm; indifferent.

lull *vt* to calm; to send to sleep; to allay (fears etc) usually by deception. * *n* a calm interval.

lullaby *n* a cradle song.

lumbago *n* rheumatism in the lower back.

lumbar *n* pertaining to the lower back.
lumber *n* useless articles; rubbish; felled timber.
luminary *n* an enlightening, influential or famous person.
luminous *adj* shining; clear.
lump *n* a small shapeless mass; an abnormal swelling; a stupid or boring person.
lunacy *n* mental derangement; utter folly.
lunar *adj* pertaining to the moon.
lunatic *adj* insane. * *n* a madman.
lunch, luncheon *n* a midday meal.
lung *n* either of the two organs of respiration.
lunge *n* a sword thrust; a plunge forward.
lurch *vi* to roll or sway to one side. * *n* a sudden roll.
lure *n* a bright fishing bait; something that tempts or entices. * *vt* to entice.
lurid *adj* vivid; glaring; sensational; ghastly pale; wan.
lurk *vi* to lie hidden in wait; to loiter furtively.
luscious *adj* very sweet; delicious.
lush *adj* luxuriant; juicy.
lust *n* longing desire; sensual appetite * *vi* to desire eagerly; to feel lust.
lustily *adv* stoutly; vigorously.
lustre *n* brightness; renown; a glossy surface.
lustrous *adj* bright; shining.
lusty *adj* vigorous; robust.
luxuriant *adj* profuse; abundant.
luxuriate *vi* to give oneself up to luxury.
luxurious *adj* given to luxury.
luxury *n* indulgence and pleasure in sumptuous things; *pl* something costly and enjoyable but not a necessity.
lymph *n* colourless fluid in the body contained in and collected from the tissues.
lynch *vt* to put to death by mob law.
lyre *n* an ancient stringed instrument re lated to the harp.
lyric, lyrical *adj* of the nature of song.

M

macaroni *n* pasta rolled into tubes.
macaroon *n* a cake or biscuit of ground almonds.
mace *n* a spiked club; an ensign of office; an aromatic spice made from the outside covering of the nutmeg.
machine *n* a structure of fixed and moving parts, for doing useful work; an organization functioning like a machine; the controlling group in a political party.
machine gun *n* an automatic gun.
machinery *n* machines in general; mechanism.
machinist *n* one who works a machine.
machismo *n* excessive masculine pride.
macrocosm *n* great world or the universe regarded as a whole.
mad *adj* insane; crazy; frantic; angry.
madam *n* a polite form of address a woman; a woman in charge of a brothel.
madcap *n, adj* (a) frolicsome girl, reckless, lively (person).
madden *vt* to make mad.
madman (madwoman) *n* an insane person.
madness *n* insanity; folly.
maelstrom *n* a whirlpool.
magazine *n* a storehouse; a munition depot; a periodical publication containing feature articles, fiction etc.; a supply chamber as in a camera, a rifle etc.
magenta *n* a bright purplish-crimson dye or colour.
maggot *n* a worm like grub.
magic *n* the use of charms, spells etc. to supposedly influence events by supernatural means; any mysterious power; the art of producing illusions by sleight of hand, etc.
magical *adj* marvellous.
magician *n* a conjurer.
magistrate *n* a public officer who administrates justice.
magnanimity *n* greatness of soul or mind; noble and generous conduct.
magnanimous *adj* noble and generous; unselfish.
magnate *n* a man of rank, wealth or influence.
magnesium *n* a white malleable metal.
magnet *n* a piece of iron or steel that has the property of attracting iron.
magnetic *adj* of magnetism or a magnet.
magnetism *n* the science which treats of

magnetic phenomena; personal charm.
magnificence *n* grandeur; pomp.
magnificent *adj* imposing; splendid; superb.
magnify *vt* to enlarge; to extol; to glorify; to exaggerate.
magnitude *n* greatness; importance.
mahogany *n* a hard reddish wood much used for furniture; a reddish-brown colour.
maid *n* a young girl; a female servant.
maiden *n* a young unmarried woman; a runless over in cricket.
mail *n* letters etc. conveyed and delivered by the post office; a postal system.
maim *vt* to mutilate; to disable.
main *adj* chief; leading. * *n* strength; the greater part; the ocean.
mainland *n* the land, other than islands.
mainstay *n* the chief support.
maintain *vt, vi* to keep up; to sustain.
maintenance *n* upkeep; the support (esp financial) given to a spouse after divorce.
maize *n* corn; a light yellow colour.
majestic *adj* august; stately.
majesty *n* grandeur; nobility; dignity.
major *adj* the greater in number, quantity, or extent; very serious; life-threatening; (music) higher than the corresponding minor by half a tone. * *n* an army officer; below lieutenant colonel.
majority *n* the greater number.
make *vt, vi* to create; to construct; to produce; to cause to be; to perform; to force; to act or do; to earn; to reach. * *n* style; brand or origin; manner of production.
make-believe *n* pretence; sham.
makeshift *n* a temporary substitute.
maladjustment *n* poor adaptation, esp to social environment.
maladministration *n* bad management.
malady *n* illness; disease.
malaise *n* a feeling of discomfort.
malaria *n* an infectious disease.
malcontent *n* a discontented person.
male *n* a man or boy; an animal or plant of that sex. * *adj* of the sex of a man.
malefactor *n* a criminal; a felon.
malevolent *adj* spiteful; malicious.
malformation *n* deformity.
malfunction *n* faulty functioning.
malice *n* spite; ill will.
malicious *adj* spiteful; intentionally destructive.
malign *adj* harmful; evil; malignant.
malignant *adj* malevolent; virulent.
malinger *vi* to feign illness.
mall *n* an avenue; an area of shops.
malleable *adj* capable of being beaten out by hammering; pliable.
mallet *n* a wooden hammer.
malnutrition *n* lack of nutrition.
malpractice *n* evil practice; misconduct.
malt *n* barley prepared by various processes for brewing and distilling.
maltreat *vt* to abuse.
mammal *n* an animal of the class Mammalia; a warm-blooded vertebrate that suckle their young.
mammoth *n* an extinct species of elephant. * *adj* gigantic.
man *n* a human being; a male adult; mankind; a male servant; a husband; an ordinary soldier; a member of a team.
manacle *n* a handcuff * *vt* to fetter.
manage *vt* to wield; to conduct or direct.
manageable *adj* able to be managed; tractable.
management *n* direction; the directors of a business, organization etc.
manager *n* a person who manages a company, organization etc.; an agent who looks after the business affairs of an actor, writer etc..
mandarin *n* any high-ranking official; (with *cap*) the Beijing dialect that is the official pronunciation of the Chinese language.
mandate *n* a command; written authority to act for another.
mandatory *adj* compulsory.
mandible *n* an animal's jaw.
mandolin *n* a stringed instrument.
mane *n* the long hair on the neck of the horse, lion etc.
manequin a woman who models fashion clothes.
manful *adj* bold; energetic.
mange *n* a skin disease of dogs, etc.
mangle *vt* to mutilate; to smooth; to press.
manhole *n* a hole giving entrance.

manhood *n* virility; manliness.
mania *n* great enthusiasm; a craze.
maniac *n* a madman; an enthusiast.
manicure *n* the fingernails and care of the hands.
manifest *adj* clearly visible; evident. * *vt* to display. * *n* a list of a ship's or aircraft's cargo.
manifestation *n* evidence; revelation.
manifestly *adv* evidently.
manifesto *n* a public declaration of policy issued by a government or a party.
manifold *adj* numerous and various.
manipulate *vt* to handle; to manage skilfully or craftily.
mankind *n* the human race.
manly *adj* brave; hardy.
man-made *adj* manufactured or created by man; artificial, synthetic.
manner *n* the mode in which anything is done; bearing or conduct; *pl* behaviour.
mannerism *n* a personal peculiarity.
manoeuvre *n* a tactical movement; a planned and controlled movement of troops, ships etc.; a stratagem.
manor *n* the land or house belonging to a lord.; a police district.
mansion *n* a large imposing house.
manslaughter *n* the killing of a person without malice.
mantel, mantelpiece *n* the ornamental work round a fireplace; the shelf above.
mantle *n* a loose sleeveless cloak.
manual *adj* done by the hand. * *n* a textbook; a book of instructions.
manufacture *n* the making of goods on large scale.
manure *n* dung or other substance for fertilizing soil. * *vt* to treat with manure.
manuscript *n* a paper written with the hand.
many *adj* numerous.
map *n* a plan of any part of the earth's surface. * *vt* to make a map; to plan.
mar *vt* to injure; impair; to spoil.
marauder *n* a robber; a rover.
marble *n* a valuable building and monumental stone; a small ball of stone, etc.
march *vi* to walk in step * *vt* to cause to march. * *n* a measured or military walk; a distance walked; a musical composition; a boundary; (*cap*) the third month of a year.
mare *n* the female of the horse.
margarine *n* a butter substitute made from vegetable and animal fats, etc.
margin *n* an edge; the blank border of a printed page; surplus; the difference between the cost and the selling price.
marginal *adj* written in the margin; situated at the margin or border; close to the lower limit of acceptability; very slight, insignificant.
marina *n* a harbour for pleasure craft.
marine *adj* pertaining to the sea; naval.
mariner *n* a seaman.
marionette *n* a puppet.
marital *adj* pertaining to marriage.
maritime *adj* relating to the sea or ships; bordering on or living near the sea.
mark *n* a visible sign or stamp; eminence; token; aim; a cross made instead of a signature; a symbol, e.g. a punctuation mark; a grade for academic work; impression; influence; the basic monetary unit of Germany.
marked *adj* pre-eminent; obvious.
market *n* a meeting of people for buying and selling merchandise; a space or building in which a market is held; the chance to sell or buy; demand for (goods, etc.); a region where goods can be sold.
marketable *adj* fit for sale.
marketing *n* all the processes involved in moving goods from the producer to the consumer.
marksman *n* one skilled at shooting.
marmalade *n* a preserve made from oranges, sugar and water.
maroon *n* a brownish-crimson colour; a distress rocket. * *vt* to abandon esp on a desert island.
marquee *n* a large tent used for entertainment.
marquetry *n* inlaid work.
marriage *n* wedlock; a wedding; a union.
marrow *n* a soft substance in cavities of bones; a kind of gourd eaten as a vegetable.
marry *vt, vi* to unite in wedlock.

marsh *n* a swamp; boggy land.
marshal *n* one who is in charge of ceremonies etc.; a military officer of the highest rank. * *vt* to arrange in order.
marsupial *adj, n* (an animal) carrying its young in a pouch.
martial *adj* warlike; military.
martyr *n* one who is tortured and suffers death for his faith.
martyrdom *n* the death of a martyr; torture.
marvel *n* a wonder. * *vi* to feel astonishment; to be filled with wonder.
marvellous *adj* wonderful; miraculous; astonishing.
mascot *n* a charm; someone or something thought to bring good luck.
masculine *adj* male; manly; robust.
mash *n* a soft thick mixture of ingredients, esp as food for horses and cattle; mashed potatoes.
mask *n* a covering to conceal or protect the face; a moulded likeness of the face; anything that conceals or disguises; a respirator placed over the nose and mouth to aid or prevent inhalation of a gas; (photog) a screen used to cover part of a sensitive surface to prevent exposure by light.
mason *n* a worker or builder in stone.
masonry *n* stonework; the craft of freemasons.
masquerade *n* a fancy-dress ball at which masks are worn; a pretence; false show.
mass *n* a lump; magnitude; a large quantity; bulk; size; the main part; in physics, the property of a body expressed as a measure of the amount of material contained in it; *pl* the common people; *cap* the celebration of the Eucharist.
massacre *n* ruthless slaughter. * *vt* to slaughter.
massage *n* the rubbing and kneading of parts of body.
masseur, masseuse *n* one who gives massage professionally.
massive *adj* bulky and heavy; solid.
mast *n* an upright on which a ship's sails are set.
master *n* one who rules or directs; an employer; an owner; a ship's captain; a teacher; an expert of craftsman; a writer, painter etc. regarded as pre-eminent; an original from which copies are made; a holder of an advanced academic degree.
masterful *adj* imperious; headstrong.
masterly *adj* skilful; expert.
masterpiece *n* an artist's greatest work; any extraordinary piece of work.
masterstroke *n* a supremely able act.
mastery *n* command; ascendancy.
masticate *vt* to chew and prepare for swallowing.
masturbate *vi* to manually stimulate one's sexual organs to achieve orgasm without sexual intercourse.
mat *n* a fabric of plaited fibre, straw, etc., for protection purpose.
match *n* any person or thing which goes with another; an equal; a contest; a marriage; a strip of wood or cardboard tipped with a chemical that ignites when struck.
matchless *adj* unrivalled.
mate *n* an associate; an animal's sexual partner; a companion; a husband or wife; four as a pair; a ship's officer.
material *n* consisting of matter; important; not spiritual; essential. * *n* the substance of which anything is made; a person suitable for a task, a position etc.
materialism *n* the doctrine of materialists.
materialist *n* one whose interest lies in acquiring possessions.
materialize *vt* to give concrete form to.
maternal *adj* of, like a mother.
maternity *n* motherhood. * *adj* relating to pregnancy.
mathematician *n* one concerned with mathematics.
mathematics *n* the science dealing with quantities, forms, space, etc. and their relationships by use of numbers and symbols.
matin *n* morning; (*pl*) morning prayers.
matinée *n* an afternoon performance.
matriarch *n* a woman who rules.
matricide *n* the killing of a mother; the person guilty of it.
matriculate *vt, vi* to enrol or be enrolled.
matrimonial *adj* pertaining to marriage.

matrimony *n* marriage.
matrix *n* a mould.
matron *n* a woman in charge of domestic and nursing arrangements.
matted *adj* entangled.
matter *n* what a thing is made of; material; whatever occupies space and is perceptible to the senses.
matting *n* a course material, such as woven straw or hemp.
mattress *n* a casing of strong cloth filled with cotton, foam rubber, springs, etc.
mature *adj* ripe; fully developed; due payable. * *vt, vi* to make or become ripe.
maturity *n* ripeness; perfection.
maul *vt* to handle roughly; to paw.
mausoleum *n* a large tomb.
mauve *n* a shade of pale purple.
maxim *n* an established principle.
maximum *n* the greatest quantity.
May *n* the fifth month of the year; hawthorn blossom. * *v aux* used to imply possibility, desire, etc.
maybe *adv* perhaps.
mayhem *n* violent destruction, confusion.
mayonnaise *n* a salad dressing.
mayor, mayoress *n* the chief administrative officer of a municipality.
maze *n* a labyrinth; a perplexity.
me *pers pron* the objective case of I.
meadow *n* a piece of land where grass is grown for hay.
meagre *adj* thin; scanty.
meal *n* the food taken at one time; any edible ground grain.
mean *adj* selfish; ungenerous; despicable; base; middle; moderate. * *n* the middle; average; *pl* resources; measures. * *vt, vi* to intend; to signify.
meander *n* a winding course. * *vi* to wind about; to wander aimlessly.
meaning *adj* significant. * *n* significance.
meantime *adv* during the intervening time; at the same time.
meanwhile *adv, n* meantime.
measles *n* (used as sing) an acute, contagious viral disease.
measurable *adj* that may be measured.
measure *n* the extent, capacity or magnitude of a thing; a standard; an instrument for measuring; just degree; a course of action; a legislative proposal; a musical time. metre.
measured *adj* set, marked off by a standard; rhythmical; regular; deliberate; stately.
measurement *n* dimensions.
meat *n* food in general; animal flesh as food; the essence of something.
mechanic *n* a person skilled in operating, maintaining, repairing machines.
mechanical *adj* of or using machinery or tools; produced or operated by machinery; done as if by a machine, lacking thought or emotion.
mechanics *n* the science of motion and force; knowledge of machinery; the technical aspects of something.
mechanism *n* the working parts of a machine; any system of interrelated parts.
medal *n* a piece of metal struck to celebrate an event; a reward of merit.
medallist *n* a winner of a medal.
meddle *vi* to interfere in another's affairs.
meddlesome *adj* interfering.
mediate *vi* to try to reconcile; to intercede.
mediation *n* intercession for another.
mediator *n* an intercessor; an advocate.
medical *adj* pertaining to medicine.
medicament, medication *n* a medicine.
medicinal *adj* healing.
medicine *n* the science of preventing, treating or curing disease; any healing substance.
medieval, mediaeval *adj* pertaining to the Middle Ages.
mediocre *adj* of moderate quality.
mediocrity *n* moderate skill, ability, etc.
meditate *vi* to think deeply; reflect.
meditation *n* reflection; contemplation of spiritual or religious matters.
meditative *adj* thoughtful.
medium *n* (*pl* **media, mediums**) the middle state or condition; a substance for transmitting an effect; any intervening means, instrument, or agency; (*pl* **media**) a means of communicating information (e.g.) newspapers, television, radio); (*pl* **mediums**) a person claiming to act as an intermediary between the living and the dead.
medley *n* (*pl* **medleys**) a miscellany; a

musical piece made up of various tunes.
meek *adj* patient, submissive.
meet *vt, vi* to come face to face; to encounter; to light on; to receive; to satisfy; to assemble.
meeting *n* an assembly; an encounter.
melancholy *n* mental depression; dejection; sadness. * *adj* dejected.
mellifluent, mellifluous *adj* sweet; honeyed.
mellow *adj* soft and ripe; matured (of wine); genial; kind hearted.
melodious *adj* tuneful; pleasing to the ear.
melodrama *n* a sensational drama, film.
melodramatic *adj* over-emotional.
melody *n* a tuneful composition.
melon *n* a large juicy fruit.
melt *vt, vi* to liquefy; to soften; to dissolve; to fade; to disappear.
member *n* a limb; one of a society or company; a representative in parliament etc.
membership *n* the members of a body.
membrane *n* a thin flexible sheet or film.
memento *n* a souvenir.
memoir *n* a biography or autobiography.
memorabilia *npl* things worthy of record; objects, souvenirs of famous people.
memorable *adj* worthy to be remembered; easy to remember; famous.
memorandum *n* (*pl* **memorandums, memoranda**) a note to help the memory; a communication in writing.
memorial *adj* bringing to memory. * *n* a monument; a remembrance.
memorize *vt* to commit to memory.
memory *n* the faculty of remembering; the sum of the things remembered; an individual recollection.
menace *n* a threat. * *vt* to threaten.
mend *vt* to repair; to improve.
mendacious *adj* lying; false.
mendacity *n* deceit.
menial *adj* low; servile descriptive of work of little skill.
meningitis *n* inflammation of the membranes enveloping the brain.
menopause *n* the time of life during which a woman's menstrual cycle ceases.
menstrual *adj* monthly.
menstruation *n* the monthly discharge of blood from the uterus.
mental *adj* pertaining to the mind; occuring or performed in the mind; having a psychiatric disorder; crazy; stupid.
mention *n* a brief reference or notice; an official recognition or citation.
mentor *n* a wise adviser.
menu *n* a bill of fare; a list of options.
mercantile *adj* relating to trade.
mercenary *adj* hired; grasping. * *n* a soldier hired for service in a foreign army.
merchandise *n* goods; trade.
merchant *n* a trader on a large scale; a retailer.
merchant navy *n* commercial shipping.
merciful *adj* compassionate; tender.
merciless *adj* pitiless; cruel.
mercurial *adj* volatile; sprightly.
mercury *n* a heavy silvery liquid metallic element used in thermometers etc.
mercy *n* pity; compassion; pardon.
mere *adj* sole; simple; nothing more than.
meretricious *adj* gaudy; insincere.
merge *vt* to absorb; to blend.
merit *n* excellence; worth; *pl* the rights and wrongs (of a case); desert. * *vt* to deserve; to be worthy of.
meritorious *adj* praiseworthy.
merriment *n* mirth; noisy gaiety.
merry *adj* joyous; jovial, cheerful.
mesh *n* the wires of a screen etc; engagement of geared wheels.
mesmeric *adj* hypnotic.
mesmerism *n* the power by exercise of will to control the actions of another.
mesmerize *vt* to subject to mesmerism; to hypnotize; to hold spellbound.
mesozoic *adj* belonging to one of the geological periods or formations.
mess *n* a state of disorder or untidiness, esp if dirty; a building where service personnel dine.
message *n* a communication; an errand; the chief idea a writer, artist etc. seeks to communicate in a work.
messenger *n* one who bears a message.
messy *adj* dirty; confused; untidy.
metabolism *n* the total processes in living organisms by which tissue is formed, energy produced and waste product eliminated.
metal *n* any of a class of chemical ele-

ments which are often lustrous, ductile solids, and are good conductors of heat, electricity, etc, such as gold, iron, copper, etc.
metallurgy *n* the science of extracting metals from their ores.
metamorphic *adj* altered in structure.
metamorphosis *n* (*pl* **metamorphoses**) a complete change of form.
metaphor *n* a figure of speech in which a word or phrase is used for another of which it is an image.
metaphoric, metaphorical *adj* figurative.
metaphysical *adj* pertaining to metaphysics; abstract.
metaphysics *n* the branch of philosophy dealing with the nature of being and reality.
mete *vt* to dole out or distribute.
meteor *n* a small particle of matter which travels at great speeds through space.
meteoric *adj* brilliant but transitory.
meteorite *n* a spent meteor.
meteorology *n* the study of the atmosphere and of weather-forecasting.
meter *n* an instrument for registering consumption of gas, water, time etc.
method *n* mode of procedure; system; orderliness of thought or arrangement.
methodical *adj* systematic; orderly.
methylated spirit *n* a form of alcohol, used as a solvent.
meticulous *adj* over careful; precise about small details.
metre *n* pattern in verse or music.
metre *n* the basic unit of length in the metric system (39.37 in.).
metric *adj* pertaining to the decimal system.
metrication *n* conversion of an existent system of units into the metric system.
metric system *n* a decimal system of weights and measures.
metronome *n* an instrument that beats musical tempo.
metropolitan *adj* belonging to a metropolis.
mettle *n* spirit; courage.
mezzanine *n* an intermediate storey between others; a theatre balcony.
mezzo *adj* in music, middle; mean.
mezzoprano *n* a female voice, singer with a range between soprano and contralto.
mice *npl* of mouse.
microbe *n* a germ; a bacillus.
microcosm *n* man as an epitome of the universe or macrocosm; a very small copy.
microfilm *n* film on which documents, etc, are recorded in reduced scale.
microphone *n* an instrument for transforming sound waves into electric signals, esp for transmission, or recording.
microscope *n* an optical instrument for magnifying.
microscopic, microscopical *adj* minute; visible only through a microscope.
mid *adj* middle; intervening.
midday *n* the middle of the day; noon.
middle *adj* equally distant from the extremes.
middle age *n* the time between youth and old age.
Middle Ages *npl* the period of European history between about AD500 and 1500.
middle class *n* people between the working classes and the aristocracy.
midnight *n* twelve o'clock at night.
midriff *n* the diaphragm.
midst *n* the middle. * *prep* amidst; among.
midsummer *n* the middle of summer.
midway *n* halfway.
midwife *n* a woman that assists women in childbirth.
might *n* power; strength.
mighty *adj* strong; powerful; large.
migrant *n* a person or animal who migrates.
migrate *vi* to remove from one region or country to another.
migratory *adj* roving; wandering.
mild *adj* gentle; merciful; soft.
mildew *n* a mouldy deposit or coating caused by fungus.
mile *n* 1760 yards or 1.61 km.
mileage *n* distance in miles.
milestone *n* a stone or post marking each mile of a road; an important event in life.
militancy *n* aggressiveness.
militant *adj* warring; combative.
militarism *n* military spirit; reliance on force.

military *adj* pertaining to soldiers.
militate *vi* (with against) to influence, to have an adverse effect on.
militia *n* an army composed of civilians.
milk *n* a fluid secreted by female mammals to feed their young. * *vt* to draw milk from; to extract money etc. from; to exploit.
mill *n* a machine for grinding corn, etc; a factory. * *vt* to grind.
millennium *n* a period of 1000 years.
milligram(me) *n* the thousandth part of a gram(me).
millimetre *n* the thousandth part of a metre.
million *n* a thousand thousands; 1,000,000.
millionaire *n* a person worth a million pounds; one who is extremely rich.
millstone *n* a stone used in grinding corn.
mime *n* a drama enacted through gestures.
mimic *adj* imitative. * *n* one who imitates; an actor skilled in mimicry.
mimicry *n* imitation.
mince *vt, vi* to chop into small pieces; to act or walk affectedly; to clip (words).
mincemeat *n* a mixture of chopped apples, raisins, etc used as a pie filling.
mind *n* the intellectual faculty or power; intellect; reason; understanding; inclination; opinion; memory. * *vt* to heed; to pay attention to; to obey; to take care of; to care about; to object.
mindful *adj* attentive; heedful.
mine *pron* my; belonging to me. * *n* an excavation from which minerals are dug; an explosive device concealed in the water or ground to destroy enemy ships, personnel, or vehicles that pass over or near them; a rich supply or source.
minefield *n* an area in which explosive mines are laid; a situation containing hidden problems.
miner *n* a person who works in a mine.
mineral *n* an inorganic substance found in or on the earth.
mineralogist *n* an expert on mineralogy.
mineralogy *n* the science of minerals.
mingle *vt* to mix together; to blend.
miniature *n* a small-scale portrait; a reduced copy.
minim *n* a note in music; the smallest liquid measure; a single drop.
minimize *vt* to estimate at the lowest; to disparage.
minimum *n* the smallest amount.
minister *n* a member of a government heading a department; a diplomat; a clergyman serving a church. * *vt* to give help to. * *vi* to perform a service.
ministration *n* service; a giving of aid; the work of a minister of the church.
ministry *n* service; office of a minister; clergy; a government department headed by a minister.
minor *adj* lesser; smaller; petty. * *n* a person under full legal age.
minority *n* the state of a minor; the smaller of two parties voting; any smaller group.
minstrel *n* a bard; a travelling musician of the Middle Ages.
mint *n* the place where money is coined; a large amount of money; an aromatic plant with leaves used for flavouring. * *vt* to coin. * *adj* in perfect condition.
minuet *n* a slow graceful dance; the music played for it.
minus *adj* less. * *n* the sign of subtraction (-).
minute *adj* very small; precise: exact.
minute *n* the sixtieth part of an hour or a degree; *pl* a summary of proceedings; an official record of a meeting. * *vt* to record, summarize the proceedings (of).
minutiae *npl* small details.
miracle *n* a marvel; a supernatural event.
miraculous *adj* marvellous; supernatural.
mirage *n* an optical illusion caused by light reflection from hot air.
mire *n* wet, muddy soil; mud.
mirror *n* a looking glass; a faithful depiction.
misadventure *n* a mishap; bad luck.
misalliance *n* an unsuitable marriage.
misanthrope, misanthropist *n* a hater of mankind.
misapply *vt* to apply wrongly.
misapprehend *vt* to misunderstand.
misapprehension *n* a mistake.
misappropriate *vt* to appropriate dishonestly; to embezzle.
misbehave *vi* to behave badly.

miscalculate *vt* to reckon wrongly.
miscarriage *n* a failure; mismanagement; the premature expulsion of a foetus.
miscellaneous *adj* mixed; diverse.
mischance *n* ill luck; mishap.
mischief *n* wayward, prankish behaviour.
mischievous *adj* troublesome; hurtful.
misconduct *n* immoral or bad behaviour.
misconstrue *vt* to interpret wrongly.
miscount *vt, vi* to make an error in counting; a wrong counting.
misdeed *n* an evil action.
misdemeanour *n* a minor offence.
miser *n* a skinflint; a hoarder of money.
miserable *adj* wretched; despicable.
misery *n* wretchedness; sorrow; poverty.
misfit *n* a bad fit; a maladjusted person.
misfortune *n* ill fortune; calamity.
misgiving *n* a doubt; mistrust.
misguided *adj* foolish; mistaken.
mishap *n* a slight or unfortunate accident.
misinform *vt* to give wrong information to.
misinterpret *vt* to interpret wrongly.
misjudge *vt* to judge erroneously.
mislay *vt* to lose temporarily; to put down in the wrong place.
mislead *vt* to deceive; to misinform.
mismanage *vt* to manage badly.
misnomer *n* an incorrect or unsuitable name for someone or something.
misogynist *n* a woman-hater.
misplace *vt* to put out of place.
misprint *n* a mistake in printing.
mispronounce *vt, vi* to pronounce wrongly.
misquote *vt* to quote incorrectly.
misrepresent *vt* to represent falsely.
misrule *n* misgovernment.
miss *vt* to fail to hit, find, meet, etc.; to lose; to omit; to fail to take advantage of; to feel the loss of. * *n* a failure to hit; loss; want; an unmarried woman; a girl.
misshapen *adj* ill-formed.
missile *n* an object, a a rock, spear, rocket.
missing *adj* lost; absent.
mission *n* a group of people sent by a church, government, etc to carry out a special duty or task.
missionary *n* one sent to a foreign country to propagate religion.
missive *n* an official letter.
misspell *vt* to spell wrongly.
misspend *vt* to squander; to waste.
mist *n* a mass of visible water vapour.
mistake *vt* to misunderstand or misinterpret. * *vi* to err. * *n* a blunder, an error of judgment; a misunderstanding.
mistaken *adj* erroneous; ill-judged.
mistress *n* the feminine of master; a woman with whom a man is having a prolonged affair.
mistrust *n* suspicion. * *vt* to suspect; to doubt.
misunderstand *vt* to take the wrong meaning from.
misuse *vt* to use for wrong purpose; to abuse. * *n* improper use.
mite *n* a minute parasitic animal; a very small object or person.
mitigate *vt* to lessen, to abate, to moderate.
mitre *n* the headdress of a bishop; a diagonal joint between two pieces of wood to form a corner.
mitten *n* a fingerless glove.
mix *vt, vi* to unite or blend; to mingle; to join; to combine (ingredients etc.).
mixed *adj* blended; assorted; of different kinds, classes, races etc.; confused.
mixture *n* a compound; a medley; a jumble.
mix-up *n* a mistake; confusion, muddle.
mnemonics *n* art of memory; rules for assisting memory.
moan *vi* to utter a mournful sound.
moat *n* a ditch round a castle or fort.
mob *n* a crowd; a rabble; a gang of animals.
mobile *adj* movable, not fixed; easily changing; characterized by ease in change of social status; capable of moving freely and quickly; having transport.
mobilize *vt* to organize troops in readiness for service.
moccasin *n* a deerskin shoe; any soft flexible shoe.
mock *vt* to imitate or ridicule; to behave with scorn; to defy; (*with* **up**) to make a model of. * *n* ridicule; an object of scorn. * *adj* false, sham, counterfeit.
mockery *n* derision; a sham.

mock-up *n* a full-scale working model of a machine, etc.

mode *n* way of acting, doing, existing; manner; fashion; (music) any of the scales used in composition; (statistics) the predominant item in a series of items; a mood in grammar.

model *n* a pattern; an ideal; a standard worth imitating; a representation on a smaller scale, usu three-dimensional; a person who sits for an artist or photographer; a person who displays clothes by wearing them.

moderate *vt* to restrain from excess; to temper, to lessen. * *vi* to preside over.

moderation *n* temperance; restraint.

modern *adj* of the present or recent times; contemporary; up-to-date.

modernism *n* modern thought or practice.

modernize *vt* to make modern.

modest *adj* retiring; bashful; diffident; moderate.

modesty *n* bashful reserve; chastity.

modicum *n* a small quantity.

modification *n* the act of modifying.

modify *vt* to change slightly; to lessen the severity of; to limit in meaning.

modulate *vt* to measure; to vary (the voice) in tone.

module *n* a unit of measurement; a self-contained unit, esp in a space-craft.

moist *adj* slightly wet; damp.

moisten *vt* to make damp or moist.

moisture *n* dampness; humidity.

moisturize *vt* to add moisture to the skin, air etc. with various preparations.

mole *n* a dark spot on human skin; a breakwater; a spy within an organization.

molecular *adj* belonging to or consisting of molecules.

molecule *n* the simplest unit of a substance; a small particle.

molest *vt* to annoy; to vex; to assault esp sexually.

mollify *vt* to soften; to appease; to tone down.

mollusc *n* a soft-bodied invertebrate animal with a hard shell (e.g. oyster, etc.).

molten *adj* melted by heat.

moment *n* an indefinitely brief period of time; importance; gravity.

momentary *adj* lasting only for a moment.

momentous *adj* important; weighty.

momentum *n* (*pl* **momenta**) the force possessed by a moving body.

monarch *n* a sovereign ruling by hereditary right.

monarchy *n* government headed by a monarch; a kingdom.

monastery *n* the residence of monks.

monastic *adj* of monks or monasteries.

monasticism *n* the monastic life or system.

Monday *n* the second day of the week.

monetary *adj* relating to money.

money *n* current coin or its equivalent in bank notes, etc.

moneyed *adj* wealthy.

mongrel *adj* of mixed or unknown breed.

monitor *n* a prefect; any device for regulating the performance of a machine, aircraft etc. * *vt, vi* to check on; to regulate, control a machine etc.

monk *n* a male member of a religious order in a monastery.

monkey *n* (*pl* **monkeys**) any of the primates except man and the lemurs, esp the smaller, long-tailed primates; a mischievous child.

monocle *n* a single eyeglass.

monogamy *n* marriage to one wife or husband only.

monogram *n* letters (esp initials) interwoven in one design.

monograph *n* an essay on one subject.

monolith *n* a standing stone or pillar.

monologue *n* a soliloquy.

monopolize *vt* to obtain entire control of.

monopoly *n* an exclusive trading privilege; exclusive use or possession.

monosyllable *n* a word of one syllable.

monotone *n* speaking without inflection; a sameness of style, colour etc.

monotonous *adj* unvarying; tedious.

monotony *n* an irksome sameness.

monsoon *n* a seasonal wind of Southern Asia.

monster *n* a huge frightsome creature.

monstrosity *n* an unnatural, misshapen creature or thing.

monstrous *adj* unnatural; horrible.

montage *n* the art or technique or assembling various elements.

month *n* any of the twelve divisions of the year; a calendar month; a period corresponding to the moon's revolution.

monthly *adj* continuing for a month; done, happening, payable etc, every month.

monument *n* a tomb, pillar, statue etc, erected as a memorial.

monumental *adj* of, like, or serving as a monument; colossal; lasting.

mood *n* a temporary state of mind; (grammar) the form of the verb indicating mode of action.

moody *adj* in low spirits; temperamental.

moon *n* the natural satellite that revolves around the earth and shines by reflected sunlight; any natural satellite of another planet; something shaped like the moon.

moonbeam *n* a ray of light from the moon.

moonlight *n* the light of the moon. * *vi* to have a secondary (usu night-time) job.

moor *n* a heath; wasteland. * *vt* to secure a ship by cable or anchor.

mooring *n* the anchors, buoys, etc, by which or to which a boat is moored.

moot *adj* debatable; hypothetical.

mop *n* a rag, sponge etc.fixed to a handle for washing floors or dishes, a thick, unruly head of hair.

mope *vi* to be downcast and uninterested.

moral *adj* of or relating to character and human behaviour, particularly as regards right and wrong; virtuous, esp in sexual conduct; capable of distinguishing right from wrong.

morale *n* the tone, spirit, or mental condition prevailing with regard to courage, discipline, confidence etc.

morality *n* the doctrine of moral duties; ethics; virtue; an old form of drama.

moralize *vt, vi* to reflect on, moral questions.

morass *n* a marsh; a bog; a fen.

moratorium *n* legal permission to defer payments due; a temporary stoppage.

morbid *adj* diseased; sickly; gruesome.

more *adj comp* of much and many greater in amount, extent, etc. * *adv* in a greater degree.

moribund *adj* in a dying state.

morning *n* the first part of the day.

morose *adj* surly; sullen; glum.

morphia, morphine *n* an alkaloid derived from opium.

morsel *n* a bite; a small piece.

mortal *adj* subject to death; deadly; fatal; human. * *n* a human being.

mortality *n* the state of being mortal; the death rate.

mortar *n* a bowl in which substances are pounded with a pestle; an artillery piece that fires shells at low velocities and high trajectories; a cement.

mortgage *n* a conveyance of property as security for loan; the deed of conveyance. * *vt* to pledge as security.

mortification *n* gangrene; humiliation.

mortify *vt, vi* to affect with gangrene; to shame.

mortifying *adj* humiliating.

mortise lock *n* a lock set into a mortise in a door.

mortuary *n* a place for temporary storage of dead bodies; a morgue.

mosaic *n* inlaid work of marble, precious stones, etc.

Moslem, Muslim *n* a Mohammedan; an adherent of Islam.

mosque *n* a Moslem place of worship.

moss *n* a very small green plant that grows in clusters on rocks, moist ground, etc.

mossy *adj* overgrown with moss.

most *adj superl* of **more** greatest in any way. * *adv* in the greatest degree.

motel *n* an hotel for motorists with adjacent parking.

moth *n* a nocturnal insect allied to the butterfly.

mother *n* a female parent; source or origin; the head of a nunnery, etc. * *adj* of, like a mother; native. * *vt* to be or care for as a mother.

mother-in-law *n* the mother of one's spouse.

motherly *adj* of, proper to a mother.

motion *n* activity, movement; a formal suggestion made in a meeting, law court, or legislative assembly; evacuation of the bowels. * *vt, vi* to signal or direct by a gesture.

motionless *adj* not moving; still.
motion picture *n* a film, movie.
motive *n* something (as a need or desire) that causes a person to act.
motley *adj* composed of diverse element.
motor *n* anything that produces motion; a machine for converting electrical energy into mechanical energy; a motor car. * *adj* producing motion; of or powered by a motor; of, by or for motor vehicles. * *vi* to travel by car.
motorbike *n* a motorcycle.
motorboat *n* a boat propelled by an engine or motor.
motorist *n* a person who drives a car.
motorway *n* a road with controlled access for fast-moving traffic.
mottled *adj* marked with blotches of various colours.
motto *n* (*pl* **mottoes**) a short saying adopted as a maxim or ideal.
mould *n* a fungus producing a furry growth on the surface of organic matter; a hollow form in which something is cast. * *vt* to make in or on a mould; to form, to shape, to guide.
moulder *vt, vi* to decay; to crumble.
moulding *n* anything cast in a mould; ornamental contour along an edge.
moult *vi* to shed or cast the hair, horns, skin, etc.
mound *n* an artificial elevation of earth or stones; a rampart; a hillock.
mount *n* a hill; a mountain; a setting for photographs, etc; a backing; a horse. * *vi* to rise; to get on horseback; to provide with horses; to amount. * *vt* to climb; to fix, place in position.
mountain *n* a high hill, a vast number.
mountaineer *n* a mountain climber.
mourn *vi* to sorrow. * *vt* to grieve for.
mournful *adj* expressing grief or sorrow.
mourning *n* lamentation; clothes worn by mourners.
mouse *n* (*pl* **mice**) a small rodent with a pointed snout, long body and slender tail; a timid person; a hand-held device used to position the cursor and control software on a computer screen.
moustache *n* the hair on the upper lip.
mouth *n* the opening in the head through which food is eaten, sound uttered or words spoken; the lips; opening, entrance, as of a bottle, etc. * *vt* to say, esp insincerely; to form words with the mouth without uttering sound. * *vi* to utter pompously; to grimace.
mouthpiece *n* the part of a musical instrument or tobacco pipe placed between the lips; a spokesman for others.
mouthwatering *adj* appetizing; tasty.
movable *adj* portable. * *npl* furniture; belongings; personal property.
move *vt* to cause to change place; to set in motion; to affect; to rouse; to prevail on; to make a motion. * *vi* to stir; to go from one place to another; to walk; to change residence.
movement *n* motion; change of position; a gesture; joint action; the policy of a group; a trend; a division of a musical work.
movies *npl* the cinema.
moving *adj* touching; pathetic.
mow *vt, vi* to cut down; to cut grass.
much *adj* (*comp* **more**, *superl* **most**) great in quantity. * *adv* considerably.
mucous, mucose *adj* slimy. * mucous membrane, a membrane lining the nose and other cavities of the body.
mucus *n* a viscid fluid secreted by mucous membrane.
mud *n* moist soft earth; mire.
muddle *vt* to make a mess of; to mix up; to confuse. * *n* a mess; confusion.
muddy *adj* like, covered in mud; confused; not bright; unclear.
muff *n* a fur cover for both hands.
muffin *n* a baked roll.
muffle *vt* to wrap up close; to conceal; to deaden sound.
muffler *n* a long scarf; the silencer of a motor vehicle.
mug *n* a large cup. * *vt* to assault (and rob).
mule *n* the offspring of a male donkey and a female horse; an obstinate person.
mull *vt* to heat, sweeten, and spice (as wine, etc); to ponder.
multifarious *adj* many and varied.
multilateral *adj* many-sided.
multiple *adj* manifold; various; complex.

* *n* a number which contains another an exact number of times.
multiplication *n* the act or process of multiplying.
multiplicity *n* great number or variety.
multiply *vt, vi* to make or become many; to increase; to find the product of by multiplication.
multipurpose *adj* able to be used for many tasks or functions.
multistorey *adj, n* (building) with many storeys.
multitude *n* a crowd; a throng; the populace.
mumble *vi, vt* to mutter; to speak indistinctly.
mummify *vi* to embalm as a mummy.
mummy *n* an embalmed human body, esp an embalmed corpse of ancient Egypt.
mumps *n* a contagious disease.
munch *vt, vi* to chew steadily.
mundane *adj* routine; everyday; banal.
municipal *adj* of or concerning a city, town, etc or its local government.
municipality *n* the corporation or governing body of a town.
munificent *adj* bountiful; generous.
mural *adj* pertaining to a wall. * *n* a picture or design painted onto a wall.
murder *n* unlawful and intentional manslaughter. * *vt* to kill (with malice aforethought); to mar.
murderous *adj* cruel; savage.
murky *adj* dark; gloomy; obscure.
murmur *n* a low continuous, indistinct sound; an abnormal sound made by the heart.
muscle *n* fibrous tissue that contracts and relaxes, producing body movement; strength; power.
muscular *adj* brawny; sinewy.
muse *n* poetic inspiration. * *vi, vt* to ponder; to meditate.
museum *n* a building housing a collection of curios, works of art, etc.
mushroom *n* an edible fungus. * *vi* to gather mushrooms; to spread rapidly.
music *n* melody or harmony; the art of producing musical compositions featuring vocal or instrumental sounds having rhythm, harmony, melody.
musical *adj* melodious; harmonious; having an interest in or talent for music. * *n* a play or film incorporating story, song and dance.
musician *n* one skilled in music.
musing *n* meditation.
Muslim see **Moslem.**
muslin *n* a fine cotton cloth.
must *aux vb* expressing necessity or certainty. * *n* something that must be done or possessed.
mustard *n* a plant with pungent seeds; the condiment got from them; a brownish-yellow colour.
muster *vt* to collect, as troops. * *vi* to assemble. * *n* an assembling of troops.
musty *adj* mouldy; stale; damp.
mutable *adj* changeable; unstable.
mutation *n* change; alteration.
mute *adj* silent; dumb; not pronounced. * *n* a person who cannot speak.
mutilate *vt* to cut off a part; to maim.
mutineer *n* one guilty of mutiny.
mutinous *adj* rebellious.
mutiny *n* a revolt against authority in military service. * *vi* to rise in revolt.
mutter *vi* to mumble; to murmur to grumble. * *n* indistinct speech.
mutual *adj* reciprocal; shared alike; having the same feelings one for the other.
muzzle *n* the projecting mouth and nose of an animal; the open end of a gun; a strap fitted over an animal's jaws to prevent biting. * *vt* to gag.
muzzy *adj* bewildered; tipsy.
my *pron* the possessive case sing of I.
myopia *n* short-sightedness.
myriad *n* a countless number.
myself *pron* emphatic and reflexive form of I; in my normal state.
mysterious *adj* very obscure; incomprehensible; secret.
mystery *n* something beyond human intelligence; something unexplained; a secret; an old form of drama.
mystic *adj* having a meaning beyond normal human understanding; magical.
mystify *vt* to perplex; to bewilder.
myth *n* a tradition or fable embodying the primitive ideas of a people.
mythology *n* the study of myths.

N

nab *vt* to catch; to seize or arrest.
nadir *n* the lowest point.
nag *n* a horse; a person who nags. * *vt*, *vi* to plague; to pester; to scold constantly.
nail *n* a horny substance covering the tip of the finger or toe; a metal spike. * *vt* to fasten, secure or hang with nails.
naïve *adj* ingenuous; unsophisticated.
naïveté *n* lack of sophistication.
naked *adj* bare; nude; destitute.
name *n* the word by which a person or thing is designated; title; reputation; a family. * *vt* to give a name to.
nameless *adj* unknown; unspeakable.
namely *adv* that is to say.
namesake *n* one named after, or with the same name as another.
nap *n* the woolly substance on the surface of cloth, etc; a short sleep.
napalm *n* a substance added to petrol to form a jelly-like compound used in firebombs and flame-throwers.
nape *n* the back of the neck.
napery *n* table and household linen.
naphtha *n* a volatile oil distilled from coal.
napkin *n* a serviette; a small square of cloth or paper used at table to protect clothes or wipe the mouth and fingers.
nappy *n* a piece of absorbent material wrapped around a baby to absorb or retain its excreta.
narcotic *n* a sedative; a drug often addictive used to induce sleep or relieve pain.
narrate *vt* to tell or relate.
narration *n* a narrative; a story.
narrative *adj* pertaining to narration. * n a history or tale spoken or written.
narrow *adj* of little breadth; very limited; not liberal; near. * *vt, vi* to make or become narrow.
narrow-minded *adj* illiberal; prejudiced.
nasal *adj* pertaining to or sounded through the nose. * *n* a sound made through the nose.
nascent *adj* budding; dawning; opening.
nasty *adj* filthy; indecent; disagreeable.
natal *adj* pertaining to birth.
nation *n* people living under the same government and of common descent, culture, language and history.
nationalist *n* one who supports a policy of independence or Home Rule.
nationality *n* national character; patriotism; a nation or national group.
nationalize *vt* to convert land, mines, etc, into state property.
native *adj* pertaining to the place of one's birth; indigenous; inborn. * *n* a person both in the place indicated; a local inhabitant; an indigenous plant or animal; an indigenous inhabitant.
nativity *n* birth; time, place, manner of birth.
natural *adj* pertaining to nature; native; inborn; normal; unaffected; simple; naïve; (music) not sharp or flat.
natural history *n* the study of nature, esp the animal, mineral and vegetable world.
naturalist *n* a person who studies natural history.
naturalization *n* the giving of citizen rights to one of foreign birth.
naturalize *vt* to acclimatize; to confer.
naturally *adv* in a natural manner, by nature; of course.
nature *n* the phenomena of physical like not dominated by man; the entire material world as a whole, or forces observable in it; the essential character of anything.
naught *n* nought; nothing.
naughty *adj* bad; mischievous; titillating.
nausea *n* sickness; disgust.
nauseate *vt, vi* to arouse feelings of disgust or revulsion.
nauseous *adj* loathsome; disgusting.
nautical *adj* pertaining to ships.
naval *adj* pertaining to ships or to a navy.
nave *n* the central part of a church.
navel *n* a depression in the centre of the abdomen.
navigable *adj* affording passage to ships.
navigate *vi, vt* to guide the course of a ship, aeroplane, etc; to sail.
navigation *n* the method of calculating the position of a ship, aircraft etc.
navvy *n* a labourer, who works on roads.
navy *n* the warships of a nation with their

crews and equipment.

near *adj* not distant; intimate; closely related; approximate; narrow (of escape etc.). * *prep* close to. * *adv* almost; close by. * *vt, vi* to approach.

nearly *adv* almost; closely.

near-sighted *adj* short-sighted.

neat *adj* trim; (of alcohol) undiluted.

nebula *n* (*pl* **nebulae**) celestial objects like white clouds, generally clusters of stars.

nebulous *adj* cloudy; hazy; indistinct.

necessary *adj* indispensable; essential. * *n* a proved need, *pl* essential needs.

necessitate *vt* to compel; to constrain.

necessity *n* urgent need; compulsion.

neck *n* the part of body connecting the head and shoulders; an isthmus; the narrowest part of a bottle.

necklace *n* a string of beads worn round the neck.

necropolis *n* cemetery.

nectar *n* the fabled drink of the gods; a delicious drink; the honey of flowers.

need *n* want; necessity; poverty. * *vt, vi* to lack; to require; to be obliged.

needful *adj* needy; necessary.

needle *n* a small steel instrument for sewing; an indicator on a dial; the thin, short leaf of trees such as the pine or spruce.

needy *adj* indigent; very poor.

negation *n* a denial; a saying no.

negative *adj* expressing denial or refusal; the opposite of positive. * *n* a photographic print from which positive prints are taken. * *vt* to veto; to contradict.

neglect *vt* to disregard; to slight; to pay no attention to; to leave uncared for; omit. * *n* want of care.

neglectful *adj* heedless; careless.

negligé *n* a woman's loose dressing gown.

negligence *n* carelessness.

negotiable *adj* capable of being negotiated or transferred.

negotiate *vi* to treat; to bargain in order to reach an agreement or settlement.

negotiation *n* bargaining.

neigh *vi* to whinny. * *n* the cry of a horse.

neighbour *n* a person living near; a fellow human being. * *vt* to adjoin.

neighbourhood *n* a particular area, district or community; the vicinity.

neighbouring *adj* adjoining.

neighbourly *adj* friendly.

neither *pron, adj* not either. * *conj* not either; also not.

nephew *n* the son of a brother or sister.

nepotism *n* favouritism to relatives shown by influential people.

nerve *n* one of the fibrous threads which convey messages to and from brain; courage; audacity. * *vt* to strengthen.

nervous *adj* timid; excitable; forcible.

nest *n* a bird's hatching place.

nestle *vi* to lie close and snug.

net *n* a meshwork of cord, twine, etc; a piece of this used to catch fish, to divide a tennis court etc.; a snare. * *vt* to snare; to twine.

net, nett *adj* clear of deductions, allowances or changes; the opposite of gross.

netball *n* a game for two teams, in which points are scored by putting a ball through an elevated horizontal ring.

nether *adj* lower.

netting *n* a piece of network.

nettle *n* a weed with stinging hairs. * *vt* to irritate.

network *n* an interconnecting arrangement of lines; a group cooperating with each other; a chain of interconnected operations, computers etc.

neuralgia *n* pain in a nerve.

neuritis *n* inflammation of nerve.

neurology *n* the study of nerves.

neurosis *n* (*pl* **neuroses**) a mental disorder with symptoms such as anxiety.

neurotic *adj* suffering from neurosis; highly strung.

neuter *adj* (of nouns) neither masculine nor feminine; (*biol*) having no sex organs. * *vt* to castrate or spay.

neutral *adj* nonaligned; not taking sides with either party in a dispute or war; having no distinctive characteristics; (chem) neither acid nor alkaline. * *n* a position of a gear mechanism in which power is not transmitted.

neutralize *vt* to render neutral.

never *adv* at no time; in no case.

nevertheless *adv* for all that; notwithstanding.

new *adj* recent; novel; fresh; unused.

news *npl* current events; recent happenings; the mass media's coverage of such events.
newsagent *n* a retailer of newspapers.
newspaper *n* a paper published periodically giving latest news.
next *adj* nearest; immediately preceding or following; adjacent. * *adv* in the nearest time, place, rank, etc; on the first subsequent occasion.
nexus *n* tie; connexion.
nibble *vt, vi* to bite little by little.
nice *adj* fastidious; pleasant; dainty.
nicety *n* precision; exactness.
niche *n* a recess in a wall for a statue, etc.
nick *n* a notch; a score; a critical moment; a police station. * *vt* to make a small cut in; to wound superficially.
nickname *n* a name given to an individual in jest or ridicule. * vt to give a nickname to.
nicotine *n* a poisonous alkaloid present in tobacco.
niece *n* the daughter of one's brother or sister.
nigh *adj* near. * *prep.* near to.
night *n* the period from sunset to sunrise.
nightcap *n* a cap worn in bed; an alcoholic drink taken just before bedtime.
nightclub *n* a place of entertainment for drinking, dancing, etc, at night.
nightdress *n* a loose garment worn in bed by women and girls.
nightfall *n* evening.
nightly *adj* done or happening by night or every night; nocturnal.
nightmare *n* a frightening dream; any horrible experience.
nil *n* nothing.
nimble *adj* active; agile.
nine *adj, n* cardinal number; one more than eight, (9 or IX).
nineteen *adj, n* nine and ten (19 or XIX).
ninety *adj, n* nine times ten (90 or C).
ninth *adj, n* next after eighth; one of nine equal parts of a thing.
nip *vt* to pinch; to snip. * *n* a pinch; a small bite from a dog; frost or cold.
nippers *npl* small pincers.
nipple *n* the small protuberance on a breast or udder through which the milk passes, a teat; a teat-like rubber part on the cap of a baby's bottle.
nitrogen *n* a gaseous element forming nearly 78 per cent of air.
nitrogenous *adj* pertaining to nitrogen.
nitroglycerine *n* a powerful explosive.
no *adv* expressing negation. * *n* a denial; a refusal; a negative vote or voter. * *adj* none.
noble *adj* of high rank; famous; lofty in character; stately. * *n* a peer; a person of high rank.
nobleman *n* a noble; a peer.
nobody *n* no one; a person of no importance.
nocturnal *adj* nightly; by night.
nod *vi, vt* to make a slight bow, to incline the head quickly in assent or greeting.
node *n* a knot; a knob; the joint of a stem.
nodule *n* a little knot or lump.
noise *n* a din; clamour; a harsh sound. * *vt* to make public.
noisome *adj* noxious; offensive.
nomad *n* a wanderer; one of a people or tribe who travel in search of pasture.
nomenclature *n* a system of names; vocabulary of scientific terms.
nominal *adj* formal; existing in name only; having only token worth.
nominate *vt* to name; to designate; to appoint to an office or post; to propose someone as a candidate (for election).
nominee *n* a person nominated for office, etc.
nonchalance *n* indifference; coolness.
noncommittal *adj* not revealing one's opinion.
nonconductor *n* a substance which does not conduct heat, electricity, etc.
nonconformist *n* one who does not conform to the established church.
nondescript *adj* hard to classify, indeterminate; lacking individual characteristics. * *n* a nondescript person of thing.
none *n, pron* not one; not any.
nonentity *n* a person of no significance.
nonsense *n* words without meaning.
nonstop *adj* making no intermediate stops (of train etc.). * *adv* never ceasing; never stopping or pausing.
noodle *pl* pasta in thin strips.

noon *n* twelve o'clock in the day.
noose *n* a loop on a running knot; a lasso.
nor *conj* and not; not either.
norm *n* a rule; a pattern; a standard.
normal *adj* according to a rule; regular.
north *n* the cardinal point opposite the midday sun. * *adj* in, of, towards, from the north. * *adv* in or towards the north.
northeast *n* the point midway between north and east.
northward *adv, adj* towards the north.
northwest *n* the point midway between the north and west.
nose *n* the part of the face above the mouth, used for breathing and smelling, having two nostrils; the sense of smell. * *vt* to discover as by smell. * *vi* to sniff for; to inch forwards; to pry.
nostalgia *n* yearning for past times or places.
nostalgic *adj* feeling or expressing nostalgia; longing for one's youth.
nostril *n* one of the two apertures of the nose for breathing and smelling.
not *adv* expressing denial, refusal or negation.
notable *adj* worthy of being noted or remembered; distinguished; memorable.
notation *n* act of recording anything by symbols.
notch *n* an incision; nick. * *vt* to indent.
note *n* a mark, a sign or token; an explanation; an epistle; a musical sound or its symbol; the sound of a bird's call. * *vt* to mark down; to observe.
noted *adj* famous; celebrated.
notepaper *n* paper for writing down notes.
nothing *n* not anything; a trifle; a zero; thing of no importance or value. * *adv* in no way; not at all.
notice *n* heed; regard; intimation; warning; information. * *vt* to observe.
noticeable *adj* worthy of notice; remarkable; easily seen or noticed.
notice board *n* a board on which notices are pinned for public information.
notification *n* intimation; warning.
notify *vt* to make known; to inform.
notion *n* a concept; an idea; an opinion.
notoriety *n* publicity (esp discreditable).
notorious *adj* widely known, esp unfavourably.
notwithstanding *prep, conj* in spite of; nevertheless; although.
nougat *n* a chewy sweet consisting of sugar paste and nuts.
nought *n* not anything; a zero.
noun *n* the name of anything.
nourish *vt* to feed; to foster; to encourage the growth of; to raise.
nourishment *n* food, nutriment.
novel *adj* new and striking. * *n* a fictitious story or narrative in book form.
novelty *n* a new or strange thing; *pl* cheap, small objects for sale.
November *n* the eleventh month of the year.
novice *n* a beginner; a person in a religious order before taking vows.
now *adv,* at the present time. * *conj* since; seeing that.
nowhere *adv* not in, at, or to anywhere.
noxious *adj* hurtful; pernicious.
nozzle *n* the projecting spout of something; e.g. a nose or pipe.
nuance *n* a fine shade; a delicate distinction of meaning etc.
nuclear *adj* of or relating to a nucleus; using nuclear energy.
nuclear energy *n* energy released as a result of nuclear fission or fusion.
nuclear fission *n* the splitting of a nucleus of an atom either spontaneously or by bombarding it with particles.
nuclear fusion *n* the combining of two nuclei into a heavier nucleus.
nuclear power *n* electrical or motive power produced by a nuclear reactor.
nuclear reactor *n* a device in which nuclear fission is maintained and harnessed to produce energy.
nucleus *n* (*pl* **nuclei, nucleuses**) the central part of core around which something may develop, or be grouped or concentrated; the centrally positively charged portion of an atom.
nude *adj* naked; bare. * *n* a naked human figure esp in a work of art; nakedness.
nudge *n* a light jog with the elbow. * *vt* to jog with the elbow; to remind.
nugget *n* a lump, as of gold.
nuisance *n* that which annoys.

null *adj* of no force; void; invalid.
nullify *vt* to render null; to cancel out.
numb *adj* benumbed; having no feeling through shock or cold. * *vt* to deaden.
number *n* a symbol or word indicating how many; a numeral identifying a person or thing by its position in a series. * *vt, vi* to count; to give a number to; to include or be included as one of a group; to limit the number of; to total.
numberplate *n* a plate on the front or rear of a motor vehicle that displays its registration number.
numeral *adj* pertaining to number. * *n* a figure or symbol representing a number.
numerate *adj* able to use and understand numbers and arithmetic.
numerical *adj* denoting number; consisting of numbers.
numerous *adj* many.
numismatics *n* the study of coins and medals.
nun *n* woman belonging to a religious order.
nuncio *n* an ambassador of the Pope.
nunnery *n* a convent.
nuptials *npl* marriage.
nurse *n* one trained to care for the sick, or infirm. * *vt* to tend; to suckle; to foster.
nursery *n* a place where children may be left in temporary care; a place where young trees and plants are raised for transplanting.
nursery rhyme *n* a short traditional poem or song for children.
nursery school *n* a school for young children, usu under five.
nursery slope *n* a gently inclined slope for novice skiers.
nursing *n* the profession of a nurse.
nursing home *n* an establishment providing care for convalescent, chronically ill, or disabled people.
nurture *n* upbringing; education; nourishment. * *vt* to nourish; to educate.
nut *n* a fruit containing a kernel in a hard covering; a screw fastening a bolt.
nutcracker *n* an instrument for cracking nuts; a bird with speckled plumage.
nutmeg *n* the aromatic kernel produced by a tree, grated and used as a spice.
nutriment *n* food; nourishment.
nutritious *adj* nourishing; health-giving.
nylon *n* any of numerous tough, synthetic materials used esp in plastics.
nymph *n* the larva of the dragonfly, mayfly etc.

O

oaf *n* a lout; a stupid clumsy person.
oak *n* a tree with a hard durable wood, having acorns as fruits.
oar *n* a pole with a flat blade for rowing.
oarsman *n* one who rows at the oar.
oasis *n* (*pl* **oases**) a fertile tract in a desert.
oast *n* a kiln to dry hops or malt.
oats *npl* a cereal grass widely cultivated for its edible grain; the seeds.
oath *n* a solemn affirmation.
oatmeal *n* ground oats; porridge or this.
obdurate *adj* unrelenting.
obedience *n* the doing of what is commanded.
obedient *adj* submissive; dutiful; complaint.
obeisance *n* a bow or curtsy; an act of respect.
obese *adj* very stout; corpulent.
obesity *n* excessive fatness.
obey *vt, vi* to do as commanded; to yield to; to comply with.
obfuscate *vt* to darken; to confuse.
obituary *n* an announcement of a person's death, often with a short biography.
object *n* the end aimed at; a purpose; anything present to the senses. * *vt, vi* to oppose; to disapprove.
objection *n* the act of objecting; a ground for; or expression of, disapproval.
objectionable *adj* causing an objection; disagreeable.
objective *adj* not influenced by opinions or feelings; impartial; having an independent existence of it sown, real. * *n* the thing or placed aimed at.
obligation *n* the binding power of a promise, contract or law.
obligatory *adj* binding; compulsory.
oblige *vt* to constrain; to compel; to do or favour; to gratify.

obliging *adj* civil; kind; agreeable.
oblique *adj* slanting; indirect; allusive.
obliterate *vt* to blot out; to destroy.
oblivion *n* the state of forgetting or being utterly forgotten.
oblivious *adj* forgetful; unaware.
oblong *adj* rectangular and longer than broad. * *n* an oblong figure.
obnoxious *adj* odious; unpopular.
oboe *n* a wind instrument of wood with a mouthpiece with a double reed.
obscene *adj* indecent; vile; offensive to a moral standard.
obscure *adj* darkened; dim; abstruse; unimportant; humble. * *vt* to darken; to hide from view; to confuse; to make unclear.
obscurity *n* darkness; dimness; an obscure thing or person.
obsequious *adj* cringing; fawning.
observance *n* the observing of a rule or practice; the performance of rites, etc.
observant *adj* attentive; watchful.
observation *n* the act or faculty of observing; a comment or remark.
observatory *n* a building for astronomical observations.
observe *vt, vi* to take notice of; to remark; to keep religiously; to celebrate.
observer *n* a person who observes; a delegate who attends a formal meeting but may not take part; an expert analyst and commentator in a particular field.
obsess *vt* to possess or haunt the mind of.
obsession *n* the complete capture of the mind by some idea; a persistent preoccupation.
obsolescent *adj* going out of date.
obsolete *adj* antiquated; out of date.
obstacle *n* an obstruction; a hindrance.
obstetrics *n* the branch of medicine concerned with the care and treatment of women during pregnancy and childbirth.
obstinate *adj* stubborn; self-willed.
obstreperous *adj* unruly; disorderly.
obstruct *vt* to block up; to impede; to hinder; to keep light from.
obstructive *adj* causing delay; preventing.
obtain *vt* to acquire; to gain; to earn. * *vi* to prevail; to hold good.
obtrusive *adj* forward; interfering; pushy.
obtuse *adj* blunt; stupid; greater than a right angle.
obvious *adj* plain; evident.
occasion *n* an occurrence; an incident; an opportunity; a cause; a juncture.
occasional *adj* casual; happening now and then; incidental.
occult *adj* hidden; mysterious; belonging to the supernatural arts; mystic.
occupancy *n* tenancy.
occupation *n* possession; tenure; business; vocation; employment.
occupy *vt* to take possession of; to fill; to employ; to engage; to engross.
occur *vi* to happen.
occurrence *n* an event, an incident.
ocean *n* the vast body of water surrounding the land or one of its divisions.
octagon *n* a plane figure having eight angles and sides.
octave *n* in music, the eighth full tone above or below a given tone, the interval of eight degrees between a tone and either of its octaves.
octavo *n* a book with eight leaves to a sheet, abbreviated 8vo.
October *n* the tenth month of the year.
ocular *adj* pertaining to the eye; visual.
oculist *n* one skilled in diseases of the eyes.
odd *adj* eccentric; peculiar; occasional; not divisible by two; extra or left over.
oddity *n* the state of being odd; an odd thing or person; peculiarity.
oddment *n* a remnant esp of fabric.
odds *n, sing, pl* inequality; excess; difference in favour of one; advantage.
ode *n* a lyric poem of exalted tone.
odious *adj* hateful; offensive; disgusting.
odium *n* hatred; dislike; blame.
odorous *adj* fragrant.
odour *n* any scent or smell; reputation.
oesophagus *n* the gullet.
of *prep* denoting source, cause, etc.
off *adv* away; distant; detached; out of condition. * *adj* cancelled; having gone bad (of food). * *prep* away from; not on.
offence *n* injury; insult; displeasure; crime; law; misdemeanour.
offend *vt* to displease; to affront; to shock.

* *vi* to break the law.

offensive *adj* causing offence; disgusting; impertinent; aggressive. * *n* an attack.

offer *vt* to present for acceptance or rejection; to tender; to bid. * *vi* to present itself * *n* a bid; a proposal.

offering *n* a gift; a sacrifice.

offhand *adv* without thinking. * *adj* inconsiderate; curt; brusque.

office *n* duty; public employment; function; service; place of business.

officer *n* the holder of an office; one who has a commission in the army or navy.

official *adj* pertaining to an office properly authorized; formal. * *n* an officer; one holding public office.

officious *adj* fussy; meddling; interfering.

offing *n* the near or foreseeable future.

off-licence *n* a licence to sell alcohol for consumption off the premises.

off-peak *adj* denoting use of a service, etc., in a period of lesser demand.

offset *n* a method of printing in which an image is transferred form a plate to a rubber surface and then to paper.

offshoot *n* a shoot; a sprout.

offshore *adv* at sea some distance from the shore.

offside *adj, adv* illegally in advance of the ball.

offspring *n, sing, pl* children; progeny.

offstage *adj, adv* out of sight of the audience; behind the scenes.

often *adv* frequently; many times.

ogle *vt, vi* to gape at; to look at lustfully.

ohm *n* the unit of electric resistance.

oil *n* a greasy liquid, often inflammable, got from animal, vegetable, and mineral sources.

oilskin *n* waterproof cloth; a garment of this.

oil slick *n* a mass of oil floating on the surface of water.

oil well *n* a well from which petroleum is extracted.

oily *adj* like or covered with oil; greasy; too suave or smooth, unctuous.

ointment *n* a fatty substance for applying to skin for healing or cosmetic purposes.

old *adj* aged; not new or fresh; out of date; former; not modern; worn out.

old-fashioned *adj* out of date.

olfactory *adj* pertaining to sense of smell.

oligarchy *n* rule by a small select body.

olive *n* an evergreen tree; its edible fruit yielding oil; a greenish colour.

olympiad *n* a four-year period, being the term between successive Olympic games.

omega *n* the last letter of Greek alphabet.

omelette, omelet (US) *n* eggs beaten and cooked flat in a pan.

omen *n* a sign of a future event.

ominous *adj* foreboding; ill-omened.

omission *n* a failure to do something; a leaving out of something.

omit *vt* to neglect; to leave out.

omnipotence *n* unlimited power.

omnipotent *adj* all-powerful.

omniscience *n* the faculty of knowing all things; universal knowledge.

omniscient *adj* all-knowing.

omnivorous *adj* all-devouring.

on *prep* in contact with the upper surface of; supported by, attached to, or covering; at the time of; concerning, about; immediately after; using. * *adv* (so as to be) covering or in contact with something; forward; (device) switched on; continuously in progress; due to take place; (actor) on stage; on duty.

once *adv* on the occasion only; formerly; at some time. * *conj* a soon as. * *n* one time.

oncoming *adj* approaching.

one *adj* single; undivided; united; the same; of a certain unspecified time. * *n* the figure I; unity; unit. * *pron.* any single person; any individual; anything.

onerous *adj* burdensome; heavy.

one-sided *adj* partial; unfair.

one-way *adj* requiring no reciprocal action or obligation.

ongoing *adj* progressing, continuing.

onion *n* an edible bulb with a pungent taste and odour.

onlooker *n* a spectator.

only *adj* single; sole. * *adv* for one purpose; merely; just; not more than. * *conj* but; except that.

onomatopoeia *n* forming words by imitation of sounds, as *hiss*.

onrush *n* a rapid onset.
onset *n* an attack; an assault; a beginning.
onslaught *n* a fierce attack.
onus *n* a burden; a duty; a responsibility.
onward *adj* advancing.
onwards *adv* forward; ahead.
ooze *n* soft mud or slime. * *vi* to issue gently; to percolate; to seep.
opal *n* a precious stone, remarkable for its changing colours.
opaque *adj* not transparent.
open *adj* not shut; uncovered; accessible; unfenced; treeless; public; candid; clear. * *vt; vi* to begin; to declare open. * *n* a sporting competition that any player can enter.
open-hearted *adj* frank; generous.
opening *adj* beginning. * *n* a way in or out; a breach; a vacancy; a chance.
opera *n* a musical drama.
operate *vt, vi* to work; to act; to produce an effect; to treat surgically; to control.
operation *n* action; process; procedure; surgical treatment; military action.
operative *adj* effective; functioning; in force. * *n* a workman; factory hand.
operetta *n* a light musical drama.
ophthalmology *n* the branch of medicine dealing with the eyes.
opiate *n* a narcotic drug containing opium.
opinion *n* a belief; a notion; a judgement; an evaluation; expert advice.
opium *n* a drug obtained from poppies.
opponent *n* an adversary.
opportune *adj* timely; convenient.
opportunist *n* a person who seizes opportunities for his or her benefit.
opportunity *n* a fit or convenient time.
oppose *vt, vi* to act against; to resist; to obstruct; to bar.
opposed *adj* adverse; hostile.
opposite *adj* facing; adverse; contrary.
opposition *n* the act of opposing; contradiction; antagonism; contrast; the party opposing the government.
oppress *vt* to treat harshly; to subjugate; to weigh down in the mind.
oppression *n* cruelty; severity; persecution; physical or mental distress.
oppressive *adj* burdensome; tyrannical; sultry, close of weather.
opt *vi* to chose or exercise an option.
optical *adj* of or relating to the eye or light; optic; aiding or correcting vision; visual.
optician *n* one who makes or sells optical aids.
optics *n* the science of light and sight.
optimism *n* the tendency to take the most hopeful and cheerful view.
optimist *n* a sanguine person.
option *n* choice; free choice; the right to buy, sell or lease at a fixed price within a specified time.
optional *adj* voluntary; left to choice.
opulence *n* wealth; riches; luxury.
or *conj* denoting; an alternative.
oracle *n* a very wise person.
oral *adj* spoken; of the mouth; taken by mouth. * *n* a spoken examination.
orange *n* a juicy, a trees fruit; its tree; its colour, reddish-yellow.
oration *n* a public speech.
oratory *n* eloquence in public speaking.
orb *n* a sphere, esp one ornamented and surmounted by a cross as part of royal insignia.
orbit *n* the path of a planet; the eye socket; the path of an electron around the nucleus of an atom. * *vt, vi* to put (a satellite) into orbit; to circle round.
orchard *n* an area planted with fruit trees.
orchestra *n* a group of musicians playing together under a conductor.
orchestral *adj* suitable for or performed by an orchestra.
ordain *vt* to consecrate (for ministry).
ordeal *n* a severe trial or test.
order *n* arrangement; method; relative position; sequence; tidiness; rules of procedure; a religious fraternity; an honour of decoration; an instruction or command. * *vt, vi* to arrange; to command.
orderly *adj* in good order; well-behaved; methodical. * *n* a hospital attendant; a soldier attending an officer.
ordinal *adj, n* a number showing position in a series.
ordinance *n* a statute; an edict.
ordinary *adj* regular; usual; normal; commonplace; unexceptional.
ordination *n* the act of ordaining or being ordained; admission to the ministry.

ore *n* rock substance containing metal.
organ *n* a complex musical wind instrument with pipes, stops, and a keyboard; a part of an animal or plant that performs a vital or natural function.
organic *adj* pertaining to or affecting a bodily organ; of the class of compounds that are formed from carbon; (vegetables etc.) grown without the use of artificial fertilizers or pesticides.
organism *n* anything living; an organized body.
organization *n* suitable arrangements for effective work; system; structure.
organize *vt* to put in working order; to establish; to institute; to arrange for.
orgasm *n* the climax of sexual excitement.
orgy *n* a wild party, with excessive drinking and indiscriminate sexual activity.
orient, orientate *vt, vi* to adjust (one-self) to a particular situation.
oriental *adj* of the Orient.
orifice *n* an opening or mouth of a cavity.
origin *n* a source; a beginning; ancestry or parentage.
original *adj* relating to the origin or beginning; novel; unusual; inventive, creative. * *n* an original work, as of art; something from which copies are made.
originality *n* initiative; freshness and independence of thought.
originate *vt, vi* to bring into being.
ornament *n* decoration. * *vt* to beautify.
ornamental *adj* decorative, not useful.
ornate *adj* richly ornamented; highly.
ornithology *n* the study of birds.
orphan *n, adj* a child without parents.
orphanage *n* an institution for the care of orphans.
orthodox *adj* conforming with established behaviour or opinions; not heretical.
orthopaedics *n* the study and surgical treatment of bone and joint disorders.
oscillate *vi* to swing back and forth as a pendulum.
ossification *n* the formation of bone.
ossify *vt, vi* to change into bone; (of habits etc.) to become rigid and inflexible.
ostensible *adj* apparent; pretended.
ostentation *n* a showing off.
ostentatious *adj* showy; pretentious.
osteopathy *n* the treatment of disease by manipulation of the bones and muscles.
ostracize *vt* to exclude; to banish from society.
other *adj, pron* not the same.
ought *vi* to be bound; to be obliged.
ounce *n* a unit of weight, equal to one sixteenth of a pound or 28.34 grams.
our *adj, pron* pertaining or belonging to us.
ourselves *pron* emphatic and reflexive form of we.
oust *vt* to eject, expel, esp by underhand means; to remove forcibly.
out *adv* not in; outside; in the open air; beyond bounds; ruled out, no longer considered; on strike; at an end; extinguished; into the open; published. * *prep* out of; out through; outside. * *adj* external; outward. * *n* means of escape.
outbid *vt* to bid more than another.
outboard *n* an engine attached to the outside of a boat.
outbreak *n* a sudden eruption of anger, war, disease, etc.
outburst *n* an explosion of anger etc.
outcast *n* a person rejected by society.
outclass *vt* to surpass or excel greatly.
outcome *n* the issue; the result.
outcrop *n* the exposure of strata at the surface.
outcry *n* clamour; protest.
outdistance *vt* to get ahead of.
outdo *vt* to excel; to surpass.
outdoors *adv* in or into the open air.
outer *adj* external.
outer space *n* any region of space beyond the earth's atmosphere.
outfit *n* the equipment used in an activity; clothes worn together, an ensemble.
outfitter *n* a supplier of clothes.
outgoing *adj* departing; sociable, forthcoming. * *n* an outlay; *pl* expenditure.
outgrow *vt* to surpass in growth; to grow too large for (clothes); to change one's ideas, habits etc. as one develops.
outhouse *n* a small building.
outing *n* a short excursion for pleasure.
outlandish *adj* strange; unconventional.
outlaw *vt* to declare illegal. * *n* an outlawed person; a notorious criminal.

outlay *n* expenditure.
outlet *n* an opening.
outline *n* a profile; a draft.
outlive *vt* to live longer than; to outlast.
outlook *n* a view; a prospect; a viewpoint.
outlying *adj* detached; remote, distant.
outmanoeuvre *vt* to surpass in strategy.
outmoded *adj* old-fashioned.
outnumber *vt* to exceed in number.
outpatient *n* a non-resident hospital patient.
outpost *n* a military post or detachment at a distance from a main force.
output *n* the quantity (of goods, etc.) produced, esp over a given period; information delivered by a computer; esp to a printer.
outrage *vt* to injure; to ravish. * *n* a gross offence, injury or insult.
outright *adv* completely; utterly.
outset *n* the beginning.
outside *n* the external surface; the exterior. * *adj* outer; outdoor; slight (of a chance). * *adv* on or to the outside.
outsider *n* a person or thing not included in a set, group, etc., a non-member; a contestant not thought to have a chance in a race.
outsize *adj* of a larger than usual size.
outskirts *npl* districts remote from the centre, as of a city.
outspoken *adj* frank; candid; blunt.
outstanding *adj* excellent; distinguished, prominent; unpaid; unresolved.
outstrip *vt* to outrun; to excel.
outward *adj* directed towards the outside; external.
outweigh *vt* to count for more than, to exceed in value, weight, or importance.
outwit *vt* to defeat by cunning.
oval *adj* egg-shaped.
ovary *n* one of the two female reproductive organs producing eggs.
ovation *n* enthusiastic applause.
oven *n* an enclosed cooking or baking compartment.
over *prep* higher than; on top of; across; to the other side of; above; more than; concerning. * *adv* above; across; in every part; completed; up and down; in addition; too. * *adj* upper; excessive; surplus; finished; remaining.
overact *vt, vi* to act in an exaggerated manner, to overdo a part.
overall *adj* including everything. * *adv* as a whole; generally. * *n* a loose protective garment.
overawe *vt* to restrain by awe; to daunt.
overbalance *vt* to lose balance and fall.
overbearing *adj* haughty; domineering.
overboard *adv* over the side of a ship; to extremes of enthusiasm.
overburden *vt* to overload; to oppress.
overcast *adj* clouded over.
overcharge *vt* to charge too much; of battery, to overload; to fill to excess.
overcoat *n* a warm topcoat.
overcome *vt* to subdue; to conquer; to get the better of; to render helpless or powerless, as by tears, laughter etc.
overdo *vt* to do to excess; to overcook.
overdose *n* too great a dose.
overdraft *n* an overdrawing, an amount overdrawn, at a bank.
overdue *adj* past the time fixed or due.
overestimate *vt* to set too high an estimate on or for.
overflow *vt, vi* to flood; to abound (with emotion etc.). * *n* surplus; excess; an outlet for surplus water etc.
overflowing *adj* abundant, copious.
overgrown *adj* grown beyond the normal size; rank; ungainly.
overhang *vt, vi* to project over.
overhaul *vt* to examine thoroughly with a view to repairs; to overtake.
overhead *adj, adv* above the head; in the sky. * *n* (often *pl*) the continuing costs of a business, as of rent, light, etc.
overhear *vt* to hear by accident.
overjoyed *adj* highly delighted.
overland *adj, adv* by on or across land.
overlap *vt* (*pt* **overlapped**) to extend over so as to coincide in part.
overlay *vt* to coat; to smother.
overload *vt* to overburden.
overlook *vt* to superintend; to pardon; to fail to notice.
overnight *adv* for, through or during the night.
overpass *n* a road crossing another road, path, etc., at a higher level.

overpower *vt* to overcome; to subdue.
overpowering *adj* overwhelming.
overrate *vt* to rate or assess too highly.
overreach *vt* to fail by attempting too much or going too far.
override *vt* to nullify; to prevail.
overrule *vt* prevail over.
overrun *vt* to ravage; to outrun, to swarm over. * *vi* to overflow.
overseas *adj, adv* across or beyond the sea; abroad.
overseer *n* an inspector; a superintendent.
overshadow *vt* to throw a shadow over; to cast into the shade; to outdo.
overshoot *vt* (*pt* **overshoot**) to shoot or send beyond (a target, etc.); (aircraft) to fly or taxi beyond the end of a runway when landing or taking off.
oversight *n* a mistake; an omission.
oversleep *vi* (*pt* **overslept**) to sleep beyond the intended time.
overstate *vt* to exaggerate.
overstep *vt* to exceed.
overt *adj* public; openly done; unconcealed; deliberate.
overtake *vt* to come up with and pass; to catch.
overtax *vt* to overstrain oneself.
overthrow *vt* to overturn; to defeat. * *n* ruin; defeat.
overtime *n* time beyond the regular hours; (payment for) extra time work.
overtone *n* an additional subtle meaning; an implicit quality; (music) an instrumental introduction to an opera, etc.
overture *n* a proposal; an offer; a musical introduction to an opera, etc.
overturn *vt* to capsize; to overthrow.
overweight *adj* weighing more than the proper amount. * *n* excess weight.
overwhelm *vt* to submerge; overpower.
overwhelming *adj* irresistible; uncontrollable; vast; vastly superior; extreme.
overwork *vt* to work beyond one's strength or too long.
overwrought *adj* overexcited.
owe *vt* to be indebted to; to feel the need to do or give out of gratitude.
own *adj* belonging to oneself or itself. * *vt* to possess by right; to avow; to concede.
owner *n* one who owns or possesses, a proprietor.
oxide *n* a compound of oxygen with another element.
oxtail *n* the tail of an ox, esp skinned and used for stews, soups, etc.
oxygen *n* a colourless, odourless, tasteless, highly reactive gaseous element forming part of air, water, etc., and essential to life and combustion.
oxygen mask *n* an apparatus worn over the nose and mouth through which oxygen passes from a storage tank.
oxygen tent *n* a canopy over a hospital bed, etc., within which a supply of oxygen is maintained.
ozone *n* a condensed form of oxygen.
ozone layer *n* a layer of ozone in the upper atmosphere that absorbs ultraviolet rays from the sun.

P

pace *n* the measure of a single stride; gait; rate of progress. * *vi* to step; to walk slowly. * *vt* to walk up and down; to determine the pace in a race.
pacific *adj* peaceable; calm.
pacify *vt* to calm; to allay; to restore peace to.
pack *n* a set of cards; a set of hounds; a gang. * *vt* to make up into a bundle; to fill; to stuff; to crowd; to dismiss. * *vi* to form into a hard mass, to assemble.
package *n* a parcel; a wrapped bundle.
packet *n* a small box.
packet *n* a small parcel; a mailboat.
pack ice *n* ice masses packed together.
packing *n* wrapping material; stuffing.
pact *n* a contract; an agreement.
pad *n* a peice of stuffing, esp absorbant material; block of writing paper.
padding *n* anything added to achieve length or amount, esp in a book.
paddle *vi* to wade in shallow water; to row. * *vt* to propel by an oar or paddle. * *n* a broad short oar.
paddock *n* a grassy enclosure for horses.
paddy *n* threshed, unmilled rice; a rice field.

padlock *n* a detachable lock. * *vt* to secure with a padlock.
pagan *n* a person who has no religion.
page *n* an attendant at a formal function; a sheet of paper in a book, newspaper.
pageant *n* a spectacular procession, etc.
pageantry *n* a spectacular display.
pagoda *n* an Eastern temple.
pail *n* a bucket.
pain *n* bodily suffering; distress; ; labour; effort. * *vt* to cause pain to.
painstaking *adj* laborious and careful.
paint *vt* to coat with colour; to portray. * *vi* to make a picture. * *n* a pigment.
painter *n* one whose occupation is to paint; an artist in colour; a rope for fastening a small boat.
painting *n* the act or art of painting.
pair *n* two things of like kind; a couple; a man and his wife. * *vi* to join in pairs.
palace *n* a royal residence.
palaeography *n* the art of deciphering ancient writing.
palaeontology *n* the science of fossil organic remains.
palatable *adj* having a pleasant taste; pleasant and acceptable.
palate *n* the roof of the mouth; taste.
palatial *adj* spacious; magnificent.
pale *n* a pointed stake; a boundary. * *vi* to grow pale. * *adj* light in colour.
palette *n* an artist's mixing board.
paling *n* a fence formed with stakes.
pall *n* a mantle, as of smoke; covering on a coffin. * *vi* to shroud.
pallet *n* a portable platform used in bulk storage.
palliate *vt* to alleviate; to excuse.
palliative *adj* mitigating. * *n* something that eases pain, sorrow, etc.
pallid *adj* pale; wan.
pallor *n* paleness.
palm *n* the underside of hand; a tropical tree; symbol of victory.
palmistry *n* fortune-telling by lines on the hand.
palpable *adj* perceptible by the touch; plain; obvious.
palpitate *vi* to throb; to tremble.
palpitation *n* violent pulsation of the heart.
paltry *adj* mean; trifling.
pamper *vt* to indulge to excess; to spoil.
pamphlet *n* a small unbound book.
pan *n* a broad shallow vessel for cooking, the bowl of a lavatory.
panacea *n* a remedy for all ills.
panache *n* stylish behaviour.
pancake *n* a thin cake of cooked batter.
pancreas *n* a fleshy gland secreting digestive juice.
pandemonium *n* chaos; scene of disorder and noise.
pander *vi* to gratify or exploit the weaknesses of others.
pane *n* a plate of glass in a window.
panegyric *n* a eulogy.
panel *n* a rectangular section of door, ceiling, etc; a group of selected persons; a board for instruments or controls.
pang *n* a sudden pain or feeling.
panic *n* a sudden blind fear.
panoply *n* splendid display.
panorama *n* a complete view.
pant *vi* to gasp; to long for.
pantomime *n* a Christmas theatrical show.
pantry *n* a small cupboard for provisions.
papacy *n* the office of the pope.
paper *n* thin sheets used for writing, printing, etc, a newspaper; an essay. * *adj* made of paper. * *vt* to cover with paper.
papyrus *n* (*pl* **papyri**) reed from which the ancients made paper.
par *n* state of equality; original, normal, or face value of shares.
parable *n* a religious allegory; a story with a moral lesson.
parachute *n* a fabic canopy used to retard speed of fall from an aircraft.
parade *n* display; show, muster; a promenade. * *vt, vi* to show off; to marshal; to walk up and down.
paradise *n* the garden of Eden; heaven; supreme bliss.
paradox *n* something containing seeming contradictory qualities or phrases.
paraffin *n* a distilled oil used as fuel.
paragon *n* a model of excellence.
paragraph *n* a subdivision in a piece of writing, marked by a new line.
parallax *n* the apparent change of position of object when viewed from differ-

ent points.

parallel *adj* equidistant at all points; corresponding. * *n* a circle of latitude.

parallelogram *n* a quadrilateral, whose opposite sides are parallel and of equal length.

paralyse *vt* to affect with paralysis; to render helpless.

paralysis *n* the loss of sensation and movement in any part of the body.

parapet *n* a wall breast-high.

paraphernalia *npl* belongings; trappings.

paraphrase *n* an interpretation of a passage of the sake of clarity. * *vt* to interpret.

parasite *n* a hanger-on; a plant or animal that lives on another.

parasol *n* a sun shade.

parboil *vt* to boil partly.

parcel *n* a small bundle or packet. * *vt* to divide into portions.

parch *vt* to become hot, dry or thirsty; to scorch.

parchment *n* a skin prepared for writing on.

pardon *vt* to forgive; to excuse. * *n* forgiveness; remission of penalty.

pardonable *adj* excusable.

pare *vt* to trim by cutting; to peel.

parent *n* a father or mother; a progenitor; a source.

parentage *n* extraction; birth.

parenthesis *n* (*pl* **parentheses**) a written explanatory 'aside', usually in brackets thus ().

pariah *n* an outcast.

parish *n* a district served by one clergyman. * *adj* parochial.

parity *n* equality; a likeness.

park *n* a recreation field; a glebe; a grass field; artillery and ground occupied by it; a stance for motors. * *vt* to enclose; to store.

parlance *n* conversation; talk.

parley *vi* to confer, to discuss. * *n* conference, esp with an enemy during cessation of hostilities.

parliament *n* a legislative assembly made up of representatives of a nation.

parlour *n* a sitting room.

parochial *adj* provincial in outlook; narrow-minded.

parody *n* a humorous imitation of a literary or musical work or style.

parole *n* word of honour; conditional release of a prisoner.

paroxysm *n* a fit (of rage, grief, etc).

parquet*n* wood flooring.

parse *vt* to tell the parts of speech and their relations in a sentence.

parsimonious *adj* miserly.

parsimony *n* excessive economy; stinginess.

parson *n* a parish minister; a clergyman.

part *n* a portion; a section; a share; a role. *pl* ability; a region. * *vi* to divide; share; break; separate; depart.

partake *vi, vt* to get a share of; to have or take a share in a meal.

partial *adj* only; incomplete; biased.

participate *vi, vt* to share in.

participle *n* a word partly verb and partly adjective.

particle *n* an atom; a word that cannot be used alone; a prefix; a suffix.

particular *adj* single; special; careful; fastidious. * *n* a detail; a single item.

parting *adj* separating; final. * *n* departure; a division; a shed of the hair.

partisan *adj* biased; one-sided.

partition *n* division; a dividing wall or screen. * *vt* to divide up.

partner *n* a sharer in business, etc; either of a couple, married or unmarried.

partnership *n* fellowship; joint interest; the state of being a partner.

party *n* a company; faction; a social entertainment; a side; a political group.

pass *vi* to go past; to change; to die; to elapse; to be enacted; to succeed at examination; to cross; to utter; to become law. * *n* an approval; passport; an uninvited sexual approach.

passable *adj* allowable; fairly good.

passage *n* a way through; transit; road; channel; journey; part of book.

passenger *n* a traveller in a conveyance.

passing *adj* current; fleeting.

passion *n* strong feeling; great suffering; anger; love.

passionate *adj* moved by passion; hasty.

passive *adj* submissive; inert; acted on.

passport *n* a licence to travel abroad; ticket of admission or acceptance.

password *n* a secret word which gives ready entrance.

past *adj* gone by; spent; ended. * *n* former time. * prep. beyond. * *adv* by.

paste *n* a plastic mass of varied materials.

pastel *n* a crayon drawing.

pasteurize *vt* to inoculate; to sterilize (milk, etc).

pastime *n* recreation; play.

pastor *n* a minister of a church.

pastoral *adj* rustic; rural; relating to a pastor. * *n* a poem of rural life.

pastry *n* crust of pies, tarts, etc.

pasture *n* grass for cattle; grass land. * *vi* to graze.

pasty *adj* like paste; pallid apperance.

pat *n* a tap; a small lump. * *vt* to tap. * *adj* apt; glib.

patch *n* a repair piece; a small piece of ground. * *vt* to mend.

patchwork *n* something made of various bits, esp in needlework.

patella *n* the kneecap.

patent *n* grant of sole right to make or sell patented article. * *adj* open; obvious; secured by patent. * *vt* to obtain patent for.

paternal *adj* fatherly; hereditary.

paternity *n* fatherhood; origin; descent.

path *n* a footway; a track; a course; a direction.

pathetic *adj* inspiring pity.

pathologist *n* a medical specialist in pathology.

pathology *n* the study of diseases.

pathos *n* expression or exciting deep feeling of pity.

patience *n* endurance; composure under trial; a card game.

patient *adj* uncomplaining; calm * *n* an invalid.

patriarch *n* the chief of a tribe or family.

patrician *adj* high born; aristocratic. * *n* a nobleman.

patriot *n* a lover of his country.

patriotism *n* love of country.

patrol *n* a unit of persons, esp employed for security; their going of the rounds. * *vti* to go the rounds, inspect, etc.

patron *n* one who encourages, helps, or protects.

patronage *n* support; conferring of favours or benefits.

patronize *vt* to act as patron of; to favour; to treat with condescension.

patter *vi* to make a sound like that of rain or hail, or feet; to mumble; *n* chatter.

pattern *n* a model; a design.

paucity *n* fewness; poverty.

paunch *n* the belly; esp of a potbelly.

pauper *n* a very poor person.

pause *n* a temporary stop; suspense. * *vi* to stop; hesitate.

pave *vt* to make a smooth roadway with blocks, flags, etc.

pavement *n* paved path for walkers.

pavilion *n* a large tent; a clubhouse; temporary building for exhibitions.

paw *n* the foot of animals with claws. * *vt* to scrape with the forefoot.

pawn *n* a security; pledge; piece of least value (chess). * *vt* to give in pledge.

pawnbroker *n* a person licensed to lend money on pledged goods.

pay *vt,vi* to give money for goods, service, etc; to reward; to bestow (attention, etc). * *n* wages; salary; reward.

payable *adj* due on a certain date.

payee *n* one to whom money is to be paid.

payment *n* act of paying; what is paid.

peace *n* quiet; calm; freedom from war or disorder; a treaty ending a war.

peaceable *adj* disposed to peace.

peaceful *adj* quiet; calm; mild.

peacemaker *n* one who restores good feeling; a reconciler.

peak *n* pointed top of hill; projection on cap; highest point.

peal *n* a loud clash; a clang; chime; loud laughter. * *vi* to ring out.

pearl *n* a lustrous gem found in oyster.

peasant *n* a rural labourer.

peasantry *n* peasants; country people.

peat *n* partly carbonized turf used as fuel.

pebble *n* small water-worn stone.

peccable *adj* liable to sin.

peccadillo *n* a petty fault or sin.

peck *n* a quick kiss. * *vi, vt* to strike or pick up with the beak.

peckish *adj* hungry.

pectoral *adj* pertaining to the breast.

peculiar *adj* one's own; particular; special; odd.

peculiarity *n* a characteristic; an oddity.

pecuniary *adj* financial; relating to money.

pedal *adj* pertaining to a foot. * *n* foot lever in cycle, etc. * *vt, vi*to work a pedal; to cycle.

pedant *n* one who parades his knowledge esp of insignificant details.

pedantry *n* a vain display of learning.

peddle *vi, vt* to sell small items from place to place.

pedestal *n* the base of a column, etc.

pedestrian *adj* going on foot; commonplace. * *n* a person who walks.

pedigree *n* lineage; ancestry.

pedlar *n* one who sells small goods from place to place.

peel *vt* to strip off skin, esp of fruit; to bare. * *vi* to lose the skin, bark, or rind. * *n* the skin or rind.

peep *vi* to chirp; to begin to appear; to look through a slit. * *n* a furtive or hurried glance.

peer n an equal; a nobleman. * *vi* to peep out; to look closely or with dificulty.

peerage *n* the rank or title of a peer.

peerless *adj* matchless.

peevish *adj* fretful; querulous.

peg *n* a wooden nail, pin, or bolt.

pellet *n* a little ball; a pill; small shot.

pelt *n* a raw hide; a blow. * *vti* to assault (with stones, etc); to fall heavily (as rain); to hurry; to rush.

pelvis *n* the bony framework which joins the lower limbs to the body.

pen *n* an instrument for writing, drawing, etc; enclosure for livestock. * *vt* to write; to coop up.

penal *adj* involving punishment.

penalty *n* due punishment; a fine.

penance *n* punishment imposed for sin.

pence *n* plural of penny.

penchant *n* bias; liking.

pencil *n* an instument for drawing; a fine paintbrush.

pendant n a hanging ornament.

pendent *adj* hanging; pendulous.

pending *p.a* in suspense. * *prep* during.

pendulous *adj* hanging; swinging.

pendulum *n* a weight suspended and swinging (as in clock).

penetrate *vti* to enter or pierce; to discern.

penetrating *adj* sharp; discerning.

peninsula *n* land almost surrounded by water.

penitence *n* repentance; sorrow.

penitent *adj* repentant; contrite.

pennant *n* a long pointed flag at masthead.

penny *n* (*pl* **pennies** or **pence**: pennies denotes the number of coins; pence the value) a low value coin .

pension *n* a periodic payment for past services or old age; a boarding house.

pensioner *n* one in receipt of a pension.

pensive *adj* thoughtful; grave.

pentagon *n* a plane figure having five sides.

pentameter *n* a verse of five feet.

penthouse *n* a top floor apartment.

penultimate *adj* the last but one.

penury *n* poverty; want.

people *n* human beings; a nation; a race; a person's family. *pl* persons; the masses. * *vt* to populate.

pepper *n* a seasoning; fruit of the pepper plant.

peptic *adj* promoting digestion.

perambulate *vt* to walk up and down.

perceive *vt* to apprehend; understand.

percentage *n* the duty, rate, etc, on each hundred.

perceptible *adj* discernible.

perch *n* a freshwater fish; a roost for fowls; an elevated position.

percolate *vt* to filter through.

percolator *n* a strainer or filter.

percussion *n* collision; impact; sounding (medical); musical instruments usu played with sticks or hammers.

perdition *n* entire ruin; eternal death.

peremptory *adj* urgent; insistent; dictatorial.

perennial *adj* lasting through the year; never-ending.

perfect *adj* finished; complete; faultless. * *vt* to make perfect.

perfection *n* great excellence; flawlessness.

perfidious *adj* treacherous.
perfidy *n* treachery.
perforate *vt* to bore through; to pierce.
perform *vt* to accomplish; to do. * *vi* to act a part; to play a musical instrument.
performance *n* achievement; deed; entertainment (musical, etc).
performer *n* an actor, musician, etc.
perfume *n* a pleasant scent; fragrance. * *vt* to scent.
perfunctory *adj* careless; half-hearted; indifferent.
perhaps *adv* it may be; possibly.
peril *n* risk; danger.
perimeter *n* the total measurement round any figure; a boundary around.
period *n* a portion of time; an age; full stop (.); menstruation; a stage in life.
periodic *adj* regular.
periodical *n* a publication issued weekly, monthly, etc.
periphery *n* the boundary line of a figure.
periscope *n* an instrument by which observer in trench or submarine can see objects on surface.
perish *vi* to die; to decay.
perjure *vt* to bear false witness; to commit perjury.
perjury *n* false evidence on oath.
permanence*n duration;* fixedness.
permanent *adj* lasting; abiding.
permeable *adj* allowing the passage of fluid, gases, etc.
permeate *vt* to pass through the pores; to pervade.
permissible *adj* allowable.
permission *n* leave; consent.
permissive *adj* allowing but not compelling.
permit *vt* , i.to allow; to grant; to concede. * *n* permit. a written permission.
permutation *n* interchange; in mathematics, all the possible variations of a series.
pernicious *adj* injurious; deadly; noxious.
perpend *vt* to consider; to ponder.
perpendicular *adj* upright; at right angles. * *n* a line at right angles to another.
perpetrate *vt* to commit.
perpetration *n* commission.
perpetual *adj* unending; eternal.
perpetuate *vt* to make lasting.
perpetuity *n* endless duration; an annuity payable forever.
perplex *vt* to confuse; to puzzle.
perplexity *n* bewilderment.
perquisite *n* a reward or benefit, other than salary, attaching to an office; a gratuity.
persecute *vt* to harass with unjust punishment; to ill-treat; to oppress, esp minority group, race, etc.
persevere *vi* to pursue steadily any design.
persevering *adj* constant in purpose.
persist *vi* to persevere; stand firm.
persistence, persistency *n* steadfastness; obstinacy.
persistent *adj* persisting; steady.
person *n* a human being; the body; a verb inflexion.
personal *adj* individual; private; one's own; unkind (remarks).
personality *n* one's individual characteristics; a celebrity; a person with distinct qualities.
personification *n* embodiment; a metaphor ascribing life to inanimate objects.
personify *vt* to embody; to endow with human qualities.
personnel *n* the staff.
perspective *n* the art of representing objects on a flat surface as they are to the eye; objectivity.
perspicacity *n* acuteness of mind.
perspicuity *n* clearness; lucidity.
perspiration *n* sweat.
perspire *vi* to sweat.
persuade *vt* to influence by argument, etc; to induce.
persuasive *adj* convincing; winning.
pert *adj* lively; saucy; forward.
pertain *vi* to belong; to concern.
pertinent *adj* to the point.
perturb *vt* to disturb; to disquiet.
perturbation *n* uneasiness; disquiet.
perusal *n* reading; study.
peruse *vt* to read through; to examine carefully.
pervade *vt* to permeate; to spread throughout.

perverse *adj* obstinate in being wrong; stubborn; contrary.
perversion *n* corruption; misuse; an abnormal way of obtaining sexual satisfaction.
perversity *n* obstinacy; wickedness; a perverse act.
pervert *vt* to corrupt; to misapply. * *n* a person who is sexually perverted.
pervious *adj* penetrable.
pessimism *n* tendency to make or expect the worst of everything.
pessimist *n* one who takes a gloomy view of life.
pest *n* a plague; a nuisance.
pestilence *n* a deadly epidemic.
pestilential *adj* destructive; hurtful.
pestle *n* an instrument for grinding material.
pet *n* a darling; a favourite; a domestic animal kept as a companion. * *adj* cherished. * *vt* to fondle.
petal *n* a flower leaf.
petite *adj* tiny; dainty.
petition *n* an entreaty; a written demand for government action etc. signed by many. * *vt* to ask humbly for; to present a petition.
petrify *vt* to turn into stone; to paralyse or stupefywith terror.
petrol *n* refined petroleum.
petroleum *n* natural mineral oil.
petrology *n* the study of rocks.
petty *adj* small; trivial; small minded.
petulance n peevishness; ill-humour.
petulant *adj* irritable; fretful.
pew *n* a seat in a church.
pewter *n* an alloy of tin and lead.
phantom *n* an apparition; a spectre.
pharmaceutic, pharmaceutical *adj* pertaining to the dispensing of drugs.
pharmacy *n* the preparation and dispensing of drugs; a drug store.
phase *n* a stage; an aspect; apparent shape (moon).
phenomenal *adj* astounding.
phenomenon *n* (*pl* **phenomena**) an appearance; anything visible; a remarkable thing or person.
phial *n* a small glass bottle.
philander *vi* to flirt.
philanthropic, philanthropical *adj* benevolent.
philanthropy *n* the love of mankind; benevolence; charitable actions.
philatelist *n* a collector of postage stamps.
philately *n* stamp collecting.
philologist *n* one versed in philology.
philology *n* the study of language, linguistic science.
philosopher *n* a person who studies philosophy.
philosophically *adv* calmly; wisely; serenely.
philosophy *n* the science of mind, conduct, and phenomena; a particular system of ethics.
phlegm *n* the secretion of the mucous membrane discharged in coughing, etc; lack of emotion.
phlegmatic *adj* sluggish; unemotional.
phoenix *n* a fabled bird, said to burn itself and rise again from its own ashes; emblem of immortality.
phone *n* contraction for telephone.
phonetic *adj* pertaining to vocal sound.
phonetics *npl* the science of sounds of human voice and their representation.
phonograph *n* an instrument for reproducing sounds.
phosphate *n* a salt of phosphoric acid.
phosphorescence *n* emission of light without heat as from fish in the dark.
phosphorescent *adj* luminous.
phosphorus *n* a nonmetallic element, luminous in dark.
photograph *n* a picture obtained by photography. * *vt* to take or produce a photograph.
photography *n* the art of recording images permanently and visibly by action of light on prepared plates.
phrase *n* a related group of words; diction; style.
phrenetic *adj* frantic.
phrenology *n* theory that intelligence is related to shape of skull.
phylloxera *n* an insect which attacks vines.
physical *adj* relating to matter and energy, the human body, or natural science. **n* a general medical examination.

physician *n* a doctor of medicine.
physicist *n* a specialist in physics.
physics *n* the science of matter in relation to force.
physiognomy *n* reading character from study of facial expression.
physiology *n* the science of bodily structures, organs, and functions.
physique *n* physical frame.
pianist *n* a performer on the piano.
piano *n* a large stringed keyboard instrument.
piazza *n* a square surrounded by colonnades.
pica *n* a standard printing type, equal to twelve points.
picaresque *adj* describing the fortunes of adventurers.
piccolo *n* a small flute.
pick *vti* to strike with something sharp; to pick at; to pluck; to choose; to nibble. * *n* an excavating axe; choice.
pickaxe *n* a pick.
picket *n* a pointed stake; a military guard; a preventive guard against strikebreakers. * *vt* to post (soldiers, etc); to tether.
pickle *n* brine; vegetables preserved in vinegar; plight. * *vt* to preserve in pickle.
picnic *n* an informal meal taken on an outing and eaten outdoors.
pictorial *adj* illustrated by pictures.
picture *n* a painting, drawing, likeness, etc; mental image; vivid description; motion picture * *vt* to portray.
picturesque *adj* striking, vivid, usually pleasing.
pie *n* meat or fruit with paste covering baked; unsorted type.
piece *n* a portion; a distinct part; a short composition or writing; a picture; a coin.
piecemeal *adv* in or by pieces.
piecework *n* work paid by quantity, not by time.
pied *adj* of various colours.
pier *n* stone column supporting arch, etc; a wharf or landing stage.
pierce *vt* to thrust through; to perforate.
piercing *adj* penetrating; cutting.
pierrot *n* a humorous entertainer in clown-like dress.
piety *n* religious devoutness.
pig *n* a hog; a bar of smelted iron.
pigeon *n* a bird with a small head and a large body.
pigeonhole *n* a compartment in a desk for papers.
pig-headed *adj* stupidly obstinate.
pigment *n* colouring matter.
pigtail *n* a plait of hair hanging down back.
pile *n* a heap; a large amount; a massive building; a supporting pillar driven into the ground. * *vt* to heap.
piles *npl* a swelling of the rectum veins.
pilfer *vi* to steal on a small scale.
pilgrim *n* a person who makes a pilgrimage.
pilgrimage *n* a journey, esp to a holy place.
pill *n* a medicine in a tablet form; an oral contraceptive.
pillage *n* plunder; spoil. * *vt* to plunder.
pillar *n* a supporting column.
pillion *n* a cushion on back of saddle for second rider.
pillory *n* the stocks or frame once used for punishment of offenders. * *vt* to expose to ridicule.
pillow *n* a cushion for the head while sleeping; something which supports and distributes pressure.
pilot *n* a person who operates a ship or an aircraft; a guide. * *vt* to direct the course of; to act as a pilot; to guide.
pimp *n* a prostitute's agent
pimple *n* a small red swelling on skin.
pin *n* a short pointed piece of metal for fastening clothes; a peg; a bolt. * *vt* to fasten.
pinafore *n* a sleeveless garment worn over a dress, blouse, etc..
pincers *npl* nippers; gripping claws.
pinch *vt* to cramp; to be sparing. * *n* a nip; distress; need; small portion.
pine *n* a coniferous tree. * *vi* to languish.
pinfold *n* a pen; enclosure for cattle.
pinion *n* the outer joint of a bird's wing. * *vt* to restrain; to bind arms to sides.
pink *n* a garden flower; a pale red colour; excellence. * *vt* to stab.
pinnace *n* a boat with oars and sails.
pinnacle *n* a turret; pointed peak; the highest point; climax.

pint *n* a liquid measure equal to one eighth of a gallon.
pioneer *n* a person who initiates or explores new areas of enterprise, research, etc; an explorer; an ealy settler. * *vt* ti initiate; to explore; to act as a pioneer.
pious *adj* devout; religious; sanctimonious.
pip *n* the seed of a fleshy fruit; spot on cards, dice, etc.
pipe *n* a musical instrument; long tube conveying gas, water, etc; shrill voice; tobacco-smoking apparatus. * *vt* (musical) to play on a pipe.
piping *adj* giving out a whistling sound. * *n* sound of pipes; system of pipes.
piquant *adj* sharp; pungent.
pique *n* irritation; resentment. * *vti* to cause resentment in; to offend.
piracy *n* a person who commits robbery at sea; infringement of copyright.
pirate *n* a sea robber; an infringer of copyright.
pirouette *n* spinning round on toe in ballet.
piscatorial *adj of or* relating to fish or fishing.
Pisces *npl* the Fishes, a sign in the zodiac.
pistil *n* the seed-bearing organ of a flower.
pistol *n* a small firearm fired with one hand.
piston *n* a metal plug which slides to and fro in the hollow cylinder of an engine, pump, etc.
pit *n* a hollow in the earth; shaft of a mine; a depression in skin; orchestra space in a theatre. * *vt* to mark with little hollows; to set in competition.
pitch *vt* to fix in ground; to set; to throw; to set the keynote of; to set in array. * *vi* to fall headlong; to encamp; to rise and fall, as a ship. * *n* a throw; highest rise; elevation of a note; a thick dark substance obtained from tar.
pitcher *n* a vessel for carrying liquids.
pitchfork *n* a fork for pitching hay.
piteous *adj* arousing pity.
pitfall *n* concealed danger; a trap.
pith *n* the soft centre of stem of plant; marrow; essence.
pitiable *adj* deserving pity.
pittance *n* a small quantity or allowance of money.
pity *n* sympathy or compassion. * *vt* to grieve for.
pivot *n* that on which something turns or depends.
placard *n* a poster or notice for public display.
placate *vt* to appease.
place *n* an open space in a town; a locality; position; room; passage in book; rank; office. * *vt* to put or set; to locate.
placid *adj* calm; tranquil.
plagiarism *n* the stealing words or ideas of another.
plague *n* a deadly epidemic; pestilence; nuisance.
plaid *n* a large woollen shawl-like wrap; cloth with tartan or checkered pattern.
plain *adj* smooth; level; clear; simple; evident; unflavoured. * *n* a tract of level land.
plaint *n* a lamentation; formal statement of grievance.
plaintiff *n* a person who brings a lawsuit against another.
plaintive *adj* mournful.
plait *n* a fold; a braid, as of hair, etc. * *vt* to fold; to braid.
plan *n* the ground shape of an object; scheme; process; method. * *vt* to scheme; to design.
plane *adj* level; flat. * *n* smooth surface; joiner's smoothing tool; an aeroplane. * *vt* to make smooth.
planet *n* a celestial body moving round sun or other star.
planetary *adj* under the influence of one of the planets; wandering.
plank *n* a flat broad piece of timber.
plant *n* a vegetable organism; an herb; a shoot; industrial machinery and equipment. * *vt* to set in ground; to implant; to establish.
plantation *n* a cultivated planting of trees; a tropical estate.
plaque *n* an ornamental plate; a film of mucus on the teeth that harbours bacteria.
plasma *n* the colourless liquid part of blood, milk or lymph.

plaster *n* a cement for covering walls; a preparation for casts, etc; adhesive dressing for wounds or relief of pain.

plastic *adj* easily shaped or moulded; any of various non-metallic compounds, syntheticaly produced.

plasticine *n* a modelling clay.

plate *n* a flat piece of metal, glass, etc; a shallow dish for meals. * *vt* to coat with gold, etc.

plateau *n* a flat, elevated piece of land; a stable period.

platform *n* a raised structure for speaking from, entering trains, etc; a statement of political policy.

plating *n* the art of covering articles with metal.

platinum *n* a heavy metal very difficult to fuse.

platitude *n* a dull truism; a commonplace remark.

platonic *adj* free from physical desire.

platoon *n* a military unit divided into squads or sections.

platter *n* a large, oval serving dish.

plaudit *n* a commendation (*usu pl*).

plausibility *n* quality of being plausible; speciousness.

plausible *adj* apparently truthful or reasonable.

play *vi, vt* to sport; frolic; gamble; act; engage in games; perform upon. * *n* free movement; a game; sport; gaming; a drama.

player *n* an actor; musician; sportsman, sportswoman.

playful *adj* full of fun, humorous, sportive.

playhouse *n* a theatre; a small house for children to play in.

playschool *n* a nursery for pre-school children.

plaything *n* a toy; a thing or person treated as a toy.

playwright *n* a writer of plays.

plea *n* an answer to a charge; an entreaty; a request.

plead *vi, vt* to argue for or against; to answer to a charge; to urge; to beg earnestly; to urge in excuse.

pleading *n* statement of facts for or against a claim.

pleasance *n* pleasure; a shady grove.

pleasant *adj* pleasing; agreeable.

pleasantry *n* a polite or amusing remark.

please *vti* to satisfy; to give pleasure to; to be willing. * *adv* a word to express politeness or emphasis in a request; an expression of polite affirmation.

pleasing *adj* agreeable; giving pleasure.

pleasure *n* enjoyment; recreation; preference.

plebian *adj, n* relating to the common people; base; vulgar.

plebiscite *n* a vote of the whole electorate on a political issue.

plectrum *n* a thin piece of metal, etc for plucking strings of guitar, etc.

pledge *n* something given in security; a surety; a toast. * *vt* to pawn; to toast; to bind by solemn promise.

plenary *adj* full; complete; attended by all members.

plenitude *n* fullness; abundance.

plentiful *adj* ample; abundant.

plenty *n* abundance; more than enough. * *adj* plentiful.

plethora *n* overabundance; a glut; (med) an excess of red corpuscles in the blood.

pleura *n* (*pl* **pleurae**) membrane enveloping the lungs.

pleurisy *n* an inflammation of the pleura.

pliable *adj* supple; easily persuaded; pliant.

pliant *adj* pliable; flexible.

pliers *npl* a hand tool for cutting, shaping wire.

plight *vt* to pledge (word, honour, etc). * *n* a pledge; predicament.

plinth *n* square slab forming base of column.

plod *vi* to work or walk laboriously.

plot *n* a small piece of ground; a plan; a conspiracy; the story of a play, novel, etc. * *vt* to devise; to conspire; to mark on a map.

plough, plow *n* an implement for turning up the soil. * *vt, vi* to furrow; to work at laboriously.

pluck *vt* to pick or gather; to snatch; to strip off feathers. * *n* courage or spirit.

plug *n* a stopper used for filling a hole; a

device for connecting an appliance to an electrical supply; a cake of tobacco. * *vt* to stop with a plug.

plumage *n* the feathers of a bird.

plumb *n* a lead weight attached to a line used to determine depth or true vertical. * *adj* true vertical * *adv* vertically. * *vt* to supply or install as plumbing; to test with a plumb line.

plumber *n* a person who installs and repairs water or gas pipes.

plumbing *n* the system of pipes used in water or gas supply, or drainage.

plume *n* a bird's feather; an ornament of feathers in hat, etc. * *vt* to preen.

plummet *n* a plumb. * *vt* to fall in a perpendicular manner; to drop abruptly.

plump *adj* rounded; chubby * *vti* to make plump; to favour or give support. * *adv* staight down, straight ahead; suddenly.

plunder *vt* to stel goods by force; to loot. * *n* plundering; booty.

plunge *vt* to thrust into water; to immerse; to penetrate quickly. * *vi* to dive into water, etc; to rush into. * *n* a dive.

plunger *n* a large rubber suction cup used to free clogged drains.

plural *adj* denoting more than one. * *n* (*gram*) the form referring to more than one person or thing.

plurality *n* a majority; being plural; a large number.

plus *prep* added to; in addition to. **n* the sign (+) of addition.

plush *n* a velvety fabric; * *adj* (*inf*) luxurious.

plutocracy *n* the power or rule of wealth.

ply *vti* to work at; to wield skilfully; to press hard; to voyage or journey regularly; (goods)to sell. * *n* a layer or thickness

pneumatic *adj* concerning wind, air or gas; operated by or filled with compressed air.

pneumonia *n* an acute inflammation of the lungs.

poach *vt* to cook (eggs) by breaking into boiling water. * *vi* take game illegally; to trespass; to encroach upon.

pocket *n* a small pouch in a garment, etc; a deposit, as of gas, minerals, etc; an isolated or closed area. * *vt* to put in one's pocket; to take dishonestly.

pod *n* the seed vessel of plants; a detachable compartment on a spacecraft; a protective container.

poem *n* an imaginative arrangement of words, esp in meter, often ryhmed.

poet *n* the author of a poem.

poetry *n* the art of writing poems; poems collectively; poetic spirt or quality.

pogrom *n* an organized extermination of a minority group.

poignant *adj* incisive; deeply moving.

point *n* the sharp end of anything; a headland; a dot; a moment in time; exact spot; purpose; a place in a cycle, scale or course; essence; feature; railway switch; a unit in printing equal to one seventy-second of an inch * *vti* to indicate; to sharpen; to aim.

point-blank *adj* aimed straight at a mark; direct, blunt.

pointed *adj* sharp; personal.

pointer *n* an indicator; a rod for pointing with; a dog trained to point out game.

poise *n* a balanced state; bearing; carriage * *vt* to balance; to put into readiness; * *vi* to hover.

poison *n* a substance which when absorbed is fatal or injurious to an organism; any corrupt influence. * *vt* to give poison to; to taint; to corrupt.

poke *n* a bag or sack; a prod or nudge. * *vt* to prod; to hit. * *vi* to pry or search (about or around)..

poker *n* an iron rod for poking a fire; a card game.

polar *adj* of or near the North or South pole; of a pole; having positive and negative electricity; directly opposite.

polarity *n* the condition of being polar; the magnet's property of pointing north; diametrical opposition.

pole *n* a long slender piece of wood, metal, etc; either end of an axis, esp of the earth; either of two opposed forces, parts, etc, as the ends of a magnet.

polemic *n* a controversy or argument over doctrine; strong criticism. * *adj* involving dispute, controversial.

pole star *n* a star near North Pole; a lodestar.

police *n* the government department for maintaning public order, detecting crime, law enforcement, etc. **vt* to control, protect, etc with police or similar body.

policy *n* system or manner of government; principle or course of action; an insurance contract.

polish *vti* to make smooth and glossy; to refine. * *n* gloss; elegance.

polite *adj* polished in manners; refined; elegant.

politic *adj* prudent; astute.

political *adj* relating to politics or govenment.

politician *n* a person engaged in politics.

politics *n* the science and art of government; political activities; factional scheming for power.

polka *n* a lively dance.

poll *n* a counting, listing, etc of persons; the number of votes recorded; an opinion survey. * *vt* to cast a vote.

pollen *n* the fine, powder-like material found in the anthers of flowers.

pollinate*vt* to fertilize by uniting pollen with seed.

pollute *vt* to contaminate with harmfull substances; to make corrupt; to profane.

pollution *n* the act of polution; contamination by chemicals, noise, etc.

polo *n* a game resembling hockey, played on horseback.

polygamy *n* the practice of being married to more than one person at a time.

polyglot *adj* having command of many languages; composed of several languages. * *n* a person who speaks several languages.

polygon *n* a plane figure of three or more sides.

polygraph *n* an instrument used for measuring involuntary changes in blood pressure, breathing, etc, often used as a lie detector.

polystyrene *n* a rigid plastic material used for packing insulating, etc.

polysyllable *n* a word of more syllables than three.

polytechnic *n* an institution that provides instruction in many aplied sciences and technical subjects.

polyurethane*n* any of various polymers that are used esp in flexible and rigid foams, resins, etc.

pommel *n* a knob or ball, as on sword hilt, saddle bow. * *vt* to pummel.

pomposity *n* the state of being pompous; a pompous act or utterance.

pompous *adj* pretentious; self-importabt.

pond *n* a body of standing water smaller than a lake.

ponder *vt* to consider carefully.

ponderous *adj* heavy; awkward; dull.

pontiff *n* the Pope; a bishop.

pontifical *adj* of a pontiff; pompous.

pontoon *n* a boat or float forming a support for a bridge.

pony *n* a small horse.

pool *n* a small pond; a swimming pool; a puddle; a combination of resources for a common purpose; a form of billiards.

poop *n* the stern of a ship.

poor *adj* having little money; needy; unfortunate; deficient; inferior; disappointing. **n* those who have little.

pop *n* a short, explosive sound; any carbonated beverage; a shot. * *adj* in a popular modern style.

pope *n* the head of the Roman Catholic church.

populace *n* the common people; all the peaple in a country, region, etc.

popular *adj* well-liked; common; prevalent.

population *n* the inhabitants; total number of people in an area.

populous *adj* densely inhabited.

porcelain *n* the variety of ceramic ware.

porch *n* a covered entry to a building.

pore *n* a minute opening in the skin; a small interstice. * *vi* to examine or study with care.

pork *n* the flesh of a pig, used as food.

pornography *n* pictues, films, etc, intended primarly to arouse sexual desire, and usu considered obscene.

porridge *n* a food made from oatmeal boiled in water or milk.

port *n* a harbour; a gate; a porthole; the left side of a ship; a circuit in a compu-

ter for the transferring of data
port *n* a fortified red wine.
portable *adj* able to be carried; not heavy.
portal *n* a door or gate; the main entrance.
portcullis *n* a sliding or falling grating at portal of a castle.
portend *vt* to give warning of; to foreshadow.
portent *n* an omen; a warning.
porter *n* a doorkeeper; a carrier; a dark brown beer.
portfolio *n* a case for drawings, papers, etc; office of minister of state; a list of stocks, shares, etc.
portico *n* a covered walkway.
portion *n* a part; a share; fate. * *vt* to divide.
portly *adj* dignified; stout.
portrait *n* a picture of a person; a vivid description.
portray *vt* to make a portrait of; to depict.
pose *n* attitude or position. * *vi*, *vt* to strike an attitude; to assert; to sit for a painting, photograph, etc..
poser *n* a difficult problem; a person who poses.
position *n* place; situation; posture; rank; a job; point of view.
positive *adj* explicit; absolute; confident; affirmative; noting the simple form of an adjective; a form of electricity; greater than zero.
possess *vt* to have and hold; to own.
possession *n* ownership; occupancy.
possessive *adj* denoting possession. * *n* the possessive case.
possible *adj* that may be or exist; practicable.
post *n* a piece of timber, etc, set upright; a place assigned; a military or other station; office or employment; a letter carrier; the postal system * *vti* to place in letter box; to enter in ledger; to travel by post horses.
postage *n* the charge for conveyance by post.
postal *adj* relating to the carrying of mails.
postcard *n* a letter card.
poster *n* a large printed bill for advertising.
posterior *adj* later or subsequent. * *n* the buttocks.
posterity *n* descendants; future generations.
postern *n* a back or private entrance.
postgraduate*n* a person persuing further study after a degree.
posthaste *adv* with all speed.
posthumous *adj* (child) born after the father's death; given or occurring after one's death.
postman *n* a mail carrier.
postmortem *adj* an autopsy; after death..
post office *n* a place where postal business is conducted ;the public department in charge of postal service.
postpone *vt* to delay; defer.
postscript *n* an addition to a letter after signature.
postulate *n* self-evident truth; assumption. * *vt* to state; assume.
posture *n* an attitude; a body position; a stand.
pot *n* a vessel for holding or boiling liquids; vessel for holding plants; frame for catching fish, lobsters, etc. * *vt* to plant in pot; to shoot.
potash *n* potassium carbonate.
potassium *n* the metallic element.
potato *n* a tuber eaten as a vegetable.
potency *n* power; force.
potentate *n* one who possesses great power; a monarch.
potential *adj* possible. * unrealized ability.
potion *n* a mixture of liquids.
potpourri *n* a mixture of scented, dried flowers;a medley.
pottery *n* earthenware; workshop where it is made.
pouch *n* a pocket; a small bag.
poultice *n* a moist dressing applied to sore parts of the body.
poultry *n* domestic birds kept for meat or eggs.
pounce *n* to fall on suddenly.
pound *n* a monetary unit; a place of confinement or temporary holding. * *vt* to beat; to pulverize. * *vi* to strike repeatedly; to throb; to work hard.
pour *vi* to flow continuously; to rain heav-

ily; to serve liquid refreshment.

pout *vi* to thrust out the lips; to look sulky. * *n* a sullen look.

poverty *n* want; the condition of being poor.

powder *n* fine particles; dust; gunpowder. * *vti* to reduce to, or sprinkle with, powder; to salt.

powdery *adj* dusty; friable.

power *n* ability to act or do; strength; influence; talent; command; authority; a state or government; warrant; a mechanical advantage or effect.

practicable *adj* feasible; possible.

practical *adj* skilful in work; useful; handy.

practice *n* custom; habit; exercise of any profession; training; drill.

practise *vti* to do frequently or habitually; to exercise, as any profession; to commit; to form a habit.

practitioner *n* one who practises a profession (esp. medicine).

pragmatic*adj* practical; testing all concepts by their practical results.

prairie *n* an extensive tract of grassy land.

praise *vt*to express approval of; to commend; to worship. * *n* commendation.

pram *n* four-wheeled carriage for a baby.

prance *vi* to spring on the hind legs; to swagger.

prank *n* a mischievous trick or joke.

prattle *vi* to talk much and idly; to prate. * *n* trifling talk.

pray *vi, vt* to beg or implore; to ask reverently.

prayer *n* supplication; entreaty; praise or thanks to God.

preach *vi* to deliver a sermon; to give earnest advice. * *vt* to proclaim.

preamble *n* introductory part of a story, speech, etc.

precarious *adj* uncertain; insecure.

precaution *n* a preventative measure; careful foresight.

precede *vt* to go before; to preface.

precedence *n* priority; order according to rank.

precedent *n* a parallel case serving as example.

precept *n* rule of conduct; maxim; mandate.

precinct *n* a bounding line; an urban area where traffic is prohibited. *pl* neighbourhood; environs.

precious *adj* of great worth or value; very fastidious; affected.

precipice *n* a cliff or overhanging rock face.

precipitate *vti* to hurl headlong; to hasten rashly; to sink to the bottom of a vessel; to bring down (moisture). * *adj* headlong; overhasty. * *n* a deposit from a liquid.

precipitation *n* rash haste; rain, snow, etc.

precipitous *adj* very steep.

précis *n* a summary; abstract.

precise *adj* exact; definite; punctilious; particular.

precision *n* exactness; accuracy.

preclude *vt* to shut out; to prevent; to make impossible.

precocious *adj* prematurely ripe; forward.

precocity *n* too early development.

preconceive *vt* to form an opinion beforehand.

preconcerted *adj* pre-arranged.

precursor *n* a forerunner; omen.

precursory *adj* forerunning.

predator *n* a person who preys, plunders or devours.

predecessor *n* one who was in office before another.

predestinate *vt* to foreordain. * *adj* foreordained.

predetermine *vti* to determine beforehand.

predicament *n* a quandary; critical position.

predicate *vti* to affirm one thing of another. * *n* that which is affirmed.

predict *vt* to foretell.

prediction *n* a prophecy.

predilection *n* a previous preference.

predispose *vt* to incline beforehand.

predominant *adj* outstanding; superior.

preen *vt* (birds) to trim and trim the feathers; to groom oneself.

preface *n* an introduction; foreword. * *vt* to introduce by preliminary remarks.

prefect *n* person placed in authority over others; a student monitor in a school.

prefer *vt* to like better; to promote or advance.
preferable *adj* more desirable.
preference *n* choice; favour; prior claim.
preferential *adj* implying preference.
preferment *n* promotion.
prefix *vt* to put at the beginning. * *n* a letter or syllable put at beginning of a word.
pregnant *adj* having a fetus in the womb; significant; fulled with.
prehistoric *adj* prior to time of written records.
prejudge *vt* to condemn beforehand.
prejudice *n* bias; prejudgment; intolerance. * *vt* to affect or injure through prejudice.
preliminary *adj* introductory. * *n* preface.
prelude *vt* to preface. * *n* a musical introduction.
premature *adj* too early; untimely; hasty.
premeditate *vti* to plan beforehand.
premier *adj* first; principal * *n* the prime minister.
premiere *n* the first public performance of a play, film, etc.
premise *n* a proposition on which reasoning is based; something assumed.
premises *n* a building and its adjuncts.
premium *n* a reward; a bonus; sum paid for insurance; increase in value.
premonition *n* a foreboding; a feeling that something is about to happen.
preoccupied *adj* engrossed; lost on thought.
preparartory *adj* introductory.
prepare *vti* to make ready.
preponderance *n* superiority of weight, influence, etc; ascendancy.
preponderant *adj* superior in power, influence, etc..
preposition *n* a word used before a noun or pronoun to show its relation to another part of the sentence.
prepossess *vt* to influence in advance; to prejudice.
prepossessing *adj* attractive.
prepossession *n* preconceived opinion; prejudice.
preposterous *adj* absurd; utterly ridiculous.
prerogative *n* a prior claim; an exclusive privilege; hereditary right.
presage *n* a presentiment; omen. * *vti* to betoken; to forebode.
prescience *n* foreknowledge.
prescribe *vti* to lay down authoritatively; to direct medically; to appoint.
prescription *n* a written direction for preparing a medicine; a claim or title based on long use.
prescriptive *adj* based on and acquired by long use.
presence *n* state of being visible; appearance; personality; something (as a spirit) felt or believed to be present.
present *adj* being at hand, in view; now existing; ready at hand; quick. * *n* present time; a gift; *pl* law term for document itself (these presents).
present *vt* to introduce; to show; to give or bestow; to nominate to a benefice; to point or aim.
presentable *adj* suitable for presenting.
presentation *n* act of presenting; thing presented; a gift; a display or exhibition.
presently *adv* in a short while; soon; now.
preservation *n* the act of preserving.
preservative *adj* tending to preserve. * *n* something that preserves, esp a food additive.
preserve *vt* to save from injury; to keep in a sound state; to maintain; to restrict the hunting of, as game. * *n* fruit, vegetables, etc, treated with a preservative; jam; a restricted area.
preside *vi* to direct or control (a meeting); to take the chair.
presidency *n* office of president.
president *n* highest officer in a republic; chairman.
press *vt* to weigh down; to urge; to enforce; to emphasize; to embrace. * *vi* to push with force. * *n* a pressing; a crowd; a machine for crushing or squeezing; a printing machine; printing; newspapers.
pressing *adj* urgent.
pressure *n* a weighing down; force; influence; urgency.
prestige *n* influence based on character or conduct.
presume *vti* to take for granted; to infer; to act in a forward way.

presumption *n* arrogance; supposition.
presumptuous *adj* over-confident; arrogant.
presuppose *vt* to take for granted.
pretence *n* act of pretending; pretext; false claim.
pretend *vti* to claim, represent, or assert falsely; to feign.
pretentious *adj* claiming great importance; ostentatious.
pretext *n* a pretence; excuse.
pretty *adj* attractive; pleasing. * *adv* moderately; fairly.
prevail *vi* to overcome; to be in force; to succeed; to persuade.
prevalence *n* superior strength or influence; general diffusion.
prevalent *adj* prevailing; dominant; widespread.
prevaricate *vi* to make evasive or misleading statements.
prevent *vt* to stop or impede.
prevention *n* hindrance; obstruction.
previous *adj* antecedent; prior.
prey *n* a victim; animal killed for food by another. * *vi* to victimize.
price *n* the value of a commodity; cost; worth.
priceless *adj* invaluable.
prick *n* a sharp point; puncture or piercing. * *vt* to puncture.
pride *n* self-esteem; conceit; delight. * *vt* to be proud of.
priest *n* in various churches, a person authorized to perform sacred rites.
priesthood *n* the office of a priest; the order of priests.
priggish *adj* conceited; affected.
prim *adj* formal; demure.
primacy *n* the office of primate or archbishop.
prima donna *n* the chief female singer in an opera; (*inf*) a temperamental and affected person.
primal *adj* primary; primitive; fundamental.
primary *adj* first; chief; elementary; first in order of time.
primate *n* any of the highest order of mammals, including man..
prime *adj* original; not divisible by any smaller number; best quality.
primer *n* child's first reader; first coat of paint; a detonating device.
primeval *adj* primitive; original.
primitive *adj* original; antiquated; primary.
primordial *adj* first of all; original.
prince *n* the son of a king or emperor.
princely *adj* noble; august; magnificent.
principal *adj* first; chief; most important. * *n* head of a school, firm, etc; chief in authority; capital sum lent at interest.
principality *n* sovereignty; territory of a prince.
principally *adv* chiefly; mainly.
principle *n* cause or origin; a general truth; a fundamental law; a rule of conduct; uprightness.
print *vt* to mark by pressure; to stamp; to copy by pressure. * *vi* to publish. * *n* a mark made by pressure; an engraving, etc; a newspaper; printed calico.
printing *n* the art or process of making impressions on paper, cloth, etc; typography.
prior *adj* preceding; earlier. * *n* a monk next in dignity to an abbot.
priority *n* precedence; first claim.
priory *n* a religious house ruled by a prior(ess).
prise *vt* to force up.
prism *n* a solid whose ends are any similar, equal, and parallel plane figures; a kind of lens for decomposing light.
prison *n* a place of confinement; a jail. * *vt* to imprison.
pristine *adj* original; first.
privacy *n* seclusion; secrecy.
private *adj* separate from others; solitary; personal; secret. * *n* a common soldier.
privation *n* destitution; hardship.
privilege *n* a prerogative, benefit, or right. * *vt* to authorize; to exempt.
privy *adj* private; clandestine; admitted to the knowledge of (with to).
prize *n* that which is seized from an enemy; a reward of merit. * *vt* to value highly.
prizefight *n* a boxing match for a prize.
probability *n* likelihood.
probable *adj* likely; credible.

probate *n* the official proof of a will; confirmation.
probation *n* proof; trial; period of trial.
probe *n* a surgeon's instrument for examining a wound. * *vt* to explore; to examine carefully.
probity *n* uprightness; honesty.
problem *n* a question for solution; a knotty point.
proboscis *n* the trunk of an elephant, etc; the sucking tube of insects.
procedure *n* mode of conducting business; conduct.
proceed *vi* to go forward; to issue; to take legal action.
proceeding *n* transaction; procedure.
proceeds *npl* money brought in by a transaction.
process *n* progressive course; method of operation; lapse; legal proceedings; a writ.
procession *n* a body of people on the march.
processional *adj* relating to a procession. * *n* a service book as guide for religious processions.
proclaim *vt* to announce publicly; to publish.
proclamation *n* an official public announcement.
proclivity *n* inclination; tendency.
procrastinate *vti* to put off; to postpone unduly.
procreation *n* the begetting of young.
procurator *n* the manager of another's affairs; legal agent or prosecutor.
procure *vt* to obtain; to cause.
prod *n* a goad; a nudge; a stab. * *vt* to goad.
prodigal *adj* lavish; wasteful. * *n* a waster; a spendthrift.
prodigious *adj* portentous; enormous.
prodigy *n* a gifted child; an extraordinary person, thing or act.
produce *vti* to bring forward; to exhibit; to bear, yield; to cause; to extend. * *n* outcome; yield.
product *n* result; effect.
production *n* fruit; product; performance.
productive *adj* fertile; fruitful.
profane *adj* not sacred; secular; blasphemous; impure. * *vt* to treat with irreverence; to pollute.
profanity *n* profane language or conduct.
profess *vt* to avow; to acknowledge; to pretend. * ni. to declare openly.
profession *n* open avowal; vocation; calling; members of a profession.
professional *adj* pertaining to a profession. * *n* one who makes his living by arts, sports, etc, as distinguished from an amateur.
professor *n* a university teacher of highest rank.
professorship *n* the office of a professor.
proffer *vt* to offer for acceptance.
proficiency *n* expertness; degree of advancement.
proficient *adj* fully versed; competent. * *n* an adept or expert.
profile *n* an outline; the side face or outline of it.
profit *n* any advantage, benefit, or gain. * *vt* to benefit. * *vi* to derive profit; to improve.
profitable *adj* yielding profit;lucrative; useful.
profligacy *n* depravity; vicious course of life.
profligate *adj* dissolute; openly vicious. * *n* a depraved man.
profound *adj* deep; deep in skill or knowledge; far-reaching.
profundity *n* depth.
profuse *adj* lavish; exuberant.
progeny *n* offspring; descendants.
prognosis *n* a forecast of the course of a disease.
prognosticate *vt* to foretell; to predict.
programme *n* a plan of proceedings; list of items at concert, etc; policy of political party.
progress *n* a going forward; a journey of state; advance. * *vi* to advance; to improve.
progressive *adj* forward; liberal; increasing by degrees; relating to whist drive where some players move forward.
prohibit *vt* to forbid; to prevent.
prohibition *n* an interdict; veto on sale of intoxicants.
prohibitive *adj* excessive.

project *vti* to hurl; to scheme; to delineate; to jut. * *n* a scheme, plan.

projectile *adj* throwing forward. * *n* a missile; a bullet or shell.

projection *n* a prominence; plan or outline on a plane surface.

projector *n* a company promoter; schemer.

prolapse*n* a displacement of an internal organ.

proletariate *n* the lower classes.

prolific *adj* fruitful.

prologue *n* introduction; speech, usually in verse, introducing a drama.

prolong *vt* to lengthen out.

promenade *n* a walk for pleasure; a public walk. * *vi* to walk up and down.

prominence *n* a projection; distinction.

prominent *adj* jutting out; eminent.

promiscuous *adj* indiscriminate, esp in sexual relations.

promise *n* an undertaking to do or not do something; pledge. * *vti* to give one's word; to show promise of.

promissory *adj* containing a promise. * a signed promise to pay.

promontory *n* a headland.

promote *vt* to forward; to encourage; to exalt; to form (a company).

promotion *n* advancement; furtherance.

prompt *adj* ready; unhesitating. * *vt* to incite to action; to whisper (words to actor, etc).

promulgate *vt* to publish.

prone *adj* lying face-downwards; inclined; apt.

prong *n* a spike, as of a fork.

pronominal *adj* of the nature of a pronoun.

pronoun *n* a word used instead of a noun.

pronounce *vti* to articulate; to utter; to affirm.

pronouncement *n* a definite statement of policy.

pronunciation *n* articulation.

proof *n* trial; convincing evidence; argument; test; standard strength (spirit); print copy for revision. * *adj* impenetrable; able to resist.

prop *n* a support. * *vt* to hold up; to sustain.

propaganda *n* methods or system of spreading beliefs, doctrines, etc.

propagandist *n* a popularizer of special doctrines; a missionary.

propagate *vt* to multiply; to diffuse. * *vi* to have young.

propel *vt* to drive or thrust forward.

propeller *n* a screw for propelling steamboats, etc.

propensity *n* natural tendency.

proper *adj* one's own; peculiar; correct; real.

property *n* a quality or attribute; characteristic; ownership; goods; estate; a stage requisite.

prophecy *n* a prediction; inspired utterance.

prophet *n* a seer; inspired preacher.

prophylactic *adj, n* preventive of disease.

propitious *adj* favourable; merciful.

proportion *n* comparative relation; symmetry; equal share; lot; ratio.

proposal *n* proposition; offer (esp of marriage).

propose *vt* to offer for consideration. * *vi* to make a proposal; to purpose.

proposition *n* a proposal; offer of terms; a statement or assertion; a problem or theorem for solution.

propound *vt* to propose; to put, as a question.

proprietary *adj* belonging to a proprietor.

proprietor *n* an owner.

propriety *n* fitness; justness.

propulsion *n* the driving forward (as of an engine).

prosaic *adj* like prose; commonplace.

proscribe *vt* to outlaw; to forbid.

proscription *n* outlawry; vetoing.

prose *n* ordinary speech.

prosecute *vti* to carry on; to pursue at law.

prosecution *n* a suit at law; the party prosecuting.

prosecutor *n* one who prosecutes.

proselyte *n* a convert.

proselytize *vti* to make or seek to make converts.

prospect *n* a distant view; scene; outlook; expectation. * *vti* to search, explore (for metals, oil, etc).

prospective *adj* looking forward; probable.
prospectus *n* a statement or outline of some enterprise.
prosper *vi, vt* to thrive or cause to thrive.
prosperity *n* success; a thriving state; good fortune.
prostitute *n* a person who performs sex acts for money.
prostitution *n* the act or activity of being a prostitute; to corrupt for unworthy purposes.
prostrate *adj* lying flat; lying at mercy. * *vt* to lie flat, to humble oneself.
protagonist *n* chief actor in a drama; the principal leader in an affair.
protean *adj* assuming different shapes; changeable.
protect *vt* to shield from danger, loss, etc.
protection *n* defence; shelter; taxation of foreign goods to protect home products.
protégé (*m*), **protégée** (*f*) *n* one under the care of another.
protein *n* an essential element in food of animals.
protest *vi* to affirm with solemnity. * *vt* to assert; to mark for nonpayment, as a bill. * *n* a formal declaration of dissent.
protestation *n* a solemn affirmation; a strong protest.
protocol *n* first draft of a treaty; ceremonial etiquette.
protoplasm *n* the life germ of animals and plants.
prototype *n* model; pattern.
protozoa *npl* the lowest class of animal life.
protract *vt* to prolong; to delay.
protractor *n* an instrument for measuring or plotting angles.
protrude *vti* to thrust forward; to project.
protrusion *n* a sticking out.
protuberance *n* a prominence; a knob.
proud *adj* haughty; arrogant; high-spirited.
prove *vti* to test; to establish the truth of; to demonstrate; to obtain probate of; to turn out to be.
proverb *n* a popular saying; an adage; a maxim.
proverbial *adj* well-known; notorious.
provide *vti* to make ready beforehand; to prepare; to supply.
provided *conj* on condition.
providence *n* foresight; divine foresight and care.
provident *adj* foreseeing; prudent; frugal.
providential *adj* due to divine providence.
province *n* a division of a country; sphere of action.
provincial *adj* rustic; countrified.
provision *n* preparation; stores provided; proviso; *pl* food.
provisional *adj* temporary.
proviso *n* a stipulation; condition.
provisory *adj* conditional.
provocation *n* cause of resentment.
provocative *adj* inciting; rousing.
provoke *vti* to incite; to irritate.
prow *n* the forepart of a ship.
prowess *n* bravery; skill.
prowl *vi, vt* to sneak around.
proximate *adj* nearest; next.
proximity *n* nearness.
proxy *n* agency of a substitute; a deputy; a warrant to act or vote for another.
prude *n* a person who affects excessive modesty.
prudence *n* caution; discretion.
prudent *adj* provident; cautious; discreet.
prune *vt* to trim; to lop off * *n* a dried plum.
prurience, pruriency *n* a lustful craving.
prurient *adj* lustful; filthy-minded.
pry *vi* to scan closely; to peer.
psalm *n* a sacred song or hymn.
pseudo *pref* signifying false or spurious.
pseudonym *n* a name assumed by a writer.
psychiatry *n* treatment of mental disease.
psychic*adj* belonging to the soul; spiritualistic.
psychology *n* the science concerned with the human mind aand behaviour.
puberty *n* beginning of manhood and womanhood; sex maturity.
pubescent *adj* arriving at puberty.
public *adj* not private; pertaining to a whole community; open to all; common. * *n* the people. * In public, in open view.
publican *n* keeper of a public house.
publication *n* act of publishing; book, etc, published.

publicity *n* any information or action that brings a person or cause to public notice; work concerned with such matters.
publish *vt* to make public; to proclaim; to print and offer for sale.
pucker *vti* to wrinkle. * *n* a fold or wrinkle.
pudding *n* a dessert dish.
puddle *n* a small pool of dirty water; clay impervious to water.
puddling *n* process of working clay so as to be impervious or of converting cast iron into wrought iron.
puerile *adj* boyish; childish.
puff *n* whiff of wind or breath; a puffball; light pastry; undeserved praise. * *vti* to breathe hard; to praise overmuch.
pugilism *n* the practice of boxing.
pugnacious *adj* quarrelsome.
pugnacity *n* aggressiveness; quarrelsomeness.
pull *vti* to draw towards one; to tug; to rend; to pluck; to gather. * *n* act of pulling; an effort.
pulley *n* a grooved wheel with running cord for raising weights.
pulmonary *adj* pertaining to the lungs.
pulp *n* the fleshy part of fruit, etc; soft substance obtained by mashing down cloth, wood, etc.
pulpit *n* preacher's raised desk or platform.
pulsate *vi* to beat or throb.
pulse *n* the beating of heart or artery; vibration; beans, pease, etc.
pulverize *vi* to reduce to dust.
pumice *n* a porous stone, used for polishing.
pummel *vt* to strike with fists.
pump *n* a machine for raising water or extracting air; a shoe used in dancing. * *vi* to work a pump. * *vt* to raise with a pump; to quiz.
pun *n* a play upon words. * *vi* to make puns.
punch *n* a tool for perforating; a blow; a spirituous beverage; a puppet show figure. * *vt* to stamp or perforate; to strike.
punctilious *adj* formal; precise.
punctual *adj* exact; prompt.
punctuality *n* scrupulous exactness.
punctuate *vt* to mark with points or stops.
punctuation *n* the art of inserting stops in sentence.
puncture *n* hole made by sharp point. * *vt* to pierce.
pungent *adj* biting; acrid; caustic.
punish *vt* to inflict pain as a penalty; to chastise.
punishment *n* pain, loss, or penalty.
punitive *adj* penal; designed to punish.
punt *n* a flat-bottomed boat.
puny *adj* small and weak.
pup *n* a young dog, seal, fox, etc.
pupa *n* (*pl* **pupae**) the chrysalis form of an insect.
pupil *n* a learner; a scholar; opening in centre of eye.
puppet *n* a mechanical figure moved by strings; a person who is a mere tool.
purchase *vt* to buy; to acquire. * *n* buying; thing bought; leverage.
pure *adj* clean; clear; unmixed; chaste.
purgative *adj* cleansing. * *n* an aperient or purging medicine.
purge *vti* to make pure or clean; to clear from accusation.
purification *n* a cleansing from guilt.
purify *vt* to make pure or clear.
puritan *n* one very strict in religious and moral matters.
purity *n* cleanness; innocence; chastity; freedom from adulteration.
purl *n* gentle murmur of a stream; a stitch in knitting. * *vi* to ripple.
purloin *vt* to steal or pilfer.
purple *n* a colour; red and blue blended; purple robe or the imperial rank denoted by it; regal power. * *adj* blood-red; royal.
purport *n* meaning. * *vt* to signify; to intend.
purpose *n* end or aim; design; intention. * *vt* to propose.
purse *n* a small pouch for money; funds. * *vt* to pucker.
purser *n* the ship's officer in charge of accounts.
pursuance *n* the carrying out (of a design).
pursuant *adj* agreeable; conformable to.
pursue *vti* to follow for some end; to chase.
pursuit *n* chase; quest; business occupa-

tion.

purvey *vti* to provide; to supply provisions.

purveyor *n* a caterer.

purview *n* the scope; limit; sphere.

pus *n* yellow matter of a sore.

push *vti* to press against with force; to shove; to urge. * *n* vigorous effort; emergency.

pusillanimous *adj* cowardly; timid.

pustule *n* a small blister or pimple.

put *vt* to place or set; to ask; to apply; to state.

put, putt *vt* to throw (a heavy stone) from the shoulder; in golf, to play the ball into the hole.

putative *adj* supposed; reputed.

putrefaction *n* decay; rottenness.

putrefy *vt* to render putrid. * *vi* to decay; to rot.

putrescence *n* a putrid state.

putrid *adj* rotten; corrupt.

putter *n* a kind of golfing club.

putty *n* a paste made of whiting and linseed oil. * *vt* to cement with putty.

puzzle *vt* to perplex. * *vi* to be bewildered. * *n* perplexity.

pyjamas *npl* sleeping clothes.

pylon *n* a tower like structure supportingelectric power lines.

pyramid *n* a solid body having triangular sides meeting in a point at the top.

pyre *n* a funeral pile.

pyrotechnics *n* the art of making or the use of fireworks.

pyrrhic *n* a metrical foot of two syllables.

Q

qua *adv* in the quality of; as.

quack *vi* to cry like a duck. * *n* the cry of a duck; an untrained person who practices medicine faudulently. * *adj* sham.

quad *n* a quadrangle or court.

quadragesima *n* lent.

quadrangle *n* a plane figure, having four angles and sides; an inner square of a building.

quadrant *n* the fourth part of a circle or its circumference; an instrument for taking altitudes; a sextant.

quadratic *adj* in algebra, involving the square of an unknown quantity.

quadrennial *adj* lasting or occurring once in four years.

quadrilateral *n* a plane figure having four sides and angles.

quadrille *n* a dance for four couples, each forming side of a square.

quadruped *n* an animal with four feet.

quadruple *adj* fourfold. * *vt* to make fourfold. * vi to become fourfold.

quaff *vti* to drink deep.

quaggy *adj* boggy.

quagmire *n* wet boggy ground.

quaich *n* a silver or wooden drinking cup.

quail *vi* to flinch; to cower. * *n* a bird allied to partridge.

quaint *adj* attractive or pleasant in an old-fashioned style.

quaintly *adv* oddly; whimsically.

quake *vi* to shake; to tremble, esp with fear or cold.

Quaker *n* a member of the Society of Friends.

qualification *n* quality which fits a person for office or occupation; ability; capability; restriction.

qualified *adj* competent; limited.

qualify *vt* to render or to become fit for office, etc; to modify or limit.

qualitative *adj* determining the nature of the component parts of bodies.

quality *n* sort, kind, or character; attribute; high rank.

qualm *n* a sudden fit of nausea; a scruple.

quandary *n* a state of perplexity; a predicament.

quantitative *adj* relating to the size or amount.

quantity *n* bulk; measure; amount; large portion.

quantum *n* a quantity; a sufficient amount.

quarantine *n* isolation period imposed to prevent the spread of disease.

quarrel *n* an angry dispute; a brawl. * vi to dispute violently.

quarrelsome *adj* apt to quarrel; contentious.

quarry *n* an excavation for the extraction

of stone, slate, etc; a place from which stone is excavated; a source of information, etc. * *vti* to excavate (from) a quarry; to research.

quart *n* 2 pints or one-fourth of a gallon.

quarter *n* the fourth part of anything; any point of the compass; a district; locality; one of four divisions of heraldic shield; proper position; mercy to a beaten foe; *pl* shelter or lodging. * *vt* to divide into four equal parts; to cut to pieces; lodge.

quarterly *adj* recurring each quarter. * *adv* once in a quarter. * *n* a periodical published quarterly.

quartermaster *n* a petty officer in charge of steering, signals, etc (navy); an officer in charge of stores, rations, etc (army).

quartet, quartette *n* a musical composition in four parts; the four performers.

quarto *n* a page size, approx 9 by 12 inches (23 by 30.5mm).

quartz *n* silica in crystalline form.

quash *vt* to quell; to suppress; to make void.

quasi. *pref* meaning sort of, sham, almost, as quasi-religious.

quassia *n* a medicinal bark with bitter taste.

quatercentenary *n* a four-hundredth anniversary.

quatrain *n* a stanza of four lines rhyming alternately.

quaver *vi, vt* to shake; to tremble; to quiver. * *n* a voice tremor; half a crotchet.

quay *n* a landing stage for vessels; wharf.

queasy *adj* squeamish.

queen *n* the wife of a king; a female sovereign.

queenly *adj* royal; gracious.

queer *adj* odd; droll; peculiar.

quell *vt* to subdue; to allay.

quench *vt* to put out, as fire; to slake, as thirst.

querulous *adj* complaining; peevish.

query *n* a question; the mark of interrogation (?). * vi to ask questions. * *vt* to question.

quest *n* search; pursuit; inquiry.

question *n* an interrogation; inquiry; discussion. * vi to ask a question; to doubt. * *vt* to interrogate.

questionable *adj* doubtful.

questionnaire *n* a series of questions designed to collect statistical information.

queue *n* a line of people, vehicles, etc awaiting entry, a turn etc.

quibble *n* a minor objection or criticism. * vi to evade the question by play on words; to prevaricate.

quick *adj* alive; brisk; swift; keen; living. * *n* the living flesh.

quicken *vti* to give life to; to vivify; to cheer; to speed up.

quicklime *n* lime burned but unslaked.

quicksand *n* a sandbank yielding under pressure, therefore dangerous.

quicksilver *n* mercury.

quickstep*n* a ballroom dance in quicktime.

quidnunc *n* one always on the alert for news; a newsmonger.

quiescent *adj* resting; still; tranquil.

quiet *adj* at rest; calm; peaceful; secluded. * *n* rest; peace. * *vt* to calm; to lull; to allay.

quietism *n* tranquillity; resignation; a form of mysticism.

quill *n* the hollow stem of a feather; anything made of this as a pen; the spine of a porcupine. * *vt* to plait.

quilt *n* a padded bedcover.

quince *n* pear-shaped fruit used for preserves.

quincentenary *n* a five-hundredth anniversary.

quinine *n* a bitter drug from bark of cinchona tree, used as an anti-malarial.

quinquennial *adj* lasting for, or occurring once every five years.

quinquennium *n* the space of five years.

quinsy *n* inflammation of tonsils or throat.

quintessence *n* purest form of a substance; vital part.

quintet, quintette *n* a musical composition in five parts.

quintuple *adj* fivefold.

quintuplet *adj* one of five offspring produced at one birth.

quip *n* a gibe; retort.

quire *n* twenty-four sheets of paper.
quirk *n* an unexpected turn or twist; a peculiarity of mannerism.
quit *adj* discharged; free. * *vti* to discharge; to depart; to acquit.
quite *adv* completely; wholly.
quiver *n* a sheath for arrows. * vi to shake; to shiver.
quixotic *adj* romantic or chivalrous to extravagance.
quiz *n* a short written or oral test; a form of entertainment where players are asked questions of general knowledge.
quoit *n* a flattish ring of iron, thrown at a mark.
quondam *adj* former.
quorum *n* minimum number needed to constitute a meeting.
quota *n* share assigned to each.
quotation *n* passage quoted; estimated price.
quote *vt* to cite (from writings or speeches); to give prices of articles.
quotient *n* the answer to a division sum.

R

rabbi *n* (*pl* **rabbis**) the religious and spiritual leader of a Jewish congregation.
rabble *n* a noisy crowd; a mob.
rabid *adj* infected with rabies; fanatical.
rabies *n* an acute viral disease transmitted by the bite of an infected animal.
race *n* any of the divisions of human kind; a contest in speed; a course or career; a rapid current. * *vt* to run swiftly; to compete in speed.
racecourse *n* a track on which races are run.
racehorse *n* a horse bred for racing.
raceme *n* a flower cluster on common stem.
racial *adj* characteristic of race.
rack *vt* to stretch unduly; to torture. * *n* a frame for holding or stretching articles; a frame for setting up snooker balls for play, anguish; instrument of torture.
racket *n* a din; clamour; the bat in tennis, etc; (*pl*) a game like tennis.
racy *adj* strongly flavoured; risqué.
radial *adj* branching from a common centre.
radiance *n* brilliancy; lustre.
radiant *adj* emitting rays; brilliant; beaming.
radiate *vi, vt* to emit rays; to broadcast; to spread; to shine.
radiation *n* emission of rays.
radiator *n* apparatus for warming a room.
radical *adj* pertaining to the root; original; fundamental; inherent. * *n* a root; a political reformer.
radically *adv* root and branch; thoroughly.
radicle *n* the first rootlet of a seed.
radioactivity *adj* giving off radiant energy in the form of particles or rays caused by the disintegration of atomic nuclei.
radiograph *n* image given by rays.
radiography *n* process of taking pictures by X-rays for use in medicine.
radium *n* a metallic element which is highly radioactive.
radius *n* (*pl* **radii, radiuses**) distance from the centre of a circle to the circumference; a bone of the forearm.
raffle *n* a kind of lottery. * *vi* to engage in a raffle. * *vt* to dispose of by raffle.
raft *n* logs fastened together and floated; a floating structure.
rafter *n* one of several sloping beams supporting a roof.
rag *n* a tattered cloth; a shred; a sensational newspaper.
rage *n* violent anger; fury. * *vi* to be furious with anger.
ragged *adj* tattered.
ragwort *n* a common weed.
raid *n* a hostile incursion; a sudden foray. * *vt* to make a raid on.
rail *n* a bar of wood or metal; a connected series of posts; a railway. * *vt, vi* to enclose with rails; to scold; to jeer.
railing *n* a fence.
raillery *n* banter; chaff.
railroad *n* a railway.
railway *n* a road or track with parallel lines of rails along which vehicles travel.
rain *n* moisture falling in drops. * *vi* to fall in drops.
rainbow *n* a many-coloured bow that of-

ten appears in the sky during sunshine and showers containing the colours of the spectrum.

raise *vt* to cause to rise; to lift upward; to excite; to stir up; to levy; to breed; to abandon (siege).

rake *n* a toothed implement for scraping ground or for gleaning; a dissolute person. * *vt* to glean; to gather.

rakish *adj* dissolute; sloping, as masts; jaunty.

rally *vt* to reunite, as disordered troops; to collect; a large gathering of people. * *vi* to recover strength. * *n* a stand; recovery of health, morale, etc.

ram *n* a male sheep; sign (Aries) of Zodiac; a battering engine; pile-driving machine. * *vt* to batter; to charge.

ramble *vi* to roam about; to talk incoherently. * *n* an aimless walk.

rambler *n* a climbing plant; a person who rambles.

rambling *adj* unsettled; disconnected.

ramification *n* a branching; a network of parts; a consequence.

ramify *vti* to subdivide; to branch out.

ramp *n* a sloping walk or runway.

rampage *vi* to prance; to rage and storm.

rampant *adj* in heraldry, standing on hind legs; unchecked; unrestrained.

rampart *n* a defensive earthwork.

ramshackle *adj* broken-down; shaky.

ranch *n* a large cattle or sheep farm.

rancid *adj* rank; tainted.

rancorous *adj* spiteful; virulent.

rancour *n* deep-seated hatred.

random *n* chance; at random, without aim * *adj* haphazard.

range *vti* to set in a row; to place in order; to roam over; to rank. * *n* a row; a series of mountains; compass or extent; a place for gun practice.

ranger *n* a park warden.

rank *n* a row; a line; a social class; dignity. * *vti* to classify; to place in line. * *adj* overgrown; tainted.

rankle *vi, vt* to grow bitter; to irritate.

ransack *vt* to plunder; to search thoroughly.

ransom *n* release from captivity by payment; price paid for release. * *vt* to redeem.

rant *vi* to rave, declaim * *n* bombast.

rap *n* a smart blow; a knock. * *vi, vt* to strike smartly; (*inf*) talk, conversation.

rapacious *adj* greedy of plunder; grasping.

rapacity *n* excessive greed; extortion.

rape *n* the act of forcing a woman to have sexual intercourse against her will; a plundering. **vt* to commit rape (upon)

rapid *adj* very swift; speedy. * *n* a swift current.

rapier *n* a long narrow sword.

rapt *adj* transported; enraptured.

rapture *n* extreme joy; ecstasy.

rapturous *adj* ecstatic; enthusiastic; intense joy.

rare *adj* sparse; uncommon; infrequent; precious; underdone.

rarefy *vti* to make or become less dense.

rarity *n* scarceness; thinness; a rare article.

rascal *n* a scoundrel; a rogue.

rase *vt* to wipe out; to destroy; to level to the ground.

rash *adj* precipitate; hasty. * *n* an eruption on the skin.

rasher *n* a thin slice of bacon.

rasp *vt* to rub with something rough; to grate. * *n* a coarse file; a raspberry.

ratchet *n* a catch which checks a toothed wheel and moves only one way.

rate *n* proportion; standard; degree of speed; price; a tax; assessment. * *vt* to fix the value, rank, etc, of; to reprove. * *vi* to classify.

rather *adv* more readily; preferably.

ratification *n* sanction; confirmation.

ratify *vt* to approve and sanction.

ratio *n* proportion of two classes of objects to each other.

ration *n* a fixed amount allowed.

rational *adj* endowed with reason; wise; judicious.

rationale *n* exposition of reasons for any opinion or action.

rattan *n* a walking stick or cane.

rattle *vi, vt* to clatter; to chatter. * *n* a clattering noise; a toy which makes a clatter.

raucous *adj* hoarse; harsh; loud.

ravage *n* havoc; devastation. * *vt* to lay waste.
rave *vi* to be delirious; to dote.
ravenous *adj* excessively hungry.
ravine *n* a gorge or pass.
ravish *vt* to carry off by force; to captivate; to rape.
ravishing *adj* enchanting.
raw *adj* uncooked; in natural state; crude; unripe; cold and damp; sore.
ray *n* a line of light; a gleam of intelligence; a radius; a flatfish.
rayon *n* a textile fibre made from a cellulose solution; a fabric of such fibres.
raze *vt* to blot out; to demolish.
razor *n* an instrument for shaving off hair.
reach *vt* to extend; to hand; to stretch out; to arrive at; to gain. * *vi* to extend. * *n* extent; scope.
react *vi, vt* to act in return; to return an impulse.
reaction *n* an action in response to a stimulus;(*chem.*) an action set up by one substance in another.
reactionary *adj* retrograde. * *n* one who opposes progress.
read *vt* to peruse; to utter aloud; to explain. * *vi* to peruse; to study; to stand written or printed; to make sense. * *adj* well-informed.
reader *n* a person who reads; a proof corrector; a university lecturer.
readily *adv* promptly; cheerfully.
reading *adj* bookish; studious. * *n* perusal; study of books; interpretation; rendering.
ready *adj* prepared; prompt; willing.
real *adj* actual; true; genuine; in law, applied to things fixed as land, houses, etc.
real estate *n* property; land.
realism *n* doctrine that the things of sense are the only reality; truth to nature in art; the practical as opposed to the ideal.
realist *n* one who believes in realism.
realistic *adj* life-like; vivid.
reality *n* fact; truth.
realize *vt* to make real; to convert into money; to make tangible; to gain.
really *adv* actually; in truth; positively.
realm *n* kingdom; domain; sphere.
realty *n* real property.
ream *n* 20 quires or 480 sheets of paper.
reap *vti* to harvest; to gather in; to receive as a reward.
rear *n* the part behind; the part of army or fleet behind van. * *vti* to raise; to educate; to breed, as cattle; to stand on hind legs.
rearguard *n* troops guarding the rear.
reason *n* mental faculty; power of thinking; a motive or cause; justice; moderation. * *vi, vt* to use reason; to argue.
reasonable *adj* rational; just; moderate.
reasoning *n* the exercise of faculty of reason; arguments used.
reassure *vt* to give confidence.
rebate*n* abatement in price; deduction; discount.
rebel *n* one who refuses to cooperate with lawful authority. **adj* rebellious. * *vi* to revolt; to act as rebel.
rebellion *n* a rising up against authority.
rebound *n* a recoil;*vi* to spring back; to bounce back.
rebuff *n* a check; a repulse. * *vt* to check; snub.
rebuke *vt* to reprimand. * *n* a reproof.
recalcitrant *adj* obstinate.
recall *vt* to call back; to revive in memory.
recant *vti* to withdraw or retract; to abjure.
recantation *n* withdrawal of previous statements or beliefs.
recapitulate *vt* to summarize; to go over chief points.
recapitulation *n* a summary.
recast *vt* to mould anew.
recede *vi* to go back; to grow less. * *vt* to give back.
receipt *n* a written acknowledgment of something received. * *vt* to discharge, as an account.
receive *vt* to take, as a thing offered; to accept; to welcome; to take in.
receiver *n* a person who receives; one who knowingly takes stolen goods from a thief; equipment that receives electronic signals; (law) a person appointed to manage or hold in trust property in bankruptcy or lawsuit.
recent *adj* new; late; fresh.
receptacle *n* a place or vessel for holding

articles.

reception *n* welcome; a formal receiving of guests; admission.

receptionist *n* a person employed to receive visitors in an office, hospital, hotel, etc.

receptive *adj* quick to absorb knowledge.

receptivity *n* power of absorbing ideas or knowledge.

recess *n* withdrawal; a nook or alcove; holiday.

recession *n* a time of severe economic downturn.

recipe *n* a list of ingredients and directions for preparing food; a method for achieving an end.

recipient *n* a person who receives.

reciprocal *adj* mutual; alternating.

reciprocate *vi* to move backward and forward; to give in return. * *vt* to interchange.

reciprocity *n* interchange on even terms; equality of tariffs; fair trade.

recital *n* a narration; musical entertainment, esp. by one performer.

recite *vti* to repeat aloud from memory; to relate.

reckless *adj* heedless; rash; incaution.

reckon *vti* to count; consider; to calculate.

reckoning *n* calculation; a statement of accounts.

recline *vti* to lean backwards; to lean down on one side.

recluse *adj* retired; solitary. * *n* a hermit.

recognition *n* the act of recognizing; identification; acknowledgement; admission.

recognize *vt* to know again; to acknowledge.

recoil *vi* to start back; to shrink; to rebound. * *n* a rebound, as of a gun.

recollect *vt* to remember.

recommend *vt* to praise to another; to advise.

recommendation *n* a favourable notice; repute.

recompense *vt* to compensate; to reward. * *n* compensation; amends.

reconcile *vt* to make friendly again; to harmonize; to settle.

reconciliation *n* act of reconciling; renewal of friendship.

recondition *vt* to repair and restore to good working order.

reconnaissance *n* a survey for military purposes.

reconnoitre *vti* to survey or spy out an area or position.

reconsider *vt* to consider again.

reconstruct *vt* to rebuild.

record *vt* to preserve in writing; to chronicle. * *n* a written memorial; a register; best result in contests; gramophone disc.

recorder *n* an official registrar; a device that records; a tape recorder.

recount *vt* to relate in detail; to count again.

recoup *vt* to make good; to indemnify.

recourse *n* a going to for help or protection.

recover *vt* to get back; to regain; to revive; to obtain as compensation. * *vi* to grow well.

recovery *n* restoration from sickness, etc; a winning back.

recreant *adj* craven; cowardly. * *n* a coward; renegade.

recreate *vt* to revive; to amuse.

recreation *n* relaxation after toil; amusement or sport.

recrimination *n* mutual accusations.

recrudescence *n* renewed outbreak.

recruit *vt* to enlist new soldiers. * *vi* to gain new supplies. * *n* a soldier newly enlisted; a beginner.

rectangle *n* a four sided geometric figure having all its angles right angles.

rectangular *adj* right-angled.

rectification *n* refining by distillation; adjustment.

rectify *vt* to set right; to correct or redress.

rectitude *n* uprightness; honesty.

rector *n* a ruler; a clergyman in charge of a parish; a headmaster.

recumbent *adj* leaning; reclining.

recuperate *vti* to recover health.

recuperative *adj* healing; strengthening.

recur *vi* to return; to happen again and again.

recurrence *n* a happening occuring again and again.

recurrent *adj* returning repeatedly.
red *adj* blood-coloured. * *n* a primary colour.
redeem *vt* to buy back; to ransom; to save; to atone for; to perform (a promise).
redemption *n* ransom; release.
redolent *adj* fragrant; reminiscent.
redoubtable *adj* formidable; valiant.
redress *vt* to set right; to adjust; to relieve. * *n* relief; compensation.
reduce *vt* to bring down; to decrease; to degrade; to subdue.
reduction *n* act of reducing; diminution; conversion into another state or form; subjugation.
redundant *adj* superfluous to requirements; deprived of one's job as being no longer necessary.
reduplicate *vti* to double again; to repeat.
reed *n* a tall grass with jointed hollow stem; a pastoral pipe.
reedy *adj* harsh and thin, as a voice.
reef *n* a fold in a sail; a low line of rocks in sea; a vein of ore * *vt* to reduce sail.
reek *n* vapour; smoke. * *vi* to smoke; to exhale.
reel *n* a bobbin; an appliance for winding a fishing line; a lively dance; a length of film. * *vt* to wind upon a reel; to stagger.
refectory *n* a dining hall of a college.
refer *vt* to trace back; to submit (a matter) to another person; to assign. * *vi* to appeal; to allude.
referee *n* an umpire; a judge.
reference *n* allusion; relation; scope.
referendum *n* the settling of a national question by a direct vote of the people.
refine *vti* to purify; to polish; to become purer.
refinement *n* fineness of manners or taste; an improvement; a fine distinction..
refinery *n* a place for refining sugar, metals,oil, etc.
refit *vti* to fit anew; to repair. * *n* repair.
reflect *vti* to throw back, esp. rays of light or heat; to mirror; to meditate; to consider; to cast reproaches on.
reflection *n* act of reflecting; meditation; reproach; a reflected image.
reflective *adj* thoughtful; meditating.
reflector *n* a polished surface for reflecting light, etc.
reflex *adj* bent or directed back; involuntary response to a stimulus. * *n* a reflex action.
reflexive *adj* in grammar, referring back to subject.
reform *vti* to improve; to better; to amend; to form anew. * *n* a beneficial change; amendment.
reformer *n* one who effects reforms in religion, politics, etc..
refract *vt* to bend back sharply; to deflect (a ray of light).
refraction *n* deflection of rays on passing from one medium to another.
refrain *vt* to restrain. * *vi* to forbear. * *n* the recurring phrase or chorus of a song.
refresh *vt* to revive; to freshen.
refreshment *n* that which refreshes, as food and drink.
refrigerate *vt* to cool.
refrigerator *n* an apparatus for keeping things cool or for making ice.
refuge *n* protection from danger or distress; a retreat; a shelter; a plea.
refugee *n* one who seeks refuge in another land; to escape persecution.
refund *vt* to repay.
refusal *n* rejection; option.
refuse *vti* to deny what is asked.
refuse *adj* worthless. * *n* waste matter; rubbish.
refutation *n* disproof.
refute *vt* to disprove; to rebut.
regain *vt* to recover possession of; to reach again.
regal *adj* royal; relating to a king or queen.
regale *vti* to entertain sumptuously.
regalia *npl* ensigns of royalty, as crown, sceptre, etc.
regard *vt* to notice carefully; to observe; to heed; to consider; to value. * *n* look or gaze; respect; deference; attention; (*pl*) good wishes.
regarding *prep.* respecting; concerning.
regardless *adj* heedless; careless.
regatta *n* a yacht (or boat) race.
regency *n* government of a regent.
regenerate *vt* to produce anew; to produce again in the original form.

regent *adj* ruling. * *n* a ruler; one who governs during minority, illness, or absence of a king.

regime *n* mode or system of government; administration.

regimen *n* orderly government; regulation of diet, exercise, etc.

regiment *n* a miltary unit smaller than a division; *vt* to organize in a strict manner.

region *n* a tract of land; country.

register *n* an official record; a roll of voters; a recording machine; a meter.

registrar *n* official keeper of records.

registration *n* act of registering; enrolment.

registry *n* place where a register is kept.

regret *n* grief; remorse; penitence. * *vt* to grieve at; lament.

regrettable *adj* deplorable; unwelcome.

regular *adj* according to rule, law, etc; normal; constant; uniform * *n* a soldier.

regulate *vt* to adjust by rule; to direct.

regulation *n* a rule; order.

regurgitate *vti* to pour or cause to surge back.

rehabilitate *vt* to put back in good condition.

rehearsal *n* a trial performance.

rehearse *vt* to repeat; to recite; to perform (by way of practice).

reign *vi* to be sovereign; to rule; to prevail. * *n* royal authority; duration of kingship.

reimburse *vt* to refund.

rein *n* the strap of a bridle; restraint. * *vt* to govern by a bridle. * *vi* to obey the reins.

reinforce *vt* to supply with fresh strength or assistance.

reinstate *vt* to restore to a former position.

reissue *vt* to issue a second time. * *n* a second issue.

reiterate *vt* to repeat again and again.

reject *vt* to cast off; to discard; to forsake; to decline; to refuse to accept.

rejoice *vi, vt* to be glad; to exult; to cheer.

rejuvenate *vt* to make young again.

relapse *vi* to fall back into a worse state. * *n* a falling back into bad health; a backsliding.

relate *vt* to tell; to narrate. * *vi* to refer.

related *adj* connected by blood or by some common bond.

relation *n* act of relating; account; connection; kindred; a relative; proportion.

relationship *n* kinship.

relative *adj* comparative; pertinent; relating to a word, clause, etc. * *n* a kinsman; a relating word, esp. relative pronoun.

relax *vt* to slacken; to unbend. * *vi* to become feeble or languid.

relaxation *n* recreation; the condition of being relaxed.

relay *n* supply of horses to relieve jaded ones; fresh supply of men or materials; a relayed broadcast. * *vt* to broadcast signals.

release *vt* to set free; to deliver from; to allow cinema film to be shown. * *n* liberation from; discharge from.

relegate *vt* to send away; to move to an inferior position; to demote.

relent *vi* to relax severity; to grow milder.

relentless *adj* unmerciful; pitiless.

relevance, relevancy *n* pertinence; pointedness; applicability.

relevant *adj* applicable; to the purpose.

reliable *adj* trustworthy; dependable.

reliance *n* trust; confidence.

reliant *adj* confident; self-reliant.

relic *n* something treasured for connection with a saint or hero; a memento; (*pl*) bones of saints.

relief *n* ease of pain; remedy; redress; assistance given to the needy or victims of a disaster; raised design in sculpture; prominence; relief from duty by another person.

relieve *vt* to ease or lessen pain; to succour; to release from duty; to give variety to.

religion *n* a system of faith or worship; a belief in God or gods.

relinquish *vt* to give up; to renounce.

relish *vt* to enjoy the taste of; to have a taste for. * *vi* to have a pleasing taste. * *n* taste; flavour; savour.

reluctance *n* unwillingness.

reluctant *adj* loath; averse.

rely *vt* to depend upon; to trust in.

remain *vi* to continue in a place; to survive; to be left; to last. * *npl* a dead body.
remainder *n* residue; remnant.
remand *vt* to recommit to jail for further enquiries.
remark *n* notice; a comment * *vt* to observe; to note; to utter.
remarkable *adj* noteworthy; uncommon; striking.
remediable *adj* curable; correcting.
remedy *n* a cure; redress; a specific. * *vt* to cure; to repair; to put right..
remember *vti* to recollect; recall; observe; bear in mind.
remembrance *n* memory; recollection; memorial; keepsake.
remind *vt* to put in mind.
reminder *n* a jog to memory.
reminisce *vi* to write, think or talk about past events.
reminiscence *n* recollections; what is recalled to mind; (*pl*) personal memories.
reminiscent *adj* recalling the past.
remiss *adj* careless; heedless.
remission *n* pardon; abatement.
remit *vt* to send payment; to relinquish; to forgive; to transmit. * *vi* to slacken.
remittance *n* sum of money remitted.
remnant *n* a scrap; fragment.
remonstrance *n* a protest against something; expostulation.
remonstrate *vi* to protest against; to warn.
remorse *n* sorrow for a fault; compunction; bitter regret.
remorseless *adj* ruthless; merciless.
remote *adj* distant; foreign; slight; inconsiderable.
remount *vti* to mount again. * *n* a fresh horse.
removable *adj* able to be removed.
removal *n* change of place; dismissal.
remove *vti* to move from its place; to take away; to dismiss. * *n* a removal; departure; a stage in gradation.
remuneration *n* pay for service; reward.
remunerative *adj* profitable; lucrative.
renaissance *n* revival.
renal *adj* pertaining to the kidneys.
renascent *adj* becoming active again.
rend *vti* to tear away and apart; to split; to rive.
render *vt* to give in return; to give back; to afford; to furnish; to translate; to interpret; to boil down.
rendering *n* translation; interpretation.
rendezvous *n* appointed meeting place.
renegade *n* a deserter; a person who is faithless to a principle, party, religion, or cause.
renounce *vt* to disown; to forsake. * *vi* to revoke.
renovate *vt* to renew; to make like new.
renovation *n* act of renovating; renewal.
renown *n* fame; glory; celebrity.
renowned *adj* famous; eminent.
rent *n* money paid for use of lands or houses; a tear; a schism * *vti* to let or hire for rent.
rental *n* rent; rent roll.
renunciation *n* act of disowning or rejecting; disavowal.
reorganize *vt* to organize anew.
repair *vt* to restore; to mend; to retrieve. * *vi* to betake one's self; to resort. * *n* return to good condition; renovation.
reparation *n* amends; compensation.
repartee *n* a witty retort.
repatriate *vt* to restore to one's own country.
repay *vt* to pay back; to refund; to requite.
repayment *n* act of repaying; money repaid.
repeal *vt* to revoke; to annul; to abrogate. * *n* a cancelling; revocation.
repeat *vt* to do or utter again; to recite; to recapitulate. * *n* repetition.
repel *vti* to drive back; to repulse; to shock.
repellent *adj* repulsive; unattractive.
repent *vi, vt* to feel regret for one's conduct; to be penitent.
repentance *n* penitence; sorrow for wrong-doing.
repentant *adj* feeling or showing sorrow.
repercussion *n* reverberation; echo; a far-reaching, often indirect reaction to an event.
repertoire *n* actor's or company's stock of plays, etc.
repetition *n* repeating; saying from memory; recitation.
replace *vt* to put back in place; substitute; supersede.

replenish *vt* to fill again; to stock anew.
replete *adj* filled up; stuffed; gorged.
repletion *n* surfeit; plethora.
replica *n* an exact copy; a reproduction.
replication *n* an answer; echo; plaintiff's answer to defendant's plea.
reply *vt, vt* to answer; to respond. * *n* an answer; a rejoinder.
report *vti* to bring back as answer; to relate; to take down speaker's exact words; to give account of; to inform against. * *n* an official statement; account; rumour; loud noise.
reporter *n* one who reports for newspaper, radio or television.
repose *vt* to lay at rest. * *vti* lie at rest; to rely. * *n* sleep; quiet; composure; serenity.
repository *n* a storehouse; warehouse.
reprehend *vt* to reprove; to censure.
reprehensible *adj* deserving censure; culpable.
reprehension *n* reproof; blame.
represent *vt* to show; to typify; to describe; to act part of; to stand for; to be entitled to speak for (constituency).
representation *n* an image or likeness; dramatic performance; a remonstrance; the representing of a constituency.
representative *adj* typical; representing; acting as delegate. * *n* a member of parliament; an agent, delegate.
repress *vt* to check; to quell; to keep under control.
repression *n* check; restraint.
repressive *adj* tending to repress.
reprieve *vt* to grant a respite to; suspension of punishment of a criminal; respite.
reprimand *n* a severe reproof * *vt* to rebuke sharply.
reprint *vt* to print again. * *n* a new edition.
reprisal *n* something done by way of retaliation.
reproach *vt* to reprove, rebuke. * *n* censure; blame; disgrace.
reproachful *adj* abusive; upbraiding.
reprobate *adj* dissolute; profligate. * *n* a hardened sinner. * *vt* to condemn strongly; to cast off.
reproduce *vt* to generate, as offspring; to make copies of.
reproduction *n* a copy; a facsimile.
reproductive *adj* generative; producing again (as seed).
reproof *n* rebuke; censure.
reprove *vt* to censure; to reprimand.
reptile *adj* creeping; grovelling. * *n* any of a class of cold-blooded, air-breathing vertebrates with horny scales or plates; a grovelling or despised person.
reptilian *adj* like reptiles.
republic *n* a state governed by rulers popularly elected.
republican *adj* pertaining to a republic. * *n* one who favours republican government.
repudiate *vt* to reject; to disown; to deny.
repudiation *n* rejection; disavowal.
repugnance *n* aversion; reluctance.
repugnant *adj* offensive; highly distasteful.
repulse *n* a check or defeat; a refusal; a rebuff * *vt* to repel.
repulsion *n* aversion; the tendency of certain bodies to repel each other.
repulsive *adj* forbidding; disgusting.
reputable *adj* held in esteem; respectable.
reputation *n* good name; repute; character.
repute *vt* to estimate; to deem * *n* reputation; character.
reputed *adj* supposed; seeming.
request *n* an expressed desire; a petition. * *vt* to ask; to beg.
requiem *n* a mass for the dead; music for this mass.
require *vt* to ask as of right; to demand; to exact.
requirement *n* demand; an essential condition.
requisite *adj* necessary; essential.
requisition *n* a demand, esp. for supplies.
requite *vt* to repay; to reward; to avenge.
rescind *vt* to annul; to revoke.
rescue *vt* to free from danger or harm. * *n* deliverance.
research *n* careful investigation; a scientific study.
resemblance *n* likeness.
resemble *vt* to be like; to compare.

resent *vt* to be indignant about; to begrudge; to take badly.
resentment *n* deep sense of injury; indignation.
reservation *n* something kept back; doubt; scepticism; land reserved for special purpose, as big game, etc; a proviso.
reserve *vt* to keep in store; to retain. * *n* that which is retained; stiffness of manner; caution; limitation; shyness; (*pl*) emergency troops.
reserved *adj* shy; distant.
reservoir *n* a place where water is stored for use.
reside *vi* to dwell; to live.
residence *n* abode; dwelling.
residential *adj* pertaining to or suitable for residence.
residual *adj* left after part is taken.
residue *n* remainder; part of estate left after paying all charges.
resign *vt* to give up; to renounce; to submit calmly.
resignation *n* calm submission; giving up of office.
resigned *adj* submissive; patient.
resilient *adj* rebounding; elastic.
resin *n* a sticky substance that oozes from trees and plants etc.
resist *vti* to withstand; to oppose.
resistance *n* opposition; stopping power or effect.
resolute *adj* determined; bold.
resolution *n* firmness of purpose; formal decision; the picture definition on a television.
resolve *vti* to split up into elements; analyse; solve; determine. * *n* fixed purpose.
resonance *n* power of sending back or intensifying sound.
resonant *adj* resounding; ringing.
resort *vi* to have recourse; to go. * *n* recourse; a popular holiday destination.
resource *n* any source of aid; an expedient; (*pl*) funds; means.
respect *vt* to regard; to esteem; to concern. * *n* regard; deference; reference to.
respectable *adj* worthy of respect; decent; moderate.
respectably *adv* worthily; pretty well.
respectful *adj* civil; courteous.
respective *adj* relating severally each to each.
respiration *n* act of breathing.
respiratory *adj* pertaining to breathing.
respite *n* temporary intermission; a delay; interval; reprieve. * *vt* to reprieve.
resplendent *adj* very bright; glittering.
respond *vi* to answer.
respondent *adj* answering; corresponding. * *n* defendant in a lawsuit, esp. in divorce.
response *n* an answer; to reply.
responsibility *n* liability; charge; trust.
responsible *adj* answerable; liable; important.
responsive *adj* responding; sensitive to influence or stimulus; sympathetic.
rest *n* cessation of action; peace; sleep; a pause; remainder. * *vi* to cease from action; to repose; to die; to remain. * *vt* to lean or place for support.
restaurant *n* a place where meals can be bought or eaten.
restful *adj* giving rest; quiet; peaceful.
restitution *n* a giving back; reparation; amends.
restless *adj* always on the move; uneasy; anxious.
restoration *n* act of restoring; renewal; repair.
restorative *adj* having power to renew strength.
restore *vt* to make strong again; to cure; to give back.
restrain *vt* to hold back; to curb; to check.
restraint *n* the ability to hold back; something that restrains; control of emotions, impulses, etc.
restrict *vt* to limit; to curb.
result *vi* to follow as a consequence; to ensue; to end. * *n* consequence; outcome.
resultant *adj* following as a result or consequence.
resume *vt* to begin again; to continue after stopping.
resumé *n* a recapitulation; a summary.
resumption *n* act of resuming.
resurgent *adj* rising again.
resurrection *n* a rising again.

resuscitate *vti* to revive.
resuscitation *n* recovering from seeming death.
retail *vt* to sell directly to the consumerin small quantities. * *n* the sale of goods in small quantities; used also as *adj.*
retain *vt* to hold back; to keep in possession; to engage (a barrister) for a law case.
retainer *n* a follower; a dependant; a retaining or preliminary fee paid to barrister for his services.
retaliate *vi, vt* to return like for like; to take revenge.
retaliation *n* the return of like for like.
retard *vt* to render slower; to impede; to delay.
retch *vi* to strain in vomiting.
retention *n* a holding back; power of retaining (ideas); memory.
retentive *adj* good at remembering.
reticence *n* silence; reserve.
reticent *adj* uncommunicative; reserved.
retina *n* inner part of eye where visual nerves are.
retinue *n* a body of attendants.
retiral *n* act of retiring.
retire *vi, vt* to go back; to withdraw from active working life; to go to bed.
retired *adj* secluded; private; withdrawn from business.
retirement *n* retired life; seclusion.
retiring *adj* reserved; unobtrusive; shy.
retort *vt* to retaliate; to make a smart reply. * *n* a ready answer; a repartee; a vessel used in distilling.
retract *vti* to take back; to recant; to unsay.
retraction *n* act of drawing back; recantation.
retreat *n* seclusion; a shelter; the retiring of an army from an enemy. * *vi* to draw back; to retire from an enemy.
retribution *n* just punishment; requital for evil done.
retrievable *adj* that may be retrieved or recovered.
retrieve *vt* to recover; to regain.
retrograde *adj* going backwards; declining morally.
retrogressive *adj* declining; backward.
retrospect *n* a review of the past.
return *vi* to come or go back. * *vt* to send back; to report officially; to elect. * *n* repayment; yield on investment; election of representative; official report; (*pl*) tabulated statistics.
reunion *n* a social gathering, esp. of old associates.
reveal *vt* to disclose; to divulge.
revel *n* a noisy feast. * *vi* to carouse; to make merry.
revelation *n* act of making known; an illuminating experience.
revelry *n* noisy festivity; jollity.
revenge *vti* to take vengeance for; to avenge. * *n* retaliation; vindictive feeling.
revenue *n* income from lands, etc; yearly income of a state; produced by taxation.
reverberate *vti* to return, as sound; to echo.
revere *vt* to regard with awe and respect.
reverence *n* awe combined with respect; veneration; a title of the clergy. * *vt* to revere; to pay reverence to.
reverent *adj* expressing reverence.
reverie *n* a daydream.
reversal *n* the act of reversing.
reverse *vt* to alter to the opposite; to annul; to move backwards. * *n* a defeat; a set back; a check; the back surface (of coin, medal, etc). * *adj* opposite.
reversible *adj* able to be reversed, turned outside in, etc.
reversion *n* a return to a former condition or type; right to future possession.
revert *vt* to go back; * *vi* to return to a former position, habit, etc.
review *vt* to re-examine; reconsider; inspect. * *vi* to write reviews. * *n* a survey; retrospect; a criticism; a magazine which reviews books; official inspection of troops.
revile *vi* to vilify; to abuse.
revise *vt* to go over carefully and correct. * *n* a second proof sheet in printing.
revival *n* a reawakening; a religious awakening.
revive *vi* to recover new vigour. * *vt* to refresh; to reproduce (a play, etc).
revoke *vt* to repeal; to annul. * *vi* in card playing, to neglect to follow suit.

revolt *vi* to rebel; to be disgusted; with at * *vt* to shock. * *n* rebellion; mutiny.
revolting *adj* exciting extreme disgust; shocking.
revolution *n* act of revolving; rotation; circuit; a radical change in government as from a monarchy to a republic.
revolutionary *adj* involving radical changes. * *n* a revolutionist.
revolutionize *vt* to bring about a complete change in.
revolve *vi, vt* to turn round an axis or centre; to consider attentively.
revolver *n* a pistol capable of firing several shots without reloading.
revue *n* a topical play usually interspersed with music.
revulsion *n* disgust; aversion.
reward *n* recompense. * *vt* to repay.
rhapsody *n* an enthusiastic speech or writing;(mus) an irregular instrumental composition of an epic.
rhetoric *n* the art of speaking or writing correctly and effectively; eloquence; declamation.
rheum *n* watery fluid secreted by mucous glands of the nose, eyes, etc.
rheumatism *n* a painful disease of the muscles and joints.
rhombus *n* a parallelogram with equal sides but angles not right angles.
rhomboid *n* a quadrilateral whose opposite sides only are equal, and whose angles are not right angles.
rhyme *n* the repitition of like endings in words or verse lines; poetry; verse. * *vt* to make rhymes; to put into rhyme.
rhythm *n* regular recurrence of accent in music and poetry.
rib *n* one of the curved bones springing from the backbone; something resembling a rib, as in an umbrella.
ribald *adj* irreverant; humorously vulgar.
ribbon *n* a narrow band of silk, satin, etc.
rice *n* a cereal extensively cultivated in hot countries.
rich *adj* wealthy; costly; fertile; plentiful; bright; mellow; highly flavoured.
rickets *npl* a disease of children marked by softening and distortion of the bones.
rickety *adj* ramshackle; shaky.
ricochet *n* a rebounding from a surface.
rid *vt* to free (from something objectionable); to disencumber. * *adj* free; clear.
riddance *n* deliverance; clearance.
riddle *n* a puzzling question; an enigma; a coarse sieve. * *vt* ; to sift; to perforate with shot.
ride *vi* to be borne on horseback, in a vehicle, etc; to practise horsemanship; to be at anchor. * *vt* to sit on, so as to be carried; to domineer over. * *n* an excursion on horseback, or in a vehicle.
ridge *n* a narrow elevation as crest of hill, or edge of roof.
ridicule *n* laughter with contempt; mockery. * *vt* to make sport of.
ridiculous *adj* absurd; laughable.
riding *adj* used in riding (a riding habit).
rife *adj* abundant; prevalent; widespread.
rifle *n* a shoulder gun with a grooved barrel. * *vt* to plunder; to groove a gun barrel.
rift *n* an opening; a cleft; a split.
rig *vt* to manipulate fraudulently; to fit with tackling. * *n* style of masts and cut of sails of a ship.
rigging *n* a ship's spars, ropes, etc.
right *adj* straight; upright; just; correct; opposite of left; perpendicular. * *adv* justly; very; to the right hand. * *n* uprightness; truth; justice. * *vti* to put right; to do justice; to make erect.
righteous *adj* moral; virtuous; just.
rightful *adj* lawful.
rightly *adv* properly; fitly; justly.
rigid *adj* stiff; unyielding; stern.
rigidity *n* stiffness; harshness.
rigmarole *n* confused or disconnected talk.
rigor *n* a sudden chill attended with severe shivering.
rigorous *adj* severe; stringent.
rigour *n* stiffness; austerity; severity.
rim *n* border; edge; margin.
rind *n* outer coat of fruits, trees, etc; bark.
ring *n* anything in the form of a circle; a gold hoop for finger; a circular area for contests, a group with mutual interests; sound of bell. * *vt* to encircle; to cause to sound. * *vi* to sound.
ringleader *n* the leader of a faction.

rink *n* a space on the ice reserved for curling; a place for roller-skating.
rinse *vt* to flush under clean water to remove soap.
riot *n* an uproar; a tumult; noisy revelry. * *vi* to engage in a riot; to revel.
riotous *adj* noisy; turbulent; disorderly.
rip *vt* to tear or cut open. * *n* a rent; a scamp.
ripe *adj* ready for harvest; mature.
ripple *n* a little wave on the surface of water.
rise *vi* to ascend; to stand up; to swell; to slope upwards; to rebel. * *n* ascent; elevation; source; increase (in price).
risible *adj* prone to laugh; laughable.
rising *adj* increasing in power, etc; approaching. * *n* a mounting up; an insurrection; a prominence.
risk *n* hazard; jeopardy. * *vt* to hazard; to venture.
risky *adj* dangerous; full of risk.
rite *n* a solemn religious act; form; ceremony.
ritual *n* a fixed (religious) ceremony.
rival *n* a competitor for the same goal. * *adj* competing. * *vt* to emulate; to strive to excel.
rivalry *n* competition; emulation.
river *n* a large running stream of water.
rivet *n* a fastening bolt clinched by hammering. * *vt* to clinch; to fasten firmly.
rivulet *n* a small stream.
road *n* a public way for travellers, vehicles, etc; a highway;a surfaced track for travelling.
roam *vi* to wander; to travel.
roan *adj* of mixed colour, red predominating. * *n* a horse of roan colour.
roar *vi* to cry with a loud voice; to bellow. * *n* the full loud cry of large animal; a shout.
roaring *adj* boisterous; noisy; brisk.
roast *vt* to cook with little or no moisture; to expose to great heat. * *n* roasted meat, or meat for roasting.
rob *vt* to take by force; to steal from.
robbery *n* theft with violence.
robe *n* a gown, or long, loose garment. * *vt* to invest with robes.
robot *n* a mechanical device that acts in a seemingly human; a mechanism guided by automatic controls.
robust *adj* sturdy; healthy and strong.
rock *vt* to move to and fro; to swing. * *vi* to reel. * *n* a large mass of stone; a reef; a sweetmeat.
rockery *n* an artificial mound of earth and stones for growing ferns, etc, on.
rocket *n* any device driven forward by gases escaping through a rear vent. **vi* to move in or like a rocket; to soar.
rococo *n, adj* a florid style of decoration prevalent in 18th century.
rod *n* a straight slender stick; a wand; a fishing rod.
rodent *adj* gnawing. * *n* an animal that gnaws, as the rat.
rodeo *n* the rounding up of cattle; a display of cowboy skill.
roe *n* the spawn of fishes.
rogue *n* a knave; a rascal.
roguery *n* trickery; fraud; mischievousness.
roister *vt* to bluster; to swagger.
roll *n* a scroll; anything wound into cylindrical form; a list or register; a rolling movement; a small cake of bread; an undulation; the sound of thunder; the beating of drumsticks. **vti* to move by turning over or from side to side; to move like a wheel; to press with a roller.
roller *n* a cylinder for smoothing, crushing, etc; a long, swelling wave.
rolling *adj* revolving; undulating.
romance *n* a tale in prose or verse; a novel of adventures; a love story; a love affair.
romantic *adj* imaginative; fanciful; picturesque.
romp *n* a noisy game; a frolic. * *vi* to play boisterously.
rood *n* a cross or crucifix.
roof *n* the cover of any building; a canopy; an upper limit.
rook *n* a kind of crow; a cheat; a piece in chess.
rookery *n* a nesting place for crows.
room *n* space; scope; opportunity; stead; apartment in a house.
roost *n* a bird's perch or sleeping place.
root *n* that part of a plant which fixes it-

self in the ground foundation; origin; a form from which words are derived.

rooted *adj* fixed; deep; radical.

rope *n* a stout cord; a series of things connected; a cable. * *vi, vt* to fasten with a rope; to curb.

rosary *n* a string of beads for keeping count of prayers.

rose *n* a plant and its flower, of many species; knot of ribbons; a perforated nozzle. * *adj* rose colour.

rosette *n* an ornamental knot of ribbons.

roster *n* a list showing order in which officers, etc, are to take up certain duties (army).

rostrum *n* a platform for public speaking.

rot *vi, vt* to decompose; to decay. * *n* putrid decay; a fatal sheep disease; nonsense.

rota *n* a turn in succession; a list or roster of duties.

rotary *adj* turning on an axle.

rotate *vi* to revolve round a centre or axis; to act in turn.

rotation *n* motion round a centre or axis; regular succession (as of crops).

rote *n* repetition without understanding.

rotten *adj* decomposed; decayed.

rotund *adj* round; spherical; plump.

rouble *n* Russian monetary unit.

rouge *n* a red cosmetic for tinting cheeks and lips.

rough *adj* not smooth; rugged; harsh; rude; uneven; ill-mannered.

round *adj* circular; spherical; plump; curved; not minutely accurate, as a number. * *n* rung of a ladder; a circular course; circuit made by one on duty; a vocal composition in parts; ammunition for firing once; a turn or bout. * *vt* to make round; to encircle. * *vi* to make a circuit. * *adv* in a circle; around. * prep about; around.

roundabout *adj* indirect; circuitous. * *n* a merry-go-round.

rouse *vt* to arouse; to awaken. * *vi* to awake.

rout *n* a noisy crowd; a disorderly retreat. **vti* to grub up, as a pig; to make a furrow.

route *n* a course or way.

routine *n* regular habit or practice.

rove *vi* to roam; to wander.

row *n* a line of objects; a rank; a line of seats.* *vt* to impel by oars, as a boat.

row *n* a noisy disturbance; a riot.

rowdy *n* a turbulent fellow; a rough. * *adj* disreputable.

royal *adj* regal; relating to a king or queen.

royalist *n* an adherent of a king or queen.

royalty *n* state of being royal; a royal personage; share paid to a superior, inventor, or author.

rub *vti* to move one thing along surface of another with pressure or friction; to scour; to chafe. * *n* impediment; friction; pinch; gibe.

rubber *n* that which rubs; an eraser; in card playing, winning two out of three games.

rubbish *n* refuse; debris; trash; nonsense.

rubble *n* broken stones of irregular shapes.

ruby *n* a valuable gem of various shades of red.

rucksack*n* a bag worn on the back by hikers.

rudder *n* the steering apparatus of a ship.

ruddy *adj* reddish; a healthy red.

rude *adj* rough-hewn; uncivilized; ill-mannered; vulgar.

rudiments *npl* the origin, first principle, or germ of anything, esp. learning, art, etc.

rudimentary *adj* undeveloped; primitive.

rue *vt* to feel remorse for.

rueful *adj* woeful; piteous; remorseful.

ruff *n* a plaited collar or frill; a ruffle; act of trumping at cards. * *vt* to trump at cards.

ruffian *n* a brutal lawless person.

ruffle *vt* to rumple; to derange. * *vi* to bluster. * *n* a frill for the neck or wrist; agitation.

rug *n* a heavy fabric used as a mat or coverlet.

rugged *adj* rough; uncouth; rocky.

rugby *n* a football game for two teams of fifteen players played with an oval ball.

ruin *n* destruction; fall; overthrow; (*pl*) remains of old buildings. * *vt* to destroy; to impoverish.

rule *n* a ruler or measure; a guiding principle; a precept, law, maxim; government; method. * *vti* to govern; to manage; to mark with lines; to decide; to reign.

ruling *adj* reigning; predominant. * *n* a point settled by a judge, chairman, etc.

rum *n* spirit distilled from molasses.

rumble *vi* to make a dull, continued sound. * *n* a low, continued sound.

ruminant *n* an animal that chews the cud.

ruminate *vi* to regurgitate food after it has been swallowed; to meditate.

rummage *vt* to search narrowly but roughly; to ransack. * *n* a careful search.

rumour *n* an unconfirmed report. * *vt* to spread abroad.

rump *n* end of an animal's backbone; buttocks.

rumple *vt* to wrinkle; to ruffle.

rumpus *n* a great disturbance; a din.

run *vi* to move rapidly; to take part in a race; to flee; to spread or flow. * *vt* to incur; to smuggle; to melt. * *n* act of running; course run; trip; general demand; distance sailed or travelled.

rung *n* the round or step of a ladder.

runner *n* a messenger; an athlete; a creeping plant; that on which anything slides.

rupture *n* a break; fracture; breach; disagreement; quarrel; hernia.

rural *adj* pertaining to the country; rustic.

ruse *n* artifice; trick; deception.

rush *vi* to dash forward. * *n* a headlong advance; hurry; a reed; an unedited film print.

rusk *n* a light hard cake or biscuit.

rust *n* the red oxide formed on iron exposed to moisture; a parasite fungus.* *vi* to contract rust; to degenerate in idleness.

rustic *adj* rural; homely; unpolished.

rustle *vi, vt* to make a sound as of rubbing of dry leaves. * *n* the crinkling sound of blown leaves.

rusty *adj* covered with rust; impaired by inaction.

rut *n* the track of a wheel; a groove; routine.

ruthless *adj* cruel; pitiless.

rye *n* a cereal plant and its seed; a whiskey made from rye.

S

sabbath *n* a day of rest and worship, observed on a Saturday by Jews, Sunday by Christians and Friday by Muslims.

sabbatical *n* a year's leave from a teaching post, often paid, for research or travel.

sabotage *n* a deliberate damage of machinery, or disruption of public services, by enemy agents, disgruntled employees, etc, to prevent their effective operation. **vt* to practise sabotage on; to spoil, disrupt.

saccharin *n* a non-fattening sugar substitute.

sachet *n* a small bag for perfume, etc.

sack *n* a bag made of coarse cloth used as a container; pillage of a town. * *vt* to pillage, as a town; to dismiss.

sacrament *n* a solemn religious ordinance; a sacred symbol or pledge.

sacred *adj* set apart for a holy purpose; consecrated; religious.

sacrifice *n* something given up in the interests of another; loss; the thing offered up. * *vt* to give up.

sacrum *n* the bone at base of vertebral column.

sad *adj* sorrowful; gloomy.

sadden *vt* to make sad. * *vi* to become sad.

saddle *n* a seat for a rider on a horse or bicycle. * *vt* to put a saddle on.

sadism *n* sexual pleasure obtained by inflicting cruelty on another; extreme cruelty.

safe *adj* secure; free from danger; trustworthy. * *n* a strong box for securing valuables; a burglar-proof chamber; a cupboard.

safeguard *n* a defence; protection. * *vt* to guard.

safety *n* freedom from danger, hurt, or loss.

safety belt *n* a belt worn by a person working at great height to prevent falling; a seatbelt in a car.

safety valve *n* a valve which opens when pressure of steam in boiler becomes too great.
sag *vi* to sink in the middle; to droop.
sagacity *n* shrewdness; high intelligence.
sage *adj* wise; grave. * *n* a wise man; an aromatic plant.
Sagittarius *n* the archer, a sign of the zodiac.
sail *n* a canvas spread to catch the wind; a voyage in a sailing vessel. * *vi, vt* to move by means of sails; to glide; to navigate.
sailor *n* a seaman; a mariner.
saint *n* one eminent for piety.
sake *n* behalf; purpose; benefit; interest.
salad *n* raw herbs as lettuce, cress, etc, dressed.
salary *n* a fixed, regular payment for work.
sale *n* act of selling; market; auction.
salesman *n* one employed to sell goods.
salience *n* projection; protrusion.
salient *adj* springing; projecting; conspicuous.
saline *adj* consisting of salt; salt.
saliva *n* the fluid secreted by glands of mouth that aids digestion.
sallow *adj* having a sickly, yellowish colour. * *n* a kind of willow.
sally *n* a sudden attack or outburst; a lively remark, a quip.
salon *n* a reception room; a gallery.
saloon *n* a spacious apartment; main cabin of a steamer.
salt *n* a substance for seasoning and preserving food; a compound produced by the combination of a base with an acid; savour; an old sailor. * *vt* to sprinkle with salt.
saltire *n* a cross (X) dividing heraldic shield into four parts.
salubrious *adj* healthful.
salutary *adj* beneficial, wholesome.
salutation *n* a greeting; a salute.
salute *vt* to greet; to welcome; to greet with a bow; kiss, etc. * *vi* to make a salute.
salvable *adj* that may be saved.
salvage *n* the saving of a ship or its cargo at sea; the saving of property from fire; payment for such service.
salvation *n* redemption of man from sin.
salve *n* a healing ointment; remedy. * *vt* to apply salve to.
salver *n* a small tray.
salvo *n* a salute of guns; a sudden burst.
same *adj* identical; exactly similar; unchanged; uniform; monotonous.
sample *n* a specimen; a small part representative of the whole.
sanatorium *n* an establishment for the treatment of convalescents or the chronically ill.
sanctification *n* a purifying from sin; consecration.
sanctified *adj* made holy; consecrated.
sanctify *vt* to make holy.
sanctimonious *adj* making a show of sanctity; hypocritical.
sanction *n* permission; authority; a penalty by which a law is enforced. * *vt* to ratify; to authorize.
sanctity *n* saintliness; holiness.
sanctuary *n* a sacred place; part of a church where the altar is placed; a sure refuge.
sanctum *n* a sacred place; a private room.
sand *n* fine particles of stone; *pl* tracts of sand on the seashore, etc.
sandal *n* a shoe consisting of a sole strapped to the foot.
sandpaper *n* paper coated with sand for smoothing and polishing.
sandstone *n* a stone composed of compressed sand.
sandwich *n* slices of bread, with meat or savoury between. * *vt* to fit between two other pieces.
sane *adj* sound in mind; sensible.
sanguine *adj* full of blood; cheerful; hopeful.
sanitary *adj* healthful; hygienic.
sanitation *n* measures for securing good health in a community; hygiene; drainage and dispoal of sewage.
sanity *n* soundness of mind.
sanskrit *n, adj* the ancient language of Hindus.
sap *vti* to undermine. * *n* a trench; vital juice of plants.
sapient *adj* wise; sage; discerning.

sapling *n* a young tree.
sapphire *n* a precious stone of a rich blue colour.
sarcasm *n* a bitter cutting jest; gibe.
sarcastic *adj* biting; taunting; satirical.
sarcophagus *n* (*pl* sarcophagi) a coffin of stone.
sardonic *adj* bitter; mocking; grimly jocular.
sartorial *adj* pertaining to a tailor.
sash *n* a long band or scarf worn for ornament; a window frame.
satan *n* the devil; the adversary of God.
satchel *n* a little bag for carrying books, papers, etc.
sate *vt* to satisfy the appetite of; to glut.
satellite *n* a small planet revolving round a larger; a man-made object orbiting the earth to gather scientific information, etc.
satiate *vt* to satisfy fully; to surfeit. * *adj* glutted.
satin *n* a glossy close-woven silk cloth.
satire *n* a composition in prose or verse, ridiculing or censuring manners and customs of the time.
satirize *vt* to ridicule; to hold up to scorn.
satisfaction *n* pleasure; contentment; atonement; payment.
satisfactory *adj* adequate; up to expectation.
satisfy *vti* to gratify fully; to convince.
saturate *vt* to soak thoroughly.
saturation *n* state of being soaked or filled with another substance to utmost limit.
Saturday *n* the seventh day of the week.
saturn *n* a planet.
sauce *n* a liquid relish or seasoning for food.
saucepan *n* a deep cooking pan with a handle and a lid.
saucer *n* a curved plate in which cup is set.
saucy *adj* pert;impudent; rude.
saunter *vi* to stroll about idly. * *n* a stroll.
sausage *n* minced seasoned meat, esp pork, packed into animal gut or other casing.
savage *adj* wild; barbarous; brutal. * *n* a barbarian.
savagery *n* cruelty; barbarity.
save *vt* to preserve; to protect; to rescue; to spare. * *vi* to be economical. * *prep* except.
saving *adj* thrifty; preserving; excepting. * *n* what is saved. * *prep* excepting.
saviour *n* a preserver; rescuer.
savour *n* taste; flavour; a distinctive quality. * *vi* to have a particular taste.
savoury *adj* tasty; palatable; spicy not sweet.
saw *n* a cutting instrument with toothed edge; a maxim * *vti* to cut with a saw.
sawdust *n* small fragments of wood produced in sawing.
sawmill *n* a mill for sawing timber.
say *vti* to utter in words; to speak; to declare; to relate.
saying *n* a proverb; maxim.
scab *n* crust formed over a sore on healing; itch; mange.
scabbard *n* the sheath of a sword.
scabies *n* contagious itching skin disease.
scaffolding *n* a framework to aid in building houses, etc.
scald *vt* to burn with hot liquid. * *n* a burn from hot liquid or steam; scurf.
scale *n* a thin flake on skin of animals; instrument for weighing; series of steps; gradation; a measure; rank; series of musical notes. * *vt* to weigh; to strip of scales; to climb. * *vi* to peel.
scallop *n* an edible shellfish; a curving or indentation on edge. * *vt* to indent or curve edges.
scalp *n* the skin and hair of top of head. * *vt* to cut off scalp.
scalpel *n* a short, thin, very sharp knife.
scamp *n* a knave; rogue.
scamper *vi* to scurry. * *n* a hurried run.
scan *vt* to look through quickly; to examine with a radiological device; to mark the rhythm of verse.
scandal *n* a disgraceful event or action; a feeling of moral outrage; shame.
scandalous *adj* shameful; disgraceful.
scant *adj* limited; meagre. * *vt* to stint; to grudge. * *adv* scarcely.
scapegoat *n* one who bears the blame of others.
scapula *n* the shoulder blade.
scar *n* the mark of a wound; a blemish; a

cliff; a steep bare bank. * *vt* to form a scar; to wound.

scarab *n* egyptian beetle; a gem cut in the form of a beetle.

scarce *adj* rare; deficient; hard to find.

scarcity *n* dearth; deficiency.

scare *vt* to terrify; to scare. * *n* a causeless alarm; panic.

scarecrow *n* anything set up to scare away birds.

scarf *n* a broad band or sash for neck wear; a joint in timber.

scarify *vt* to make small incision in the skin; to shock; to criticize savagely.

scarlet *n, adj* a bright red colour.

scarp *n* a precipitous slope.

scathing *adj* severe; bitterly critical; withering.

scatter *vt* to disperse; to throw loosely about, to occur at random. * *vi* to straggle apart.

scatterbrain *n* a giddy, thoughtless person.

scattered *adj* thinly spread; dispersed.

scenario *n* summary of leading incidents in a play.

scene *n* a stage; a distinct part of a play; a painted device on the stage; place of action; a view; display of emotion.

scenery *n* the painted scenes and hangings of the stage; landscape; view.

scenic *adj* relating to natural scenery.

scent *n* an odour left by an animal, by which it can be tracked , a perfume; sense of smell; . * *vt* to discern by smell.

sceptic *n* a doubter; disbeliever.

sceptical *adj* doubting; doubting truth of revelation.

scepticism *n* doubt; incredulity.

sceptre *n* the rod borne by a ruler as a symbol of power.

schedule *n* a timetable; a list or inventory. **vt* to plan.

scheme *n* a plan of proceedings; a system; a project. * *vti* to plan; project; plot.

schism *n* a separation; a disruption.

scholar *n* a school pupil; a learned person.

scholarship *n* learning; an annual grant to a student, usu won by competitve examination.

school *n* a place of instruction; a body of pupils; disciples; sect or body; a shoal (of fishes). * *vt* to instruct; to train.

schooner *n* a vessel with two masts.

sciatica *n* neuralgia of the sciatic nerve.

science *n* knowledge; knowledge reduced to a system; study of natural laws and principles; trained skill.

scientific *adj* skilled in science.

scientist *n* a specialist in a branch of science.

scimitar *n* a short curved sword.

scintillate *vi* to sparkle; to twinkle.

scion *n* a cutting; a young shoot; a descendant.

scissors *npl* a cutting instrument of two blades, whose edges slide past each other.

sclerosis *n* a hardening of tissue.

scoff *n* an expression of scorn; a gibe. * *vi* to jeer; to mock. * *vt* to mock at.

scold *vi, vt* to rebuke angrily; to find fault with harshly; to tell off.

scoop *n* a short-handled shovel for grain, etc; a coal scuttle; a hollowing out spoon or gouge for cheese, etc. * *vt* to hollow out.

scooter *n* a child's two wheeled vehicle with a footboard and steering handle; a motor scooter.

scope *n* an aim or end; range; opportunity.

scorch *vti* to singe; parch; shrivel; to drive at reckless speed.

score *n* a notch; a line; a furrow; an account or reckoning; runs, points, etc, made in games; twenty; reason; copy of concerted musical piece. * *vt* to mark; record; register.

scorn *n* extreme contempt. * *vt* to disdain; to deride. * *vi* to feel or show scorn.

scornful *adj* disdainful; mocking; contemptuous.

scotch *vt* to stamp out.

scoundrel *n* a rogue, rascal.

scour *vti* to clean by rubbing; to purge violently; to pass swiftly over.

scourge *n* a lash; a whip; a grievous affliction; a plague. * *vt* to lash; to afflict sorely.

scout *n* an exploring or reconnoitering

messenger; a person employed to find new talent. * *vi* to act as scout.

scowl *vi* to frown in anger. * *n* a sullen frowning look.

scraggy *adj* lean and bony; gaunt.

scramble *vi* to clamber on all fours; to push rudely; to break and stir eggs; to make unintelligible in transit. * *n* a pushing and struggling for something.

scrambling *adj* irregular; straggling.

scrap *n* a small piece; a fragment; a cut-out picture.

scrape *vti* to rub with something hard; to grate; to erase; to gather money laboriously; to make a grating noise. * *n* a rasping sound; serious trouble.

scratch *vti* to tear or mark with something sharp; to tear with nails; to erase or cancel * *n* a slight mark or wound; starting line; competitor without start. * *adj* haphazard.

scrawl *vti* to scribble. * *n* slovenly writing.

scream *vi* to shriek. * *n* a shrill cry.

screen *n* a shield from draughts, heat, etc; a sieve; a partition in a church; a sheet on which pictures are projected; an electronic display. * *vt* to shelter; to conceal; to sift.

scree *npl* debris of rocks; shingle.

screw *n* a cylinder with a spiral ridge; a screw propeller; a twist or turn. * *vt* to fasten by a screw; to twist; to oppress.

screwdriver *n* an instrument for turning screw nails.

screw nail *n* a nail grooved like a screw.

scribble *vti* to write carelessly. * *n* a scrawl.

scribe *n* a writer; copyist.

scrimp *vt* to make too small or short. * *adj* scanty.

script *n* handwriting; type imitating handwriting; the text of a play or a film.

scripture *n* any sacred writing.

scroll *n* a roll of paper; a first draft; a spiral design.

scrotum *n* the bag which contains the testicles.

scrounge *vti* to seek or obtain (something) for nothing.

scrub *vt* to rub hard; to make clean or bright. * *n* a stunted tree or bush; a mean person.

scrubby *adj* stunted; niggardly.

scruple *n* (*usu pl*) a moral principle or belief causing one to doubt or hesitate about a course of action. **vt, vi* to hesitate owing to scruples.

scrupulous *adj* conscientious; exact.

scrutinize *vti* to examine closely; to investigate.

scrutiny *n* close search; careful investigation.

scuffle *n* a confused struggle. *vi* to strive confusedly at close quarters.

scull *n* a short oar, used in pairs. * *vt* to propel by sculls.

scullery *n* a back kitchen where dishes, etc, are washed.

sculptor *n* an artist in stone, wood, clay, etc.

sculpture *n* the art of carving wood or stone into images; an image in stone, etc.

scum *n* impurities which rise to the surface of liquids; offscourings.

scupper *n* hole to carry off water from ship's deck; to sink deliberately.

scurrilous *adj* foul-mouthed; abusive.

scurry *vt* to hurry. * *n* hurry; haste.

scurvily *adv* basely; shabbily.

scurvy *n* a disease caused by insufficiency of vitamin C. * *adj* vile; mean.

scuttle *n* a pail for coals; a hatchway; a short run; a quick race. * *vt* to sink by making holes in (a ship). * *vi* to scurry.

scythe *n* an implement for mowing grass, etc.

sea *n* an expanse of salt water; ocean or part of it; a vast quantity; a great wave.

seagoing *adj* applied to vessels going to foreign ports.

seal *n* a stamp or die with motto or device; wax with stamp impression; guarantee; carnivorous marine animal. * *vt* to set a seal to; to confirm; to close.

sea level *n* the level of the sea's surface.

seam *n* the joining line of edges of cloth; a vein of metal; a scar.

seamy *adj* sordid; disagreeable; shabby.

séance *n* to try to communicate with the dead; a meeting of spiritualists.

seaport *n* a town on the sea or estuary

accesible to oceangoing ships.
sear *vt* to brand; to burn; to deaden.
search *vt* to look or rummage for; to explore, examine. * *n* quest; pursuit; inquiry.
searching *adj* penetrating; severe; testing.
seashore *n* land beside the sea or between high and low water marks.; the beach.
seasick *adj* affected with sickness by rolling of ship.
seaside *n* the seacoast.
season *n* a division of the year; a suitable time; time of greatest activity. * *vt* to accustom; to acclimatize; to flavour.
seasonable *adj* opportune; timely.
seasoning *n* salt, spices, etc used to enhance the flavour of food.
seat *n* that on which one sits; a chair, stool, etc; place of sitting; a right to sit; residence; station; manner of sitting. * *vt* to place on a seat; to settle.
seaward *adj, adv* toward the sea.
seaweed *n* a mass of plants growing in or under water; a sea plant, esp a marine alga.
sebaceous *adj* containing fatty matter.
secede *vi* to withdraw from fellowship.
secession *n* disruption; withdrawal from membership.
secluded *adj* retired; remote; private.
seclusion *n* solitude; privacy.
second *adj* next after the first; inferior; other. * *n* one who comes next after first; one who supports another; to place in temporary service elsewhere; sixtieth part of a minute. * *vt* to support.
secondary *adj* subordinate; not elementary; inferior.
secrecy *n* concealment; seclusion; habit of keeping secrets.
secret *adj* not made public; concealed from others; hidden; private; remote. * *n* something hidden; a mystery; a hidden cause.
secretariat *n* an administrative office or staff, as in a government.
secretary *n* a person employed to deal with correspondence, filing, answering telephone calls etc; head of a state department; executive officer of company.
secrete *vt* to hide; to produce and release (a substance) out of blood or sap.
secretion *n* act or process of secreting; matter secreted, as bile, etc.
secretive *adj* given to secrecy; reticent.
sect *n* a body of persons united in doctrine; a denomination.
sectarian *adj* pertaining to a sect; bigoted. * *n* member of a sect.
section *n* a cutting; part cut off; subdivision of chapter, etc; slice; distinct part; the plane figure formed when solid is cut through.
sectional *adj* made up of sections; partial.
sector *n* part of circle between two radii; a mathematical instrument.
secular *adj* worldly; temporal; not sacred.
secularize *vt* to free from religious influence; to hand over church property to state.
secure *adj* free from care or danger; safe; confident. * *vt* to make safe; to seize and confine; to guarantee; to fasten.
security *n* safety; confidence; protection; a guarantee; a surety; *pl* bonds, stocks, etc.
sedate *adj* staid; sober; calm; composed.
sedately *adv* calmly; tranquilly.
sedative *adj* soothing. * *n* an opiate; a soothing drug.
sedentary *adj* inactive; requiring much sitting.
sediment *n* that which settles to bottom of liquids; matter deposited by water or wind.
sedition *n* action or speech against law and order.
seditious *adj* inciting to rebellion; inflammatory.
seduce *vt* to lead astray; to corrupt.
seduction *n* allurement; temptation; attraction.
seductive *adj* enticing; alluring.
sedulous *adj* assiduous; diligent.
see *vt* to perceive by the eye; to notice; to understand. * *vi* to have the power of sight. * *interj* Look! * *n* diocese or sphere of a bishop.
seed *n* the small hard part of a plant from which a new plant grows; descendant. * *vti* to sow; to produce seed.

seedling *n* a plant reared from the seed.
seedy *adj* abounding with seeds; shabby; out of sorts.
seeing *n* vision, sight. **adj* having sight; observant. **conj* in view of the fact that; since.
seek *vti* to search for; to ask for; to resort to.
seem *vi* to appear; to look as if; to pretend.
seemingly *adv* apparently.
seemly *adj* becoming; decent.
seer *n* a prophet.
seesaw *n* a swinging movement up and down; a children's game on balanced plank; vacillation.
seethe *vi* to be very angry outwardly.
segment *n* a section; part of circle cut off by straight line; a portion.
segregate *vt* to set apart or separate from others; to isolate.
seismic *adj* pertaining to earthquakes.
seismology *n* the science of earthquakes.
seize *vti* to lay hold of forcibly; to apprehend; to attack, as fear, illness, etc.
seizure *n* act of seizing; a sudden attack of illness.
seldom *adv* rarely; not often.
select *vt* to choose; to pick out. * *adj* chosen.
selection *n* process of choosing; things chosen.
self *n* (*pl* **selves**) one's individual person or interest. * *adj* or pron same; uniform.
self-conscious *adj* thinking about one's self overmuch; shy.
self-defence *n* the act of defending oneself.
self-denial *n* the forbearing to gratify one's desires; unselfishness.
self-esteem *n* high opinion of one's self; vanity.
self-evident *adj* obvious; needing no proof.
self-important *adj* pompous.
self-imposed *adj* voluntarily undertaken.
selfish *adj* absorbed in one's self; ungenerous.
self-respect *n* proper pride.
self-righteous *adj* stressing one's own goodness; pharisaical.
self-seeking *adj* selfish.
self-sufficient *adj* needing no help.
sell *vt* to give for a price; to betray. * *vi* to practise selling; to be sold.
semaphore *n* a system of visual signalling using the operators arms, flags etc.
semblance *n* similarity; appearance.
semibreve *n* a musical note = 2 minims.
semicircle *n* a half circle.
semicolon *n* the point (;) marking a longer pause than a comma.
seminal *adj* pertaining to seed; germinal.
seminar *n* a group of students engaged in research or study under supervision; any group meeting to pool and discuss ideas.
seminary *n* a school, academy, or college.
semiquaver *n* half a quaver in music.
semitic *adj* hebrew.
semolina *n* granular flour.
senate *n* a legislative or deliberative council; governing body in some universities.
senator *n* a member of a senate.
send *vt* to cause to go or be carried; to transmit; to dispatch.
senile *adj* aged; doting; tottering.
senility *n* a state of being mentally weakened by old age.
senior *adj* older; higher in rank or standing. * *n* one older in age or office.
seniority *n* priority in rank or office.
sensation *n* perception through the senses; feeling; a thrill.
sensational *adj* causing excited feeling; emotional.
sense *n* one of the five senses, sight, hearing, taste, smell, touch; understanding; good judgment; discernment; meaning.
senseless *adj* stupid; foolish; meaningless; purposeless.
sensibility *n* acuteness of perception; delicacy of feeling.
sensible *adj* having good sense; judicious; reasonable; appreciable.
sensitive *adj* susceptible to impressions; easily affected; touchy; tender.
sensitize *vt* to make (paper) susceptible to rays of light.
sensory *adj* relating to the sensorium; conveying sensation.
sensual *adj* bodily, relating to the senses

rather than the mind; arousing sexual desire.
sensuous *adj* giving pleasure to the body or the mind through the senses.
sentence *n* opinion; judgment of a court; a number of words containing complete sense. * *vt* to pass sentence upon; to condemn.
sententious *adj* abounding in maxims; terse; judicial.
sentient *adj* making use of the senses.
sentiment *n* tenderness of feeling; thought prompted by emotion; a toast.
sentimental *adj* apt to be swayed by feelings; romantic.
sentinel *n* a guard; sentry.
sentry *n* a soldier on guard to give warning of danger.
separable *adj* that may be separated; capable of separation.
separate *vt* to put or set apart; to sever; to divide apart. * *vi* to go apart. * *adj* detached; distinct.
separation *n* the act of separating or the state of being seperate; a formal arrangement of husband and wife to live apart.
separatist *n* one who advocates separation; a seceder.
sepia *n* a brown pigment.
September *n* the ninth month of the year.
septenary *adj* consisting of or proceeding by sevens; lasting seven years.
septennial *adj* occuring every, or lasting seven years.
septic *adj* promoting or causing putrefaction.
septicaemia *n* blood poisoning.
septuagenarian *n* a person seventy years of age.
septum *n* (*pl* septa) a membrane separating organs or cavities.
sepulchral *adj* grave; hollow, as a voice.
sepulchre *n* a tomb. * *vt* to bury.
sequel *n* that which follows; a consequence; issue.
sequence *n* a coming after; succession; series.
sequester *vt* to set apart; to withdraw; to seize goods till debt is paid; to confiscate.
sequestrate *vt* to seize and dispose of goods for benefit of creditors.
sequestration *n* confiscation of debtor's goods in interest of creditors.
serenade *n* music played at night under a person's window, esp by a lover. * *vti* to perform such music.
serene *adj* clear; bright; calm; unruffled.
serenity *n* calmness; peace; equanimity.
sergeant *n* a noncommissioned officer above corporal in the army etc; a police officer.
serial *adj* appearing periodically. * *n* a story issued in parts.
series *n* a succession of things; sequence.
serious *adj* grave; earnest; attended with danger; important; critical.
sermon *n* a religious discourse; an admonition.
serpentine *adj* spiral; winding; crafty. * *n* a mineral.
serrated *adj* notched; toothed.
serum *n* the watery part of bodily fluid, esp liquid that seperates out from the blood when it coagulates; such fluid taken from the blood of an animal immune to a disease, used as an anti-toxin.
servant *n* a domestic; an attendant.
serve *vt* to work for and meet the needs of; to minister to; to deliver or execute; to supply with (food). * *vi* to be a servant; to suit.
service *n* work of servant; employment; kindness; official duties; public worship; liturgy; table dishes; the services, army, navy, etc.
serviceable *adj* useful; beneficial.
serviette *n* a table napkin.
servile *adj* slavish; fawning; subservient.
servility *n* meanness of spirit; excessive deference.
servitude *n* slavery; bondage.
sessile *adj* stalkless; growing direct from stem.
session *n* the meeting of a court; a series of such meetings; aperiod of study; a university year.
set *vt* to place in position; to fix; to appoint; to regulate or adjust; to fit to music; to adorn; to spread (sails). * *vi* to sink below horizon; to solidify; to tend; to point out game; to apply one's self.

* *n* direction; tendency; attitude; bent; collection of things used together; a group of games; persons associated.

settee *n* a short sofa.

setting *n* descent below horizon; hardening of plaster; the mounting of a gem; fitting to music; a background scene; enviroment.

settle*vt, vi* to fix permanently; to quiet; to decide; to pay; to agree; to subside; to become calm; to clarify; to take up residence.

settled *adj* established; steadfast.

settlement *n* an arrangement; a newly established colony; subsidence (of buildings).

settler *n* a colonist.

seven *adj* one more than six.

sevenfold *adj* seven times.

seventeenth *adj, n* the ordinal of seventeen.

seventh *adj* the ordinal of seven.

seventieth *adj, n* the ordinal of seventy.

seventy *adj, n* seven times ten.

sever *vt* to seperate; to divide into parts; to break off.

several *adj* separate; more than two; but not very many.

severally *adv* separately.

severance *n* separation.

severe *adj* serious; grave; harsh; searching; austere.

severity *n* harshness; cruel treatment; intensity.

sew *vti* to make by needle and thread.

sewage *n* waste matter carried off by sewers.

sewer *n* a subterranean drain, to carry off water, filth, etc.

sewerage *n* the system of sewers; sewage.

sex *n* the characteristics that distinguish male and female organisms on the basis of their reproductive function.

sexagenarian *n* a person sixty years of age.

sexism *n* discrimination on the basis of sex.

sextant *n* instrument for measuring angles and altitudes.

sextuple *adj* sixfold.

sexual *adj* pertaining to sex.

sexual intercourse *n* the act of copulation.

sexuality *n* state of being sexual.

shabbily *adv* in a shabby manner; with shabby clothes; meanly.

shabby *adj* threadbare; mean; stingy.

shackle *n* a fetter; a manacle. * *vt* to fetter; hamper.

shade *n* interception of light; obscurity; darkness; a shady place; a screen; dimness; gradation of light; a ghost.

shading *n* light and shade in a picture.

shadow *adj* a figure projected by interception of light; shade; an inseparable companion; a spirit. * *vt* to shade; to cloud; to follow closely.

shadowy *adj* faint; dim; unsubstantial.

shady *adj* abounding in shade; of doubtful character.

shaft *n* the handle of a tool, etc; body of a column; pole of carriage; a critical remark or attack; well-like entrance to mine.

shaggy *adj* long and unkempt; rough; untidy.

shake *vt* to move quickly to and fro; to agitate. * *vi* to tremble. * *n* a tremor; shock; a trill.

shaky *adj* unsteady; feeble.

shale *n* a clay rock having a slaty structure.

shall *vb aux* in first person it is a future tense; in the second and third it implies authority.

shallow *adj* not deep; superficial; simple. * *n* a shoal.

sham *n* a pretence; a fraud. * *adj* false. * *vti* to feign; pretend.

shambles *npl* a place of great disorder.

shambling *adj* walking with awkward, unsteady gait.

shame *n* a painful emotion excited by guilt, disgrace, etc. * *vt* to make ashamed; to disgrace.

shameful *adj* disgraceful; infamous.

shameless *adj* immodest; unblushing.

shampoo *n* a liquid cleansing agent for washing the hair. **vt* to wash the hair with shampoo.

shandy *n* beer diluted with a nonalchoholic drink (as lemonade).

shank *n* the leg; the shinbone; the stem or shaft of tool, anchor, etc.

shanty *n* a hut or mean dwelling; sailors' song.

shape *vt* to form; to mould. * *vi* to suit. * *n* form or figure; make; a model.

shapely *adj* well-proportioned.

shard *n* a fragment of pottery.

share *n* a part, lot, or portion; ploughshare; one of equal parts of company's capital. * *vti* to divide; to apportion among others; to have part.

shareholder *n* owner of shares in company.

shark *n* a voracious sea fish; a swindler.

sharp *adj* having a cutting edge or point; keen; shrewd; piercing; biting; barely honest. * *n* a note raised a semitone.

sharpen *vt* to make sharp; to whet.

sharpshooter *n* an expert shot; a sniper.

shatter *vti* to break in pieces; to smash.

shave *vt* to cut hair close with razor; to pare; to miss narrowly; to graze; to fleece. * *n* a cutting off of the beard; a narrow escape.

shaving *n* a thin slice pared off.

shawl *n* a loose covering for the shoulders.

she *pron nominative* third person sing. feminine.

sheaf *n* (*pl* **sheaves**) a bundle of stalks of wheat, etc; a collection of papers tied in a bundle.

shear *vti* to clip or eat through; to remove (a sheep's fleece) by clipping; to break off.

shears *npl* a large kind of scissors.

sheath *n* a close fitting cover; a condom.

sheathe *vt* to put into sheath; to protect by a casing.

sheathing *n* covering of metal to protect ship's bottom.

shed *vti* to cast off; to diffuse; to let fall in drops; to spill. * *n* a watershed; a hut; a roofed shelter.

sheen *n* brightness; gloss.

sheer *adj* mere; downright; precipitous. * *vi* to swerve; to shy.

sheet *n* a broad, thin piece of anything; broad expanse; bed linen; a single piece of paper; a newspaper.

shelf *n* (*pl* **shelves**) a horizontal board fixed in position to support books, etc; a ledge.

shell *n* hard outer crust or case; an explosive projectile. * *vt* to strip off shell; to fire shells.

shellfish *n* an aquatic animal with a shell covering.

shelter *n* a protection; asylum; refuge. * *vt* to protect. * *vi* to take shelter.

shelve *vt* to place on a shelf; to defer consideration. * *vi* to slope.

shelving *n* shelves collectively.

shepherd *n* a person who looks after sheep.

sheriff *n* chief law officer or judge of a county.

sherry *n* a fortified wine of southern Spain.

shield *n* a protective covering or guard; a piece of armour carried for defence on the left arm. * *vt* to protect; to screen.

shieling *n* see Shealing.

shift *vi* to change; to move; to contrive; to manage; *n* a change; expedient; a dodge; relay time.

shiftless *adj* improvident; useless; without resource.

shifty *adj* unreliable; changeable; tricky.

shillyshally *vi* to wobble; to vacillate.

shimmer *vi* to glisten softly. * *n* a flicker.

shin *n* the front of lower leg.

shine *vi* to emit light; to beam; to be bright, lively, conspicuous.

shingle *n* thin wood used in roofing; loose gravel. **vt* to roof with shingles.

shingles *n* a viral disease marked by a painful rash of red spots.

shining *adj* bright; illustrious.

shinty *n* a form of hockey.

ship *n* a large seagoing vessel; **vti* to put or take on board; to transport for service in a ship; to fix in place.

shipmate *n* a fellow sailor.

shipment *n* a consignment; goods shipped.

shipper *n* one who exports or imports goods by sea.

shipping *n* ships in general; the business of transporting goods.

shipshape *adj* in seamanlike fashion; trim.
shipwreck *n* the wreck of a ship; the loss of a vessel at sea.
shipyard *n* a shipbuilding establishment.
shirk *vti* to try to evade a duty.
shirt *n* a sleeved garment of cotton etc for the upper body.
shiver *vt* to shatter. * *vi* to tremble, as from cold; to shudder. * *n* a splinter; shaking fit.
shoal *n* a large number of fish swimming together.
shock *n* a violent collision; a sudden emotional disturbance; the effect of an electrical charge on the body. * *vt* to horrify; to disgust.
shocking *adj* dreadful; offensive.
shoddy *n* made of inferior quality. **adj* made of shoddy; trashy.
shoe *n* outer covering for foot; metal plate on hoof of horse; a drag for a wheel.
shoehorn *n* a curved piece of horn (or metal) to aid in putting on shoe.
shoot *vt* to discharge with force; to hit or kill with missile; to propel quickly.* *vi* to dart along; to sprout. * *n* a young branch or bud; a chute.
shooting *n* killing game; land rented to shoot over.
shop *n* a place where goods are sold by retail; a workshop. * *vi* to visit shops.
shore *n* land along edge of sea; coast; a prop. * *vt* to prop up.
short *adj* not long or tall; scanty; concise; curt; brittle. **npl* short trousers. * in short, briefly.
shortage *n* a deficit.
shortcoming *n* a defect.
shorten *vt* to make short; to reduce amount.
shorthand *n* abbreviated writing.
short-sighted *n* unable to see far; wanting foresight.
shortwave.*n* a radio wave sixty metres or less in length.
shot *n* act of shooting; a projectile; a bullet; range or reach; a marksman.
shoulder *n* the joint connecting arm, foreleg, or wing to body; a projection. **vt* to jostle; to put on shoulder.
shout *vi* to utter a loud cry. * *n* a loud cry.
shove *vti* to push forward; to jostle. **n* a push.
shovel *n* a kind of spade with slightly curved blade.
show *vt* to display to view; to let be seen; to prove. * *vi* to appear. * *n* display; pageant; pretence; a theatrical performance.
shower *n* a brief fall of rain, etc; a copious supply. * *vti* to rain; to pour down; to bestow liberally.
showroom *n* a room in which goods are exhibited.
shrapnel *n* an artillery shell filled with small pieces of metal that scatter on impact.
shred *vt* to tear into small pieces. * *n* a fragment or scrap.
shrew *n* a scold; a kind of mouse.
shrewd *adj* astute; clever.
shrewish *adj* given to scolding.
shriek *vi* to scream * *n* a shrill cry.
shrill *adj* piercing in sound; strident.
shrine *n* a hallowed place; an altar; a tomb.
shrink *vi* to contract; to shrivel; to flinch.
shrive *vt* to confess and absolve.
shrivel *vi, vt* to shrink into wrinkles; to wither up.
shroud *n* a burial cloth; anything that covers or conceals.
shrub *n* a bush with separate stems from same root.
shrubbery *n* a plantation of shrubs.
shrug *vti* to raise one's shoulders in surprise, doubt, indifference, etc.
shudder *vi* to tremble with fear; to quake. * *n* a tremor.
shuffle *vt* to shove one way and the other; to confuse; to mix cards. * *vi* to quibble; to drag one's feet. **n* an evasion; a shuffling gait or step.
shuffling *adj* moving with irregular gait; evasive.
shun *vt* to avoid; to refrain from.
shunt *vi, vt* in railways, to switch from one track to another.
shut *vti* to close or stop up; to bar.
shutter *n* a movable screen for a window.
shuttle *n* a boat-shaped contrivance for shooting cross threads in loom; an aircraft, spacecraft, etc, making back-and-forth trips over a given route..

shuttlecock *n* a cork stuck with feathers, used in game of badminton.

shy *adj* timid; retiring; very self-conscious; coy. * *vi, vt* to start aside, as horse; to throw. * *n* a throw.

shyness *n* reserve; coyness.

sibilant *adj* hissing. * *n* a letter uttered with a hissing as s and z.

sic *adv* thus; it is so; usually written (sic).

sick *adj* ill; disgusted; uhealthy; vomiting.

sicken *vt* to make sick; to disgust. * *vi* to become sick.

sickening *adj* disgusting.

sickle *n* a reaping hook.

sickness *n* disease; ill-health.

side *n* the broad or long surface of a body; edge, border; slope (of hill); bias (of ball). * *vi* to support; espouse (a cause). * *adj* oblique.

sideboard *n* a piece of furniture used to hold dining utensils, etc.

sidelong *adv* indirect. * *adj* oblique.

sidetrack*vt* to prevent action by diversionary tactics; to shunt aside.

sideways *adv* see Sidewise.

sidewise *adv* toward one side; on one side.

siding *n* a short line of rails for shunting purposes.

siege *n* the surrounding of a fortified place to cut off supplies and compel its surrender; the act of beseiging; a continued attempt to gain something.

sienna *n* a reddish-brown pigment.

siesta *n* a nap in hottest part of day.

sieve *n* a strainer; sifter.

sift *vt* to separate coarser parts from finer with a sieve.

sifter *n* a sieve.

sigh *vi* to draw a deep and audible breath, as in grief, weariness or relief. * *n* a long and deep breath.

sight *n* act or power of seeing; view; visibility; estimation; a show. * *vt* to see.

sightless *adj* blind.

sightseeing *n* the visiting of interesting places.

sign *n* a mark, token, stamp, or symbol; an emblem; indication; gesture. * *vti* to affix signature; to make a sign.

signal *n* a sign to give information, orders, etc, at a distance. * *adj* notable. * *vti* to convey by signs.

signally *adv* remarkably; notably.

signatory *n* party to signing a treaty or other agreement.

signature *n* one's name written by oneself; a printed sheet when folded before being used.

signboard *n* a board marked with person's name or business.

significant *adj* weighty; important; highly expressive; momentous.

signify *vt* to make known; to mean; to imply.

silence *n* quiet; secrecy; stillness; absence of sound. * *vt* to still; to cause to be quiet.

silent *adj* mute; taciturn; making no noise.

silhouette *n* a shadow outline of a shape against light.

silicon *n* nonmetallic element whose oxide is silica.

silk *n* the fine thread produced by silkworm; cloth made of silk.

silky *adj* like silk; smooth and glossy.

sill *n* the timber or stone at foot of window.

silly *adj* foolish; unwise; frivolous; being stunned or dazed.

silo *n* a pit or tower for storage (fodder).

silt *n* sediment from moving water.

silver *n* a ductile, malleable, precious metal of a white colour used in jewellery, cutlery etc.. * *vti* to coat with silver.

silvering *n* coating with silver or quicksilver.

silversmith *n* a worker or dealer in silver.

silver-tongued *adj* persuasive; musical.

similar *adj* like; resembling.

similarity *n* likeness; resemblance.

simile *n* a figure of speech containing a comparison.

similitude *n* likeness; resemblance.

simmer *vi* to boil gently.

simper *vi* to smile in a silly manner. * *n* an affected smile.

simple *adj* not complex; single; artless; plain; silly; easy to understand or solve * *n* a medicinal herb.

simplicity *n* sincerity; artlessness; innocence; folly.

simplify *vt* to make simple.
simulate *vt* to pretend to have or feel; to feign.
simulation *n* reproducing specific conditions or conduct.
simultaneous *adj* taking place at the same time.
sin *n* a transgression of the divine law; iniquity; a wicked act; an offence. * *vi* to do wrong.
since *adv* from that time; ago. * prep after. * conj because that.
sincere *adj* genuine, real, not pretended; honest; straightforward.
sincerity *n* honesty of mind; freedom from pretence.
sinecure *n* a paid office with few, if any, duties.
sinew *n* the fibrous cord which joins muscle to bone.
sinful *adj* wicked; erring.
sing *vi, vt* to utter melodious sounds; to celebrate in song.
singe *vt* to burn surface. * *n* a slight burn.
single *adj* being one or a unit; individual; unmarried; sincere. * *vt* to select individually (with out).
singly *adv* one by one; sincerely.
singular *adj* denoting only one person or thing; remarkable; quaint; rare. * *n* singular number.
singularly *adv* peculiarly; remarkably.
sinister *adj* left; evil; malevolent; ominous.
sink *vi* to fall below surface (water); to subside; to fall in value, strength, etc. * *vt* to immerse; to dig (shaft); to degrade. * *n* a drain or receptacle to carry off dirty water.
sinking *adj* depressing, as in feeling.
sinner *n* a transgressor; offender; a person who sins.
sinuate *vt* to wind. * *adj* winding.
sinuosity *n* a wavy line; a bend.
sinuous *adj* winding; curved; tortuous.
sinus *n* an air cavity in the skull that opens in the nasal cavities.
sip *vt* to drink in small quantities. * *n* a drop; a taste.
siphon *n* a bent tube for drawing off liquids.
sir *n* a word of respect used to men; a title.
siren *n* a device producing a loud wailing sound as a warning signal; a sea nymph who lured sailors to destruction; an alluring, dangerous woman.
sirloin *n* the upper part of loin of beef.
sirocco *n* a hot wind blowing over southern Europe from south.
sister *n* a female born of the same parents; a member of a religious sisterhood.
sister-in-law *n* a husband or wife's sister.
sit *vi* to rest oneself on the buttocks, as on a chair, to perch (birds); to incubate; to have a seat (in Parliament); to suit; to take an examination.
site *n* situation; a building plot; the scene of something.
sitter *n* one who sits for his portrait.
sitting *n* a session, as of a court.
situated *adj* placed; located; circumstanced.
situation *n* position; station; post.
six *adj, n* one more than five.
sixfold *adj, adv* six times.
sixteen *adj, n* six and ten.
sixteenth *adj* ordinal of sixteen.
sixth *adj* ordinal of six.
sixtieth *adj, n* ordinal of sixty.
sixty *adj, n* six times ten.
size *n* magnitude; the dimensions or proportions of something; a thin pasty glue used by painters to glaze paper, etc. * *vt* to arrange according to size; to cover with size.
skate *n* a steel bar fastened to boot for moving on ice; a coarse flat fish. * *vt* to go on skates.
skateboard *n* a short, oblong board with two wheels at each end for standing on and riding.
skein *n* a small hank of thread.
skeleton *n* the bony framework of an animal; outline.
sketch *n* an outline; a first rough draught quickly made. * *vt* to draw; to outline.
skewer *n* a pin for fastening meat.
ski *n* (*pl* **skis**) a long narrow runner of wood, metal or plastic that is fastened to a boot to enable movement across snow. * *vi* to travel on skis.

skid *vti* to slide without rotating; to slip sideways as cycle, aeroplane, etc. * *n* a drag to reduce speed.
skiff *n* a small light boat.
skilful *adj* skilled; dexterous; adroit.
skill *n* ability; expertness; aptitude; proficiency.
skim *vt* to remove the scum from the surface of; to glance over (book). * *vi* to glide along (water).
skin *n* the natural outer coating of animals; a hide; rind. * *vt* to strip the skin from; flay.
skin-deep *adj* superficial.
skinflint *n* a stingy person.
skinny *adj* very thin.
skip *vi* to leap; to bound; to spring. * *vt* to omit. * *n* a light leap; captain of curling or bowling team.
skipper *n* the captain of a ship.
skirmish *n* a minor fight in a war. * *vi* to fight when reconnoitering.
skirt *n* lower part of a coat; woman's garment that hangs from the waist; border. * *vti* to border; to pass along edge.
skit *n* a short humorous sketch.
skittish *adj* excitable; frisky; fickle.
skulk *vi* to lurk; to keep out of sight; to shirk duty.
skull *n* the bony case which contains the brain; the cranium.
sky *n* the vault of heaven.
skylight *n* a window in a roof.
skyward *adj, adv* toward the sky.
slab *n* a flat piece of stone, wood, etc. * *adj* thick and slimy.
slack *adj* loose; easy-going; not busy; relaxed. * *n* loose part of a rope, etc. * *vti* to idle; less active; to slacken.
slacken *vi* to become slack; * *vt* to relax; to reduce; to loosen.
slag *n* fused dross of metal; clinkers.
slake *vt* to quench; to mix (lime) with water.
slam *vti* to shut with a bang. * *n* a bang; winning of all tricks at bridge.
slander *n* a false and injurious report. * *vt* to vilify; to defame.
slang *n, adj* expressions in common use but not approved as good English; jargon.
slant *adj* sloping. * *vti* to slope; to incline; to tell in such a way as to have a bias.* *n* a slope.
slap *n* a blow with the open hand. * *vt* to strike with the open hand.
slapdash *adv* carelessly; at random.
slash *vti* to strike at wildly with knife, sword, etc; to slit, as a sleeve. * *n* a long cut; slit.
slate *n* rock which splits into thin layers; a thin roofing slab; a writing plate. * *vt* to cover with slates; to criticize harshly.
slater *n* one who slates buildings.
slating *n* the roof or roofing; harsh criticism.
slaughter *n* a slaying; carnage; massacre. * *vt* to slay; to kill for market.
slave *n* a person without freedom or personal rights.
slaver *n* saliva dripping from mouth. * *vti* to let saliva drip; to fawn upon.
slavery *n* bondage; drudgery.
slavish *adj* servile; oppressively laborious.
slay *vt* to kill by violence; to murder.
sledgehammer *n* a large, heavy hammer for two hands.
sledge *n* a vehicle on runners used over snow; a sleigh.
sleek *adj* smooth and glossy; plausible.
sleep *vi, vt* to rest with mind and body inactive; to slumber; to lie dormant. * *n* slumber; repose; death.
sleeper *n* one who sleeps; a beam for support joists, floors, rails, etc; a sleeping car (railway).
sleepy *adj* drowsy; sluggish; not alert.
sleet *n* hail or snow mingled with rain.
sleeve *n* part of a garment enclosing arm.
sleight *n* manual dexterity; **sleight of hand** jugglery.
slender *adj* thin; slim; scanty.
slice *vt* to cut into thin pieces; a stroke that makes the ball curl to th right (golf). * *n* a thin broad piece cut off.
slide *vi, vt* to slip or glide over surface, as ice. * *n* a slope or track for sliding on.
slight *adj* small; trifling; frail. * *n* intentional disregard. * *vt* to treat as of no account.
slim *adj* slight; slender; cunning.
slime *n* oozy sticky mud; mucus.

sling *vt* to hurl; to suspend; to place in a sling. * *n* a contrivance for hurling stones; a hanging bandage for injured limb.

slink *vt* to steal away.

slip *vi* to move smoothly along; to glide; to miss one's foothold; to let go (anchor); to err; to escape (memory). * *n* act of slipping; omission; error; leash; narrow strip (paper, etc); incline on which ships are built.

slipper *n* a light soft shoe for household wear.

slippery *adj* causing to slip; unreliable.

slipshod *adj* down at heels; slovenly.

slit *vi* to cut lengthwise. * *n* a long cut or opening.

sliver *n* a splinter.

slobber *vi, vt* to drool; to run at the mouth.

slogan *n* a catchy phrase used in advertising or as a motto by a political party etc.

sloop *n* a sailing vessel with one mast.

slop *vt* to spill. * *n* unappetising; semi-liquid food; spilled water; poor liquor; (*pl*) dirty or waste water.

slope *n* a slant.* *vti* to incline.

sloppy *adj* careless; untidy; slovenly.

slot *n* a long narrow opening; a slit. **vt* to fit into a slot.

sloth *n* indolence; laziness; a slow-moving mammal.

slouch *n* to sit or move in a drooping or ungainly manner * *vi, vt* to move with drooping gait.

slouching *adj* awkward; crouching.

slough *n* cast skin of snake. * *vi, vt* to cast or come off (skin).

slovenly *adj* untidy; dirty; careless.

slow *adj* not rapid; tardy; dull; stupid.

sludge *n* mire; soft mud; sediment.

sluggish *adj* lazy; slothful; slow.

sluice *n* a gate for regulating flow of water in canal, etc. * *vti* to scour with water.

slum *n* an overcrowded area.

slumber *vi* to sleep; to doze. * *n* a light sleep.

slump *n* sudden fall in value or slacking in demand. * *vt* to lump together; to fall heavily (shares).

slur *vt* to pronounce or speak indistinctly; to run together (words). * *n* a stain, stigma.

slush *n* sludge or soft mud; half-melted snow.

slut *n* a slovenly or immoral woman; a slattern.

sly *adj* cunning; crafty; wily.

smack *vi* to make a sharp noise with lips; to taste. * *vt* to slap. * *n* a loud kiss; a slap; a taste; a fishing vessel.

small *adj* little; petty; short; narrow-minded; mean.

small arms *npl* rifles, pistols, etc, as distinguished from artillery.

smallpox *n* a contagious disease, now rare, marked by pustules on skin.

small talk *n* light, social talk.

smart *n* a quick, keen pain. * *adj* keen;clever; quick; brisk; witty; spruce. * *vi* to feel a sharp pain.

smarten *vt* to make smart.

smash *vt* to dash or go to pieces. * *n* a crash; ruin; failure.

smattering *n* a superficial knowledge.

smear *vt* to daub with anything greasy.

smell *vti* to perceive by the nose; to give out an odour. * *n* sense of smell; scent; odour.

smelt *vt* to melt, as ore. * *n* a small fish allied to salmon.

smile *vi* to show joy by the features of the face. * *n* a look of pleasure.

smirk *vi* to smile affectedly. * *n* an inane smile; simper.

smite *vti* to strike; to slay; to afflict.

smock *n* a chemise; a smock frock.

smocking *n* a fancy stitch in sewing.

smoke *n* sooty vapour from burning substance; vapour; act of smoking (pipe, etc). * *vi, vt* to emit smoke; to use tobacco; to fumigate.

smoking *n* the use of tobacco. * *adj* emitting smoke.

smoky *adj* giving out smoke; filled with smoke.

smooth *adj* even on the surface; glossy; pleasant. * *vt* to make smooth; to level.

smother *n* to cover over quickly * *vti* to stifle; to suffocate.

smoulder *vi* to burn and smoke without flame.

smudge *vt* to stain with dirt. * *n* a stain; a smear.

smug *n* complacent; self-satisfied.

smuggle *vt* to import or export secretly without paying duty.

smuggling *n* the importing or exporting goods without paying duty.

smut *n* a spot or stain; a flake of soot; obscene language.

smutty *adj* soiled with smut; obscene.

snack *n* a light meal between regular meals.

snag *n* a short projecting stump; a knot; a stumbling block.

snake *n* a limbless, scaly reptile with a long tapering body, often with salivery glands modified to produce venom.

snap *vti* to bite or seize suddenly; to break with a sharp sound. * *n* a sudden bite; spring catch; sharp noise.

snapshot *n* a hasty shot at a moving animal; an instantaneous photograph.

snare *n* a running noose for catching animals; a pitfall; a trap. * *vt* to catch in snare; to trap.

snarl *vi* to growl with bared teeth, as an angry dog; to speak rudely; to become entangled. * *n* a growl.

snarling *adj* snappish;peevish.

snatch *vt* to seize abruptly or without permission. * *vi* to grasp (at). * *n* a sudden seizing; a small portion.

sneak *vi, vt* to go slyly; to steal off; to behave meanly. * *n* a telltale; a mean wretch.

sneer *vi* to show contempt by a look; to jeer. * *n* a scoff; a jeer.

sneeze *vi* to emit air violently and audibly through nose.

snick *vt* to cut; to clip; to snip.

sniff *vi* to smell; to inhale through the nose audibly.

snigger *vi* to giggle; to laugh in sly fashion. * *n* a partly suppressed laugh.

snip *vt* to cut off at a stroke. * *n* a single cut; small piece; a certainty.

snipe *vt* to lie in wait and pick off enemy by rifle fire.

snippet *n* a small part cut off; *pl* odds and ends.

snivelling *adj* whining; tearful.

snob *n* a person who wishes to be associated with those of a higher social status, whilst acting condescendingly to those whom he or she regards as inferior.

snooze *n* a short sleep. * *vi* to take a short nap.

snore *vi* to breathe noisily in sleep;noisy breathing in sleep.

snorkel *n* a breathing tube extending above the water, used in swimming just below the surface. **vi* to swim using a snorkel.

snort *vi* to eject air violently through nose, as horses. * *n* an explosive breath sound.

snout *n* animal's nose or muzzle.

snow *n* vapour frozen in the air and falling in flakes.

snowball *n* a ball of snow pressed together for throwing.

snowdrift *n* a bank of drifted snow.

snowdrop *n* an early spring flower.

snowplough *n* an implement for clearing snow from roads.

snub *vt* to humiliate with words or look; to slight. * *n* a check; rebuke.

snuff *vti* to sniff; to smell; to take snuff; to crop or trim (wick). * *n* charred part of wick; powdered tobacco.

snuffle *vi* to speak through the nose. * *n* a nasal twang; cant; *pl* cold in the head.

snug *adj* neat; trim; cosy.

snuggle *vi* to lie close for warmth; to nestle.

so *adv* in this or that manner; to that degree; thus; very. * *conj* provided that; therefore.

soak *vti* to become saturated; to wet thoroughly.

soap *n* a compound of fat with an alkali, used in washing. * *vt* to rub with soap.

soar *vi* to fly upwards; to tower.

sob *vi* to weep convulsively. * *n* a short choking sigh.

sober *adj* temperate; not drunk; staid; grave; thoughtful.

sobriety *n* temperance; saneness; gravity.

sobriquet *n* a nickname.

soccer *n* a football game played on a field by two teams of eleven players with a round inflated ball.

sociable *adj* fond of companions; social.

social *adj* living or organized in a community, not solitary; genial; affable.

socialism *n* a theory of social organization aiming at co-operative action and the nationalization of capital and land.

socialist *n* one who advocates socialism.

social security*n* financial assistance for the unemployed, the disabled, etc to alleviate economic distress.

society *n* the social relationship between human beings or animals organized collectively.

sociologist *n* one versed in social science.

sociology *n* the science of the history, nature, etc, of human society; social science.

sock *n* a short stocking covering the foot and lower leg.

socket *n* a cavity into which anything is fitted.

sod *n* small square piece of turf.

soda *n* the alkali, carbonate of sodium.

sodden *adj* saturated; soaked and soft.

sofa *n* a couch with cushioned seat, back, and arms.

soft *adj* yielding easily to pressure; delicate; smooth; not harsh; quiet.

soften *vti* to make or become soft; to tone down; to melt; to relent.

softly *adv* gently; tenderly.

soil *vti* to make dirty; to tarnish. * *n* dirt; top layer of earth; mould; country.

sojourn *vi* to reside for a time. * *n* a temporary stay.

solace *vt* to cheer or console. * *n* consolation; comfort.

solar *adj* pertaining to or proceeding from sun; sunny.

solder *vt* to unite metals by a metal alloy. **n* an alloy capable when fused of cementing metals together.

soldier *n* a person in military service.

sole *n* the under side of the foot; the bottom of a shoe; a flatfish. * *vt* to furnish with a sole. * *adj* single; only; alone.

solecism *n* a grammatical error; a breach of rules of syntax.

solely *adv* singly; alone; only.

solemn *adj* grave; formal; impressive; awe inspiring.

solemnity *n* gravity; a solemn ceremony.

solicit *vti* to ask earnestly; to invite.

solicitation *n* supplication; entreaty.

solicitor *n* a lawyer.

solicitous *adj* anxious; very concerned.

solid *adj* resisting pressure; not liquid or gaseous; not hollow; compact; firm; strongly constructed. * *n* a compact body.

solidarity *n* unity of interest and action.

solidity *n* density; firmness.

soliloquy *n* the act of talking to oneself.

solitaire *n* a gem in a single setting; a stud; a game for one player.

solitary *adj* being alone; lonely; unfrequented. * *n* a recluse.

solitude *n* loneliness; a lonely place.

solo *n* a tune or air for a single performer. *vi* to perform by oneself.

soloist *n* a solo singer or performer.

solstice *n* the time when the sun is farthest north or south of equator, 21st June and 21st Dec. respectively.

solubility *n* quality of being soluble.

soluble *adj* capable of being dissolved in a fluid; capable of solution, as a problem.

solution *n* the dissolving of a solid in a liquid; explanation; result.

solve *vt* to explain; to make clear; to unravel.

solvency *n* ability to pay debts.

solvent *adj* having the power of dissolving; able to pay all debts. * *n* a fluid that dissolves another substance.

sombre *adj* dark; gloomy; dismal.

some *adj* an indefinite number; considerable; more or less. * *pron* an indefinite part, quantity, or number; certain individuals.

somebody *n* some person; a person of importance.

somehow *adv* one way or another.

somersault *n* a leap in which the heels turn over the head.

something *n* a thing unspecified; part or portion. * *adv* to some degree.

sometime *adv* once; by and by. * *adj* former.

sometimes *adv* now and then; at times.

somewhat *n* more or less. * *adv* in some degree.

somewhere *adv* in some place.
somnambulism *n* the act of walking in sleep.
somnolence *n* sleepiness.
somnolent *adj* sleepy; drowsy.
son *n* a male child or descendant.
song *n* that which is sung; vocal music; a lyric; the call of certain birds.
sonic*adj* of, producing, or involving sound waves.
son-in-law *n* a daughter's husband.
sonnet *n* a poem of fourteen pentameter lines with varying rhymes.
sonorous *adj* resonant; deep-toned.
soon *adv* in a short time; quickly; readily.
soot *n* a black substance formed from burning matter.
sooth *adj* true. * *n* truth; reality.
soothe *vt* to calm; to comfort; to relieve pain.
soothsayer *n* one who foretells the future.
sop *n* something dipped in broth or liquid food; bribe given to pacify.
sophism *n* false reasoning but with appearance of truth.
soporific *adj* causing sleep. * *n* a drug that induces sleep.
soprano *n* the highest female voice; a singer with such a voice.
sorcerer *n* a wizard; a person who uses magic powers.
sorceress *n* a female sorcerer.
sorcery *n* magic; enchantment; witchcraft.
sordid *adj* mean; vile; base; squalid.
sore *adj* painful; tender. * *n* an ulcer, wound, etc.
sorely *adv* seriously; grievously.
sorrow *n* grief; distress of mind; sadness; regret. * *vi* to grieve.
sorrowful *adj* full of sorrow.
sorry *adj* feeling sorrow or pity; grieved; wretched.
sort *n* nature or character; kind; species; a set. * *vt* to arrange in order; to sort.
soufflé *n* a light dish of baked egg whites.
soul *n* the spiritual element in man; conscience; essence; a person.
sound *adj* whole; firm; healthy; orthodox; just. * *n* a narrow channel of water; a strait; that which is heard; noise. * *vti* to measure the depth of; to examine medically; to try to discover the opinion, etc, of; to make a noise; to probe; to pronounce; to be spread or published.
sounding *adj* resounding. * *n* the ascertaining depth of water.
soundings *npl* the depths of water in rivers, harbours, etc.
soundtrack*n* the sound accompanying a film; the area on cinema film that carries the sound recording.
soup *n* a kind of broth.
sour *adj* acid to the taste; tart; peevish; distasteful or unpleasant. * *vt* to make sour; to embitter.
source *n* that from which anything rises; the fountainhead; origin.
souse *n* pickle; to plunge into water.
south *n* one of four compass points; position of sun at noon. * *adj* being in or toward the south.
southeast *n* the point midway between south and east. * *adj* pertaining to or from the southeast.
southerly *adj* lying toward the south; coming from the south.
southern *adj* belonging to the south; southerly.
southward *adv, adj* toward the south.
southwest *n* the point midway between south and west. * *adj* pertaining to or from the southwest.
souvenir *n* a keepsake; a momento.
sovereign *adj* supreme in power; chief * *n* a monarch; a ruler.
sovereignty *n* supreme power; dominion.
sow *vti* to scatter seed over; to spread abroad.
spa *n* a resort for medicinal water.
space *n* the limitless three-dimensional expanse within which all objects exist; outer space; a specific area; an interval; empty area; room; an unoccupied area or seat. **vt* to arrange at intervals.
spacious *adj* roomy; capacious.
spade *n* an instrument for digging; one of the suits of cards.
span *n* reach or space from thumb to extended little finger; nine inches; short space of time; spread of arch. * *vt* to extend across; to measure with the fingers extended.

spank *vt* to slap with the flat of the hand, esp on the buttocks.
spanner *n* a tool with a hole or jaws to grip and turn nuts or bolts.
spar *n* a long piece of timber; a pole; a crystalline mineral; boxing match. * *vi* to box; to bandy words.
spare *adj* scanty; thin; held in reserve. * *vti* to use frugally; to dispense with; to be saving; to forbear; to have mercy on.
sparing *adj* frugal; economical.
spark *n* a particle of burning matter; a flash of light from an electrical discharge. * *vi* to emit fiery particles.
sparkle *n* a little spark; lustre. * *vi* to emit sparks; to glitter.
sparkling *adj* glittering; lively.
sparse *adj* thinly scattered; scanty.
spartan *adj* rigorously severe.
spasm *n* a violent contraction of muscles; a convulsive fit.
spasmodic *adj* intermittently.
spastic*n* a person who suffers from cerebral palsy. **adj* affected by muscle spasm.
spate *n* a sudden heavy flood; a large amount.
spatial *adj* pertaining to space.
spatter *vt* to scatter a liquid on; to sprinkle.
spatula *n* a broad thin blade, used in spreading plasters, paints, etc.
spawn *n* the eggs or ova of fish, etc. * *vti* to deposit spawn.
speak *vi, vt* to utter words; to talk; to deliver a speech; to pronounce.
speaker *n* one who speaks; the presiding official in a legislative assembly.
spear *n* a long, pointed weapon; a lance. * *vt* to pierce with a spear.
special *adj* particular; distinctive; uncommon.
specialist *n* one who devotes himself to some particular subject; an expert.
speciality *n* special characteristic; something made or sold exclusively by certain traders. * specialty *n* special characteristic; a special pursuit; a special product.
specialize *vti* to apply one's self to a particular subject.
species *n sing, pl* a kind, sort, or variety; a class of plants or animals; subdivision of a genus.
specific *adj* pertaining to a species; definite; precise. * *n* a remedy for a special disease; a sure remedy.
specifically *adv* definitely; precisely.
specification *n* a requirement; detailed statement of particulars for carrying out contracts, etc.
specify *vt* to make specific; to state in detail.
specimen *n* a sample; a part to typify the whole.
specious *adj* superficially correct; plausible.
speck *n* a small spot; a flaw; a particle.
speckled *adj* spotted.
spectacle *n* a show; an exhibition; a pageant; *pl* glasses to assist vision.
spectacular *adj* impressive; astounding.
spectator *n* an onlooker.
spectral *adj* shadowy; ghostly.
spectre *n* an apparition; a ghost.
spectroscope *n* the instrument employed in decomposition of rays of light.
spectrum *n* (*pl* **spectra**) the coloured bands produced by passing light through a prism.
speculate *vi* to theorize; to conjecture; to gamble in stocks, land, etc.
speculation *n* act of speculating; theory; hazardous financial transactions.
speculative *adj* risky; contemplative.
speculator *n* one who takes undue risks in business.
speech *n* the faculty of speaking; language; talk; a formal discourse; oration.
speechless *adj* silent; unable to speak.
speed *n* success; velocity; haste. * *vi, vt* to make haste; to prosper; to fare.
speedometer *n* indicator for showing speed of motors, cycles, etc.
spell *n* a charm; fascination; a period of work. * *vt* to give in correct order the letters of words.
spend *vti* to pay out, as money; to squander; to pass, as time; to exhaust of force.
spendthrift *n, adj* a prodigal; wasteful.
spent *adj* wearied; exhausted.
sperm *n* semen; the male reproductive cell.

spew *vti* to vomit; to flow or gush forth.
sphere *n* an orb; a ball; a sun, star, or planet; extent of motion, action, etc.
spheric, spherical *adj* globular.
spheroid *n* a body like a sphere, as earth, orange, etc.
sphincter *n* a ring-like muscle closing an opening an orifice.
sphinx *n* a fabled monster, half human, half lion.
spicate *adj* spiked; pointed.
spice *n* an aromatic seasoning for food; relish; flavour. * *vt* to flavour; to season.
spicy *adj* pungent; piquant; racy.
spider *n* a small wingless creature (arachnid) with eight legs, and abdominal spinnerets for spinning silk threads to make webs.
spike *n* a piece of pointed iron; an ear of corn, etc. * *vt* to fasten with spikes; to transfix; to plug a hole (cannon).
spill *vti* to let run out or overflow; to shed. * *n* a piece of wood or twisted paper for lighting candle, etc; a fall.
spin *vti* to draw out and twist into threads; to protract; to whirl; to rotate swiftly. * *n* a rapid run.
spinach *n* a plant with large green edibble leaves
spinal *adj* pertaining to the spine.
spinal cord *n* the cord of nerves enclosed by the spinal column.
spindle *n* a tapering rod on which thread is wound; an axis; a yarn measure; a slender stalk.
spine *n* a prickle; a pointed spike in animals; the backbone.
spinnaker *n* a triangular sail used in running before wind.
spinster *n* an unmarried woman.
spiral *adj* winding like thread of screw. * *n* a helix or coil.
spirally *adv* in spiral fashion.
spire *n* a cone-like structure; a steeple.
spirit *n* the breath of life; the soul; a spectre; vivacity; courage; mood; essence; a volatile liquid; *pl* alcoholic liquor.
spirited *adj* lively; animated.
spiritless *adj* dejected; depressed.
spirit level *n* an instrument for testing when a thing is horizontal.
spiritual *adj* not material; mental; holy; divine.
spiritualism *n* the doctrine that soul, spirit, is only reality; belief that communication can be obtained with the dead.
spiritualist *n* one who believes in spiritualism.
spirituality *n* quality of being spiritual; spiritual nature.
spit *n* a prong on which meat is roasted; low land running into the sea. * *vt* to put on a spit; to pierce.
spit *vti* to eject from the mouth, as saliva.
spite *n* ill-will; rancour; malice.
spiteful *adj* malignant; malicious.
spittle *n* saliva.
spittoon *n* a vessel to receive discharges of spittle.
splash *vti* to bespatter with liquid matter. * *n* water or mud thrown on anything; noise of heavy body striking water; a spot of mud.
splay *vt* to slope or form with an angle. * *adj* turned outward, as a person's feet.
spleen *n* a large lymphatic organ in the upper left part of the abdomen which modifies the blood structure; spitefulness; ill humour.
splendid *adj* brilliant; showy; famous.
splendour *n* brilliancy; magnificence; grandeur.
splenetic *adj* morose; sullen; spiteful.
splice *vt* to unite, by interweaving, as ropes, or overlapping, as timber. * *n* union by interweaving or joining.
splint *n* a rigid structure to keep a broken limb in position.
splinter *n* a piece of wood split off * *vt* to split into small pieces.
split *vti* to cleave; to rend; to burst; to separate. * *n* a rent; fissure; breach. * *adj* divided; rent.
splutter *n* a confused noise; a stir. * *vi* to speak incoherently; to spit when speaking.
spoil *n* pillage; booty; plunder. * *vt* to plunder; to impair; to over indulge a child. * *vi* to grow useless; to decay.
spoke *n* one of bars or rays of a wheel; rung (of ladder). * *vi pret* of speak.
spoken *adj* oral; speaking (as in fair-spoken).

spokesman *n* one who speaks on behalf of others.

sponge *n* a plantlike marine animal with an internal skeleton of elastic interlacing horny fibres; a piece of natural or manmade sponge for washing or cleaning. **vt* to wipe with a sponge. **vi* (*inf*) to scrounge.

sponger *n* one who lives on others; a parasite.

sponsor *n* a person or organization that pays the expenses connected with an artistic production or sports event in return for advertising; in US, a business firm, etc that pays for a radio or TV programme advertising its product. **vt* to act as sponsor for.

spontaneity *n* voluntary action; readiness.

spontaneous *adj* arising naturally; instinctive.

spook *n* a ghost; an apparition. **vt* to frighten.

spool *n* a reel, esp to wind thread or yarn on.

spoon *n* a domestic utensil used in feeding or cooking.

spoor *n* the track or trail of an animal.

sporadic *adj* scattered; occurring here and there.

spore *n* the reproductive body of a flowerless plant.

sport *n* a game; good humoured joking; out-of-door recreation; jest. * *vti* to play; to trifle; to wear publicly.

sporting *adj* indulging in sport; belonging to sport.

spot *n* a speck, a blemish; a flaw; a locality. * *vt* to stain; to note.

spotless *adj* blameless; stainless.

spouse *n* a husband or wife.

spout *n* a nozzle; projecting mouth of a vessel; a waterspout. * *vti* to gush forth; to mouth one's words.

sprain *vt* to overstrain as muscles or ligaments of a joint. * *n* a violent strain of a joint.

sprawl *vi* to spread the limbs untidily.

spray *n* a twig; collection of small branches; windblown water. * *vt* to sprinkle with a fluid.

spread *vti* to stretch or expand; to distribute; to apply a coating; to emit; to diffuse. * *n* extent; a meal or banquet.

spree *n* a merry frolic; a carousal.

sprig *n* a small shoot or spray; a twig with leaves on it.

sprightly *adj* lively; gay.

spring *vi* to leap; to start up; to dart; to warp. * *vt* to cease to operate suddenly; to start or rouse. * *n* a leap; resilience; elastic spiral; an issue of water; source of supply; season of the year.

springboard *n* an flexible board used in vaulting, etc.

spring-clean*vi* to clean (a house, etc) thoroughly.

sprinkle *vti* to scatter; in small drops.

sprint *n* a short foot race; a spurt.

sprit *n* a small spar to extend and raise sail.

sprite *n* a spirit; a goblin; a dainty person.

sprout *vi* to bud; to push out new shoots. * *n* a shoot of a plant; *pl* brussels sprouts.

spruce *adj* neat; trim * *n* a pine tree yielding valuable timber.

spry *adj* nimble; active; lively.

spume*n* froth; foam; surf. **vi* to froth.

spur *n* a goad or rowel worn on horsemen's heels; a stimulus; an incentive; an outgrowth; a ridge running off from main range. * *vt* to prick with a spur; to incite.

spurious *adj* counterfeit; false.

spurn *vt* to drive away, as with the foot; to reject or treat with disdain.

spurred *adj* wearing spurs.

spurt *vti* to spirt; to exert one's whole strength (in a race). * *n* a gush of liquid; a special effort.

sputter *vi* to emit saliva in speaking; to speak hastily and indistinctly.

sputum *n* spittle.

spy *vt* to gain sight of; to explore. * *vi* to pry. * *n* a secret agent; an informer.

squabble *vi* to wrangle; to quarrel noisely. * *n* a scuffle; a brawl.

squad *n* a small group of soldiers.

squadron *n* a unit of cavalry or of a fleet.

squalid *adj* sordid; wretched; dirty.

squall *vi* to scream loudly. * *n* a loud scream; a violent gust of wind.

squalor *n* wretchedness; foulness.

squander *vt* to spend lavishly; to waste.
square *adj* having four equal sides and four right angles; forming a right angle; just; honest. * *n* a parallelogram having four equal sides and right angles; an area with houses in form of square; an instrument for drawing right angles; product of a number multiplied by itself * *vti* to make square; to adjust; to settle (accounts); to suit.
squash *vt* to crush; to beat into pulp.
squat *vi* to crouch down on the heels ; to crouch; to settle on land without authority.
squatter *n* one who settles on land or property without a title.
squawk *vi* to cry with a harsh voice; as of a bird.
squeak *vi* to utter a high pitched sound. * *n* a high pitched sound.
squeal *vi* to cry with a sharp, shrill voice. * *n* a shrill, sharp cry.
squeeze *vt* to subject to pressure; to hug. * *vi* to press; to crowd. * *n* pressure; an embrace.
squint *adj* looking obliquely. * *n* a oblique look. * *vi* to half close or cross the eyes.
squire *n* an attendant on a knight; a country gentleman. * *vt* to escort.
squirm *vi* to wriggle; to writhe.
squirrel *n* a rodent with a long bushy tail.
squirt *vt* to throw out in jets. * *vi* to spirt. * *n* a syringe; a jet.
stab *vti* to pierce with a pointed weapon; to pain suddenly and sharply. * *n* a thrust with dagger, etc; a secret injury.
stability *n* steadiness; firmness.
stable *adj* firm; steadfast. * *n* a building for horses, etc. * *vt* to put or keep in a stable.
stabling *n* accommodation for horses.
staccato *adj* in music, a sign for separate emphasis on each note.
stack *n* a large, regularly built pile of hay, records, papers, etc; a chimney head; a tall chimney. * *vt* to pile together.
stadium *n* an arena.
staff *n* (*pl* **staves, staffs**) a stick or rod; a prop or support; a baton; the five parallel lines on which musical notes are written; the officers assisting generals, etc; in any body of assistants, e.g. in schools.
stag *n* a full grown male deer.
stage *n* a raised platform, esp. for actors; a theatre; a halting place; distance between two halting places; field of action; degree of progress. * *vt* to put on the stage.
stagger *vi, vt* to reel; to totter; to amaze. * *n* a lurch; an involuntary swaying of body.
staging *n* scaffolding.
stagnant *adj* not flowing; motionless; with a foul smell; sluggish.
stagnate *vi* to cease to flow; to become foul.
stagnation *n* state of being motionless; sluggishness.
staid *adj* sober; grave; sedate.
stain *vt* to discolour; to soil; to disgrace; to dye. * *n* a discoloration; disgrace.
stainless *adj* untarnished; pure.
stair *n* a series of connected steps.
staircase *n* a flight of stairs; space occupied by stairs.
stake *n* a sharpened piece of wood; a post; that which is pledged or wagered; hazard (preceded by at). * *vt* to mark with stakes; to pledge; to wager.
stalactite *n* a mass of calcareous matter hanging from roof of cave.
stalagmite *n* a spike-like calcareous mass rising from floor of cave.
stale *adj* not fresh; musty; trite. * *vt* to make stale.
stalemate *n* a draw in chess through one player not being able to make any move except one that puts his king in check; a deadlock.
stalk *n* the stem of a plant; a strut. * *vi, vt* to walk in stately fashion; to follow game warily.
stalker *n* one who hunts (stalks) deer.
stall *n* a compartment in a stable; a bench or shed where goods are exposed for sale; a seat near orchestra in theatre; seat in chancel or choir of church. **vti* to play for time; to postpone.
stallion *n* a male horse for breeding purposes.
stalwart *adj* stout-hearted; tall and strong.
stamen *n* the organ of flower that produces pollen.

stamina *n* staying power; strength.
stammer *vi, vt* to stutter; to halt in speech. * *n* a stutter.
stamp *vti* to strike by thrusting foot down; to impress; to imprint; to affix a postage stamp to; to coin. * *n* an instrument for crushing or for making impressions; mark imprinted; a postage stamp; character; sort.
stampede *n* a sudden panicky rush (esp. of cattle). * *vi, vt* to make or cause a sudden rush.
stance *n* posture; the attitude taken in a particular situation.
stanchion *n* a supporting prop or post.
stand *vi, vt* to be erect; stop; endure; be on end; become a candidate; not to fail; pay for. * *n* a halt; station; small table; booth for exhibiting; tiered platform for spectators.
standard *n* a flag; an ensign; a rule or measure; a test; a grade; an upright.
stand-in *n* a substitute.
standing *adj* upright; erect; permanent; stagnant. * *n* rank; position.
standpoint *n* point of view; opinion.
stanza *n* a verse or connected number of lines of poetry.
staple *n* a principle commodity of trade or industry of a region, etc; a main constituent; a U-shaped thin piece of wire for fastening. **vt* to fasten with a staple.
star *n* a celestial body other than sun or moon; a figure with radiating points; a badge of honour; an asterisk; thus *; an outstanding artiste. * *vt* to adorn with stars; to bespangle. * *vi* to shine as a star; to be pre-eminent.
starboard *n, adj* the right-hand side of a ship.
starch *n* a vegetable substance, employed for stiffening linen, etc.
starched *adj* stiffened with starch; precise; formal.
stare *vi* to look fixedly. * *vt* to affect or abash by staring. * *n* a fixed look.
stargazer *n* an astronomer; an astrologer.
stark *adj* bare; plain; blunt. * *adv* wholly.
starless *adj* having no stars visible.
starlight *n* the light from the stars.
starry *adj* abounding with stars; like stars.
start *vi, vt* to spring up; to set out; to begin; to wince; to startle. * *n* a sudden movement; a jump; a handicap; outset.
starter *n* a device for starting motor engine; one who gives signal for setting off; the first course in a meal.
startle *vi* to move suddenly. * *vt* to frighten.
startling *adj* surprising; alarming.
starvation *n* state of being starved.
starve *vi* to suffer or die through lack of food. **vt* deprive (a person) of food; to deprive (of) anything necessary.
state *n* condition; situation; rank; pomp; a nation; civil power. * *adj* national; public. * *vt* to narrate.
statecraft *n* skill in managing affairs of state.
stated *adj* fixed; regular.
stately *adj* imposing; dignified; lofty.
statement *n* something stated; narrative.
statesman *n* a well-known and experienced politician.
static *adj* fixed; stationary; at rest. **n* electrical interference causing noise on radio or TV.
station *n* position; situation; rank; class; a stopping place for trains, etc. * *vt* to assign a position to.
stationary *adj* fixed; not moving.
stationery *n* paper, pens, etc.
statistic *n* a fact expressed in numbers.
statistician *n* one versed in statistics.
statue *n* an image of a human figure or animal in marble, bronze, etc. that is moulded.
statuesque *n* statue-like.
statuette *n* a small statue.
stature *n* height; tallness.
status *n* social position; rank; state of affairs.
statute *n* a law enacted by parliament.
statutory *n* enacted by statute.
staunch *adj* loyal, dependable. **vt* to stop from running (as blood).
stave *n* a pole; one of segments in side of cask; a stanza, in music, the staff * *vt* to make a hole in. *to stave off, to put off; to delay.
stay *vt* to prop; to stop; to delay; * *vt* to remain; to reside. * *n* sojourn; stop; ob-

stacle; a prop; support; in place.
steadfast *adj* firm; constant; resolute.
steady *adj* firm; constant; regular. * *vt* to make or keep firm.
steak *n* a slice of beef or fish for grilling or frying.
steal *vti* to gain secretly; to take from someone.
stealth *n* a manner of moving quietly and secretly.
steam *n* the vapour of boiling water; energy (fig.) * *vti* to emit steam; to expose to steam.
steamy *adj* damp; misty; full of condensation.
steel *n* iron hardened by addition of carbon; a knife sharpener; sternness. * *adj* made of steel; hard. * *vt* to harden; to temper.
steep *adj* sloping greatly; precipitous. * *n* a cliff * *vt* to soak.
steepen *vi* to become steep.
steeple *n* a spire; a pointed tower; usu of a church.
steeplechase *n* a race over obstacles, esp cross-country.
steer *vti* to direct and govern, as a ship; to guide. * *n* a young ox; a bullock.
stellar *adj* pertaining to stars; starry.
stem *n* the stalk of a tree, shrub, etc; stock of a family; the prow of a vessel. * *vt* to dam up; to check.
stench *n* a foul smell.
stencil *n* a thin plate with a pattern cut through it, used for marking surface beneath. * *vt* to paint by means of a stencil.
stenographer *n* one who is skilled at writing in shorthand.
stentorian *adj* loud-voiced.
step *vi* to walk. * *vt* to measure by steps; to fix a mast. * *n* a pace; a grade; a degree; a rise; footprint; rung of ladder; (*prefix*) related by remarriage of a spouse or partner.
stepladder *n* a portable self-supporting ladder.
stepping stone *n* a stone to raise the feet above a stream or mud; a means of advancement.
stereo *n* a hi-fi or record player with two loudspeakers; stereophonic sound. **adj* stereophonic sound.
stereophonic*adj* (*sound reproduction system*) using two seperate channels for recording and transmission to create a spatial effect.
stereotype *n* a fixed general image of a person or thing shared by many people.
sterile *adj* barren; unfruitful; free from bacteria.
sterility *n* barrenness; unfruitfulness; free from bacteria.
sterilize *vt* to make sterile; to rid of bacteria by boiling, etc.
sterling *adj* genuine; pure; denoting standard British money.
stern *adj* austere; harsh. * *n* the hind part of a ship.
sternum *n* the breastbone.
stertorous *adj* marked by laboured and noisy breathing.
stethoscope *n* an instrument for sounding the chest, lungs, etc.
stevedore *n* one who loads or unloads vessels.
stew *vt* to boil slowly in a closed vessel. * *vi* to be cooked slowly. * *n* meat stewed; state of anxiety.
steward, stewardess *n* one who manages affairs for another; one who helps to manage a public function; an attendant on ship or aeroplane passengers.
stick *vti* to pierce or stab; to fasten; to fix; to adhere. * *n* a rod or wand; a staff.
stickler *n* a person who is scrupulous or obstinate about something.
sticky *adj* adhesive; gluey.
stiff *adj* rigid; formal in manner; stubborn; difficult; not flexible or supple.
stiffening *n* substance used to make anything stiff.
stifle *vti* to suffocate; to suppress; to smother.
stigma *n* (*pl* **stigmas, stigmata**) a mark or brand; a mark of infamy; top of pistil of a flower.
stigmatize *vt* to hold up to reproach.
stiletto *n* a small dagger; a pointed instrument for making eyelet holes. a shoe with a long pointed heel.
still *adj* at rest; calm; silent; not carbon-

ated. * *vt* to make still; to appease or allay. * *adv* to this time; yet * *n* a distilling apparatus.

stillborn *adj* dead at birth.

still life *n* a painting of inanimate objects such as fruits, flowers, etc; objects without life.

stilt *n* either of a pair of poles, with a rest for the foot on which one can walk.

stilted *adj* pompous; unnaturally formal.

stimulant *adj* energizing. * *n* a drug that increases energy for a time; an intoxicant.

stimulate *vt* to rouse up; to incite; to spur on.

stimulating *adj* rousing; invigorating.

stimulus *n* (*pl* **stimuli**) an incentive to action; a spur; a response in a living organism.

sting *vt* to pierce, as wasps; to prick, as a nettle. * *n* a sharp-pointed defensive organ of certain animals; secreting poison (plants); any acute mental or physical pain.

stinging *adj* sharp; keen; painful.

stingy *adj* very niggardly; scanty; mean.

stink *vi* to emit a strong offensive smell. * *n* a foul smell.

stint *vt* to restrict. * *vi* to cease. * *n* limit; restriction.

stipend *n* yearly allowance; salary.

stipple *vt* to engrave by means of dots.

stipulate *vi* to specify as terms of an agreement.

stipulation *n* a condition; item in a contract.

stir *vt* to set in motion; to agitate; to rouse. * *vi* to be in motion; to be up and doing. * *n* bustle; noise.

stirring *adj* rousing; exciting.

stirrup *n* a foot support in riding.

stitch *n* a sharp pain; movement of a needle in sewing. * *vti* to join by stitches.

stoat *n* a kind of weasel, valuable for its fur.

stock *adj* a post; stem of a tree; wooden piece of a rifle; lineage; capital; shares in state funds; goods in hand; cattle; a thick gravy for soups; a garden plant; *pl* an old instrument of torture for offenders; shares; frame on which a ship is built. * *adj* standing; permanent.

stockade *n* an area fenced round for protection; an enclosure.

stockbroker *n* one who deals in stocks and shares.

stockbroking *n* the business of a stockbroker.

stockholder *n* an owner of shares.

stocking *n* a close-fitting covering for foot and leg.

stock market, stock exchange *n* place where shares are bought and sold.

stockpile *n* a reserve supply of essentials.

stocktaking *n* a periodical valuation of goods in a shop, etc.

stodgy *adj* damp; heavy; indigestible.

stoic *n* one indifferent to pleasure or pain; one imperturbable and serene whatever fortune brings.

stoicism *n* impassiveness; serenity of spirit.

stoke *vt* to stir and keep supplied with fuel, as a fire.

stole *n* a vestment worn round neck and with hanging ends.

stolid *adj* dull; unresponsive.

stomach *n* the principal organ of digestion; appetite.

stone *n* a hard mass of earthy or mineral matter; a pebble; concretion in the kidneys or bladder; the nut of a fruit; a measure of 14 lbs/6.35kg. * *vt* to pelt with stones; to free from stones.

stony *adj* abounding in or like stone; hard; frigid; unfeeling.

stool *n* a portable seat, without a back, for one person; matter evacuated from the bowels.

stoop *vi* to bend forward and downward; to yield; to condescend. * *n* a downward bend of body; a veranda; a flagon.

stop *vti* to halt; to hinder or check; to suspend; to close up; to stay; * *n* pause; punctuation mark; device for regulating musical sounds.

stopcock *n* a tap to regulate flow of water, gas, etc.

stopgap *n* a temporary expedient.

stoppage *n* a halt.

stopper *n* that which closes a small vent or hole.

stopwatch *n* a watch that can be started and stopped instantaneously.
storage *n* act of storing; charge for storing goods; the storage of goods in a computer memory.
store *n* a large quantity for supply; a warehouse; abundance. * *vt* to amass; to hoard up.
storeroom *n* a room for reception of stores.
storey *n* a floor of a building, also story.
stork *n* a large heron-like bird.
storm *n* a heavy fall of rain, snow etc. with strong winds; tempest; a tumult. * *vti* to assail; to take by assault; to rage.
stormy *adj* tempestuous; violent.
story *n* a narrative; a tale; a fiction; a falsehood.
stout *adj* bold; valiant; corpulent. * *n* a dark-brown malt liquor.
stove *n* an apparatus for warming a room, cooking, etc.
stow *vt* to store; to pack closely.
stowaway *n* one who hides himself on a ship to avoid paying the fare.
straddle *vt* to have one leg or support on either side of something.
straggle *vi* to stray; to be scattered.
straggler *n* one who wanders from main body; a laggard.
straight *adj* continuing in one direction, not curved or bent; not crooked; upright.
straighten *vt* to make straight.
straightforward *adj* honest; open.
strain *vti* to stretch tightly; to exert to the utmost; to sprain; to filter. * *n* violent effort; tenor; theme; a poem; tune; race.
strained *adj* overstretched; forced or unnatural.
strainer *n* a filter or sieve.
strait *adj* confined; narrow; strict. * *n* a narrow passage of water; distress (often *pl*).
straiten *vt* to make narrow; to embarrass; to distress.
straitjacket *n* a strong garment used to bind arms of violent people to their bodies.
strait-laced *adj* puritanical; strict in morals.
strand *n* the shore; beach; a single peice of thread or wire twisted to make a rope or cable. * *vti* to drive or be driven ashore; to leave helpless without transport or money.
strange *adj* foreign; wonderful; odd.
stranger *n* a foreigner; an alien; a visitor.
strangle *vt* to choke; to throttle.
strangulate *vt* to strangle; to stop circulation by pressure.
strangulation *n* compression of the windpipe; constriction.
strap *n* a narrow band of leather, metal, cloth, etc; a razor strop. * *vt* to fasten with strap.
strapping *adj* tall and well made.
stratagem *n* a device or plan to deceive an enemy; a ruse.
strategic, strategical *adj* pertaining to strategy.
strategy *n* the planning and conduct of war; a political, economic, or business policy.
stratification *n* arrangement in layers.
stratify *vt* to form or deposit in strata.
stratum *n* (*pl* **strata**) a layer of rock, earth, etc.
stratus *n* a low horizontal layer of clouds.
straw *n* the stalk of threshed grain, pulse, etc.
stray *vi* to wander; to err. * *adj* strayed; straggling.
streak *n* a long mark of contrasting colour; a stripe. * *vt* to mark with streaks.
stream *n* a small river or brook; a current. * *vi*, *vt* to move in a stream; issue forth.
streamer *n* a banner; a long decorative ribbon.
streamline *vt* to shape (a car, boat etc.) in a way that lessens resistance through air or water; to make more efficient; to simplify.
street *n* a road in a town, village or city lined with trees.
strength *n* force or energy; power; numbers of an army, fleet, etc. * On the strength of, in reliance upon.
strenuous *adj* earnest; energetic; vigorous.
stress *vt* to emphasize. * *n* pressure; mental or physical tension; emphasis.

stretch *vti* to draw out tight; to extend; to strain; to exaggerate. * *n* strain; scope; expanse.
stretcher *n* a portable frame for carrying sick or wounded.
strew *vt* to spread by scattering; to scatter loosely.
stricken *pp* of **strike**; smitten; afflicted, as by something painful.
strickle *n* a hone; a grindstone.
strict *adj* rigid in enforcing rules; exact; severe.
stricture *n* an unnatural contraction of throat, intestines, etc; censure.
stride *vi* to walk with long steps. * *n* a long step.
strident *adj* harsh; grating.
strife *n* conflict; discord; quarrel.
strike *vi* to hit with force; to sound (clock); to cease work to enforce a demand for better conditions. * *vt* to smite; to mint; to come sharply against; to lower (flag); to take down (tent). * *n* a cessation of work; a military attack.
striking *adj* surprising; impressive.
string *n* a slender cord; twine; a series; cord or wire of musical instrument. * *vt* to thread on a string.
stringency *n* severity; pressure.
stringent *adj* strict; severe; binding.
strip *vt* to lay bare; to skin. * *vi* to undress. * *n* a long narrow piece.
stripe *n* a streak; a band; a lash; a weal.
stripper*n* a striptease artist; device or solvent that removes paint.
strive *vi* to endeavour; to struggle; to vie.
stroke *n* a blow; calamity; attack; striking of a clock; touch; a line; a gentle rub; the sweep of an oar; the aft-most rower who sets time to others. * *vt* to rub gently with hand.
stroll *vi* to ramble; to saunter. * *n* a short leisurely walk.
strong *adj* powerful; robust; firm; forcible; ardent.
stronghold *n* a fort; a keep; a centre of strength or support.
strongroom *n* a room where valuables are kept.
strop *n* a strip of leather for sharpening razors, etc.
structural *adj* pertaining to structure.
structure *n* a building of any kind; manner of building; make; form; organization.
struggle *vi* to strive; to contend. * *n* a violent effort; contest; strife.
strum *vi, vt* to play noisily on a stringed instrument.
strut *vi* to walk with affected dignity. * *n* a pompous gait; a support for a rafter or framework.
strychnine *n* a highly poisonous alkaloid.
stubble *n* the stumps of cornstalks left after reaping.
stubborn *adj* obstinate; wilful; mulish; dogged.
stucco *n* a fine plaster; work made of stucco.
stuck-up *adj* giving one's self airs; proud; pompous.
stud *n* a post; a nail with a large head; an ornamental button; a set of breeding horses.
student *n* a scholar; one given to study.
studied *adj* deliberate; well-considered.
studio *n* the workplace of a painter or sculptor; a building or room where motion pictures are made or TV and radio programmes are recorded.
studious *adj* given to study; earnest.
study *n* application to learning; subject studied; room set apart for study; thought, reflexion. * *vti* to apply mind to; to investigate; to reflect on.
stuff *n* material; textile fabrics; trash. * *vti* to pack; to cram.
stuffing *n* padding; seasoning packed into meat, fowls, etc, in cooking.
stuffy *adj* close; stifling; poorly ventilated.
stultify *vi, vt* to make ineffectual or foolish.
stumble *vi* to trip; to err; to light on by chance. * *n* a stagger; trip.
stump *n* part of felled tree left standing; part of limb left after amputation; a wicket (cricket). * *vt* to lop; to dismiss batsman off his ground; to pay (up).
stun *vt* to make senseless; to stupefy; to amaze.
stunning *adj* strikingly attractive.
stunt *vt* to dwarf * *n* a check in growth; a

showy turn; a feat of strength or skill.
stunted *adj* dwarfed.
stupefaction *n* insensibility; amazement.
stupefy *vt* to astound; to dull the senses.
stupendous *adj* immense; awe-inspiring.
stupid *adj* foolish; dull-witted.
stupidity *n* dullness of mind; folly.
stupor *n* torpor; insensibility.
sturdy *adj* stout; strong; hardy.
stutter *vi* to stammer. * *n* a stammer.
sty *n* a pen for swine; a foul place.
sty, stye *n* a small swelling on edge of eyelid.
style *n* manner of doing anything; title; fashion. * *vt* to designate; to term.
stylish *adj* fashionable.
stylist *n* a master of style.
stylus *n* the component in a record player which contacts with the grove of a record and transmits sound to the amplifier.
suave *adj* gracious in manner; pleasant.
sub *n* (*inf*) a submarine; a sustitute; a subscription; a subeditor. **prefix* under, below; subordinate, next in rank to.
subconscious *adj* happening without one's awareness. **n* the part of the mind that is active without one's conscious awareness.
subcutaneous *adj* immediately below the skin.
subdivide *vt* to divide into smaller parts.
subduce, subduct *vt* to take away; to subtract.
subdue *vt* to overcome; to overpower; to tone down.
subeditor *n* an under or assistant editor.
subject *adj* ruled by another; liable. * *n* one who owes allegiance to a ruler or government; theme; topic; the nominative of a verb. * *vt* to subdue; to expose.
subjection *n* authority; control.
subjective *adj* relating to the conscious subject; opposed to objective.
subjugate *vt* to subdue; to conquer.
subjunctive *adj, n* the mood of a verb which expresses condition, hypothesis, doubt.
sublet *vt* to let to another person what oneself holds as tenant.
sublime *adj* awe-inspiring; noble; majestic. * The sublime, the awe-inspiring in the works of nature or of art, as opposed to the beautiful.
subliminal *adj* under the threshold of consciousness; subconscious.
sublimity *n* loftiness of style or feeling; grandeur.
submarine *adj* being under surface of the sea. * *n* a submersible boat.
submerge *vti* to put under water; to sink.
submersed *adj* being or growing under water.
submersible *adj* capable of being submerged and propelled under water. * *n* a submarine.
submission *n* surrender; obedience; resignation.
submissive *adj* humble, compliant.
submit *vti* to yield or surrender; to refer to another's judgment; to suffer without complaint.
subordinate *adj* secondary; lower in rank. * *n* one who ranks below another. * *vt* to place in a lower rank.
subordination *n* inferiority of rank; subjection.
subpoena *n* a summons to give evidence in law court.
subscribe *vt* to pay to receive regular copies (of a magazine, etc.); to donate money (to a charity, campaign); to support or agree with (an opinion, faith).
subscriber *n* a contributor.
subscript *adj* written below.
subscription *n* sum subscribed to receive copies (of a magazine) or to be a member of a club.
subsection *n* a division of a section.
subsequent *adj* following; next.
subserviencen servility; obseqiousness.
subservient *adj* serving to further some end; helpful; servile; inferior.
subside *vi* to sink or fall to the bottom; to abate; to settle.
subsidence *n* a sinking down of land or sea; a landslip.
subsidiary *adj* minor; subordinate; supplementary.
subsidize *vt* to assist with money; to purchase help by a subsidy.
subsidy *n* government financial aid to a private person or company to assist an

enterprise.
subsist *vi* to have existence; to live.
subsistence *n* existence; livelihood.
subsoil *n* the stratum of earth just below surface.
substance *n* that of which a thing consists; material; a body; essence.
substantial *adj* of considerable value or style; real; solid; strong.
substantiate *vt* to give proof for; to verify.
substantive *adj* expressing existence; real. * *n* a noun.
substitute *vt* to put in the place of another; to exchange. * *n* a deputy.
substructure *n* a foundation; basis.
subterfuge *n* an artifice; evasion.
subterranean *adj* underground.
subtile *adj* subtle; thin; fine.
subtitle *n* an explanatory, usu secondary, title of a book; a printed translation superimposed on a foreign language film.
subtle *adj* thin; acute; sly; artful.
subtlety *n* nicety of distinction.
subtract *vt* to take from; to deduct.
subtraction *n* the taking of a number from a greater.
suburb *n* an outlying residential part of a city.
suburban *adj* situated in the suburbs.
subvention *n* a government grant; a subsidy.
subversion *n* the act of undermining the authority of a government or institution.
subversive *adj* destructive.
subvert *vt* to ruin utterly; to overturn.
subway *n* an underground passage.
succeed *vt* to follow in order; to come after. * *vi* to ensue; to become heir; to accomplish what is attempted.
success *n* favourable result; good fortune.
successful *adj* prosperous; fortunate.
succession *n* a following in order; lineage.
successive *adj* coming in succession; consecutive.
successor *n* one who succeeds or follows another.
succinct *adj* brief; concise.
succour *vt* to help when in difficulty; to aid. * *n* aid; help.
succulent *adj* full of sap; juicy.
succumb *vi* to yield; to submit.
such *adj* of like kind or degree; similar.
suck *vti* to draw (liquid, etc) into the mouth. * *n* milk drawn from breast.
sucker *n* a person who is easily taken in or deceived.
suckle *vt* to nurse at the breast.
suckling *n* an unweaned child or animal.
suction *n* act of sucking; the sucking up of a fluid by exhaustion of air.
sucrose *n* sugar.
sudden *adj* happening without warning; abrupt.
sue *vt* to bring a legal action against.
suet *n* white, solid fat in animal tissue, used in cooking.
suffer *vt* to endure; to permit. * *vi* to undergo pain.
sufferance *n* endurance of pain; passive consent.
suffering *n* the bearing of pain; distress.
suffice *vi* to be sufficient. * *vt* to satisfy.
sufficiency *n* an ample supply; competence.
sufficient *adj* adequate; enough.
suffix *n* a letter or syllable affixed to the end of a word.
suffocate *vti* to stifle; to choke; to be stifled.
suffrage *n* a vote; right of voting; the franchise.
suffuse *vt* to spread over or fill, as with colour or light.
sugar *n* a sweet granular substance, manufactured from sugar cane, maple, beet, etc. * *vt* to sweeten.
sugary *adj* sweet; flattering.
suggest *vt* to hint; to propose; to intimate.
suggestion *n* a hint; a tentative proposal.
suggestive *adj* hinting at; stimulating; prompting thought; rather indecent; risqué.
suicidal *adj* fatal; self-destructive.
suicide *n* self-murder or self-murderer.
suit *n* a petition; a courtship; an action at law; a set of matching garments. * *vti* to adapt; to fit; to satisfy.
suitable *adj* fitting; appropriate; becoming.
suite *n* a retinue; a set, as of rooms.
suitor *n* a wooer.

sulk *vi* to be sullen or pettish.
sulky *adj* sullen; morose.
sullen *adj* ill-natured; morose; sour; dismal.
sully *vti* to soil; to tarnish.
sulphur *n* brimstone; a yellow nonmetallic element.
sulphurous *adj* impregnated with sulphur; like sulphur.
sultry *adj* very hot; oppressive.
sum *n* the whole; aggregate; essence; substance; quantity of money; arithmetical problem *vt* to add up; to review main facts.
summarize *vt* to set forth main facts; to make an abstract or outline.
summary *adj* concise; brief; dispensing with formalities. * *n* an abridged account; an abstract.
summation *n* addition; aggregate.
summer *n* the warmest season of year; between spring and autumn.
summit *n* the top; highest point.
summon *vt* to call by authority; to cite to appear in court.
summons *n* a notice to appear, esp. in court; an earnest call.
sumptuous *adj* very costly; magnificent.
sun *n* the star around which the earth and other planets revolve which gives light and heat to the solar system; the sunshine. **vt* to expose oneself to the sun's rays.
sunbeam *n* a ray of the sun.
sunburn *vt* inflamation of the skin from exposure to the sun.
Sunday *n* the day after Saturday; the Christian day of worship; the Christian Sabbath.
sunder *vt* to part; to separate.
sundial *n* an instrument to show time by shadow cast by sun.
sundry *adj* miscellaneous; various.
sunglasses *npl* tinted glasses to protect the eyes from sunlight.
sunlit *adj* lit by the sun.
sunny *adj* like the sun; brilliant; bright or cheerful.
sunrise *n* first appearance of sun in morning.
sunset *n* descent of sun below horizon.
sunshine *n* the light of the sun; warmth; brightness.
sunstroke *n* acute illness caused by over exposure to sun's rays.
sup *vt* to sip; to imbibe. * *vi* to take supper. * *n* a sip; a small mouthful.
super*adj* (*inf*) fantastic; excellent; (*inf*) a superintendent, as in the police. **n* a variety of high octane fuel.
superannuation *n* regular contributions from employee's wages towards a pension scheme.
superb *adj* magnificent; grand; of the highest quality.
supercilious *adj* haughty; scornful; disdainful.
superficial *adj* being on the surface; shallow.
superfluous *adj* needless; redundant.
superhuman *adj* more than human.
superimpose *vt* to lay upon something else.
superintend *vt* to supervise; direct; manage.
superior *adj* higher; better; preferable. * *n* one higher in rank; head of monastery, convent.
superiority *n* pre-eminence.
superlative *adj* highest in degree; supreme. * *n* the highest degree of adjectives or adverbs.
supermarket *n* a large, self-service shop selling food and household goods.
supernatural *adj* that which cannot be explained by nature.
superpower*n* a nation with great economic and military strength.
superscribe *vt* to write upon or over.
supersede *vt* to set aside; displace; supplant.
supersensitive *adj* oversensitive.
supersonic*adj* faster than the speed of sound.
superstition *n* credulity in regard to the supernatural; a belief without reason.
superstitious *adj* credulous.
superstructure *n* anything resting on a foundation; a building.
supervise *vt* to oversee and direct; to superintend.
supervision *n* oversight.

supine *adj* lying on the back; indolent. * *n* a part of the Latin verb.
supper *n* the evening meal.
supplant *vt* to supersede; to oust, esp. by craft.
supple *adj* pliant; flexible.
supplement *n* an addition; appendix. * *vt* to make additions to.
supplicant *adj* suppliant. * *n* one who begs earnestly for some favour.
supplication *n* earnest prayer; entreaty.
supply *vt* to furnish; to satisfy. * *n* store; *pl* stores; money provided for government expenses; a substitute.
support *vt* to uphold; to prop; to maintain; to endure; to back up. * *n* a prop; aid; maintenance.
supporter *n* a defender; adherent; prop.
suppose *vt* to assume; to imagine; to imply; to expect.
supposition *n* assumption; surmise.
suppress *vt* to put down; to quell; to conceal; to crush.
suppression *n* concealment; stoppage.
suppressive *adj* tending to suppress.
suppurate *vi* to form or discharge pus.
suppuration *n* a gathering of pus.
supremacy *n* supreme authority.
supreme *adj* highest in authority; sovereign; paramount.
surcharge *vt* to overload. * *n* an excessive load; an overcharge; unauthorized expenditure of public bodies and charged against members.
sure *adj* certain; positive; unfailing; stable.
surety *n* security against loss, etc; guarantee; bail.
surf *n* the swell of sea breaking on shore.
surface *n* the outside part of anything; external appearance.
surfeit *n* an excess of food or drink; satiety. * *vti* to feed to excess.
surge *n* the swelling of a wave; a billow. * *vi* to swell; to heave.
surgeon *n* a medical man skilled in surgery.
surgery *n* the operative branch of medical practice; a doctor's consulting room.
surgical *adj* pertaining to surgery.
surly *adj* morose; churlish.
surmise *n* a supposition; conjecture. * *vt* to guess; to suspect.
surmount *vt* to rise above; to overcome.
surname *n* the family name of an individual.
surpass *vt* to go beyond; to excel.
surplus *n, adj* excess beyond what is required; balance.
surprise *n* act of taking unawares; astonishment. * *vt* to take unawares; to startle; to astonish.
surprising *adj* amazing; remarkable.
surrender *vt* to deliver up; to resign; to cede. * *n* a yielding or giving up. * *vt* to yield.
surreptitious *adj* done by stealth; underhand.
surrogate *n* a person or thing substituting for another person or thing, esp bearing a child.
surround *vt* to encompass.
surrounding *n* an environment; generally in *pl.*
surveillance *n* a keeping watch over; oversight.
survey *vt* to oversee; to inspect; to measure and value as land, etc. * *n* a general view; examination; plan.
surveying *n* the art or practice of measuring land.
surveyor *n* a measurer; an inspector.
survival *n* a living or continuing longer; a relic or custom of the past.
survive *vt*to outlive; to outlast; to endure.
susceptible *adj* easily affected; sensitive.
suspect *vt* to mistrust; to conjecture. * *n* a suspected person.
suspend *vt* to hang; to postpone; to discontinue; to debar tempoarily from a privelege, etc.
suspender *n* a supporting strap or brace.
suspense *n* uncertainty; anxiety.
suspension *n* abeyance; temporary cessation of office; postponement; (chem) a dispersion of fine particles in a liquid.
suspension bridge *n* a bridge suspended by cables anchored to towers at either end.
suspensory *adj* giving support.
suspicion *n* act of suspecting; mistrust; a belief held or formed without sure proof;

a trace.

suspicious *adj* mistrustful; doubtful.

sustain *vt* to hold up or support; maintain; endure.

sustenance *n* nourishment.

suture *n* a seam; the line of junction of bones of skull; the stitching of a wound.

swab *n* a wad of aborbant material, usu cotton, used to clean wounds, take specimens, etc; a mop. * *vt* to clean with a swab.

swaddle *vt* to swathe; to bind tight with clothes.

swagger *vt* to strut; to bluster. * *n* swinging gait.

swallow *vt* to receive through the gullet into the stomach; to engulf; to accept without question. * *n* a well-known migratory bird; gullet.

swamp *n* a bog; a fen. * *vt* to overwhelm; to capsize, as a boat.

swap *vt* to barter; to exchange.

swarm *n* a multitude, esp. of insects. * *vi* to throng together; to leave hive in a body; to climb a tree, etc.

swarthy *adj* tawny; dark-complexioned.

swashbuckler *n* an adventurous person.

swath *n* a line of mown grass or grain; sweep of a scythe.

swathe *vt* to wrap around, as with a bandage.

sway *vi* to move backwards and forwards; to vacillate in judgement or opinion * *n* influence; control.

swear *vi, vt* to make a solemn declaration; to curse; to use obscene language.

sweat *n* perspiration; labour. * *vi, vt* to emit moisture through pores.

sweater *n* a knitted pullover.

sweaty *adj* moist with sweat.

sweep *vt* to remove(rubbish, dirt) with a brush; to carry along. * *vi* to pass with swiftness or pomp; to move with a long reach. * *n* reach; range; rapid survey; one who sweeps chimneys.

sweeping *adj* comprehensive.

sweepstake *n* a gamble in which the stakes go to drawers of winning horses, etc.

sweet *adj* agreeable to the taste; having taste of honey or sugar; fragrant; melodious; kind; gentle. * *n* a dessert; *pl* confectionery.

sweetheart *n* a lover.

swell *vi* to grow larger; to heave; to bulge out. * *vt* to expand. * *n* gradual increase; a rise of ground; a wave of surge.

swelling *adj* inflamation.

swelter *vi* to be overcome with heat; to perspire.

swerve *vi* to turn aside; to alter course suddenly.

swift *adj* speedy; fleet; prompt. *n* a species of swallow.

swig *n* a long drink, esp from a bottle.

swill *vi* to drink greedily; to rinse with a large amount of water.* *n* a liquid refuse fed to pigs.

swim *vi* to float; to move through water; to be dizzy. * *vt* to pass by swimming. * *n* act of swimming.

swimmingly *adv* smoothly; with great success.

swindle *vt* to cheat. * *n* a gross fraud.

swindler *n* a cheat.

swine *n sing, pl* a pig; *pl* pigs collectively.

swing *vi* to move to and fro; to turn round at anchor; to change opinion or preference. * *vt* to achieve; to bring about. * *n* sweep of a body; rhythm; apparatus for swinging on; free course; a form of jazz music.

swipe *vti* to strike with sweeping blow. * *n* a sweeping blow.

swirl *vi* to turn with a whirling motion.

swish *vt* to move with a soft, whistling sound.* *n* swishing sound.

switch *n* a sudden change; a swap; a device for changing the course of an electric current. * *vt* to change.

swivel *n* a coupling that permits parts to rotate. * *vt* to turn as if on a pivot.

swoon *vi* to faint.

swoop *vi* to dart upon prey from a height. * *n* the pounce or dart as of a hawk.

sword *n* a weapon with a long blade and a handle at one end.

sworn *adj* bound by oath.

sycophant *n* a person who flatters to win favor.

syllable *n* a sound or combination of sounds uttered with one effort.

syllabus *n* an outline or summary, esp of a course of study.

sylph *n* a slender, graceful female.

sylviculture *n* forestry.

symbol *n* a sign; an emblem; a type; a figure.

symbolism *n* the lavish use of symbolic language.

symbolize *vt* to represent by a symbol; to typify.

symmetry *n* the corresponding arrangement of one part to another in size, shape and position.

sympathetic*adj* compassionate; showing sympathy.

sympathy *n* fellow feeling; compassion.

symphonist *n* a composer of symphonies.

symphony *n* unison of sound; an orchestral piece of music.

symposium *n* (*pl* **symposia**) a discussion (oral or written) on some subject by experts.

symptom *n* a bodily sensation indicative of a particular disease; an indication.

symptomatic *adj* indicative; relating to symptoms.

synagogue *n* a place where Jews assemble for worship and religious study.

synchronize *vi, vt* to agree or make to agree in time.

synchronous *adj* happening at the same time; simultaneous.

syncopate *vt* to contract words by omission of middle letters; in music, to pass from one bar to another by a slur.

syncopation *n* word shortening; interruption of musical rhythm.

syndicate *n* a company formed for a special purpose.

synonym *n* a word having same meaning as another.

synonymous *adj* of similar meaning; interchangeable.

synopsis *n* a summary.

syntax *n* correct arrangement of words in sentences.

synthesis *n* the combining of parts to make a whole.

synthetic*adj* inflectional; artificially produced.

syringe *n* a hollow tube with a plunger and a sharp needle at either end by which liquids are injected or withdrawn, esp in medicine. * *vt* to inject or cleanse with a syringe.

syrup *n* a thick sweet substance made by boiling sugar with water; the concentrated juice of a fruit or plant.

system *n* a method of working or organizing by following a set of rules; the body as a functional unity; a plan; method.

T

tab *n* a small flap; a tag.

table *n* an article of furniture with flat surface set on legs; fare; persons round the table; a list or index. * *vt* to lay on a table.

tableau *n* (*pl* **tableaux**) a picture; a striking group or dramatic scene.

table d'hôte *n* dinner served in hotel or restaurant at fixed price.

tableland *n* a plateau; a region of elevated flat land.

tablet *n* a set of ivory or paper slips for memoranda; a slab bearing an inscription; a small cake, as of soap, etc.

tabloid *n* a small format newspaper.

taboo *n* a ban or prohibition. * *vt* to forbid approach to or use of.

tabular *adj* in form of a table; flat.

tacit *adj* implied, but not expressed; silent.

taciturn *adj* of few words; silent.

tack *n* a small nail; a stitch; course of a ship as regards the wind. * *vt* to fasten by tacks; to attach slightly. * *vi* to change course of a ship to catch the wind.

tackle *n* gear or apparatus; pulleys, ropes, rigging. * *vt* to grapple with; to seize.

tact *n* fineness of touch; judgment; taste; adroitness.

tactical *adj* pertaining to tactics.

tactics *npl* stratagem; ploy; the science and art of military manoeuvring.

tactile *adj* having the sense of touch.

tactless *adj* lacking tact.

taffeta *n* a silk fabric.

tag *n* a metallic point to end of a lace; an appendage; a catchword.

tail *n* appendage to hinder part of animal's body; hinder part; reverse of a coin.

tailor *n* a maker of clothes, esp.. for men.

taint *vt* to defile; to infect. * *vi* to be infected. * *n* infection; a stain.

take *vti* to receive or accept; to capture; to understand; to employ; to be infected; to bear; to conduct.

taking *adj* alluring; attracting.

talc *n* a smooth mineral used in ceramics and talcum powder.

talent *n* any innate or special aptitude.

talisman *n* a charm; a mascot.

talk *vi* to utter words; to converse. * *vt* to discuss. * *n* familiar conversation; rumour; discussion.

talkative *adj* garrulous; fond of talking.

tall *adj* high in stature; lofty.

talon *n* the claw of a bird of prey.

tambourine *n* a percussion instrument.

tame *adj* domesticated; spiritless; insipid. * *vt* to make tame; to subdue.

tamper *vi* to meddle or interfere; to use bribery.

tampon *n* a plug of absorbant material inserted in the vagina during menstruation.

tan *vt* to convert into leather, as skins; to make sunburnt. * *n* bark used for tanning.

tandem *adv* one behind another. * *n* a pair of horses yoked single file; a bicycle with riders single file.

tang *n* a taste; characteristic flavour; part of tool which fits into handle.

tangent *n* a straight line touching a circle but not cutting it.

tangible *adj* perceptible to touch; real; actual.

tangle *vt* to interweave; to involve. * *n* a knot; a muddle; complication.

tango *n* a Latin American ballroom dance.

tank *n* a large cistern; a reservoir; a covered armoured car with caterpillar wheels and containing men and weaponry.

tankard *n* a large drinking vessel with a lid.

tannery *n* a place for tanning leather.

tanning *n* process of converting hides into leather.

tantalize *vt* to torment by raising false hopes.

tantamount *adj* equal; equivalent.

tantrum *n* a fit of bad temper.

tap *n* pipe for drawing off liquor; a spigot; a stopper or plug; a touch. * vti to broach; to strike lightly.

tape *n* a narrow band of linen; magnetic tape, as in an audio cassette or videotape.

taper *n* a long wick coated with wax. * *adj* narrowing to a point. * *vt* to narrow to a point.

tapestry *n* rich woven hangings of wool and silk, with pictorial representations.

tapeworm *n* a long tape-like worm found sometimes in intestines.

taproot *n* main root of a plant.

tar *n* a thick, dark, viscous substance obtained from pine, coal, etc; a sailor. * *vt* to smear with tar.

tarantella *n* a lively Italian dance.

tardily *adv* slowly.

tardy *adj* slow; late; backward.

target *n* a circular shield; a shooting mark or butt.

tariff *n* a schedule of dutiable goods; a scale of charges.

tarnish *vti* to sully; to dim.

tarpaulin *n* canvas covered with tar.

tarry *vi* to stay; to delay. * *vt* to wait for.

tart *adj* sharp to the taste; acid; snappish. * *n* a small fruit pie.

tartan *n* a woollen checkered cloth of many colours.

task *n* a piece of work imposed by another; lesson to be learned; toil. * *vt* to burden.

tassel *n* a small ornament with hanging threads.

taste *vti* to perceive flavour of by tongue or palate; to partake slightly of; to experience; to have a flavour. * *n* flavour; trial; sample; discernment; good style.

tasteful *adj* showing good taste.

tasteless *adj* stale; void of taste.

tasty *adj* savoury; palatable.

tatter *n* a loose hanging rag.

tattle *vi* to talk idly; to gossip. * *n* idle talk.

tattoo *n* military call to quarters; military exhibition. * *vt* to prick ink into skin.
taunt *vt* to reproach; to upbraid. * *n* a bitter reproach.
Taurus *n* the Bull, one of twelve signs of zodiac.
taut *adj* tight; stretched.
tautology *n* repetition of same meaning in different words.
tavern *n* an inn.
tawdry *adj* showy but inelegant.
tawny *adj* tan-coloured; yellowish-brown.
tax *n* a charge made by government on property, income, etc; a burdensome duty. * *vt* to place tax on; to accuse.
taxation *n* act of levying taxes; the aggregate of taxes.
taxidermy *n* the art of stuffing animals.
tea *n* dried leaves of an Eastern shrub; beverage made from them.
teach *vti* to instruct; to inform; to give instruction.
teacher *n* one who teaches; a schoolmaster.
teaching *n* act or business of instructing.
teak *n* an Indian tree producing hard durable timber.
team *n* a brood; a litter; two or more draught animals harnessed together; a side in a game, match, etc.
tear *n* a drop of water appearing in, or falling from, the eye.
tear *vti* to pull in pieces; to wound; to pull with violence. * *n* a rent.
tease *vt* to pull apart fibres of; to torment.
teat *n* the nipple.
technical *adj* pertaining to arts, crafts, or sciences.
technicality *n* something peculiar to a special art, craft, etc.
technique *n* manner of artistic execution; manipulative skill.
technology *n* the science of the industrial arts.
techy, tetchy *adj* peevish; fretful.
tedious *adj* tiresome; fatiguing.
tedium *n* irksomeness.
tee *n* the target in quoits, curling, etc; the starting place for each hole in golf.
teem *vi* to pour (with rain); to be prolific.
teeming *adj* fruitful; prolific.
teens *npl* the years of one's age having ending teen.
teeth *npl* of tooth.
teethe *vi* to cut one's first teeth.
teetotal *adj* totally abstaining from intoxicants.
telegram *n* a telegraphic message.
telegraph *n* a contrivance for sending messages to a distance, esp.. by electricity, and with or without wires. * *vt* to send a telegraph.
telepathy *n* the transference of thought from mind to mind without aid of senses.
telephone *n* an instrument transmitting sound to a distance by electricity. * *vt* to transmit by telephone.
telescope *n* an optical instrument for viewing distant objects.
television *n* the transmission of visual images and sound via electrical and sound waves; a television receiving set; television broadcasting.
tell *vti* to number; to relate; to explain; to report; to inform; to bid.
teller *n* a bank clerk in charge of cash; one appointed to count votes.
telling *adj* very effective.
telltale *adj* revealing; informative. * *n* a blabber; a betrayer of secrets.
temerity *n* contempt of danger; rashness.
temper *vt* to mix in due proportion; to moderate; to harden. * *n* due mixture; disposition of mind; passion; mood; quality.
temperament *n* disposition; nature.
temperance *n* moderation, esp. in regard to alchoholic drink.
temperate *adj* moderate; calm.
temperature *n* degree of heat or cold.
tempered *adj* disposed; hardened, as steel.
tempest *n* a violent storm.
tempestuous *adj* very stormy; violent.
temple *n* a place of worship; a church; side of head above either cheekbone.
tempo *n* musical time.
temporal *adj* pertaining to time; secular; worldly; civil, secular.
temporarily *adv* for a time only; provisionally.
temporary *adj* lasting but for a time; provisional.

temporize *vi* to hedge; to wait and see; to trim.
tempt *vt* to entice; to put to test; to allure into evil.
temptation *n* enticement to evil.
tempting *adj* attractive; alluring.
ten *adj, n* the number next after nine.
tenable *adj* able to be held; defensible; sound.
tenacious *adj* holding fast; unyielding; tough; stubborn.
tenacity *n* doggedness; toughness.
tenancy *n* a holding land, etc, as a tenant.
tenant *n* an occupier who pays rent.
tend *vi* to incline; trend; aim * *vt* to attend; guard; to look after.
tendency *n* inclination; bias; proneness.
tender *n* a small vessel carrying stores, etc, to larger one; the part of a locomotive carrying fuel and water; an offer; an estimate. * *vt* to offer or present; to send in an estimate. * *adj* fragile; delicate; sensitive; compassionate; weak.
tendon *n* a sinew; fibrous band joining muscles to bones.
tendril *n* a slender, twining shoot by which some plants cling or climb.
tenebrous *adj* dark;gloomy.
tenement *n* block of buildings divided into separate houses.
tenet *n* a doctrine, opinion, or dogma.
tenfold *adj* ten times more.
tennis *n* a game with balls and rackets.
tenon *n* the end of piece of wood shaped to fit into mortise or hole in another piece.
tenor *n* a prevailing course; purport; drift; higher of two kinds of men's voices; one with tenor voice.
tense *n* verbal inflection to express time. * *adj* stretched tight; strained.
tensile *adj* of or relating to tension; stretchable.
tension *n* act of stretching; tightness; strain; anxiety.
tensor *n* a muscle that extends or tightens a part.
tent *n* a portable shelter of canvas.
tentacle *n* a thread-like organ of various animals, serving as limb or feeler.
tentative *adj* experimental.
tenterhook *n* one of hooks on cloth-stretching frame. *(with on) in a state of anxiety or suspense.
tenth *adj* ordinal number of 10.
tenuity *n* thinness; rarity.
tenuous *adj* thin; slender.
tenure *n* a holding or conditions of holding land, office etc.
tepid *adj* lukewarm.
tercentenary *adj* comprising three hundred years. * *n* the three-hundredth anniversary.
term *n* a limit; boundary; period of session, etc; rent day; a word; *pl* conditions. * *vt* to name; to call.
terminable *adj* capable of being ended or bounded.
terminal *adj* pertaining to the end. * *n* an extremity; the clamping screw at each end of a voltaic battery; computer keyboard and monitor.
terminate *vti* to bound; to limit; to end.
terminology *n* the terms special to science, art, etc.
terminus *n* (*pl* **termini**) a boundary; a limit; end of a transport line.
terrace *n* a raised level bank of earth; a row of houses.
terracotta *n* a reddish-brown pottery or its colour.
terrestrial *adj* pertaining to the earth; worldly.
terrible *adj* awful; terrifying.
terrific *adj* terrifying; dreadful.
terrify *vt* to scare; to affright.
territory *n* a large tract of land; a region.
terror *n* extreme fear; dread.
terrorism *n* the use of violence to intimide.
terrorize *vt* to intimidate by means of terror.
terse *adj* concise; pointed.
tertiary *adj* third; applied to a geological formation.
tessellated *adj* resembling mosaic.
test *n* a putting to the proof; examination; trial. * *vt* to try.
testament *n* in law, a person's will; (with cap.) one of two divisions of Bible.
testamentary *adj* bequeathed by will.
testator (*f* **testatrix**) *n* one who leaves a will at death.

testicle *n* one of two semen producing glands.
testify *vi, vt* to bear witness; to affirm on oath.
testimonial *n* a recommendation of one's character or abilities.
testimony *n* evidence; declaration.
testy *adj* fretful; peevish.
tête-à-tête *adv* face to face. * *n* a private talk.
tether *n* a rope confining animal within certain limits. * *vt* to confine with a tether.
tetragon *n* a plane figure having four angles.
tetrahedron *n* a solid body having four equal triangles as its faces.
text *n* a main part of a printed work; a topic; a textbook.
textbook *n* a standard book of instruction; a manual.
textile *adj* woven. * *n* a fabric made by weaving.
texture *n* the grain or feel of a thing.
thallus *n* a plant showing little difference between leaf, stem, and root.
than *conj* introduces second member of comparison.
thank *n* almost always in *pl* expression of gratitude. * *vt* to give thanks to.
thanksgiving *n* act of giving thanks, esp.. to God.
that *adj, demons pron* (*pl* **those**) pointing out a person or thing at a distance; the farther of two. * rel pron; sing, *pl* equivalent to who or which. * conj introducing noun clause; in order that.
thatch *n* straw used as cover for roofs or stacks. * *vt* to put thatch on.
thaw *vi, vt* to melt, as ice or snow; to become genial. * *n* the melting of ice or snow.
the *def art* denoting particular person or thing.
theatre *n* a playhouse; an operating room; sphere of action.
theatrical *adj* artificial; showy; pompous.
theft *n* act of stealing.
their *poss.adj, pron* belonging to them * theirs possessive case of they, used without noun.
theism *n* belief in gods.
them *per pron* the objective case of they.
theme *n* a subject or topic.
themselves *per pron pl* of himself, herself, etc.
then *adv* at that time. * conj from that place or time; therefore.
thenceforth *adv* from that time.
thenceforward *adv* from that time onward.
theocracy *n* direct government by God; a state so governed.
theologian *n* a person well versed in theology.
theology *n* the study of religious doctrine and divine things.
theorem *n* a proposition capable of being proved.
theoretical *adj* not practical; hypothetical.
theorize *vi* to conjecture; to speculate.
theory *n* speculation; hypothesis to explain something.
therapeutic *adj* pertaining to the healing art; curative.
there *adv* in or at that place.
thereafter *adv* after that; accordingly.
thereby *adv* by that means.
therefore *adv, conj* for that or this reason; consequently.
thereupon *adv* upon that or this; immediately.
therewith *adv* with that or this.
thermal *adj* pertaining to heat; warm; hot.
thermodynamics *npl* the science of heat as a force.
thermometer *n* an instrument for measuring degree of temperature.
thermos *n* a vacuum flask used to keep liquids warm.
thermostat *n* an appliance for regulating steam pressure and temperature.
thesaurus *n* a reference book of synonyms and antonyms.
these *pronominal adj pl* of **this**.
thesis *n* (*pl* **theses**) a subject for discussion; a theme; an essay.
thespian *adj* relating to dramatic acting.
they *per pron pl* the plural of he, she or it.
thick *adj* dense; close; foggy; crowded; dull.

thicket *n* a copse; a tangle of shrubs.
thickset *adj* thickly planted; stumpy.
thief *n* (*pl* **thieves**) a person who steals.
thieve *vi, vt* to steal.
thigh *n* the leg above the knee.
thimble *n* a metal cover for finger in sewing.
thin *adj* not thick; sparse; slim; lean; poor. * vti to make or become thin.
thing *n* an inanimate object; any separate entity; *pl* clothes; baggage, etc.
think *vi, vt* to have the mind working; to reflect; to judge; to believe.
third *adj* ordinal of three.
thirst *n* the desire or distress occasioned by want of water; eager desire after anything. * *vi* to feel thirst; to desire vehemently.
thirteen *adj, n* ten and three.
thirty *adj, n* thrice ten.
this *adj, pron* (*pl* **these**) that which is near or present.
thong *n* a strap of hide or leather.
thorax *n* the human chest.
thorn *n* a prickly tree or shrub.
thorough *adj* complete; entire.
thoroughbred *adj* of pure stock.
thoroughfare *n* a public or open road.
thoroughgoing *adj* downright; extreme.
those *adj, pron pl* of that.
though *conj* notwithstanding.
thought *n* the power of thinking; opinion; judgment; care.
thousand *adj, n* ten hundred.
thrash, thresh *vt* to beat out grain from husk; to flog.
thread *n* a fine cord; any fine filament; spiral part of a screw; general purpose. * *vt* to pass thread through; to make one's way through.
threadbare *adj* worn out; trite.
threat *n* declaration of intention to punish or hurt.
threaten *vt* to use threats towards.
threatening *adj* impending; menacing.
three *adj, n* the number next after two.
threescore *adj* three times a score; sixty.
thresh *vt* to beat out grain from husks.
threshold *n* a door sill; entrance.
thrice *adv* three times.
thrift *n* frugality; a plant.
thriftless *adj* wasteful.
thrifty *adj* frugal; saving.
thrill *vti* to send a quiver through. * *n* a quiver; a tingling feeling.
thrilling *adj* exciting.
thrive *vi* to prosper; to flourish.
throat *n* the opening downward at back of mouth.
throb *vi* to beat, as the heart; to palpitate.
throe *n* extreme pain; agony.
throne *n* a royal seat.
throng *n* a crowd. * *vi*, t. to crowd together.
throttle *n* the windpipe; the gullet; engine's steam or petrol regulator.
through *prep* from end to end of; by means of * *adj, adv* from end to end.
throughout *prep* quite through. * *adv* in every part.
throw *vti* to fling or cast; to propel; to twist or wind; to utter; a cast at dice, etc; a venture.
thrum *n* coarse yarn. * *vti* to drum; to strum.
thrush *n* a singing bird; an oral fungal infection.
thrust *vti* to push with force; to shove; to stab; to intrude. * *n* a violent push; a stab.
thumb *n* the short thick finger of hand. * *vt* to soil with fingers.
thump *n* a dull, heavy blow. * vti to strike with something heavy.
thunder *n* the sound which follows lightning; any loud noise. * *vi* to make a loud noise.
thunderbolt *n* a shaft of lightning.
thunderclap *n* a peal of thunder.
thundering *adj* resounding.
thunderstruck *adj* amazed.
thursday *n* the fifth day of the week.
thus *adv* in this manner.
thwart *adj* transverse. * *vt* to cross; to frustrate. * *n* rowers' seat athwart boat.
thyme *n* a small aromatic herb or shrub.
tiara *n* a diadem for head.
tibia *n* the shin bone.
tick *n* the beat of watch or clock; a tapping; a dot. * *n* insect. * vti to mark with a dot; to sound, as watch.
ticket *n* a label; a piece of cardboard giving right of entry, travel, etc.

tickle *vi, vt* to touch lightly in certain places and cause involuntary laughter; to please; to puzzle.
ticklish *adj* difficult; critical.
tidal *adj* pertaining to tides.
tide *n* time; season; the ebb and flow of sea.
tidings *npl* news; information.
tidy *adj* clean and orderly; neat; trim * *vt* to make tidy.
tie *vt* to fasten; to constrain; * *n* a fastening; a necktie; bond; an equality in numbers.
tier *n* a row; a rank.
tiff *n* a slight quarrel.
tiffany *n* a gauze or very thin silk.
tight *adj* compact; well-knit; fitting close or too close; scarce, as money; tipsy.
tights *npl* a one-piece garment covering the legs and lower body.
tile *n* a slab of baked clay for roofing, flooring, etc; a drain pipe. * *vt* to cover with tiles.
till *n* a money drawer in shop counter. * prep. until. * *vt* to cultivate; to plough and prepare for seed.
tiller *n* the handle of a rudder.
tilt *vi* to joust; to lean or slope. * *n* a slant; a joust; an awning for cart or boat.
timber *n* wood for building purposes.
timbre *n* characteristic quality of musical note.
time *n* the measure of duration; a point of duration; occasion; season; epoch; present life; rhythm * *vt* to regulate or measure.
timely *adj* opportune. * *adv* early.
timeous *adj* timely.
timetable *n* a table of school hours and classes; a schedule.
timid *adj* fearful; shy.
timorous *adj* full of fear.
tin *n* a malleable white metal.
tincture *n* a tinge, tint, or shade; flavour; extract or solution of drug in alcohol. * *vt* to tinge.
tinder *n* an inflammable substance used for kindling fire from a spark.
tine *n* a prong; tooth of harrow, etc.
tinge *vt* to tint; to imbue. * *n* a tint; a slight colour.
tingle *vi* to feel a thrilling sensation.
tinker *n* a mender of kettles, etc. * vti to mend; to patch up.
tinkle *vi* to make small, sharp sounds; to clink. * *n* a sharp, ringing sound.
tinplate *n* thin sheet iron coated with tin.
tinsel *n* glittering thread or foil; something gaudy but of little value; mere glitter.
tint *n* a tinge; hue. * *vt* to tinge.
tintinnabulation *n* a jingling, as of bells.
tiny *adj* very small; puny.
tip *n* a small end or point; a tap;a gratuity; a dump; a hint. * *vt* to cant, as a cart; to put tip on; to give gratuity to.
tipple *vi, vt* to drink strong liquors frequently; to imbibe often.
tipsy *adj* mildly intoxicated.
tiptoe *vi* to walk very quietly.
tiptop *adj* excellent; first-rate.
tirade *n* a violent speech, denunciation.
tire *n* band or hoop of iron or rubber round wheels; headdress. * *vt* to fatigue; to weary; to attire.
tiresome *adj* wearisome; tedious.
tissue *n* delicate fabric; thin paper sheet; substance (muscle, fat, etc) composing parts of animals and plants; a fabrication.
titanic *adj* huge; gigantic.
titbit *n* a tasty morsel.
titillation *n* a pleasant feeling, a teasing, esp. sexual.
title *n* an inscription; heading; name; appellation of dignity; a right.
titled *adj* having a title.
title deed *n* the legal document proving right to property.
title page *n* the page of book containing its name, author, etc.
titter *vi* to giggle. * *n* a half-suppressed laugh.
titular *adj* nominal.
to *prep.* denoting motion towards.
toadstool *n* a mushroom-like fungus.
toady *n* a base sycophant; a sponger. * *vt* to fawn upon.
toast *vt* to dry and brown before the fire; to drink health of * *n* toated bread; person or sentiment whose health is drunk.
tobacco *n* a narcotic plant whose leaves when dried are used for smoking or snuff.

toboggan *n* a snow sledge
toddle *vi* to walk with uncertain steps, as a child.
toddy *n* a mixture of spirit, hot water, and sugar.
toe *n* one of the five extremities of the foot.
toffee *n* a sweetmeat made of butter and sugar.
toga *n* a loose robe.
together *adv* in company.
toil *vi* to labour; to drudge. * *n* hard work; a snare.
toilet *n* the lavatory; the act of washing and dressing oneself.
toilsome *adj* laborious.
token *n* a mark; symbol; keepsake.
tolerable *adj* passable; middling.
tolerance *n* forbearance.
tolerant *adj* indulgent; broad-minded.
tolerate *vt* to allow or permit; to put up with.
toll *n* a tax charged for use of road, bridge, etc; sound of a bell. * *vi* to ring bell slowly.
tomb *n* a grave; burial vault.
tombstone *n* a stone erected over a grave.
tome *n* a volume; a large book.
tomfoolery *n* nonsense; silly acts.
tomorrow *n* the day after the present.
tone *n* sound or character of sound; timbre; temper; colour scheme. * *vti* to tone down, to soften.
tongs *npl* an appliance for lifting coal, sugar, etc.
tongue *n* the organ of speech and taste; speech; language; clapper of bell.
tonic *adj* strengthening; bracing. * *n* a bracing medicine; keynote.
tonight *n* the present night.
tonnage *n* weight of ship's freight; duty on ships.
tonne *n* a metric ton, 1,000 kg.
tonsil *n* one of glands on each side of throat.
tonsillitis *n* inflammation of tonsils.
too *adv* over; as well; also.
tool *n* an instrument to work with.
tooling *n* skilled work with a tool.
tooth *n* (*pl* **teeth**) one of the bony projections from gums used for chewing.
toothache *n* a pain in teeth.
toothed *adj* jagged; indented.
top *n* the highest part; summit; toy for spinning. * *vi*, t. to excel; to be at top.
top-heavy *adj* overweighted above and apt to fall over.
topic *n* a theme or text.
topical *adj* local; full of allusions.
topography *n* scientific description of a district; local geography.
topple *vi* to fall over; overbalance.
torch *n* a light to be carried in the hand.
toreador *n* a Spanish bullfighter.
torment *n* torture; anguish. * *vt* to torture; to tease.
tornado *n* (*pl* **tornadoes**) a hurricane.
torpedo *n* (*pl* **torpedoes**) a kind of electric eel; a self-propelled explosive submarine projectile.
torpid *adj* numb; inactive.
torpor *n* apathy; numbness.
torrent *n* a rushing stream.
torrid *adj* parched; violently hot.
torsion *n* act of twisting; amount or force of twist.
torso *n* a headless, limbless trunk, esp.. of statue.
tort *n* wrong; injury.
tortuous *adj* crooked; winding.
torture *n* extreme pain; agony. * *vt* to rack; to harass.
toss *vti* to throw upward; to jerk, as head; to roll about. * *n* a throw; a fall.
tot *n* anything small; a sum in addition. * *vt* to add.
total *adj, n* whole; complete.
totem *n* a tribal emblem.
totter *vi* to stagger; to reel.
touch *vti* to come in contact with; to handle lightly; to reach; to move feelings of * *n* contact; feeling; skill in some art.
touching *adj* affecting. * *prep.* concerning.
touchstone *n* a stone for testing purity of gold and silver; a test or criterion.
touchy *adj* irritable; sensitive.
tough *adj* flexible; tenacious; stubborn.
tour *n* a long trip, esp for pleaasure. * *vt* to make a tour.
tourist *n* one who makes a tour.
tournament *n* a contest in which individuals or sides are pitted against one another.

tourniquet *n* an appliance for stopping flow from cut artery.
tousle *vt* to ruffle; to disarrange.
tout *vi* to seek for custom openly; to canvas obtrusively. * *n* a shameless canvasser.
tow *vt* to haul by a rope. * *n* haulage; fibres of flax or hemp.
toward, towards *prep* in the direction of * *adv* at hand.
towel *n* a cloth for drying.
tower *n* a lofty narrow building; a fortress. * *vi* to soar.
towering *adj* lofty; violent.
town *n* an urban centre, smaller than a city and larger than a village.
toxic *adj* poisonous.
toxin *n* a poisonous substance.
toy *n* a plaything; a trifle. * *vi* to dally; to trifle.
trace *n* a mark left by anything; footstep; track; one of straps by which a carriage is drawn. * *vt* to track out; to copy by marking over.
trachea *n* the windpipe.
track *n* a footprint; rut made by wheel; beaten path; course. * *vt* to trace; to follow step by step.
trackless *adj* pathless; untrodden.
tract *n* wide region; a short treatise.
tractable *adj* docile; manageable.
traction *n* act of drawing, esp.. vehicles.
trade *n* employment; commerce; traffic. * *vi*, *vt* to buy and sell.
trademark *n* a distinctive mark put by manufacturer on his goods.
trades union *n* a union of workers in a trade to protect their interests.
tradition *n* knowledge handed down orally; a custom.
traduce *vt* to slander; defame.
traffic *n* trade; commerce; intercourse; conveyance of passengers or goods on railways, roads, etc. * *vi* to trade.
tragedy *n* an elevated drama with fatal ending; any dreadful event.
tragic, tragical *adj* fatal; disastrous.
trail *n* a track or scent. * *vt* to drag along the ground; to hang downwards.
trailer *n* a climbing plant; a vehicle towed by another.
train *vt* to draw along; to drill; to exercise; to teach; to take aim * *n* something drawn along; a series of railway carriages coupled with engine; trailing part of skirt; a retinue; process.
training *n* exercise; education; practice.
trait *n* a distinguishing feature.
traitor *n* one guilty of treason.
trajectory *n* the path of a moving body, as bullet, comet, etc.
tram *n* a tramway line; a tramcar.
trammel *n* a net for birds or fishes; a shackle; a handicap; a hindrance. * *vt* to impede.
tramp *vti* to tread under foot; travel on foot. * *n* a journey on foot; a vagrant.
trample *vt* to tread on heavily; to ride roughshod over.
trance *n* a state of insensibility; a swoon.
tranquil *adj* calm; serene.
transact *vti* to carry through.
transaction *n* management; performance; *pl* report of proceedings of societies.
transcend *vt* to rise above; to surpass.
transcendent *adj* of surpassing merit; preeminent; supernatural.
transcribe *vt* to copy.
transcript *n* a written copy.
transcription *n* act of transcribing; a copy.
transfer *vt* to convey from one place or person to another. * *n* conveyance of titles, etc, from one to another; a design that can be printed off on another surface.
transfigure *vt* to change in form or shape.
transfix *vt* to piece through.
transform *vt* to change the form of; to convert.
transformation *n* a complete change of appearance or nature.
transfuse *vt* to transfer, as blood, from one person to another.
transgress *vt* to break or violate. * *vi* to do wrong.
transgression *n* fault; offence.
transient *adj* passing quickly; fleeting.
transit *n* a passing across; passage of planet across sun's disc or of star across meridian of a place; conveyance.
transition *n* passage from one place or state to another.

transitive *adj* in grammar, said of action passing from subject to object.
transitory *adj* fleeting.
translate *vt* to remove from one place to another; to render into another language.
translation *n* removal; a turning into another language; a version.
translucent *adj* semi-transparent.
translucid *adj* translucent.
transmissible *adj* able to be passed through or along.
transmission *n* a passing through; act of sending.
transmit *vt* to convey or effect conveyance of news, light, etc; to hand down.
transmogrify *vt* to transform; to change.
transmute *vt* to change from one form into another.
transom *n* a strengthening cross beam over door or window.
transparency *n* clearness; obviousness; picture visible only when light passes through.
transparent *adj* clear; not opaque; frank.
transpiration *n* emission of vapour or moisture through pores.
transpire *vt* to emit through pores of skin. * *vt* to exhale; to become known.
transplant *vt* to remove and plant in another place.
transport *vt* to carry from one place to another; to banish; to enrapture. * *n* conveyance for goods; a ship for carrying troops, etc; rapture.
transpose *vt* to change the order of things.
transposition *n* change in order of words for effect.
transubstantiate *vt* to change to another substance.
transude *vi* to pass through pores.
transversal *adj* lying across. * *n* line cutting other straight lines.
transverse *adj* lying across; crosswise.
trap *n* a contrivance for catching animals; an ambush; a contrivance in drains to prevent foul air rising; a light uncovered vehicle; an igneous rock. * *vti* to snare; to take unawares; to set trap for.
trap door *n* a door in a floor or ceiling or roof.
trapeze *n* a swing for gymnastic exercises.
trapezium *n* (*pl* **trapezia**) a plane four-sided figure of which no two sides are parallel.
trappings *npl* finery; adornment, esp.. for horses.
trash *n* rubbish; refuse.
travail *vi* to labour; to toil. * *n* toil and pain; childbirth.
travel *n* journey to a distant country. * *vi* to journey.
traverse *adj* transverse. * *n* a crosspiece; denial of a plea in lawsuit; barrier across a trench. * *vt* to cross; to journey through; to deny. * *adv* athwart; crosswise.
travesty *n* a wilful misrepresentation.
trawl *vi* to fish by trailing a net. * *n* a large net for deep-sea fishing.
trawler *n* a fishing vessel with a trawl net.
tray *n* a broad, flat, rimmed utensil for carrying dishes, etc.
treacherous *adj* faithless; deceitful.
treachery *n* betrayal of trust; perfidy; treason.
treacle *n* the syrup obtained in the refining of sugar.
tread *vi* to step or walk. * *vt* to trample; dance. * *n* step; the part of a shoe, tyre, etc that touches the ground.
treason *n* treachery; disloyalty to king or country.
treasonable *adj* involving treason.
treasure *n* great wealth; something greatly valued. * *vt* to prize highly.
treasurer *n* one who has the charge of funds.
treasury *n* place where public money is stored; government department that controls finance.
treat *vti* to handle; to act towards; to discourse on. * *n* an entertainment; a rare pleasure.
treatise *n* an essay; pamphlet.
treatment *n* mode of dealing with.
treaty *n* an agreement between nations.
treble *adj* threefold. * *n* highest part in music; soprano.
tree *n* a woody plant with trunk and branches.
trefoil *n* a three-leaved plant, as clover; a sculptured tracery like clover.

trek *vi* to migrate by wagon.
trellis *n* a lattice-work structure.
tremble *vi* to shake; to quiver.
tremendous *adj* terrible; huge.
tremor *n* an involuntary trembling; a shivering.
tremulous *adj* trembling; quavering.
trench *vti* to dig a ditch in; to turn over and mix, as soil. * *n* a long narrow cutting; a deep ditch with rampart.
trenchant *adj* cutting; severe.
trend *vi* to incline towards. * *n* direction; tendency.
trepidation *n* consternation; fear.
trespass *vi* to intrude on another's land; to transgress; to sin. * *n* a sin; offence; intrusion on another's property.
tress *n* a lock of hair.
trestle *n* a frame for supporting things.
trial *n* a putting to the test; ordeal; attempt; hardship.
triangle *n* a figure having three sides and three angles.
triangular *adj* having form of triangle.
tribe *n* a division of a people; family; race.
tribulation *n* deep affliction; suffering.
tribunal *n* a court of justice.
tributary *adj* paying tribute; subordinate. * *n* a stream flowing into another.
tribute *n* merited praise.
trice *n* an instant.
trick *n* an artifice; fraud; a knack; a habit; a prank. * *vt* to deceive; to cheat.
trickery *n* cheating; fraud.
trickle *vi* to fall in drops.
trickster *n* a knave; cheat.
tricycle *n* three-wheeled cycle.
trident *n* three-pronged sceptre.
tried *adj* approved; reliable.
triennial *adj* happening every three years.
trifle *n* thing of little value; a confection or pudding. * *vi*, t. to toy; to idle.
trifling *adj* trivial; frivolous.
trigger *n* the catch by which a gun is fired.
trigonometry *n* the science dealing with measurement of triangles and ratios of their angles.
trilateral *adj* three-sided.
trill *n* a tremor of voice in singing. * *vt* to warble.
trilogy *n* a series of three connected dramas, poems, etc.
trim *vt* to put in order; to prune; to adjust (cargo). * *adj* spruce; neat. * *n* readiness; good condition.
trimming *n* an embellishment, esp.. of garment; *pl* accessories; parings.
trinity *n* a union of three in one.
trinket *n* a trifling ornament.
trio *n* a set of three; composition for three performers.
trip *vi* to step lightly; to skip; to stumble. * *vt* to cause to stumble. * *n* a stumble; an excursion or jaunt.
tripartite *adj* divided into three; made between three parties.
tripe *n* stomach of sheep, cow, etc, prepared as food.
triple *adj* threefold; treble.
triplet *n* three of a kind; *pl* three children at one birth.
triplicate *adj* threefold.
tripod *n* a three-legged stand.
tripper *n* a day excursionist.
trisect *vt* to cut into three equal parts.
trisyllable *n* a word consisting of three syllables.
trite *adj* commonplace; well-worn.
triumph *n* a rejoicing for victory; a great victory. * *vi* to gain a victory; to exult.
triumphal *adj* pertaining to a triumph.
triumphant *adj* victorious; exultant.
triumvirate *n* a coalition of three men in office.
trivet *n* a tripod for kettle, etc.
trivial *adj* common; trifling.
trod, trodden *v.* past and *p.p.* of tread.
troglodyte *n* a cave dweller.
troll *vti* to sing in chorus or succession; to fish by trailing bait. * *n* a part song; a fishing reel; a dwarfish elf.
trolley, trolly *n* a small truck.
trollop *n* a slattern.
trombone *n* a deep-toned wind instrument.
troop *n* a collection of people or animals; a cavalry company; *pl* soldiers in general. * *vi* to gather in large numbers.
trooper *n* a cavalryman; a mounted policeman.
troopship *n* a ship used for transport of military forces.

trophy *n* a token or memorial of victory.
tropic *n* one of the two parallel lines of latitude on either side of the equator; (*pl*) the regions lying between these lines.
tropical *adj* excessively hot; relating to the tropics.
trot *vi* to run with small steps. * *n* a medium pace.
troth *n* truth; faith.
trouble *vt* to disturb; to distress. * *n* distress; affliction.
troublesome *adj* annoying; tiresome.
trough *n* a long shallow drinking vessel; a hollow.
trounce *vt* to beat severely.
troupe *n* a company of performers.
trousers *npl* a garment for men, covering legs.
trousseau *n* a bride's outfit.
trowel *n* a hand tool for spreading mortar, etc.
truant *n* one who stays from school without leave.
truce *n* a temporary stoppage of fighting; armistice.
truck *n* a heavy motor vehicle for transporting goods. **vt* to convey by truck. * *vi* to drive a truck.
truculence *n* ferocity.
truculent *adj* aggressive; overbearing.
trudge *vi* to walk, esp.. with heavy steps.
true *adj* conformable to fact; genuine; loyal; honest; exact.
truffle *n* an edible fungus growing underground.
truism *n* a self-evident truth.
truly *adv* really; according to truth.
trump *n* a winning card; one of the favoured suit for time being; a real good fellow. * *vt* to take with a trump card; to concoct (with up).
trumpet *n* a metal wind instrument. * *vt* to proclaim; to sound.
truncate *vt* to cut off; to lop.
truncated *adj* cut short.
truncheon *n* a short staff; a baton of authority.
trundle *vi* to roll or bowl. * *n* a little wheel.
trunk *n* the stem of a tree; body of an animal; chest for containing clothes, etc; proboscis of an elephant, etc.
trunk line *n* main line of railway, telephone, etc.
truss *n* a bundle, as of hay; a bandage; crossbeams to support roof * *vt* to tie up (fowl) for cooking; to strengthen; to bind firmly.
trust *n* reliance; confidence; hope; credit; a business combine; money or property entrusted to individuals (trustees) for use in specified ways. * *vti* to rely upon; to credit; to entrust.
trustee *n* one appointed to hold property for benefit of others.
trustworthy *adj* faithful; honest.
trusty *adj* reliable; staunch.
truth *n* conformity to fact or reality; integrity; constancy; reality.
try *vt* to test; to afflict; to examine judicially; to attempt.
trying *adj* severe; searching.
tryst *n* an appointment to meet; a rendezvous.
tub *n* an open wooden vessel; a small bath.
tube *n* a pipe; a hollow cylinder.
tuber *n* an underground fleshy stem or root.
tuberculosis *n* a disease marked by presence of tubercles in tissues; consumption.
tubing *n* material for tubes series of tubes.
tubular *adj* like a tube; consisting of tubes.
tuck *vt* to gather in a fold. * *n* fold in garment; roll of drum; eatables.
tuesday *n* the second work day of the week.
tuft *n* a cluster; clump.
tug *vti* to pull with effort. * *n* a strong pull; steam towing vessel.
tuition *n* instruction; business of teaching.
tulle *n* a thin silk fabric.
tumble *vi* to roll about; to fall. * *vt* to overturn. * *n* a fall.
tumbler *n* an acrobat; a drinking glass.
tumid *adj* swollen; bombastic.
tumour *n* an abnormal growth of tissue in any part of the body.
tumult *n* uproar; riot.
tumultuous *adj* turbulent; disorderly.
tundra *n* flat, treeless arctic plain.

tune *n* a short air or melody; harmony; correct intonation; frame of mind; mood. * *vt* to put into tune; to adapt.

tunic *n* a loose garment sometimes worn by both sexes; a military jacket; a covering membrane.

tuning fork *n* a two-pronged fork which when struck gives a standard musical note.

tunnel *n* an arched underground passage, esp on railways.

turban *n* a headdress.

turbid *adj* muddy; dense.

turbine *n* a horizontal water wheel; a rotary motor driven by steam, water, etc.

turbulence *n* disorder; tumult.

turbulent *adj* disorderly; riotous.

tureen *n* a large deep dish for soup.

turf *n* the grassy layer on surface of ground; a sod. * the turf, the business of horse racing.

turgid *adj* swelling; bombastic.

turmeric *n* an E. Indian plant whose root is used as a dye, a drug, and a flavour.

turmoil *n* uproar; disorder.

turn *vt* to cause to move round; to shape by a lathe; to alter course; to reverse; to change. * *vi* to revolve; to bend or curve; to become sour. * *n* a revolution; a bend; a short walk; purpose; short spell.

turncoat *n* one who deserts his party or principles.

turning *n* a turn; bend; art of shaping articles on a lathe.

turnstile *n* a revolving barrier that serves as entrance gate.

turpentine *n* resin got from certain trees; oil distilled from this.

turpitude *n* baseness; depravity.

turquoise *n* a greenish blue precious stone.

turret *n* a little tower forming part of a building; rotary iron tower to protect guns and gunners on warship.

tusk *n* a long pointed tooth projecting from mouth as in elephant, boar.

tussle *n* a struggle; scuffle.

tussock *n* a clump of grass.

tutelage *n* guardianship.

tutelar *adj* protecting.

tutor *n* a teacher.

twaddle *vi* to prate; to chatter. * *n* silly talk.

twang *vi* to pluck a taut string or wire. * *n* sound of a taut string plucked.

tweak *vt* to pinch; twist.

tweed *n* a twilled woollen fabric.

tweezers *npl* small pincers to pluck out hairs, etc.

twelfth *adj* the ordinal of twelve

twelve *adj, n* ten and two.

twentieth *adj* the ordinal of twenty.

twenty *adj, n* twice ten.

twice *adv* two times.

twiddle *vti* to twirl idly.

twig *n* a small shoot or branch.

twilight *n* the faint light after sunset and before dawn.

twill *n* a textile fabric with parallel ribs.

twin *n* one of two born at a birth. * *adj* double.

twine *n* strong thread or cord. * vti to twist; to coil.

twinge *n* a sudden darting pain.

twinkle *vi* to sparkle; to blink. * *n* a sparkle.

twirl *vti* to turn round rapidly; to rotate. * *n* a curl; a flourish.

twist *n* something twined, as a thread; roll of tobacco; a wrench; a turn. * *vti* to twine; to writhe; to pervert.

twitch *vt* to pluck; to jerk. * *n* a quick pull; a muscular jerk.

two *adj, n* the number next above one.

tymbal *n* a kettledrum.

tympanum *n* (*pl* **tympana**) the drum of the ear.

type *n* a distinguishing mark; emblem; model; letter used in printing; such letters collectively.

typewriter *n* a machine for producing printed letters by inked type.

typhoid *n* enteric fever; a low fever with acute intestinal pain.

typhoon *n* a violent hurricane.

typhus *n* a dangerous fever.

typical *adj* characteristic; symbolic.

typify *vt* to represent; exemplify.

typography *n* the art of printing.

tyrannical *adj* despotic; overbearing.

tyrannize *vi* to act the tyrant; to oppress.

tyranny *n* oppressive government; despotism.

tyrant *n* a despot; an oppressor.
tyre *n* a protective ring, usu rubber round the rim of a wheel.
tyro *n* a novice, a beginner.

U

ubiquitous *adj* existing everywhere; omnipresent.
udder *n* the milk gland of cows, sheep, etc.
ugly *adj* unattractive; unsightly; repulsive; ill-tempered.
ulcer *n* a festering sore. .
ulceration *n* an ulcerous condition.
ulster *n* a long loose overcoat.
ulterior *adj* not evident;on further side; (motives) hidden .
ultimate *adj* utmost; final.
ultimatum *n* a last or final offer.
ultra *pref, adj* beyond; extreme.
ultramarine *n* a vivid blue pigment.
ululate *vi* to howl, as with pain.
umbilical *adj* pertaining to the navel.
umbra *n* the dark central part of a shadow.
umbrage *n* resentment; offence.
umbrella *n* a folding frame with handle and covering covering, etc, as protection from rain; general protection.
umpire *n* a judge or referee.
un- *pref* the addition of this prefix negatives or reverses the original meaning, as untrue, not true.
The sense of these 'u' words is in most cases self-evident, and only those in common use are given below, together with a fairly complete list of those whose meaning is less obvious.
unable *adj* not able; unequal to some task.
unacceptable *adj* unwelcome.
unaccountable *adj* not responsible.
unaccustomed *adj* unusual.
unacknowledged *adj* ignored.
unacquainted *adj* not familiar with.
unadorned *adj* plain; simple.
unadvisable *adj* not prudent.
unaffected *adj* simple; sincere; unmoved.
unaided *adj* without aid.
unalterable *adj* unchangeable.
unanimity *n* complete agreement. the 'un' here stands for 'unus', one.
unanimous *adj* being of one mind.
unanswerable *adj* conclusive.
unappreciated *adj* not duly prized.
unapproachable *adj* inaccessible.
unarmed *adj* defenceless.
unassailable *adj* impregnable.
unassuming *adj* modest.
unattended *adj* solitary; alone.
unattractive *adj* uninteresting.
unauthorized *adj* unwarranted.
unavailing *adj* of no avail.
unaware *adj, adv* unconscious; ignorant.
unawares *adv* unexpectedly.
unbearable *adj* intolerable.
unbecoming *adj* unseemly.
unbend *vi* to make straight.
unbiased *adj* impartial; just.
unbounded *adj* boundless, vast.
unbridled *adj* unrestrained.
unburden*vt* to rid of a load or burden.
uncanny *adj* weird; mysterious.
unceasing *adj* continual.
uncertain *adj* doubtful; variable.
unchallenged *adj* unopposed.
unchanging *adj* constant; immutable.
uncharitable *adj* harsh; ungenerous.
uncivil *adj* rude; discourteous.
uncivilized *adj* barbarous.
uncle *n* the brother of one's father or mother.
unclean *adj* dirty; impure.
uncomfortable *adj* ill at ease.
uncommunicative *adj* reserved; taciturn.
uncompromising *adj* unyielding.
unconditional *adj* unqualified.
unconnected *adj* separate; rambling.
unconscionable *adj* inordinate.
unconscious *adj* insensible; unaware.
unconstitutional *adj* not according to the principles of the constitution.
uncontrollable *adj* headstrong.
unconventional *adj* free and easy.
unconverted *adj* unchanged.
uncouple *vt* to set loose, as dogs on leash.
uncouth *adj* odd in appearance.
uncover *vt* to divest of a cover.
unctuous *adj* oily; greasy.
uncultivated *adj* not tilled; boorish.
undaunted *adj* intrepid; fearless.

undecided *adj* wavering; irresolute.
undemonstrative *adj* reserved; placid.
undeniable *adj* indisputable; true.
under *prep.* below; beneath; subject to; inferior. * *adv* in a lower condition or degree. * *adj* lower; subordinate.
underclothes*n* clothes worn under others or next skin.
undercurrent *n* a current below another.
undergo *vt* to bear; to suffer.
undergraduate *n* a student who has not taken his degree.
undergrowth *n* shrubs growing among large ones; copsewood.
underhand *adj* sly; dishonest.
underline *vt* to mark with a line underneath for emphasis.
undermine *vt* to sap; to injure by underhand means.
underrate *vt* to undervalue.
undersized *adj* dwarfish; small.
understand *vti* to comprehend.
understanding *n* comprehension; discernment; knowledge; agreement.
understudy *n* one who gets up a theatrical part to be ready as substitute.
undertake *vti* to take in hand.
undertaker *n* one who manages funerals.
undertaking *n* a task; project; promise.
undertone *n* an undercurrent of feeling.
undertow *n* the backward suction of a wave breaking on shore; undercurrent.
underwear *n* underclothes.
underworld *n* the world of criminals.
underwrite *vt* to sign one's name as answerable for a certain amount of insurance.
undisguised *adj* open; candid.
undisturbed *adj* calm; tranquil.
undo *vt* to reverse what has been done.
undoing *n* reversal; ruin.
undoubted *adj* certain; unquestionable.
undress *vt vi* to take off one's clothes.
undue *adj* unnecessary; excessive.
undulation *n* a waving motion; a gentle slope; vibratory motion.
undulatory *adj* wave-like.
unearned *adj* unmerited; (income) not earned by labour or skill.
unearth *vt* to discover; to reveal.
unearthly *adj* weird; ghostly.
uneasy *adj* restless; awkward; anxious.
unendurable *adj* intolerable.
unequable *adj* changeful; fitful.
unequal *adj* ill-matched.
unequivocal *adj* undoubted; clear.
uneven *adj* unequal; rough; odd.
unexceptionable *adj* irreproachable.
unexpected *adj* unlooked for; sudden.
unexplored *adj* unvisited.
unfading *adj* ever fresh.
unfailing *adj* sure.
unfair *adj* unjust; biassed.
unfaithful *adj* disloyal; false.
unfamiliar *adj* strange; unaccustomed.
unfasten *vt* to loose; to unfix.
unfavourable *adj* adverse.
unfeeling *adj* devoid of feeling; harsh.
unfit *adj* unsuitable; incompetent.
unflinching *adj* resolute; firm.
unfold *vti* to open the folds of; to display.
unforeseen *adj* unexpected; sudden.
unforgiving *adj* relentless; implacable.
unfortunate *adj* unlucky; unhappy.
unfounded *adj* false; groundless.
unfrequented *adj* rarely visited; solitary.
unfurl *vt* to spread out (sail, flag, etc).
unfurnished *adj* without furniture.
ungainly *adj* clumsy; awkward.
ungenerous *adj* stingy; mean.
ungovernable *adj* headstrong; unruly.
ungraceful *adj* inelegant.
ungrammatical *adj* not according to grammar.
ungrateful *adj* not thankful; irksome.
ungrudging *adj* generous; hearty.
unguent *n* an ointment.
unhappily *adv* unfortunately.
unhappy *adj* miserable; sad; unlucky.
unhealthy *adj* sickly; unwholesome.
unheeded *adj* ignored; disregarded.
unheeding *adj* careless.
unhesitating *adj* instant; prompt.
unhinge *vt* to loosen; to derange.
unholy *adj* profane; wicked.
uniform *adj* regular; unvarying. * *n* regulation dress of certain persons.
uniformity *n* sameness; agreement; conformity to one type.
unify *vt* to form into one.
unimpaired *adj* uninjured.

unimpeachable *adj* irreproachable.
uninhabited *adj* deserted; desolate.
unintelligent *adj* dull; stupid.
unintelligible *adj* incapable of being understood; meaningless.
unintentional *adj* accidental.
uninteresting *adj* tedious; wearisome.
uninterrupted *adj* continuous; unbroken.
uninviting *adj* unattractive.
union *n* concord; a league; a trade union.
unionist *n* a trade unionist.
unique *adj* being the only one of its kind.
unison *n* harmony; concord.
unit *n* a single thing or person; an individual; a standard quantity.
unite *vti* to combine; to connect.
unity *n* harmony; oneness; the number 1.
universal *adj* all-embracing, total.
universe *n* the whole creation; the world.
university *n* educational institution for higher learning.and research.
unjust *adj* unfair; bad; biassed.
unkempt *adj* uncombed; rough.
unknowingly *adv* unwittingly.
unlace *vt* to unfasten.
unlawful *adj* illegal.
unless *conj* if it be not that.
unlicensed *adj* without legal permission.
unlike *adj* different; dissimilar.
unlimited *adj* unbounded; limitless.
unlooked-for *adj* unexpected.
unlucky *adj* unfortunate; ill-fated.
unmanageable *adj* beyond control.
unmannerly *adj* rude; ill-bred.
unmask *vt* to strip off mask; to expose.
unmeasured *adj* excessive; boundless.
unmerciful *adj* ruthless; cruel.
unmerited *adj* undeserved.
unmitigated *adj* unqualified; absolute.
unnatural *adj* inhuman; affected.
unnavigable *adj* incapable of being navigated.
unnerve *vt* to unman; to deprive of power.
unobtrusive *adj* retiring; modest.
unoccupied *adj* empty; at leisure.
unopposed *adj* meeting with no opposition.
unorthodox *adj* unconventional.
unpack *vt* to empty a pack, trunk, etc.
unpalatable *adj* unpleasant to taste.
unparalleled *adj* unequalled; matchless.
unpardonable *adj* inexcusable.
unpleasant *adj* disagreeable.
unpractised *adj* raw; unskilful.
unprecedented *adj* unparalleled.
unpretentious *adj* modest.
unprincipled *adj* immoral; wicked.
unproductive *adj* barren.
unprofessional *adj* contrary to professional etiquette.
unprofitable *adj* fruitless; futile.
unqualified *adj* untrained; incompetent.
unquestionable *adj* indisputable.
unravel *vt* to disentangle; to solve.
unreadable *adj* illegible.
unreal *adj* sham; visionary.
unreasonable *adj* immoderate; absurd.
unrecorded *adj* not placed on record.
unrelenting *adj* hard; pitiless.
unreliable *adj* untrustworthy.
unremitting *adj* ceaseless; constant.
unrequited *adj* unrewarded.
unreserved *adj* frank; full; open.
unrest *n* disquiet; uneasiness.
unrestrained *adj* unbridled; loose.
unripe *adj* immature.
unrivalled *adj* peerless.
unroll *vti* to unfold; to display.
unruffled *adj* calm; composed.
unruly *adj* disorderly.
unsatisfactory *adj* not up to expectation.
unsavoury *adj* insipid; unpleasing.
unscathed *adj* uninjured.
unscrupulous *adj* unprincipled.
unseemly *adj* unbecoming; improper.
unsentimental *adj* matter-of-fact.
unserviceable *adj* useless.
unsettle *vt* to upset; to derange.
unshaken *adj* firm; resolute.
unshapely *adj* ill-formed.
unsightly *adj* ugly; repulsive.
unsociable *adj* reserved; solitary.
unsolicited *adj* unsought.
unsophisticated *adj* natural; artless.
unsound *adj* diseased; faulty.

unspeakable *adj* unutterable.
unstable *adj* unsteady; fickle.
unsteady *adj* changeable; unsafe.
unstinted *adj* lavish; generous.
unsubstantial *adj* visionary; flimsy.
unsuitable *adj* unfit; unbecoming.
unsullied *adj* pure; stainless.
unsung *adj* not celebrated in song or poetry.
unsurpassed *adj* unexcelled.
unsuspecting *adj* free from suspicion.
unswerving *adj* steadfast; straight.
untenable *adj* not fit to be occupied.
unthinkable *adj* inconcievable.
unthinking *adj* careless; heedless.
untidy *adj* slovenly; careless.
untie *vt* to loosen; to undo.
until *prep, conj* up to the time that; till.
untimely *adj* ill-timed; unseasonable.
untiring *adj* unwearied.
unto *prep* to.
untold *adj* countless; vast; unrecorded.
untouched *adj* unscathed; unmoved.
untoward *adj* unseemly; unfavourable.
untried *adj* not attempted; inexperienced.
untroubled *adj* calm; unruffled.
untrue *adj* incorrect; faithless.
untrustworthy *adj* unreliable; false.
unusual *adj* rare; peculiar.
unutterable *adj* unspeakable.
unvarnished *adj* plain; unadorned.
unvarying *adj* uniform.
unveil *vt* to uncover; to disclose to view.
unwarrantable *adj* unjustifiable; illegal.
unwavering *adj* steady; staunch.
unwearied *adj* tireless; incessant.
unwieldy *n* huge; cumbersome.
unwilling *adj* reluctant; loath.
unwind *vt* to wind off.
unwitting *adj* ignorant; unaware.
unworthy *adj* base; worthless.
unwritten *adj* understood though not expressed; traditional.
unyielding *adj* stubborn; unbending.
up *adv* aloft; in or to a higher position; upright; out of bed. * prep. from below to.
upbraid *vt* to reproach; to taunt.
upbringing *n* training; breeding.
upheaval *n* great social or political changes.
uphold *vt* to support; to sustain.
upholster *vt* to furnish (chairs, sofas, etc) with springs, stuffing, etc.
upkeep *n* maintenance.
upon *prep* up and on; on.
upper *adj* higher in place or rank.
uppish *adj* snobbish.
upright *adj* erect; trustworthy.
uproar *n* a great tumult.
uproarious *adj* noisy; boisterous.
uproot *vt* to tear up by roots.
upset *vt* to overturn; to discompose. * *n* act of upsetting. * *adj* fixed.
upshot *n* final issue; end.
upstairs *adj, adv* in or towards upper story of building; house, etc.
upstart *n* one who has suddenly risen in position; an arrogant person.
urban *adj* belonging to a city.
urbane *adj* sophisticated; polite.
urchin *n* a small mischievous boy.
urge *vt* to press to do something.
urgent *adj* pressing; imperative.
urine *n* fluid excreted from kidneys and bladder.
urn *n* a kind of vase.
us *pron* the objective case of we.
usage *n* treatment; customary practice.
use *n* employment practice; need. * *vt* to put to use; to avail one's self of; to employ.
user*n* one who uses
useful *adj* helpful; serviceable.
usher *n* a doorkeeper; an assistant.
usual *adj* customary; common.
usurer *n* one who takes exorbitant interest.
usurp *vt* to seize and hold without right.
usury *n* extortionate interest for loan.
utensil *n* a kitchen implement.
utility *n* usefulness; profit.
utilize *vt* make use of.
utmost *adj* the highest degree.
utopia *n* an ideal state or government.
utopian *adj* ideally perfect; visionary.
utter *adj* complete; total. * *vt* to speak; pronounce; spread abroad.
uvula *n* small fleshy body hanging from back palate.

V

vacancy *n* empty space; an unfilled post.
vacant *adj* empty; unfilled; silly.
vacate *vt* to quit possession of.
vacation *n* holiday time.
vaccinate *vt* to inoculate against smallpox.
vaccine *n* inoculating lymph.
vacillate *vi* to waver; to be undecided.
vacuous *adj* empty; void; vacant.
vacuum *n* a space void of air; empty space; a vacuum cleaner.
vagabond *adj* roaming; idling. * *n* a tramp.
vagrant *adj* wandering. * *n* a tramp; a sturdy beggar.
vague *adj* indefinite; hazy.
vain *adj* empty; fruitless; conceited. * In vain, to no purpose.
vale *n* a valley.
valedictory *n* farewell.
valentine *n* a love gift or missive sent on Valentine's day (14th February).
valet *n* a manservant.
valiant *adj* brave; heroic.
valid *adj* well grounded; sound.
validity *n* justness; soundness.
valley *n* the low ground between hills.
valour *n* bravery; courage.
valuable *adj* of great worth. * npl precious belongings.
valuator *n* an appraiser or valuer.
value *n* worth; importance; price. * vt to estimate; to prize; to appraise.
valve *n* a lid or flap for an opening, giving passage in one direction only.
vampire *n* a fabled bloodsucking creature; a person who preys on others; a bat.
van *n* a covered motor vehicle.
vandal *n* a barbarian; a person who willfully damages property.
vane *n* a weathercock; blade of a windmill, etc.
vanguard *n* front part of an army; the leading position of any movement.
vanilla *n* a flavouring prepared from tropical orchid.
vanish *vi* to disappear; to pass away.
vanity *n* idle show; craving for praise; emptiness; conceit.
vanquish *vt* to conquer; overcome.
vapid *adj* spiritless; flat; dull.
vaporize *vt* to convert or pass off into vapour.
vapour *n* a gas or fume given off by a body when sufficiently heated.
variable *adj* fickle; changeable.
variance *n* dispute; quarrel.
variant *n* an alternative form.
variation *n* change; alteration.
varicose *adj* enlarged, said of veins.
varied *adj* diverse; various.
variegated *pp* diversified in colour.
variety *n* diversity; change in assortment; a species.
various *adj* different; several.
varnish *n* a resinous solution used to give gloss to wood, paper, etc; a gloss; a sham.
vary *vti* to change; to alter; to differ; to disagree.
vascular *adj* pertaining to vessels, ducts, etc, of organic bodies.
vase *n* a jar-shaped vessel for ornament or use.
vast *adj* of great extent; immense.
vat *n* a huge tub or tank for holding liquors.
vaudeville *n* a light comedy with dances and songs.
vault *n* an arched roof; cellar; a leap. * *vi* to leap.
vaunt *vi, vt* to brag; to exult. * *n* a boast.
veal *n* the flesh of a calf.
veer *vi* to change direction.
vegetable *adj, n* a plant grown for food.
vegetarian *n* a person who consumes a diet that excludes meat and fish.
vegetate *vi* to live a plant's life; to lead an aimless life.
vegetation *n* plants in general.
vehement *adj* ardent; forcible.
vehicle *n* any kind of land carriage; a medium.
veil *n* a screen; a face shade; a disguise. * vt to conceal.
vein *n* a blood vessel which returns blood to heart; sap tube or rib in leaves; a seam of ore; disposition; mood; streak.
velocity *n* rate of motion; speed.

velvet *n* a rich soft fabric.
venal *adj* base; corrupt.
vend *vt* to sell.
vendetta *n* a feud.
veneer *n* a thin facing of fine wood glued on a less valuable sort; a gloss. * vt to overlay with veneer; to gloss.
venerable *adj* worthy of respect and admiration.
venerate *vt* to revere; honour.
vengeance *n* punishment in return for an injury.
venial *adj* pardonable; slight.
venison *n* the flesh of deer.
venom *n* poison; spite; malice.
venomous *adj* poisonous; spiteful.
venous *adj* pertaining to a vein.
vent *n* an outlet; a flue; expression. * vt to emit; utter.
ventilate *vt* to give air to; to discuss freely.
ventral *adj* abdominal.
ventricle *n* a small cavity in body, esp. one of those in heart or brain.
ventriloquist *n* one able to disguise his voice so that it seems to come from another speaker.
venture *n* a risky undertaking. * *vi* to dare. * vt to risk.
venturesome *adj* bold; hazardous.
venue *n* the appointed place of trial (law); meeting place.
veracious *adj* truthful; accurate.
veracity *n* truthfulness.
veranda, verandah *n* a portico or balcony along front of house.
verb *n* the predicative word in a sentence.
verbal *adj* spoken; oral.
verbally *adv* by word of mouth.
verbatim *adv* word for word.
verbiage *n* the use of too many words.
verbosity *n* superabundance of words; wordiness.
verdant *adj* green; simple; gullible.
verdict *n* the finding of a jury; considered opinion.
verdigris *n* the green rust of copper.
verdure *n* green vegetation.
verge *n* border; margin; brink. * *vi* to incline; to border.
verification *n* a proving true.
verify *vt* to prove to be true; to confirm.
verisimilitude *n* the appearance of truth; probability.
veritable *adj* true; real; actual.
verity *n* truth.
vermicular *adj* worm-like.
vermilion *n* a beautiful red colour.
vermin *n* noxious animals or insects as rats, lice, etc.
verminous *adj* infested by vermin.
vernacular *adj* native. * *n* mother tongue.
vernal *adj* pertaining to the spring.
versatile *adj* readily turning; variable; many-sided.
verse *n* a line of poetry; metre; poetry; a stanza; a short division of any composition.
versed *adj* conversant; skilled, with in.
version *n* a translation; rendering.
versus against.
vertebra *n* (*pl* **vertebrae**) one of bones of spine; *pl* the spine.
vertebrate *adj* having a backbone.
vertex *n* ; *pl* ^texes or tices. the highest point; apex; zenith.
vertical *adj* upright; plumb.
vertigo *n* giddiness.
verve *n* spirit; energy.
very *adj* true; real. * *adv* truly.
vesicle *n* a small bladder or blister.
vessel *n* a hollow utensil for holding things; a ship.
vest *n* a waistcoat; an undergarment. * *vi* to furnish with (power, property, etc). * vt to invest.
vestal *adj* virgin; pure. * a nun.
vested *adj* robed; established.
vestibule *n* lobby or hall of house.
vestige *n* footprint; mark or trace.
vestment *n* a garment, esp. priestly garment.
vestry *n* room where clerical vestments are kept.
vesture *n* dress; clothing.
veteran *adj* long experienced, esp. in war.
veterinary *adj* pertaining to diseases of domestic animals.
veto *n* the right to reject or forbid. * vt to refuse assent to.
vexatious *adj* annoying; troublesome.
vexed *adj* annoyed; much disputed.
via *prep* by way of.

viaduct *n* an arched bridge over a valley.
vial *n* a small glass bottle.
vibrant *adj* vibrating; tremulous.
vibrate *vti* to wave to and fro; to swing; to quiver.
vibratory *adj* causing to vibrate.
vicarious *adj* acting for, or on behalf of, another.
vice *n* a blemish; moral failing; profligacy; an instrument for gripping things firmly.
vice *prefix* denoting depute or one who acts in the place of another, e.g. vice-president.
vicinity *n* neighbourhood.
vicious *adj* malicious; bad-tempered.
vicissitude *n* one of ups and downs of life.
victim *n* a person who has suffered injury; a dupe.
victimize *vt* to make a victim of.
victor *n* conqueror; winner.
victory *n* defeat of enemy or rival; triumph.
victual *n* food provided; provisions; usu. in *pl* * vt to supply with food or stores.
vide see; refer to.
vie *vi* to contend; to compete.
view *n* a look; inspection; survey; range of vision; scene; intention. * vti to see; to survey; to consider.
vigil *n* a watching, esp. devotional.
vigilance *n* watchfulness.
vigilant *adj* watchful.
vignette *n* an engraving on title page, etc., without definite border; a picture without definite edges.
vigorous *adj* full of vigour.
vigour *n* energy; force; strength.
vile *adj* base; depraved.
villify *vt* to slander.
villa *n* a country or suburban house.
village *n* a collection of houses smaller than a town.
villain *n* a criminal; a scoundrel.
villainous *adj* base; vile; wicked.
vim *n* vigour; energy.
vinaigrette *n* a salad dressing of oil, vinegar and seasoning.
vindicate *vt* to justify; uphold.
vindictive *adj* revengeful.
vine *n* a plant that bears grapes.
vinegar *n* a liquid containing acetic acid, used as a condiment and preserve.
vineyard *n* a plantation of vines.
vintage *n* the yearly produce of vine; wine of particular year.
vintner *n* a wine seller.
viola *n* a large violin; genus of plants including violet, pansy, etc.
violate *vt* to injure; to outrage.
violation *n* infringement.
violence *n* great force; injury.
violent *adj* vehement; furious.
violin *n* a four-stringed musical instrument.
virago *n* a bad tempered woman.
virescent *adj* slightly green.
virgin *n* a person who has never had sexual intercourse. * *adj* untouched; pure.
virginal *adj* of or pertaining to a virgin. * *n* a kind of spinet.
virile *adj* sexually potent; strong.
virtual *adj* in effect, but not in name.
virtue *n* moral goodness; admirable quality.
virtuoso *n* a person highly skilled, esp in playing a musical instrument.
virtuous *adj* moral; upright.
virulent *adj* poisonous; malignant.
virus *n* a microorganism capable of causing ill-health; illness caused by a virus.
visa *n* an endorsement on a passport allowing the holder to travel in the country of the government issuing it.
visage *n* the face or countenance.
vis-à-vis *adv* face to face.
viscera *npl* the entrails.
viscid *adj* sticky or adhesive.
viscous *adj* glutinous; viscid.
visible *adj* perceivable by the eye.
vision *n* sight; object of sight; a dream.
visionary *adj* imaginary; fanciful. * *n* an unpractical person.
visit *vt* to call upon; to afflict. * *vi* to make calls. * *n* a call.
visor, vizor *n* the movable faceguard of a helmet.
vista *n* an extended view.
vital *adj* mortal; essential.
vitality *n* vital force; energy.
vitals *npl* parts essential to life.
vitamin *n* an essential element in diet.

vitiate *vt* to make faulty; to impair.
vitreous *adj* glassy.
vitrify *vt* to convert into glass.
vitriol *n* sulphuric acid.
vituperate *vt* to abuse; to revile.
vivacious *adj* lively; sprightly.
vivid *adj* bright; striking.
vivify *vt* to animate.
viviparous *adj* giving birth to live young.
vivisection *n* act of experimenting on a living animal.
vixen *n* a female fox; a shrew.
vocabulary *n* a list of words with definitions; an individual's command or use of words.
vocal *adj* pertaining to the voice.
vocalist *n* a singer.
vocation *n* a calling; occupation.
vocative *n* the vocative case.
vociferous *adj* clamorous; noisy.
vogue *n* temporary fashion.
voice *n* the sound uttered by the mouth; utterance; speech; sound emitted; vote; a form of verb inflection. * vt to utter or express.
void *adj* empty; null. * *n* an empty space. * vt to make vacant; to nullify.
volatile *adj* readily passing off in vapour; flighty.
volcano *n* a mountain formed by ejections of lava, ashes, etc through an opening in the earth's crust.
volition *n* will; power of choice.
volley *n* a simultaneous discharge of missiles.
volleyball *n* a team game played by hitting an inflated ball over a net with the hands; the ball used.
volt *n* unit of electromotive force.
volubility *n* fluency of speech.
voluble *adj* over fluent; glib.
volume *n* an amount of space; mass or bulk; a book.
volumetric *adj* pertaining to measurement by volume.
voluminous *adj* bulky; copious.
voluntary *adj* acting of one's own free will; without remuneration; deliberate.
volunteer *n* a person who undertakes military or other service of his own free will. * *vi* to offer one's services.
voluptuous *adj* fond of bodily pleasures; a sensualist.
vomit *vi, vt* to throw up from stomach; to eject; matter ejected from stomach.
voracious *adj* greedy; ravenous.
vortex *n* (*pl* **vortices, vortexes**) a whirling motion as in whirlpool, whirlwind.
vote *n* the recording of opinion for or against proposal; suffrage. * *vi*, vt to give a vote. * vt to grant by vote.
votive *adj* promised by vow.
vouch *vt* to attest; to guarantee.
voucher *n* a written record of a transaction; a token that can be exchanged for something else.
vouchsafe *vt* to condescend to grant.
vow *n* a solemn promise; an oath. * vt to promise solemnly.
vowel *n* a simple vocal sound; letter denoting it.
voyage *n* a journey, esp by ship.
vulcanite *n* a rubber hardened by treating with sulphur.
vulgar *adj* coarse in manners.
vulgarity *n* rudeness of manners.
vulnerable *adj* liable to injury.
vulpine *adj* crafty; foxy.
vulture *n* a large bird of prey; a rapacious person.

W

wad *n* a fibrous mass; a bundle of paper money.
wadding *n* any soft material for use in packing, padding, etc.
waddle *vi* to walk with rolling gait.
wade *vi* to walk through water; to walk with difficulty.
wafer *n* a thin crisp cracker or biscuit.
waft *vt* to sail or bear along gently.
wag *vti* to shake up and down or to and fro. * *n* a wit; joker.
wage *vt* to stake; to carry on, esp war; * *n* salary; hire; usu. in *pl*
wager *n* a bet; subject of bet. * *vt* to stake.
wagon, waggon *n* a four-wheeled cart; a truck.
waif *n* a homeless, neglected child.

wail *vi* to lament; to cry aloud. * *n* a moaning cry.
waist *n* part of body from ribs to hips.
waistcoat *n* a sleeveless undercoat; a vest.
wait *vi* to stay in expectation; to attend; to serve at table. * *n* period of waiting.
waiter *n* a servant in attendance at table.
waive *vt* to forgo; give up.
wake *vi* to be awake. * *vt* to arouse. * *n* vigil over dead; track left by ship.
waken *vti* to arouse; wake.
walk *vi* to advance step by step. * *n* a ramble; a road, path; sphere of life.
wall *n* a rigid vertical structure for enclosing, dividing or protecting.
wallet *n* a flat pocketbook for paper money, cards, etc.
wallow *vi* to roll in mud, to indulge oneself in emotion.
waltz *n* a whirling dance and its music.
wand *n* a magician's rod.
wander *vi* to ramble; to roam; to err.
wane *vt* to grow less; to decline.
want *n* need; longing; dearth; poverty. * *vti* to lack; need.
wanton *adj* frisky; lustful. * *n* a lewd person.
war *n* a fight between nations; enmity; a contest.
warble *vti* to sing like a bird; to trill.
ward *vt* to guard; to fend off * *n* guard; custody; one under a guardian; a division of a town or country; apartment of an hospital.
warden *n* a guardian; head of college or hostel.
warder *n* a guard; a keeper.
wardrobe *n* a cabinet or closet for keeping clothes; one's stock of clothes.
ware *n* merchandise; goods, usu. in *pl* * *adj* wary.
warehouse *n* a building for storing wares, goods.
warfare *n* military service; war.
warm *adj* moderately hot; zealous; excited; lively. * *vti* to make or become warm or animated.
warmth *n* gentle heat; cordiality.
warn *vt* to caution; to advise.
warning *n* caution; previous notice.
warp *vti* to twist; to pervert. * *n* lengthwise threads in loom; a twist.
warped *adj* twisted by shrinking; perverted.
warrant *vt* to guarantee; to authorize; to justify. * *n* a guarantee; writ or summons; voucher.
warranty *n* warrant; guarantee.
warrior *n* a gallant soldier.
wart *n* a hard dry growth on skin.
wary *adj* cautious; prudent.
was *vb* past tense of to be.
wash *vti* to cleanse with water; to colour lightly. * *n* flow or dash of water; a lotion; thin coat of colour.
washer *n* a ring of metal, rubber, etc, for tightening nut on screw.
washing *n* clothes washed; a cleansing.
wasp *n* a stinging winged insect.
waspish *adj* like a wasp; venomous; irritable; snappish.
wastage *n* lost by use or waste.
waste *vti* to ravage; to damage; to squander; to grow less. * *adj* unused; devastated. * *n* a wilderness; useless spending; decrease; refuse.
waste pipe *n* a pipe to carry off waste water.
watch *n* a guard; vigilance; sentry; a timepiece. * *vti* to guard; to observe carefully; to await.
watchful *adj* vigilant; cautious.
watchmaker *n* one who makes or repairs watches.
watchword *n* a password; a slogan; a motto.
water *n* the commonest of liquids, clear and transparent when pure. * *vti* to supply with water; to irrigate; to dilute; to take in water.
watercolour *n* a pigment ground up with water and gum instead of oil; a picture painted with watercolours.
watercourse *n* a channel for water.
waterfall *n* a stream falling over rocks; a cascade.
waterlogged *adj* soaked or filled with water.
waterproof *adj* impervious to water. * *n* cloth so made.
watershed *n* dividing ridge between river systems.

waterspout *n* a column of water sucked up by whirlwind.
watery *adj* like water; tasteless.
wave *vi, vt* to move up and down, or to and fro; to brandish; to beckon. * *n* a rising motion on surface of water, etc; a waving of hand as signal.
waved *adj* undulating.
waver *vi* to move to and fro; falter; flicker.
wax *n* secretion by bees; anything like wax. * *vt* to rub with wax; to grow larger.
waxwork *n* modelling in wax; *pl* figures in wax.
way *n* a track, path, or road; distance traversed; direction; condition; method; course.
wayfarer *n* a traveller.
waylay *vt* to lie in wait for; to accost.
wayside *n* the side of a road.
wayward *adj* wilful; perverse.
we *pron* plural of I.
weak *adj* feeble; frail; foolish; vacillating.
weaken *vti* to make or become weak.
weakling *n* a weak creature.
weal *n* a raised mark on skin.
wealth *n* riches; abundance.
wean *vt* to break off from any habit; to discontinue giving mother's milk.
weapon *n* any instrument of offence or defence.
wear *vt* to have on, as clothes; to waste by rubbing; to exhibit. * *vi* to last; to exhaust.
wearisome *adj* tiresome; tiring.
weary *adj* tired; jaded. * *vt* to wear out strength or patience; to become weary.
weather *n* the general atmospheric conditions at any particular time. * *vt* to affect by weather, as rocks; to bear up against (storms, etc).
weathercock *n* a vane turning with wind.
weatherglass *n* a barometer.
weave *vt* to form by interlacing threads; to compose or fabricate.
web *n* woven cloth; tissue or texture; film; membrane between toes of waterfowl.
webbed *adj* having the toes united by a membrane.
webbing *n* a strong narrow band used for girths, etc.
wed *vti* to marry; unite together.
wedding *n* marriage; nuptials.
wedge *n* a block sloping to thin edge at one end. * *vt* to cleave, fix, or fasten with wedge.
wedlock *n* marriage.
Wednesday *n* fourth day of week.
weed *n* a useless plant; tobacco; * *vt* to remove weeds.
week *n* seven consecutive days.
weep *vi, vt* to shed tears; to mourn.
weft *n* cross-threads of web.
weigh *vt* to find heaviness of; to reflect on; to raise anchor. * *vi* to have weight; to bear heavily.
weight *n* heaviness; gravity; heavy mass; pressure.
weir *n* a dam across a stream.
weird *n* fate. * *adj* unearthly; queer.
welcome *adj* pleasing. * *n* a kind reception.
weld *vt* to fuse together, esp metal; to unite.
welfare *n*well-being; state provision of financial aid to the unemployed, sick, etc.
well *n* a spring; a pit sunk for water; staircase or lift space. * *vi* to bubble up; to issue forth.
well *adv* rightly; smartly. * *adj* hale; hearty.
wellington *n* a high waterproof boot.
welter *vi* to wallow; to roll. * *n* a confused mass.
went past tense of go.
west *n* one of the four compass points; sun's setting place.
western *adj* in or from west.
wet *adj* covered with water; moist; rainy. * *n* water; rain. * *vt* to make wet.
whale *n* largest of sea animals.
whaler *n* a ship employed in whale fishery.
wharf *n* (*pl* **wharfs, wharves**) a loading place for ships; quay.
wheat *n* a cereal from which flour is obtained.
wheaten *adj* made from wheat.
wheel *n* a round spoked frame turning on axis; anything like a wheel. * *vti* to revolve or cause to revolve.

wheelbarrow *n* a hand carriage with one wheel.
wheelwright *n* a maker of wheels and carts.
wheeze *vi* to breathe hard and audibly.
whelk *n* a shellfish; a periwinkle.
when *adv, conj* at what or which time; while; whereas.
whence *adv, conj* from what place.
where *adv, conj* at or in what place.
whereas *conj* that being so.
whereby *adv, conj* by which or what.
wherefore *adv, conj* for which reason; why.
whereon *adv, conj* on which or on what.
whereupon *adv* upon which.
wherever *adv* at whatever place.
whet *vt* to sharpen; edge; stimulate.
whether *pron* which of two. * conj, *adv* which of two or more.
whetstone *n* a sharpening stone.
which *pron* an interrogative pronoun; a relative pronoun, the neuter of who.
whiff *n* a puff of air, smoke, smell.
while *n* short space of time. * conj during that time that. * *vt* to pass (time) pleasantly.
whilst *adv* while.
whim *n* a sudden fancy.
whimper *vi* to whine. * *n* a pathetic cry.
whimsical *adj* fantastic; odd.
whine *vi* utter plaintive cry. * *n* a wail.
whip *vt* to lash; flog; beat into froth.
whippersnapper *n* a forward but insignificant person.
whir *vi* to fly with buzzing sound.
whirl *vti* to revolve rapidly.
whirlpool *n* a whirling eddy of water.
whirlwind *n* a whirling eddy of air.
whisk *vt* to stir or move rapidly. * *n* a jerking motion; small brush; an egg-beater.
whisker *n* hair on cheeks.
whisky, whiskey *n* spirit distilled from barley, etc.
whisper *vti* to speak very softly. * *n* a low voice.
whist *interj* hush! * *n* a game of cards.
whistle *vi* to make a shrill sound with lips or instrument. * *n* a shrill sound; a small wind instrument.
white *adj* snow-coloured; pure.
whitewash *n* lime and water for whitening walls, etc; to coneal the truth.
whither *adv* to what or which place.
whittle *vt* to pare down.
who *pron, rel, interr* referring to persons only.
whole *adj* hale and sound. * *n* the total; all.
wholesale *n* sale of goods in large quantities. * *adj* extensive.
wholesome *adj* healthy; salutary.
wholly *adv* entirely.
whoop *n* a loud shout.
whooping cough *n* see Hooping cough.
whose *pron* the possessive case of who or which.
why *adv, conj* for what reason.
wick *n* the thread of a lamp or candle.
wicked *adj* bad; sinful; roguish.
wicket *n* a small gate; the three upright stumps in cricket.
wide *adj* broad; extensive.
widen *vti* to make or grow wide.
widow *n* a woman whose husband is deceased.
widower *n* a man whose wife is deceased.
width *n* breadth.
wield *vt* to handle; to exercise.
wife *n* ; *pl* wives. a married woman.
wig *n* an artificial head of hair.
wigwam *n* a North American Indian domed shelter.
wild *adj* in a state of nature; untamed; stormy.
wilderness *n* a desert; waste.
wildfire *n* sheet lightning.
wile *n* fraud; trick. * *vt* to entice.
wilful *adj* stubborn; headstrong.
will *vb aux* expressing futurity or resolve. * *vti* to determine by choice; to wish; to bequeath. * *n* wish; choice; determination; purpose; last testament; feeling.
willing *adj* ready; instant; ungrudging.
willow *n* a tree or shrub, valuable for basket-making, etc; a cricket bat.
wily *adj* cunning; sly.
win *vt* to gain; to allure. * *vi* to gain victory.
wince *vi* to shrink, as from pain.
winch *n* crank of wheel or axle; a windlass.

wind *n* a current of air; breath; flatulence. * *vt* to blow, as a horn. * *vt* to put out of breath; to rest.

wind *vt* to twist; to coil. * *vi* to twine; to meander.

windfall *n* fruit blown down; an unexpected financial gain.

winding *adj* bending; twisting. * *n* a turn; a bend.

windlass *n* a kind of hoisting machine; a winch.

windmill *n* a mill driven by wind.

window *n* a glazed opening in wall for light.

windpipe *n* the air passage to lungs; trachea.

windward *n* the point from which the wind blows.

wine *n* the fermented juice of grapes.

winepress *n* an apparatus for pressing juice from grapes.

wing *n* organ of flight; side extension of building, army, etc; side. * *vt* to fly; to wound.

wink *vi* to shut and open eyelids; to give hint by eyelids; to connive. * *n* a winking or hint given by it.

winning *adj* attractive; charming.

winnow *vt* to fan chaff from grain; to sift.

winsome *adj* attractive; winning.

winter *n* the cold season of year. * *vi* to pass the winter.

wipe *vt* to clean by gentle rubbing; to efface.

wire *n* a thread of metal; a telegram * *vt* to bind with wire. * *vi* to telegraph.

wiry *adj* wire-like; sinewy.

wisdom *n* sound judgment and knowledge; prudence.

wise *adj* learned; judging rightly.

wish *vi* to have a desire; to long. * *vt* to express desire. * *n* a desire.

wisp *n* a small bundle of straw, etc; anything slender.

wistful *adj* pensive; yearning.

wit *vti* to know; to be aware. * to wit, namely; that is to say. * *n* understanding; humour; a humorist.

witch *n* a woman who practices magic and is considered to have dealings with the devil.

witchcraft *n* the practice of magic.

with *prep* expressing nearness or connection; among; possessing.

withdraw *vt* to draw back; to retract. * *vi* to retire.

wither *vi* to fade or shrivel.

withers *npl* ridge between shoulder bones of horse.

withhold *vt* to hold back; not to grant.

within *prep* inside. * *adv* inwardly.

without *prep, adv* outside.

withstand *vti* to oppose; to resist.

witness *n* testimony; evidence; one who gives sworn evidence. * *vti* to see; to attest; to sign as witness.

witticism *n* a witty remark.

witty *adj* humorous; smart and droll.

wizard *n* a magician; conjuror.

wizen, wizened *adj* shrivelled.

wobble *vi* to sway from side to side.

woe *n* grief; misery.

woebegone *adj* grief-stricken.

wolf *n* ; *pl* wolves. a wild animal of the dog family.

woman *n* ; an adult female; female sex. *pl* women.

womanhood *n* the state or qualities of a woman.

won *pret, pp* of **win**.

wonder *n* something very strange; a marvel; feeling excited by something strange. * *vi* to be struck with wonder; to marvel.

woo *vt* to court with a view to marriage.

wood *n* a collection of growing trees; timber.

wooden *adj* made of wood; stiff.

woodwork *n* carpentry.

wool *n* the fleece of sheep, goats, etc.

woolgathering *n* idle dreaming.

woollen *adj* made of wool. * *n* cloth made of wool.

word *n* an articulate sound expressing an idea; information; a saying; motto; promise; *pl* wrangel.

wording *n* the mode of expressing in words.

wordy *adj* using many words; verbose.

work *n* effort; employment; a task; achievement; a book or other composition; a factory * *vi* to labour, toil; to be employed; to ferment. * *vt* to bring about; to influence; to fashion.

working class *n* people who work for wages, esp manual workers.

workman *n* an artisan; a skilled worker.

workmanship *n* skill of a worker or quality of his work.

workshop *n* a place where some craft is carried on.

world *n* the whole creation; the earth; mankind; the public.

worldly *adj* relating to this world or this life.

worm *n* a small creeping animal; thread of screw; spiral pipe in a condenser. * *vi* to work slowly and secretly. * *vt* to undermine; to extract.

worn *pp* of **wear**.

worry *vt* to harass; to fret. * *n* anxiety.

worse *adj* bad or ill in greater degree; inferior.

worship *n* religious service; adoration; reverence; title of honour. * *vt* to adore; to perform religious service.

worshipful *adj* honourable.

worst *adj* bad or evil in highest degree. * *vt* to defeat.

worsted *n* woollen yarn used in knitting.

worth *adj* equal in value to; deserving of * *n* value; price.

worthy *adj* deserving; befitting. * *n* a notable person.

would-be *adj* wishing to be; pretended.

wound *n* a cut or stab, etc; injury. * *vti* to inflict a wound; to pain.

wove *pret* of **weave**.

wrack *n* seaweed generally; wreck; a thin flying cloud.

wrangle *vi* to dispute angrily. * *n* a dispute.

wrap *vt* to fold or roll; to envelop. * *n* a shawl or rug.

wrapper *n* a loose morning gown; cover for postal packets, as books, etc.

wrath *n* violent anger; rage.

wreak *vt* to inflict, execute (vengeance, etc).

wreath *n* a garland.

wreathe *vt* to entwine; to encircle.

wreck *n* ruin; destruction of ship at sea. * *vt* to ruin; destroy.

wreckage *n* remains of wrecked ship.

wrench *n* a violent twist; tool for screwing nuts, etc. * *vt* to pull with a twist.

wrest *vt* to twist; to distort.

wrestle *vi* to contend by grappling and trying to throw down.

wretch *n* a miserable person; base creature.

wretched *adj* unhappy; worthless.

wriggle *vi, vt* to twist about.

wright *n* an artisan; a carpenter.

wring *vt* to twist and squeeze; to extort.

wrinkle *n* a crease in skin; furrow; hint. * *vti* to crease.

wrist *n* the joint uniting hand to arm.

writ *n* a written court order.

write *vti* to form by a pen, etc; to set down in words; to communicate by letter; to compose.

writer *n* an author; a clerk; a law agent.

writhe *vti* to turn and twist, as in pain.

wrong *adj* not right; false. * *n* an injury. * *vt* to treat unjustly.

wrongful *adj* injurious; unjust.

wry *adj* contorted; twisted; ironic.

wynd *n* a narrow alley; a lane.

X

xanthic *adj* yellowish; of or relating to xanthine.

xenophobia *n* fear or dislike of foreigners or strangers.

xerography *n* photocopying by using light to form an electrostatic image.

X-ray, x-ray *n* a radiation of very short wavelengths, capable of penetrating solid bodies. * *vt* to photograph by x-rays.

xylophone *n* a musical instrument of wooden bars freely suspended and vibrating when struck.

Y

yacht *n* a light sailing vessel for pleasure or racing.

yahoo *n* a rude brutish or crude person.

yak *n* a Tibetan ox.
yam *n* a tropical plant and its edible root.
yap *vi* to talk constantly.
yard *n* a standard measure of 3 feet; an enclosure; a spar hung across a mast to support a sail.
yardarm *n* either end of a ship's yard.
yarn *n* any spun thread; a spun-out story.
yaw *vi* to swerve suddenly in sailing.
yawl *n* a ship's small boat; a small yacht.
yawn *vi* to open the jaws involuntarily, as from drowsiness.* *n* act of yawning.
year *n* the period of earth's complete revolution round sun; 12 months; 365 or 366 days.
yearling *n* a one-year-old animal.
yearn *vi* to be filled with longing, love, or pity for.
yeast *n* fermenting substance for raising bread; barm.
yell *vi* to scream * *n* a shrill cry.
yellow *adj, n* a bright golden colour.
yelp *vi* to utter a sharp bark.
yesterday *n* the day before the present.
yet *adv* in addition; still. * *conj* nevertheless.
yew *n* a large evergreen tree.
yield *vt* to produce in return for labour, etc; to afford; to give up. * *vi* to submit. * *n* product; crop.
yodel *vti* to sing with changes from natural to falsetto voice.
yoga *n* a system of exercises for attaining bodily and spiritual control and well-being.
yoke *n* a neckpiece of wood binding oxen together in drawing; a pair of draught oxen; a bond or link. * *vt* to couple.
yokel *n* a country person regarded as unsophisticated.
yolk *n* the yellow part of an egg.
yonder *adv* over there.
you *pron* the 2nd person singular and plural, the person or persons spoken to.
young *adj* not old; youthful. * *n* offspring; young persons.
youngster *n* a boy; young person.
youth *n* period from childhood to manhood; a young man; young people.
yule *n* Christmas.

Z

zany *adj* comical; eccentric.
zeal *n* eagerness; ardour; fanaticism.
zealot *n* an extreme partisan; a fanatic.
zebra *n* a striped wild animal related to the horse.
zenith *n* the point of heavens right overhead; highest point.
zephyr *n* the west wind; any soft breeze.
zeppelin *n* a rigid, cigar-shaped airship.
zero *n* a cipher; nothing; point from which marking of a scale begins.
zest *n* relish; keen enjoyment.
zigzag *adj, n* a line with short sharp turns. * *vi* to turn sharply this way and that.
zinc *n* a soft bluish white metal.
zither *n* a flat, stringed musical instrument.
zodiac *n* the tract in the heavens within which the apparent path of sun, moon, and planets is confined, and containing the twelve constellations, or signs of zodiac.
zone *n* a girdle or belt; one of the five great belts of the earth; any well-defined tract.
zoolite *n* a fossil animal.
zoology *n* the science of animal life.
zoophyte *n* a plant-like animal, as sponge, coral.
zoroastrian *n* a believer in religion of zoroaster, founder of Parseeism, or fire worship.
zymotic *adj* caused by or relating to an infection or an infectious disease; producing fermentation.
zymurgy *n* the chemistry of fermentation in brewing, etc.